AVID

READER

PRESS

ALSO BY FERGUS BUTLER-GALLIE

A Field Guide to the English Clergy: A Compendium of Diverse Eccentrics, Pirates, Prelates and Adventurers; All Anglican, Some Even Practising

Priests de la Résistance! The Loose Canons Who Fought Fascism in the Twentieth Century

Twelve Churches

An Unlikely History of the Buildings

That Made Christianity

FERGUS BUTLER-GALLIE

AVID READER PRESS

New York   Amsterdam/Antwerp   London   Toronto   Sydney/Melbourne   New Delhi

AVID READER PRESS
An Imprint of Simon & Schuster, LLC
1230 Avenue of the Americas
New York, NY 10020

For more than 100 years, Simon & Schuster has championed authors and the stories they create. By respecting the copyright of an author's intellectual property, you enable Simon & Schuster and the author to continue publishing exceptional books for years to come. We thank you for supporting the author's copyright by purchasing an authorized edition of this book.

No amount of this book may be reproduced or stored in any format, nor may it be uploaded to any website, database, language-learning model, or other repository, retrieval, or artificial intelligence system without express permission. All rights reserved. Inquiries may be directed to Simon & Schuster, 1230 Avenue of the Americas, New York, NY 10020 or permissions@simonandschuster.com.

Text copyright © 2025 by Fergus Butler-Gallie
Text illustrations copyright © 2025 by James Oses
First published in Great Britain in 2025 by Hodder &
Stoughton Limited, a Hachette UK company

First published in Great Britain in 2025 by Hodder & Stoughton Limited

All rights reserved, including the right to reproduce this book or portions thereof in any form whatsoever. For information, address Avid Reader Press Subsidiary Rights Department, 1230 Avenue of the Americas, New York, NY 10020.

First Avid Reader Press hardcover edition August 2025

AVID READER PRESS and colophon are trademarks of Simon & Schuster, LLC

Simon & Schuster strongly believes in freedom of expression and stands against censorship in all its forms. For more information, visit BooksBelong.com.

For information about special discounts for bulk purchases, please contact Simon & Schuster Special Sales at 1-866-506-1949 or business@simonandschuster.com.

The Simon & Schuster Speakers Bureau can bring authors to your live event. For more information or to book an event contact the Simon & Schuster Speakers Bureau at 1-866-248-3049 or visit our website at www.simonspeakers.com.

Manufactured in the United States of America

1   3   5   7   9   10   8   6   4   2

Library of Congress Cataloging-in-Publication Data has been applied for.

ISBN 978-1-6680-7447-3
ISBN 978-1-6680-7449-7 (ebook)

Magistris discipulisque Scholae Tonbridgiensis,
quae me olim nutritum etiam nutrit

Contents

	Introduction	ix
	Author's Note	xv
1	The Church of the Nativity, Bethlehem, West Bank of Palestine	1
2	St Peter's, Rome, Italy	23
3	Hagia Sophia, Istanbul, Turkey	55
4	Canterbury Cathedral, England	87
5	Mount Athos, Greece	113
6	Bete Golgotha, Lalibela, Ethiopia	145
7	Templo de las Américas, Dominican Republic	175
8	Kirishitan Hokora, Kasuga, Japan	201
9	Site of the First Meeting House, Salem, Massachusetts, United States	223
10	Christ Church, Zanzibar, Tanzania	249
11	16th Street Baptist Church, Birmingham, Alabama, United States of America	275
12	Canaanland, Ota, Nigeria	301
	Epilogue: Surprise, Service, Belonging	327
	Acknowledgments	333
	Appendix: Dramatis Personae	335
	References	349
	Index	377

Introduction

You also, like living stones, are being built into a spiritual house

1 Peter 2:5

What is a church? Well, put simply, it's the place where humanity encounters God.

From the very earliest times humans have been setting aside specific places for this purpose. Yes, it's true, most societies and religions, as well as most expressions of Christianity, don't seek to limit God physically or geographically: they say you can encounter him anywhere. But the thing is that as soon as a person encounters God in a place, it becomes a somewhere. Christians call these "somewheres" *churches*. Places where God and humanity might meet.

But the problem with—and also the most interesting thing about—humanity is that it's messy. Specifically, it brings its mess—its violence and beauty, its competing desires for profit or sex or justice—with it wherever it goes. And that includes into churches. So the places where these encounters exist become messy too: they get caught up with the human as well as the Divine, blending the two in places made up of stones with stories to tell, in stones that live.

I first walked into a church as a child; not yet a teen, susceptible to wonder but beginning to be curious about the world, its past, and my place in it. The church was St Margaret's in Bethersden in Kent, the beautiful church that sits at the little ridge above the village nearest to my family home in the English countryside. It is a church I know well, having lived under the aegis of its parochial boundary for much of my childhood. It was there, among those centuries-old arches, that I first felt that distinctive atmosphere that comes from ancient stone. Cooling, even on the brightest summer day. It was there that I retraced the repeated names on the village war memorials—three men, boys really, with the same name. Two more with another. Brothers or cousins, I wondered of the first trinity. Perhaps a father and then his son, one in each World War, for the pair.

It was there that I read and reread the sentimental Victorian inscriptions and austere Georgian tributes that lined the walls, and ran my fingers over the medieval brasses on the north wall. It was there that I knelt and received communion as people had been doing in this same church for a thousand years, since the Conqueror sent his men around to compile a book of his possessions, which would last, so they thought, until Domesday.

This is, I acknowledge, a very particular first impression of a very particular church. For some people the equivalent will have been a very different place: perhaps it was the austerity of a Moravian meeting house in the corn fields of Iowa, the simple white walls speaking of an uncluttered God who was credible in the stark flatlands and great open skies, or for others the rambunctious brimming over of a Coptic Easter in Cairo, which told of a faith bubbling with color and action. Perhaps your first memory of a church was a Roman Catholic funeral mass, in the sweltering heat of a Goan high noon? It might be of a mega church, a great concrete dome off a highway in Manaus or Mississippi or Manila, where, inside, the signs and wonders of the Lord are shown with great gusto. It might be of silence in an ancient cloister. Or maybe it is of the child-height view of a well-loved bench in a building that's no longer there. This is the thing about churches: for all their variation, they lodge in the memory in a very particular way.

Why did I find the church of my childhood so fascinating? Why did I feel differently inside the shade and must of the building? Why did these stones draw me in? Because though all these people were dead—the farm boys who went off to the Somme, or the parson in the reign of Queen Anne memorialized in marble, the Norman civil servants stuck forever in brass—in that place, they felt, amidst the stones, alive. And I felt linked to them. Linked by a shared faith, and linked, too, by a shared space. A Church; *our* church.

Introduction xi

. . .

Since then I have known many churches, visiting sometimes dozens in one day in those places like Rome and Venice that are veritable orgies for the church-crawler. Some I have merely had brief flings with: a head poked around the door of an empty building in the back streets of Prague, or a momentary prayer at the back of a mass in rural Argentina. I have been to mega churches and barely visited chapels, churches of every flavor of denomination available. Others I have got to know really very well; going back at several stages in my life to seek the wisdom pooled in these places. In all of these churches, though, I have felt something: a sense of that wonder similar to that which I first felt all those years ago.

What links these places of worship? What is it that a corrugated-iron structure, clinging to a South African hillside, has in common with the soaring buttresses of a French cathedral town? What does an austere puritanical meeting room in the American Midwest have in common with a Rococo extravaganza in Eastern Europe? What thread is there that weaves together churches across continents and denominations and time?

I would argue that it is their stories: that is what they have in common. Specifically, *the* story, that of Christianity itself. But what these churches show is that Christianity is not just one story—the story we all know, whether believer or not—but a whole patchwork of interlinking ones, each necessarily sacred and all interwoven by their links to that first story: to that of Christ. It is those stories that mean the stones of churches are more than just building material: it is the stories that make them sing, make them shout, make them *live*.

Yet living things are complex, even when they are made of stone. So often in the stories of these places there is much that is complicated, aspects that don't seem to fit with their lofty aims to speak of the Christian faith in brick and stone. Instead, these buildings speak of other things. Tragedy sits alongside triumph, violence alongside peace, human corruption alongside a yearning for the Divine. This book is made up of their stories and, by telling their stories, seeks to tell the sometimes unlikely and surprising story of the faith that shaped them.

The story of Christianity is, as our journey will show, the story of our modern world: it's a story of who we should be, as well as who we sometimes are. Christianity has hugely formed how we all—believers or not—think about any number of issues. I hope that this book will help the reader to further understand how that came to be. I hope that the person who comes not knowing much about Christianity will see, through this human story, how their own lives have been impacted by it. To those who know the faith well, perhaps even practice it, I hope that this book will show that the history of Christianity is not as simple as sometimes suggested, its trajectory not always clear. I hope, too, that it will remind those who think of history as great sweeps of societal change that in fact, at its heart, there are people and places. And that in Christianity—both in its theology and, as we will see, from its past—people and places are accorded an even more hallowed position than any historiological trend.

With this in mind, there is another quandary, too: How were the moral values of a simple teacher from Nazareth, one who was put to death by the Roman Empire, subsumed into that self-same Empire? And how is it that those values have been used by numerous states and individuals, who manifestly wield a very different power to that which He preached about, ever since? The answer can, I think, be found by looking at those churches built in His name. This book seeks to answer these questions.

This book is an attempt to try to set out a new history of Christianity, by looking at some of those churches and the people who prayed in them. Because of that, it is an "unlikely history." Not some grandiose sweep from year zero to the present day, but a collection of stories. Some, I hope, funny, some moving, some speaking of power and grace, some of folly and wickedness. All of them human and so therefore all of them complex.

For it is in churches that we see the attempts to deal with these complexities, paradoxes rendered into stone. We see the messiness of the practical living of Christianity. We see humanity. It's why the Hagia Sophia has sheets over its mosaics; why a hillside in Japan became sacred; why a group of teenagers in colonial Massachusetts began accusing their neighbors of witchcraft; and why a Pope was prepared to split

Introduction xiii

Christendom in order to build the church of his dreams. It's why a mega church in Nigeria is about to break world records, why a tabernacle in Birmingham, Alabama, still has shrapnel holes around its front porch, why the very rocks of rural Ethiopia are hollowed out and reverberate with the praise of God. It's why there is a sword hanging in Canterbury Cathedral and why a basement in Zanzibar attracts more visitors than the sanctuary on which it stands. It's why a group of men live together, sexless, on the western side of a Greek mountain and why a group of men, driven mad by sex, power, and profit, erected a makeshift shrine on the north shore of a Caribbean island. And that messy union of God and man is why the gilded remnants of a cave once used as a stable in small-town Palestine remains one of the most iconic places on the face of the globe.

We will journey across seas and across centuries, from Bethlehem and the birth of Christ some two thousand–odd years ago, to the immediate present and future of Christianity. We will see what unites a Baptist Church in the segregationist American South with a medieval monastery in the heart of the Greek countryside; the Vatican—beautiful, imposing, vainglorious, the seat of Catholicism—with a sparse, tiny private shrine above the rocky coastline of Southern Japan.

These twelve churches have been chosen because they represent breadth and depth too. They are on almost every continent, they come from a wide range of denominations, they vary from those which date from the very beginnings of Christianity over two thousand years ago, to those which, even as Christianity enters its third millennium, are not yet complete. They have welcomed in millions of worshippers over their histories, each one bringing their own perspective on this monumental faith. Come, join them, and join me, as we journey around them. Come and see what stories they tell, what they sometimes conceal, come and be part of that bigger story as well.

Over the course of that journey together, I hope there are things we might learn, people we might meet who will change our perspective. Not only on Christianity, but on the issues with which it clashed, the movements it helped form, the world which it has undeniably shaped. There will be moments that will shock and disappoint us, people of whom we

xiv *Introduction*

will want to know more and those whom we will be glad to only meet on the page and not in the flesh. The desire to tell these stories, and to tell the story of the faith as a whole, are what inspired me to travel and to write this book. The encounters are mine initially, but I hope they might become ours, shared in the pursuit of a greater knowledge of this strange and wonderful faith.

Of course, this book cannot and does not claim to be a totally comprehensive history of Christianity. It would be mad to suggest so, as there are countless aspects that have only received a cursory mention here. The truth is that there are over 37 million church buildings on the face of the earth, and there are as many world-shaping stories about Christianity as there are Christians. The twelve chosen here are, by their very nature, a limited selection and yet, I hope, one that is diverse and gives, albeit at times in snapshot form, a sense of the full breadth of what churches are and mean across the world. In this sense it is an unlikely history, but I hope still one which will open eyes, minds, and hearts.

This is a book about human nature and human stories; but in telling these I hope to tell a story far deeper, of the impact and reach of Christianity and, by extension, a story about the world it has shaped. At heart, the stories these buildings tell are stories of people and their God and how both have made the world we live in today.

Author's Note

Choices have been made around dating systems and specific Biblical translations in particular. These are aesthetic rather than scholarly—although where it is necessary to expand on specifics of etymology or disputed translations, the original Greek and Hebrew are always referred to in the endnotes.

Invariably almost every source—Biblical and otherwise—is subject to thousands and thousands of pages' worth of debate. Again, this is a book primarily interested in telling the stories of people and places: so there has not been room for a full playing out of each of these debates. I hope those who hold such debates to be important will forgive this; and there has always been an attempt to direct the reader to the necessary scholars and articles in the endnotes.

Chapter One

The Church of the Nativity, Bethlehem, West Bank of Palestine

(Worship began between 4 BC and 1 AD)

"Of course, everyone goes to Bethlehem," Yazid tells me, over a cup of tea some several thousand miles from the city itself. It was at the very start of this project, when the idea of visiting and writing about churches was first in my mind. I knew it would be a story best told through people; and I don't know many people quite like him, an Anglican cleric, a professor of Arabic, an Israeli citizen and a Palestinian. I mooted the idea in the broadest possible terms to Yazid in Liverpool, where we both then worked, keenly aware that he knew the Holy Land much better than I. He himself is from Nazareth—proudly so—but even he acknowledges that this "other" origin center for Christianity has lost the struggle for global attention. Everyone goes to Bethlehem. Of course they do.

They go to Bethlehem because it claims to be the birthplace of Jesus Christ. They go to where he died, where he was raised, where he lived and preached, where he rejoiced and where he wept too. But where he was born has a distinct appeal. If I was going to work out how it was that Christianity developed, then, naturally, I had to start where it started. When looking at the origins of the faith that has become such a global phenomenon there was really only one place to which I could go. Two of the four Gospels—the books of the Bible which deal with the biographical details of the life of Jesus (though one, John, does so in a way different to the others)—relate that the infant who would come to be identified as Jesus, called the Christ, was born in Bethlehem.

These two are the Gospel of Matthew and the Gospel of Luke. They deal explicitly with the birth of Jesus and the very earliest origins of Christianity as an earthly phenomenon.[1] The two books are generally thought to have been written at roughly similar times. Based on the idea that they were derivative of the shorter and less grammatically polished Gospel of Mark as well as, possibly, an unknown other source known as

"Q," much twentieth-century study of the Gospels puts the dating of the final edited text (as we have it) of both Gospels in the period between 80 and 100 AD.[2] More recent scholarship has tended to err toward early dating: Matthew as being written c. 50 AD and Luke about a decade later.[3] While this, of course, might give credence to the idea that there are eyewitness statements of the crucifixion and resurrection (assumed to have happened in the early 30s) included in the Gospels, it doesn't quite make the same assumption possible for the birth of Jesus, some thirty years previously. What, then, do they actually say about the beginning of "the greatest story ever told"? And what do the origins of Christianity tell us about the faith and phenomenon which it was to become?

The tale of Christ's birth is perhaps the best-known story on the face of the planet, but it isn't as simple as it first seems. There are differences between the Gospel accounts, length being one of them: Luke actually only dedicates sixteen verses of his second chapter to the events in Bethlehem.[4] Mary and Joseph go there because Joseph is of "the house and lineage of David" and needs to be taxed as part of the census.[5] Luke sets his account in the context of a Messiah who will overturn the ways of the world and threaten the norms of the Roman Empire. Matthew places the birth in the context of extant Jewish predictions about a coming Messiah predicted by the Hebrew prophet Isaiah: "a virgin shall conceive, and bear a son."[6] Matthew, too, mentions Bethlehem explicitly, eager to underline the received Jewish wisdom that the prophecy of Micah suggested Bethlehem as the likely birthplace for a Messiah. The Wise Men visit the child in Bethlehem sometime after his birth, though Matthew seems to imply that, by this point, the family have found some more suitable accommodation as they are in "a house."[7]

A sort of composite of the two stories, the census and the prophecy, the Wise Men and the shepherds, has come to be the story of "the Nativity" which is so well known today. Yet, for most Christians who flock to hear the story every year, whether at Bethlehem or elsewhere, the differences in Luke and Matthew are less differences or contradictions and more clues to what the whole religion is about. They suggest that from the very start of Christianity there is this sense of things being bigger than they seem: both the very lowest in Jewish society and the

The Church of the Nativity, Bethlehem, West Bank of Palestine   5

very highest figures in the global order, shepherds and Magi, come to the manger.

Indeed, Matthew and Luke's subtle differences point to another truth: that throughout the Christian story there is a permanent sense of everything existing on two levels—the macro and the micro, if you will, the personal and the universal. We will see it again and again as we journey through the faith and its places and people. This phenomenon goes back to its very beginning. On one level the story of the Nativity is a fairly easy one to comprehend. True, it has some complex theology behind it, but at its heart it is something that all humans by the very fact of their existence can relate to: the birth of a baby.

This birth, however, is both like and totally unlike all other births. Not least because not all births are the traceable beginnings of a faith. Christians call this birth like no other "the incarnation." The idea that Christ is fully God and fully man, made flesh, *carnal,* is a crucial starting point for Christianity.[8] God isn't just indulging in a disguise, as the pagan Gods were wont to do, such as when Zeus became a swan or a satyr to indulge in one of his multiple rapes; rather, he really is both God and man.[9] And in so becoming, what it means to be human is changed forever as humanity is "taken into" the very center of the universe, the very moving force of creation, and the very source of love. That is what the tale of the baby in the manger means on a higher level; perhaps—as it pertains to God—on the highest level of all.

Now, you might hear that self-same story and think it untrue. You might deny the possibility of the Virgin Birth or want to dispute the historicity of the detail. You might think that the dating doesn't work—as Herod probably died in 4 BC. You might quibble on details, like those Christian scholars who argue that the "stable" wasn't a stable at all but rather that "no room at the inn" meant that Mary and Joseph got a better place to stay, not a worse one.[10] You might dispute that Roman census practice required the sort of journey that forms the necessary backdrop for the presence of Mary and Joseph in Bethlehem. You might desperately struggle with the claim of Mary's virginity or you might simply think, like Thomas Jefferson, that the whole thing was "a fable" or "artificial scaffolding" with which "reason and freedom of thought . . . will do away."[11]

But what there is no denying is the change that this story brought to the world. There is no denying that billions of people throughout history thought it to be true and that billions continue to believe it to be true. And when we say that they thought it to be true, it is impossible to deny that they really did think so. There is always a temptation to indulge in what C. S. Lewis called "chronological snobbery" and assume that those beliefs held by people in the past were inherently less reasonable or intelligent or even authentic than our own. The evidence which we have would warn us strongly against such an approach when it comes to Christianity. People lived whole lives shaped by it; people died deaths because of the depth of their belief in it. Indeed, people still do. They crafted civilizations based on it. They made the world which we now live in—for better or for worse—according to their sense of what had happened at Bethlehem.

Now, of course, that is not to say that there is a clear straight line from here and now to Bethlehem. The events said to have occurred at Bethlehem spawned a plethora of movements calling themselves Christianity. But what is Christianity? The truth is, it is many things.

What happened at Bethlehem gave the spark of life both to the might and reach of the Roman Catholic Church, with its c. 1.75 billion members, and to sects living off grid in the heartlands of America, of which we have never heard, with perhaps two or three members.[12] Christianity is a faith which encompasses socially liberal, economically comfortable people in the West and some of the poorest people on earth, for whom the traditional rhythms of life have not changed for centuries. It is the writings of bishops of Greek colonies in the first century AD and it is blogposts by underground believers in Communist China. It is old ladies in Spanish hilltop towns, who have hobbled to Mass every day since their childhood during the Civil War; it is newly baptized babies in townships and favelas and leafy suburbs; it is online communities of the newly faithful connected not by place at all but by gigabytes. It is the cultural phenomenon that undergirds many of the moral, political and societal assumptions made across the world today and it is the

The Church of the Nativity, Bethlehem, West Bank of Palestine 7

quietly uttered prayer of the desperate relative at the hospital bedside. It is a young woman, dancing and shouting in tongues that her hearers cannot understand, under the barn-like roof of a Nigerian mega church, and it is me, my knee clicking as I kneel down in a college chapel at the University of Oxford and silently repeat well-worn daily prayers in seventeenth-century English.

To repeat the question, what is Christianity? Well, it is all of these things and more than I or anyone else can possibly write. The Gospel according to St John ends with the words "there are also many other things which Jesus did, the which, if they should be written every one, I suppose that even the world itself could not contain the books that should be written."[13] The same might be said for those who have followed on in his name. It is, quite probably, the most varied and, some would argue, influential set of beliefs that humanity has ever come up with. Bethlehem itself speaks of that diversity.

The Church of the Nativity is home to multiple communities— Greek Orthodox, Roman Catholic, Armenian, Coptic, Ethiopian, and Syriac—claiming particular rights there. Even the washing of particular steps at particular times is governed by a strict code of rules and regulations designed to keep civility between the varied believers who all claim to serve the Christ child.[14] Many more so—Anglicans, Methodists, Lutherans, Uniates, and people who wouldn't even claim to be anything beyond just "a Christian"—visit and cherish its space every day. Even beyond its geography, when it is considered as a cipher or symbol for Christianity, Bethlehem speaks of the diversity of Christian faith and life around the whole world. There are hundreds of things and places named after Bethlehem: from the great tower at the entrance of Lisbon harbor, the Torre de Belem, to Bethlehem, Namibia, a tiny farming community next to the dried bed of the Skaap River. From Pennsylvanian drive-through towns, to mental hospitals in Georgian London, to a single lane in the rural Western Finnish village of Vähä-Katava, which leads, appropriately, to a stable. People don't just go to Bethlehem: wherever Christians have traveled they have sought to take the town with them as well.

Scholars studying the context from which Christianity emerged often talk about the existence of so many competing forms of first-century religion in the Holy Land that it makes more sense to refer to "Judaisms" rather than a single "Judaism" at the time.[15] Given that context it seems reasonable to say that the diversity—contradictions even—of Christian faith exhibited above means we are dealing with "Christianities" rather than a single whole. What they do have in common, though, however diverse they might be, is tracing the start of their existence to Bethlehem. And so everyone—all these wildly different types of Christians—goes there. Of course. They go to the site where all that began.

People go to Bethlehem itself, and above all the Church of the Nativity, which purports to be on the site of where that great story unfolded. Because there is something very innately human about wanting to see where something began. Not least something as world changing as Christianity. And there is a special curiosity which is attached to the fact that something so important could come from something so small. That which was once the stable—or the cave—has, quite understandably, become a center for Christian worship. At the heart of what Christians seek to do is to make God present—to bring the Divine into the mundane, Heaven into earth. They believe that this act, so central to their faith, was done in the flesh, in the manger at Bethlehem.

My friend Yazid's observation that "everyone goes to Bethlehem," casual and non-literal though I am sure it was, remained spinning around my head for weeks as I thought about this book. Others advised that I should start with Nazareth or Jerusalem or Rome or Alexandria or Ephesus or any one of the other places that were pivotal in making Christianity a global religion, but Bethlehem and its universality lingered in my brain, a guest unasked for and yet important. As I pored over manuscripts and texts, magazine articles and news reports, it occurred to me that "everyone" really does mean everyone: even today it still draws the rich, the famous, the powerful and the unknown, the powerless and the poor. All come to Bethlehem. They don't come for the olive groves or the relics of Ottoman administration. They don't even come for the watermelon hookah, speciality of the Reem al-Bawadi restaurant on the Street of the Manger, just up from the church, which I was told I must visit one day. No, they come there to visit the site of the manger itself.

The Church of the Nativity, Bethlehem, West Bank of Palestine 9

Since Mary, Joseph, the shepherds, the angels, and the Magi, Bethlehem has known many visitors of note. Crowned heads, elected presidents, authors, and celebrities have all made it a destination, bringing with them to the manger the weights of their callings and their various eccentricities.

Perhaps the first seriously important visitor in the centuries after the birth of Christ was another significant mother. The Empress Helena was the mother of Constantine, the first Christian Roman Emperor, whose various endeavors we will discuss more fully in due course. It would be anachronistic, of course, to declare Constantine a "mommy's boy," but the relationship between the two was indubitably close. Some accounts have Constantine converting due to his mother's influence, whereas most, including the ancient historian Eusebius, suggest it was the other way around.[16] Either way, in the early fourth century, the freshly devout mother and son were eager to set about giving Bethlehem the sort of buildings which they felt it deserved as the place where their new faith had begun.

Helena toured the province of Syria Palaestina in order to find what state the sites referenced in the Gospels were in. Her archaeological method was novel, to say the least. It was purported that she discovered the location of the true cross at Golgotha, where Jesus was crucified, through a combination of dramatic visions, endless interrogation of the populace, and a tactic of hitting sick people with the bits of wood she dug up until the real cross cured them.[17] Fortunately, the grotto at Bethlehem seems to have been spared Helena's techniques, as it was already known and identified by locals. Helena took particular care to beautify the place where Mary had "suffered the travails of childbirth," one mother of an extraordinary son feeling a particular pang of connection with another.[18]

In years that followed, even non-Christians seemed to treat the Church of the Nativity with a particular reverence. The "mad Caliph" Al-Hakim, who ruled over the majority of the Islamic world from Damascus to Algiers in the early eleventh century, was notorious for his controlling and eccentric behavior. Decrees issued by the caliph included the execution of all dogs, a ban on the sale of women's shoes, and a law making the serving of a dish of stewed jute leaves—*mulukhiyah*—illegal on pain of death.[19] Al-Hakim was also notorious for his persecution of Jews and Christians, even going so far as to destroy the church of the Holy Sepulchre—where Jesus had been buried—in Jerusalem. The Church of the Nativity, however, he left curiously untouched, out of a sense of respect for its particular and peculiar holiness, which it seems was apparent even to a megalomaniac.[20]

Hakim's actions in Jerusalem contributed, in part, to the Crusades, and the brief return of the church to Christian rule. It had been a destination for pilgrims while under the Byzantines and the Caliphs, but the Crusader states actively encouraged a pilgrimage industry like never before. A visit to the church in the early thirteenth century so affected St Francis of Assisi that, afterwards, he would "always pronounce the word 'Bethleheeeeem' in the manner of a bleating sheep."[21] Francis was also known to lick his lips after saying it because he believed the name of the town to have an inherent sweetness.[22] Not content with these strange ticks by way of a holiday souvenir, Francis tried to re-create the cave and crib back at his church in Italy and so gave the world the some might say dubious gift of the tradition of the holiday Nativity scene.

Christian visitors from Western Europe in the nineteenth century were a little less enthusiastic about the religiosity that they encountered, struggling to see what on earth their polite, Western religion had to do with the lines of men and women who came to kiss the stones of the manger each morning. One—Mrs. Favell Lee Mortimer, author of the creatively named Victorian children's book *More about Jesus* and a clergyman's wife from Shropshire—remarked upon the preponderance of "images of the Virgin Mary and her holy child." "They were very pretty," she observed, "but they were idols. And God *hates* idols."[23] More enthusiastic was Gertrude Bell, who spent Christmas 1899 at the Church of the Nativity, but only after consuming "tea, then wine, then beer, with biscuits and sausages." She went to the service at 11:30 p.m. and didn't get to bed till "past three," where, despite or perhaps because of the wine and sausages, she "slept soundly until 8." In spite of the length of the liturgy, she seemed to enjoy the experience, although she did observe that the singing was "awful."[24]

As Victorian visitors went, Kaiser Wilhelm II was a little less easy to

The Church of the Nativity, Bethlehem, West Bank of Palestine   11

accommodate. When the German Emperor visited in the late nineteenth century, he insisted on riding to the church from Jerusalem in the heat of the day while wearing plate armor and a metal helmet, surmounted by an eagle.[25] On arrival, his requirements were so complicated that his official protocol officer produced a whole three pages of notes simply on the subject of which door he would use to enter the church.[26]

Since the Kaiser, modern heads of state have made it a regular stopping-off point on their all-too-regular trips to such a fractious region. Recent US presidents in particular have all made sure to visit. When President George W. Bush visited the grotto of the Nativity, he spent most of his time holding hands with two elderly Greek Orthodox priests.[27] President Barack Obama received a more muted welcome, with a group of Palestinians standing grimly outside the church with a faintly bemusing sign which read "GRINGO, RETURN TO YOUR COUNTRY."[28] There was the leader of perhaps the most powerful Christian nation ever to have come into existence and he was welcomed to the birthplace of Christ with what sounded like a quote from a Clint Eastwood movie.

More recently, King Charles III of the United Kingdom spoke of his visit to Bethlehem, in his first Christmas speech after the death of his mother. The Christmas Day speech had become Queen Elizabeth II's trademark mode of communication to her people and a cherished part of many Christmas Day traditions in Britain and across her former Empire. Most people had known no other voice for seventy years. Charles chose, in what would have felt a strange moment for many listening, to take people to Bethlehem.

"Some years ago, I was able to fulfill a lifelong wish to visit Bethlehem and the Church of the Nativity. There, I went down into the Chapel of the Manger and stood in silent reverence by the Silver Star that is inlaid on the floor and marks the place of our Lord Jesus Christ's birth. It meant more to me than I can possibly express to stand on that spot where, as the Bible tells us, 'The light that has come into the world' was born."[29]

Just a week after Charles's speech, another British icon came to Bethlehem. Gemma Collins is a British reality television star, who began her professional career as a car sales executive in Essex in the East of England. Her bombastic personality caught the attention of television executives and, from 2011, she became a regular face on British screens. Collins was known for escapades that included falling through a hole in the staging at a concert, advocacy of the concept of the "designer vagina," and for screaming the words "I'm claustrophobic, Darren" at a fellow contestant on Channel 4's *Celebrity Big Brother*. Collins went to Bethlehem just before the feast of the Epiphany—which marks the visit of the Magi to the infant Jesus—in early 2023. From the interior of the Church of the Nativity, she sent a video with the following comments:

"I've got tears running down my face. It's the most breathtaking experience of my life. The feeling here; you cannot describe it and I hope everyone experiences this once in their life. The feeling in here, the hairs stand on your end. I'm just breathless, like it is just so beautiful." The video was posted alongside a still photo of Collins in tears with a fistful of candle tapers.[30]

Collins, the King, St Francis of Assisi. Not people you would necessarily expect to find in the same room. Yet all could be found in the same place. At the manger. And all, expressed in their own idiosyncratic ways, had the same reaction: one of awe and wonder.

Alongside these, the great, good, and not so good, there have been, since the days of the Magi, millions of more ordinary visitors to the Church of the Nativity. People of every race and profession and part of the world have entered to pay homage to the place where they, like those saints and emperors and presidents, believed that their savior was born. The place where God became man. While there might appear to be a disparity between the ranks or importance of these visitors, the building imposes a sort of enforced uniformity. The Door of Humility—the main entrance to the church—forces all, king or commoner, pauper or president, to bend down as they enter. All, so the thinking goes, bow down, before the babe of Bethlehem.

The church itself is therefore more than just bricks and mortar. There is a sense of it as a living set of stones itself. It is more a doctrinal statement than an architectural one. The very first place where the Christian God

The Church of the Nativity, Bethlehem, West Bank of Palestine   13

incarnate was worshipped has set the tone for all the other churches we will visit on this tour around the Christian faith.

With Bethlehem in particular, there is a very pronounced sense that both the building and the town that now so depends on the tourism that its presence brings are not quite what they seem. Some of those medieval visitors, like the Tuscan friar and traveler Niccolò da Poggibonsi, thought it "grand and imposing," but both the destructive effects of time and our modern senses of scale and proportion make it hard to necessarily agree.[31] What is impressive is that it seems to be almost a metaphor for the messiness of Christianity itself: doors within doors, building materials from different times and cultures all mashed together in a palimpsest of stone. There are almost no windows and even the famous door is a dark, squat hole in the edifice that gives no sense of the interior. It is a place that conceals as much as it reveals, raises as many questions as it answers. Everyone goes there, and everyone leaves their mark. It is more like a complex, living organism rather than a static building. As such, it is a perfect metaphor for Christianity.

And like the faith whose beginning it bears witness to, the Church of the Nativity did not spring, in its current enigmatic form, from nowhere. It was shaped entirely by the people that were drawn to it, that reviled it, that loved it, that fought in and about it, that lived in it and died in it. Medieval pilgrims might have thought it grand but, by the nineteenth century, other words sprang to the mind of one visitor to the church and its surroundings:

> O Little Town of Bethlehem, how still we see thee lie.
> Above thy deep and dreamless sleep, the silent stars go by.

I have sung Bishop Brooks's carol about the little town of Bethlehem maybe a hundred times in my life. Perhaps more. The effect wears off after a while, with the temptation to view it as a twee, Victorian invocation of a sleepy Christmas-card version of the birthplace of Christianity all the more tempting on the hundredth singing. The words are also seemingly odd because they have rarely proved true of late or, indeed, in the earlier years of its history.

As a memorial to his beloved mother, Constantine expanded and beautified the shrine she had built on the site of the grotto. It was likely a large classical structure, designed to imitate the grandeur of Rome, even while honoring one who had been killed courtesy of its Empire. Constantine's structure didn't, in terms of the history of the site, last very long. At some point during the Samaritan revolts of the 500s, Constantine's church was burned to the ground. Beneath the current structure archaeologists have found the charred remains of the ornate mosaics and layers upon layers of ash.[32]

It was rebuilt by the Byzantines but, after this drama, Bethlehem did have deep and dreamless years. Following the Islamic conquests of the seventh century, long centuries of backwater status followed. The conquering caliph, Umar ibn al-Khattab, made a deal with the Greek monks in 638 to ensure the independence of the church and its continuation as a place of Christian worship enshrined in a suitably complicated and extensive document.[33] However, any changes to it had to undergo a lengthy approval by the Islamic legal system and so nearly half a century of relatively benign neglect occurred, with the occasional mosaic snuck past the eyes of the stricter Islamic scholars.

The Crusades meant a return to the cycle of violence, with Bethlehem returning to Christian control in 1099 to great rejoicing among the Crusaders. Less happy were the Greek clergy, who found themselves unceremoniously replaced by Latin Catholic Westerners, from whom the Greek Church had formally split in the earlier part of the eleventh century. The Crusaders restored and extended the church enormously, in particular paying attention to the decoration of the interior. They even, after appropriate time for the licking of wounds, allowed Greek and Armenian decoration to feature, too, as a sign that even a divided Christendom could find some unity on the site of the birth of Christ.[34]

A series of inter-Islamic power struggles followed the fall of the Crusader Kingdom of Jerusalem in 1187 and a period of further decline followed. Assorted treaties and counter treaties favored one group of squabbling monks followed by another. The various Islamic rulers mainly viewed the church as an income source for increasingly dubiously executed building repairs, managing to fleece the Duchy of Burgundy, the Kingdom of England, and the Republic of Venice for the restoration of its roof in just a single year.[35] Eventually, its Latin Catholic bishops didn't even bother to live there, a quirk of an ex-Crusader's last will and testament meaning they were instead resident in the Burgundian village of Clamecy until the French Revolution turfed them out in turn. Eventually, in the early sixteenth century, Bethlehem and its church came under the control of the Ottoman Empire and an era of dreamless decline followed once again.

Though they were aware of, and sought to manage, its religious significance, to the Ottomans, Bethlehem was quite literally "a little town," or "kasaba," according to the meticulous system of categorization so beloved by the bureaucrats of the Sublime Porte. When François-René de Chateaubriand visited during the lazy dog star–days of the late Ottoman Empire, his primary impression was of a place that was "miserable and isolated."[36] Like tourists before and since, he too moaned about having to pay for every little thing, partly as a result of the exorbitant Ottoman tax regime. By the time the author of the carol "O Little Town of Bethlehem," the future Bishop Brooks of Connecticut, visited it in 1865, it was in much the same state. Yet in his description of the sleepy and backwards town that it had become, Brooks managed to convey something very distinct about Bethlehem and something that was probably even more accurate at the time of the Nativity itself: that it was precisely its smallness and sleepiness that made it special.

He wasn't the first, of course, to identify something special about this. Micah, who in the 700s BC made the prophecy which would be so notably alluded to by Matthew in his Gospel, predicted that Bethlehem would be the place where a new sort of savior would emerge. "And thou, Bethlehem Ephratah, though thou be little among the thousands of Judah, yet out of thee shall he come forth unto me that is to be ruler in Israel, whose goings forth have been from of old, from everlasting."[37] The idea that this of all places would be the place where a Savior would arrive seemed as unlikely in 700 BC as it did at the start of the first century AD, as it does now.

Bethlehem, therefore, is a code. A deliberate cipher for a non-place. It could be Rotterdam or anywhere, Liverpool perhaps, but certainly

16   *Twelve Churches*

not Rome. At the time of the birth of Christ, the self-styled Eternal City was the center of the universe, the nursemaid of emperors, warlords, and tyrants, the grandest and greatest urban enterprise humanity had ever attempted. Bethlehem was more than just a backwater: it was as far from Rome as Roman geography—and society—could imagine.

Perhaps the best rendering of this contrast was written by Aurelius Prudentius Clemens, a Roman poet of the fourth century AD. His poem, "O Sola Magnarum Urbium," is now most often rendered as the hymn "Bethlehem of Noblest Cities," with a first verse that reads thus:

> BETHLEHEM! of noblest cities
> none can once with thee compare;
> thou alone the Lord from heaven
> didst for us Incarnate bear.[38]

To have declared the little town as superior to Rome at its absolute height would have seemed insane to the Romans. Yet, it is a testament to just how much Bethlehem—and specifically its central church—has transfigured our expectations and concepts of what is good or noble, that we instinctively know what the inference is today: in the small and the powerless, a beauty and grace and truth might be found that are lacking in the strong or monumental.

There is another irony here, of course. What brought the great and the good to Bethlehem was exactly the message that they might find it most difficult to hear. That God in Christianity is not just a God of the powerful and that the manger isn't just their manger, though some long imagined it to be so. Bethlehem is, if anything, even more the center for the despised or damaged or rejected or those living in the supposedly uninfluential corners of the globe. Indeed, it is the hope of little towns everywhere. Why? Well, the revelation which was birthed in its dark streets, of God made man, the idea of humanity hallowed and changed, has shaped the world and will continue to do so as the silent stars go by.

However, plenty of the rulers of Bethlehem over the years weren't especially interested in the fact that it was a theological center but instead were primarily interested in its potential as a money-making machine. The Ottomans in particular viewed Bethlehem as a tax farm rather than as the site of the incarnation. As the years progressed, even the site of the Nativity itself became more than ever a place obsessed with the minor and the petty rather than the immanent or holy. As the Ottomans profited from a divide-and-rule mentality, throughout the 1800s, arguments between Catholics, Armenians, and Orthodox broke out, often resulting in physical violence. Monastic habits would turn into blurs of white, Black, and brown as various orders and denominations indulged in brawls in the church. They continue to this day. Sometimes they are small-scale: a fistfight over the color of a new curtain in 1869 or an incident as recent as 2011 when a group of rival priests bashed one another on the heads with brooms during the annual Christmas clean-up, resulting in the intervention of riot police.[39] Sometimes the fights were more serious: a dispute over who stole the star on the top of the church in the early 1850s, for example, arguably led to the Crimean War.

One day, the monks of the Latin rite noticed that their star was missing. Suspicion immediately fell upon the Greek and Syriac Orthodox monks, who hated the presence of the star, not least because they kept Christmas in early January rather than December and felt it was, at best, unseasonal. The dispute led the Ottomans into giving the Latin Roman Catholic monks a key in an attempt to stop future thefts. The Orthodox viewed this as an impingement of their ancient rights confirmed by sultans past and suspected it was all a profiteering ruse by the Catholics to benefit from wealthy Western visitors; mobs in St Petersburg, Athens, and Constantinople asked, "Must we be robbed by these wretched Turks to gratify a few French tourists?"[40] As the great powers of France and Russia piled in to back their respective sides, Europe slid toward war. The Church of the Nativity remained a focal point where global tensions could spill over.

Undoubtedly, what many believe happened at Bethlehem changed our perceptions of life and of what it is to be alive. Yet its role in provoking conflict points to another side to Bethlehem that is darker; a side to Bethlehem that is as closely linked to the history and theology that has unfolded there and yet speaks of something very different. For as much as Bethlehem is a city of life, it is also a city of death.

18   *Twelve Churches*

Unlike King Charles and Barack Obama, St Francis of Assisi and Gemma Collins, or any of the millions of people whose names go unrecorded, from little towns all over the globe, I could not visit the Church of the Nativity. Unlike other churches in this book, I cannot tell you of my time there or the people I met; for my detail I rely not on my own observations or experiences but those of others across thousands of years. The closest I got to Bethlehem was that conversation with Yazid, years before this book was even a coherent concept. In other places I could step on the very floors where saints had trod, but circumstances meant that I couldn't go and touch where kings and reality stars and widows and sinners have knelt down and felt the sense of God nearby. Indeed, I couldn't go to Bethlehem at all.

Despite the narrative of the peaceful little town and for all the sense that this is the place from where Christians mark the beginning of the story of eternal life, Bethlehem has been stalked by trauma and by death. That is the other side of Bethlehem, and the other side of Christianity as a whole. Both life and death are inherently linked. In the world of today, it is impossible to watch a news report or refresh social media without a reminder that Bethlehem has recently been at the heart of such violence as has become normal in the West Bank, where the little town now lies.

However, for all the horrors of today's news, this is no new phenomenon. Matthew's Gospel relates that pain and death came to Bethlehem almost as soon as Jesus had been born. He relates that the Magi realized that Herod's interest in their trip to visit the Christ child had not been entirely a religious one. Fearful of the political consequences of a child Messiah, Herod orders the massacre of all baby boys up to the age of two in Bethlehem and the surrounding region, in an attempt to eliminate Christ before his ministry can begin.[41] The reason for Bethlehem being made holy also became a reason for its weeping and sorrow. From the very beginning of Christianity, life and death were inseparable themes.

While some scholars now doubt the historicity of the massacre, and think it an attempt to draw a theological link between Herod and the Pharaoh of Egypt, who ordered a similar massacre in the book of Exodus, the power of the story resonated across Christian generations.[42] In medieval Coventry—the English weaving town—a carol based on the

massacre became a centerpiece of the annual pageants that characterized local religious life. Three mothers would come on stage and sing, to
a haunting melody, the following words:

> Lully, lullah, thou little tiny child,
>> Bye bye, lully, lullay.
>> Thou little tiny child,
>> Bye bye, lully, lullay.

> That woe is me, poor child, for thee
> And ever mourn and may
> For thy parting neither say nor sing,
> "Bye bye, lully, lullay."

In an age where infant mortality was between 30% and 50% of all babies
born, it must have been even more moving then than it is today.[43] Yet, the
medieval mothers of Coventry were expressing something radical about
the Christian faith. The sense that even the tragic loss of a child was
something mirrored in the story of salvation would have been a comfort
to those who grieved. Bethlehem was a place of pain and hope bound
together, and so more reflective of ordinary lives than a picture-perfect
"little town."

After these initial horrors there came those endless centuries of conquest and counter conquest, monks fighting endlessly about the smallest
details of who got to worship where and when. What is painfully ironic
is that much of that violence and pain was caused by the fact that people
did view Bethlehem as special, as a holy and symbolic place.

Perhaps the starkest recent reminder of this tension in recent years
was the incident during what became known as the Second Intifada, a
period of heightened violence in the Holy Land between Israel and Palestine, which lasted between the years 2000 and 2005. As Israeli troops
entered Bethlehem in the early hours of April 2, 2002, members of a
fragmented Palestinian resistance, both official and otherwise, retreated
to the very heart of the city and took shelter in the Church of the Nativity. Those dark streets which had once so captivated Bishop Brooks were

blockaded with burned-out cars and rubbish to prevent the advance of Israeli tanks.[44] A stand-off began between the two sides, with sixty or so monks and nuns remaining inside the church, caught in the middle and yet determined to keep the vow they had made as custodians of the holy place.

Over the following month or so, a number of people were killed, including the church's bell ringer; still more were wounded, including monks. Fires broke out and the world watched aghast—leaders from the Pope to the US president appealed for peace and for calm. The eyes of the world were on Bethlehem once more, but as much in horror as in awe.

Finally, a deal was negotiated some thirty-nine days after the siege had begun. As aid workers and clergy arrived in the building to survey the damage, there was "an overwhelming smell of urine."[45] The main body of the building found itself strewn with discarded ammunition and the full panoply of the detritus of life lived by 200 people at close quarters. The grotto and site of the manger, however, were unscathed. And yet, there was a hope, as the Intifada finished, that the negotiations around the church might provide a model for a wider resolution and that hope might yet spring from the message of the Nativity.[46] It was not to be, as the world today bears witness. Today, in 2025, as when faced with Herod's anger or during the Crusades or the Intifada, Bethlehem is a place that is troubled, where death is all too well known. The origin story and its themes are not so distant after all.

The present day, therefore, is as subversive a time as any to assert the holiness of the little town. Dreamless sleeps have become daily nightmares. In 2023 the Church of the Nativity elected, *contra* St Francis, not to have a crib scene. Instead, in light of the destruction across the Holy Land, the figure of the infant Christ lies in a heap of rubble. The beginnings of the Church, the earliest moment of Christianity, still has power and ramifications today. To view Bethlehem—and indeed to view Christianity—as merely two-dimensional in what it offers is a mistake. The origin story of the Christian faith isn't just a comforting myth of a baby on a winter's night, but rather the means by which a completely radical change to what it means to be a human in all its manifestations

The Church of the Nativity, Bethlehem, West Bank of Palestine   21

might be understood. Put another way, either the incarnation—God as man—embraces the darkest moments of human existence, and offers hope for them, or it has no real relevance at all.

This is at the heart of what Bethlehem has come to mean. The contrast of its smallness and troubled history with the hope and magnitude of the message imparted there has shaped Christianity in ways beyond all telling. The fact that this backwater—often the scene of humanity's worst instincts—is the place of the actual incarnation of the living God, with all its consequences for both divinity and humanity, is monumental precisely because of its paradoxical nature, precisely because of its ridiculousness. As we will see when we travel from imperial cities to barren hillsides, from shanty towns to opulent halls of marble, through different continents and centuries, the power of Bethlehem is that it opens up the potential for any place, however unlikely, to become holy.

Bethlehem has therefore affected more than just Christianity's theology of place: it has changed how we think about everything. Secular liberalism might like to imagine that its concern for the individual or its concern for the needy comes from the Athenian agora or the Roman senate or, perhaps most superstitiously of all, is simply magically imparted in our brains at birth, but in reality all the specific concerns for what is right or true or beautiful to people in the West flow from the manger. From Bethlehem.

Christianity might be a complex and interwoven phenomenon, its historical and societal consequences might be perhaps the most complicated and conflicting of any human idea in existence, but, as we begin our survey of those consequences, it is worth recalling that at its heart remains the message first imparted at Bethlehem, the idea of "God with us."

We will see this again and again in all of the churches which we do manage to visit. But Bethlehem's history represents that idea better than any other place. It does not say that God is with us only in times of success or particular holiness, only by being pure or proper, or only during life. If the Church of the Nativity shows us anything it is that life and death are interwoven. That is the hope that marks Christianity out: God being with us is not a statement with terms and conditions, but rather one that applies throughout history, in all times and in all places. That is the real power of the manger. The second half of the carol puts it thus:

Yet in thy dark streets shineth
The everlasting light
The hopes and fears of all the years
Are met in thee tonight.

If no place better speaks of this great encompassing of history than Bethlehem, then no building in Bethlehem speaks of it better than the Church of the Nativity. There is a reason why so many people describe their visit to this strange, higgledy-piggledy church as one of the most important moments of their lives. This mad, confusing warren of a building, with steps down one way and up another, impractically small doorways, and great, looming domes, which has seen politics, violence, profit, and death, perhaps represents the beautiful paradoxes of the Christian faith better than any other. Not least because, in the very middle of its structural contradictions, lies a simple, powerful place: the tiny chapel in a cave with a silver star inlaid in the floor. In the midst of chaos, beauty; in the midst of death, life; and in the midst of the human, the Divine.

Chapter Two

St Peter's, Rome, Italy

(First worship on the site *c.* 65 AD, foundation
of current building laid 1506)

With the earthly ministry of Christ—his incarnation, crucifixion, resurrection, and ascension—complete, the next stage of Christianity was defined by the establishment of church as a human community. The gathering together of people across the Mediterranean world in specific places to form their lives around the revelation that they believed had been made at Bethlehem. At first in houses, and later in specific, beautified buildings, communities of believers became the first "churches." In doing so, they clashed first with the religious authorities of Judaism and then, more sensationally, with the great political, military, social, economic, and aesthetic superpower of the day: Rome. The next chapter in Christianity's history was to see whether its vision of what was beautiful and true could possibly survive in the face of the dominant pagan power. Rome itself was the scene of the showdown.

Cracked pavements are not rare in Rome. As such, the one that exists a short walk from the Colosseum elicits little notice. Weeds poke through the gaps in the flagstones and the gates that sit above them seem to be ever half open or half closed. Groups of tourists tramp past the gateway with no hint of recognition at all, their eyes fixed on the waved umbrella or flag that will take them to the next church. This nonchalance would have surprised the Ancient Romans. It was here that the entrance stood to the Domus Aurea—in English, "the Golden House"—once the grandest residence in the city and therefore in the entire Empire.

Even by the standards of the Romans, no strangers to the monumental, the complex was enormous. Since the establishment of the Empire, multiple rulers had engaged in building projects in central Rome, largely to remind both the fickle populace and even more fickle elite of their power and their goodwill. The strategy, unfortunately, didn't really work. By the time of the initial construction of the Golden House, in 64 AD, plenty of Caesars had come and gone since our last encounter with them, as far-off heads of state over the Roman province of Syria. The Emperor at the time of Christ's crucifixion, the "most gloomy" Tiberius, had died, probably assassinated, as had his successor, the mad and bad Caligula, who was definitely assassinated.[1] So, too, had the quietly competent Claudius, who was quite possibly assassinated, with Nero, his stepson, acceding to the imperial throne in 54 AD. This Golden House—the most ambitious imperial building commission yet—was the brainchild and pet project of this latter emperor. Where there are now cracked pavements, opulence reigned. Contemporary chroniclers described corridors and colonnades a mile long, water of any temperature piped in across an inordinately complex canal system, and, above all else, every single surface in the palace was covered in gold and encrusted with pearls and rare jewels. At the center of the palace's main atrium stood a 120-foot statue of Nero himself. On his first inspection, the Emperor made only one comment: "Finally," he said, "I will be housed in a place fit for human habitation!"[2] The palace and its related extravagant engineering works were, in the words of the Roman historian Tacitus, a monument to Nero's "love of the impossible."[3] Perhaps more than that, it was a monument to Nero's love of beauty. And, of course, his love of himself.

And yet, despite the seeming impossibility of its scope and design, as the Domus Aurea neared the end of its construction in 68 AD, the impossible had become a reality. The network of halls, pools, and pleasure gardens had reached completion in a mere four years—a feat impressive even in modern terms. In ancient ones, it's practically miraculous. What had made it so? How had Nero managed to achieve his pursuit of the beautifully impossible? Well, as always with incidents involving the man born Lucius Domitius Ahenobarbus, but known to infamy as the Emperor Nero, the details do not make particularly pleasant reading.

Dr. Freud would have had a field day with Nero. His father, Gnaeus Domitius, described by the chronicler Suetonius as "detestable in every single way," behaved in a manner which was considered by the Romans—who were not, as we have discussed, bywords for moral rectitude—as beyond the pale.[4] He was known as a violent, drunken fraudster, once deliberately swerving his chariot in order to run over a child playing with a doll near the street. His other pastimes included blinding people, treason, and incest. Nero's mother, Agrippina, meanwhile, filled her time with poison, driving people to suicide and incest. When people congratulated Gnaeus on the birth of his son, even he remarked that he doubted any child produced by him and his wife was likely to be good news for the population at large. He was right.[5]

The revelers arrived at the party with some trepidation. Any social engagement hosted by Nero, the man who had engineered the murder of his mother during a riparian entertainment, was an event at which being on your guard was essential. What were considered horrors by ordinary people were mere practical jokes for the Emperor. The location of the party was the Emperor's own gardens. Arriving as the sun was low in the sky, the guests wondered quite how it was that Nero intended to light the proceedings, which were scheduled to go on, outside, until the small hours of the morning. It soon became very, horrifically clear. Along the pathway to the dining area, silhouetted by the dying light, were masts, dug into the ground, to which were tied bodies, men and women, young and old, some limp, some still writhing in agony. These unfortunates were covered in pitch and tar and, as the guests made their way toward dinner, they were set alight. Every one of the human torches was a Christian.

The use of human beings as candles was just one of the ways in which Christians met their deaths in Rome during the mid-60s AD. Other grisly methods of dispatch included crucifixion, the preferred Roman punishment for criminals and, of course, the fate of Christ himself, as well as death in the arenas of Rome, being ripped apart by wild dogs and other animals. Christians being "thrown to the lions" might well have become a stereotype, but Nero saw it as a convenient way of punishing Christian believers—in particular those who refused to renounce their faith under torture—and therefore provide the circuses of the "panem et circenses," which the Roman populace required so as to be kept onside. To add to the macabre amusement of it all, sometimes victims would be dressed up in or sown into animal skins in order to give the appearance of a pursuit from the natural world.[6]

28   *Twelve Churches*

Nero's narrative was clear: the Christians deserved this, and no punishment was sadistic enough. But what could they possibly have done to deserve punishments that turned even the stomachs of Roman dinner-party goers, men and women who ate putrefied fish and cow's vulva by way of entrées? Well, according to the Emperor, they had tried to destroy Rome itself.

Just as people were beginning to go to sleep on the night of July 18 64 AD, in the midst of an already hot and dry Roman summer, a fire—or perhaps a series of fires—broke out in a densely packed neighborhood near the Circus Maximus in Rome. Soon, multiple parts of the city were ablaze, and it became clear that the rudimentary fire protection measures in place were not going to stop the spread of the flames between the city's compacted residential areas. The historian Cassius Dio described how, as soon as people began trying to put out one fire, news that another fire had started or spread would reach the rescuers, causing yet more panic.[7] The Roman populace, renowned neither for their moral rectitude nor for quiet, calm deliberation, soon gave up trying to put the inferno out and turned to looting one another's houses and running about like madmen. The fire was said to have burned for nine days, with Tacitus estimating that only four areas of the city remained untouched.[8] Modern historians and archaeologists put a conservative estimate of the damage at about a third of the city, some reckon closer to 70% of it.[9] At least 200,000 people were rendered homeless. Both the vengeful instincts of the Roman population and the specific circumstances of the fire were such that someone needed to be found to take the blame for the disaster. The official answer was not long coming. The destruction, it was alleged by Nero, had been the work of the small but growing group who claimed that a Jew from one of the far-off Eastern provinces of the Empire had been the son of the one true God: the Christians.[10]

In many ways, Nero had chosen his scapegoats well. Christians were not popular in Rome. Their moral code, their preference for the weak and the poor, and the rumors that their celebration of the Eucharist—the sharing of bread and wine—was in fact a ritual where they cannibalized their founder and ate his body and blood, all made for a sense that they were outcasts, a danger to the established patterns of Roman society. Yet even among the most enthusiastic pagans of Rome, the Emperor's actions elicited disgust. The Christians might be odd, might even be dangerous to the fabric of Rome and her society in some cases, but the idea that they deserved the particularly cruel treatments meted out in the aftermath of the fire was a step too far. Many even began to articulate the thought that was on many a Roman mind: that they didn't believe the Christians were responsible for the catastrophe at all. After all, it was the fire which had enabled Nero—most conveniently—to begin the construction of his long-planned Golden House. Surely it was not a coincidence that the area most comprehensively cleared by the flames provided the perfect location for a personal pleasure palace for the Emperor of Rome? As the horrors inflicted on Christians intensified, Romans began to ask: Was this a price worth paying for beauty?

The idea that Nero himself had engineered the fire in order to begin his great construction became part of the lore about Rome's least appealing Emperor, especially after his demise, when, as with all political monsters, people who had supported and enabled him suddenly discovered just how appalling they had actually found him to be. However, such voices were few and far between in the years immediately after the catastrophe, as Nero's increasingly violent personal rule continued unabated, with the "new and maleficent" sect of the Christians in the firing line.[11]

The persecution really reached its apogee around the year 67 AD, just as the Domus Aurea was reaching its completion. Among those who died a horrific death in this final flourish of Nero's bloodlust was an elderly former fisherman from Judea. Or at least he had been a fisherman. Much had changed since he'd mended nets beside the Sea of Galilee, not least his name. Then he had been Simon, but now he was known as Peter. It is said that Peter—perhaps as a reflection of his status as a known leader of the Christians—managed to elicit a concession from those who were putting him to death.[12] Rather than the conventional method of crucifixion, where the victim would be pinned, bolt upright, to the cross until, horribly, the pressure forced their chest to collapse in on itself, he would be crucified upside down, with his legs in the air. He did so because he felt that, though he had been granted the crown of martyrdom, he did not believe that he was worthy to die in the same manner as Christ. The same Christ who had been his leader, his friend, and, he believed, his savior. For all the tenderness and piety of the sentiment, Peter's death would have been an ugly sight, the old man gasping for his final breaths, blood from the nails in his hands and feet wreathing the wood and flesh.

Despite the horror of Peter's death, if Nero thought that, by killing the community's leader, he was removing a dangerous fifth column once and for all, he was wrong. Many of the executions took place on the far side of the River Tiber from Nero's great beautification project: the Theater of Nero and the surrounding gardens were two notable arenas where the mass martyrdom of the Christians took place. They were in a part of Rome far from the fashionable hills on the other bank of the River. They were also deliberate examples of that great Roman obsession of "rus in urbe," the countryside *in* the city. These gardens, though, were not as organized and cultivated as those around Nero's palace. Rather, they were something of a wilderness. The perfect location, the Emperor decided, for the executions, including that of Peter.

The location of the amphitheater is fairly well known. It was originally built by Caligula but became associated with Nero, who expanded it. Little remains now, in the form of felled marble pillars and the outlines of foundations. These currently lie in the courtyard of the Palazzo della Rovere, a building split, in a gloriously unlikely shared tenancy, between the Four Seasons hotel chain and the Equestrian Order of the Holy Sepulchre, which began life as a group of crusading knights but later morphed into an order of chivalry whose members had the specific privileges of being allowed to legitimize bastards and riding a horse into a church. Visiting them is difficult; an elderly priest shook his head forlornly when I enquired about entry. Perhaps I should return on horseback?

Of the gardens, by contrast, very little remains. On top of them is now the Vatican, the center of the Roman Catholic Church and a symbol of Christianity more generally the world over. The church there is dedicated to none other than Peter. It is in a palace more filled with art and examples of beauty than even the Domus Aurea that the successor to the Galilean fisherman—that first Bishop of Rome, or Pope, as they became known—now lives. Even the most faithful and hopeful of the huddled outcasts, awaiting their fate upon the same site nearly 2,000 years ago, would, I suspect, struggle to believe that the place where they were to meet their horrible deaths would become symbolic of the triumph of Christianity and renowned, specifically, for its beauty. But then history—especially the history of Christianity—is a study in the unlikely and the unexpected.

Today, the site on which Nero conceived of a house of unsurpassed beauty is a hodgepodge of cracked pavements and fragmentary ruins, visited by a few in the know but often passed by. The site of Peter's martyrdom is, by contrast, perhaps the most visited building in the entire world.[13] Specifically, it is visited by millions every year on account of its beauty. It might seem odd for a faith to seek to venerate the place where such unbeautiful events took place, but Christianity has always been masterly in its reversal of the expected. We might even feel the faintest pang of sympathy for the monster Nero: he really didn't know what it was he was taking on.

Yet the very fact that Christianity, too, like the Roman Emperors, sought to pursue the beautiful in the Eternal City is its own story. The tension between the quest for beauty and its cost didn't die with the Domus Aurea, and added to it came the question—particularly pertinent for the followers of the man who chose fishermen as his disciples— of whether beauty has anything to do with God at all. All this was to play out on the site of Peter's martyrdom. In that place, symbolic above all else of the interplay between the beauty of holiness and the ugliness of history, the Christian quest for beauty would itself prove capable of getting very ugly indeed.

On the morning of Pentecost Sunday 1972, a man dressed in a full dinner suit and bow tie entered the basilica of St Peter's during the main morning Mass. He made a beeline to a statue of the Virgin Mary cradling a dead Christ, which was located on the immediate right-hand side of the entrance. He then leapt over the low altar railing that separated the side chapel from the main aisle of the church and, after taking a hammer from his pocket, began to smash the face of the Virgin. As he did so he screamed, "I am Jesus Christ, risen from the dead!"

32   *Twelve Churches*

He was not, in fact, Jesus Christ, but actually a man called Lazslo Toth, a Hungarian-born Australian geologist. Understandably, his outbreak of extreme independent thought didn't go down very well with the worshippers and tourists who had come to see St Peter's that day. He was wrestled to the ground by onlookers, but not until he managed to inflict fifteen hammer blows on the sculpture. One of the men who tackled Toth was the American sculptor Bob Cassilly, who had been staring at the sculpture for inspiration.[14] Cassilly was the first to notice what damage Toth had done and snarled, "I'll kill the guy," but, by his own admission, only managed to "get one good punch in."[15]

Toth was suddenly an international superstar. He was described, as people who do unexpectedly violent things often are in subsequent press reports, as a "nice guy" by his roommate in the Roman youth hostel in which he was living prior to the attack.[16] Toth had begun to grow his hair and his beard in a way that mimicked conventional representations of Jesus, had moved to Rome specifically to mark his thirty-third year (the age of Christ at the crucifixion), and had spent the previous few months writing letters to Pope Paul VI, inviting him to meet with and presumably then worship him.

Despite the obvious diagnosis of Messiah syndrome, as the marble dust cleared, multiple more complex explanations for Toth's actions were posited in the global press. It was suggested by terribly clever people that Toth had "lost all ability to distinguish between an image and the reality it denotes."[17] Yet cleverer still people saw in Toth a reaction against the Jungian anima, which he saw in the form of a denaturalized projection of a mother figure.[18] Toth's repeated insistence that he was Jesus Christ and his later claim that the statue deserved to be destroyed because its arms didn't move would point more reasonably in the direction eventually reached by the Italian and Vatican authorities: that he was insane.

What is perhaps more interesting than the motivation for Toth's act itself was the reaction to it. People were horrified: but not only because the statue was a religious one. Indeed, even the over-academic explanations suggested in the 1970s hinged on the fact that the statue was no ordinary depiction of the Virgin Mary and Christ. The representation of Mary cradling Christ was the "Pietà" of Michelangelo, considered

St Peter's, Rome, Italy 33

by many to be perhaps the finest example of Renaissance sculpture on earth.[19] Particularly powerful are the details of the arms of Christ, limp at his mother's side, the attention given to the ribs and muscles of the dead man, and the skill required to capture a specific human moment of anguish on the face of the Blessed Virgin. What gave it its beauty was, and is, in part the awe inspired by realizing that someone has managed to make such an accurate and moving similitude of flesh out of stone. The vandalism started a global debate about the nature of beauty. Not every eye that looked upon the smashed marble saw its damaged form as a tragedy: some praised Toth and his "gentle hammer" for challenging aesthetic standards.[20] The argument was that the standard of beauty personified by the statue was an artificial one and that a broken statue was a better embodiment of a broken world. The fact that Mary is portrayed as younger than her son in the statue was seen as preposterous, the poses contrived or formulaic. Once again, in Rome, the quest for beauty was causing trouble, though this time spilling ink rather than blood.

Toth's destructive efforts also revealed an interior life of the statue, and revealed that its beauty was more complex than first thought. As restoration work began, to try to repair the damage done by the errant Hungarian, it was discovered that the inside of the Virgin Mary's hand had an "M" carved on it: it is thought to be the only piece that Michelangelo ever signed. The artist had a mixed relationship with that particular subject. His other take on Mary cradling Christ after being taken down from the cross was also attacked, à la Toth, with a hammer. However, the person who damaged the "Florentine Pietà" was Michelangelo himself, it is said because he felt it did not match up to the form and accuracy of its Vatican counterpart. Whether it was a case of an artist driven mad by the quest for beauty—or, perhaps, that he was suffering an attack of the bipolar disorder which modern scholars believe he might have had—is unknown.[21] Either way, before he was eventually restrained, the great maestro of Renaissance sculpture smashed the arms and expressions of the figures, leaving a scarred and jarring depiction of the same scene which later provoked the wrath of Toth.

Fortunately, the Vatican statue was spared a similar fate. The Pietà has always been in St Peter's. First in a funerary chapel in the old building

34   *Twelve Churches*

and later moving to the "Secretaire," a sort of Papal locker room where the pontiff would change clothes between masses. Finally, it was moved in the eighteenth century to the front right hand of the church. Its presence as the first and last thing that visitors see is a testament to the power of beauty to inspire faith to this day. The statue has become a wider symbol of St Peter's itself and of the central role that the quest for the beautiful has in defining the place and the people who have lived and prayed there. Indeed, it has become a symbol for how the Christian faith—more than any other human phenomenon since the Roman Empire itself—has shaped our concept of what beauty is.

It wasn't always thus. St Peter's as a repository for beauty is a less likely story than one might expect. It is not known exactly when the first church was built near the Vatican. It seems odd to even imagine today, especially when standing on St Peter's Square, in the Holy See itself, a state whose modern political setup has the public practice of the Christian religion at its center, that at one point worship probably happened here only in secret. The tombs of many of the martyrs—Peter, it is assumed, included—were on the edge of the Vatican gardens. In the immediate weeks after Peter's grisly execution nearby, people began to visit the graves and, in defiance of Nero and the whole Roman imperial structure, they worshipped there too. This was common Christian practice across Rome, with some of the most active areas for the practice of the Christian religion in the first few centuries of its existence in Italy being the catacombs, underground cities of the dead that became places of worship, both subterranean and subversive, for the new believers. Such locations might seem macabre to us, but, as well as being a necessity—it's much easier to avoid becoming one of Nero's candles if you're underground—they also became a statement of the fundamental Christian belief in love, and life, being stronger than earthly death. Roman Catholicism's long fascination with death and, at times, seemingly gruesome preoccupation with human remains, seems a little more understandable when one realizes just how baked in the symbiosis between the living and the dead is to its DNA.

Yet the Christians were not destined to labor beneath the surface of the city, like holy moles, for long. The key transition in their status—and in Rome's life—came with the Emperor Constantine's conversion to Christianity. Although he would become focused on his new power-base of Constantinople, Rome was where Constantine's Christian story began, at a site near the basilica of St John Lateran. The brick octagon of the baptistry there dates from just after the Battle of the Milvian Bridge in 312 AD and is a rare complete survival of the era of Roman imperial Christianity. Why rare? Well, less than a century after Constantine's baptism, disaster struck the Empire's capital, which was to change the face of the city, and the world, forever.

At the time of the birth of Christ and for centuries after, up to and including Constantine's rebirth, Rome had been arguably the most beautiful city on earth, or certainly the most monumental and impressive. It was a very different city 500 years after the Nativity. In fact, it wasn't even really a city at all. Having reached a peak population of well over a million in the third and fourth centuries AD, Rome in the sixth and seventh centuries had perhaps barely 30,000 people in it.[22] For context, that is akin to the present-day populations of the town of Pontypridd in Wales, or St Neots near Cambridge in the UK, or Fulshear, just outside Houston, Texas, in the United States. It is roughly the number of people employed by the UK bakery firm Greggs as of 2023. The sacks of Rome in 410 by the Visigoths and in 476 by the Vandals played their parts, destroying much of the ancient infrastructure and leaving buildings like Constantine's baptistry as unusual survivors. However, the thing that had the most catastrophic impact on the city's expanse was not a single event but rather a series of failures, which made it impossible to secure sufficient grain imports to support the once vast urban population. Even in the City of Beauty, the embodiment of Italy's "Grand Bellezza," sometimes the prosaic wins out.

As political power departed conclusively to Constantinople and ordinary people left for the countryside and smaller, easier-to-defend settlements across Italy, the remaining Romans milled about the crumbling remains of what was once the most impressive conurbation on earth. It must have been like living on another planet, rattling around the monumental structures of a civilization now inescapably alien. Sheep were

36   *Twelve Churches*

grazed in the Forum where Cicero had spoken, wild animals slinked where once the crowds had cheered on the Circus Maximus; it was perhaps the closest to a post-apocalyptic landscape that there has ever been on earth. It is no wonder that the shocked, smaller populace of Rome looked to the Church not only for moral guidance but also for the return of beauty.

Theologically, the Church—now arguably the sole stable institution left in the fractured remnants of the Roman Empire—was up to the challenge. Rome—indeed all of the Europe which she once ruled—would be reshaped in the Church's image, with Christian beauty at the forefront of this reimagining of space. At exactly the same time that Cassian and others were extolling the power of simplicity in habits and aesthetics in the Christian East, a bishop in the West, Hilary of Poitiers, was writing at length that it was through "the beauty of the things that He hath made [that] the Creator of worlds is rightly discerned." The beautiful was, Hilary argued, a key attribute of God, and so finding God through the beautiful was the duty of anyone who sought to follow the Christian faith.[23] This was to find its physical expression in the new landscape of the Roman metropolis. Beautification became the physical expression of sanctification. The blood of martyrdom might have been what made a place holy theologically speaking, but the way to show that holiness was by paint and mosaic, use of light and space; in short, by beauty.

Soon it wasn't just where Peter died that was adorned and beautified. Places where he had visited became churches and basilicas on the strength of the connection, places where he probably hadn't visited did too. Perhaps most significantly, the Marmetine prison, a grim dungeon cut into the slope of the Capitoline hill, became a church too. Peter had been held there, in Rome's most infamous place of incarceration, prior to his crucifixion. The Marmetine was the place where the Roman Republic and then Empire kept their most infamous captives, from the Cataline conspirators to Gaulish chieftains. There was only one way in and out, through a narrow hatch. Sometimes food was thrown down into it, often it wasn't. A tiny, slimy spring dribbled its way along one corner of the cell, providing some water, but also bone-chilling damp. Peter made use of the trickle of water, baptizing fellow prisoners to whom he and Paul had preached. Now, the most feared dungeon in the Roman world is a small chapel. Into the stone of the altar is carved an upside-down cross: even the means of Peter's martyrdom was transformed into a symbol for veneration. As it became clear that the Papacy was going to become a political force as well as a religious one, so, one by one, the old sites that symbolized the power of Nero and his successors were converted into bastions of the new faith and its increasingly institutional expression, the Church. By the time the Middle Ages dawned, the Petrification of Ancient Rome was complete. Prisons, palaces, gardens and homes: all were churches, churches, churches. It was Peter's city now. And so, with both political and religious power in hand, Peter's successors meant to make it, once again, the most beautiful one on earth.

Naturally, the centerpiece of this new city was to be the church built on top of Peter's tomb itself. It was going to be a symbol of the victory of Christianity over the Rome of old. The process of its construction was piecemeal. Almost as soon as he had converted, Constantine himself commissioned the church which was to form the heart of the old site, a basilica on the classical Roman model, as part of his Christianization project for the imperial capital. Proliferations followed: Pope Leo the Great added monastic accommodation, Symmachus a baptistry, Gregory the Great a passage through the crypt. Alongside this there was endless fiddling with the existing fabric: a side chapel here, a new altar there.[24] Successive generations lumped their concepts of the beautiful on top of one another. Occasionally, however, beauty had to give way to practicality: yet another sack of Rome—by the Saracens in 846—resulted in the less beautiful but eminently sensible addition of a defensive wall by the practically inclined Pope Leo IV.[25] With this endless cycle of addition, the church soon became the largest in the world. From drawings and first-hand accounts, a labyrinthine and occasionally structurally dangerous vision emerges. However, as lifelike as many of these descriptions are, the truth is that we cannot know for sure exactly what the old St Peter's looked like. In particular, while it was certainly monumental and subject to the awe of pilgrims from across Europe, it's impossible to know whether it was beautiful.[26]

What we do know is that, for much of the medieval period, St Peter's was seen by the Papacy as an embarrassment at best and an outright mistake at worst. Much as we might now associate the Vatican with the Pope, most medieval pontiffs preferred the calmer surroundings of their palaces on the Lateran or Quirinal hills, or simply got out of Rome altogether. They had good reason to. The area immediately around St Peter's was now not so much a romantic Roman vision of "rus in urbe" but more a dangerous wilderness. Bandits mingled with livestock among the ruins. Indeed, the targeting of pilgrims as they made their way to St Peter's became such a problem that, in the twelfth century, Pope Celestine III had to issue a specific edict reminding people that it was not fair game to steal things from people on pilgrimage. The fact that it had to be quoted in numerous future legal cases, both in Rome itself and further along the pilgrimage routes, suggests that it wasn't a particularly effective decree.[27]

The presence of Old St Peter's (as the predecessor to the current building is now known) didn't do much to calm the populace and make the area safer. If anything, as the medieval age wore on, it became even more of a focal point for violence and disorder. The schism which affected the Church of the late Middle Ages, whereby the Pope ruled from Avignon, where he was held as a de facto puppet prisoner of the King of France and so left the City of Peter without its nominal political and religious hierarch, only worsened Rome's reputation as a place for ugly behavior. The Papal conclave of 1378 ended in farcical scenes as cardinals clambered out of windows and across roofs as a way of escaping the recalcitrant populace in the square outside the basilica, who were put out that the princes of the Church seemed unlikely to elect their preferred candidate, a Roman gangster.[28]

The return of the Popes to Rome in the early fifteenth century focused the minds of the successors of Peter on the need for a more fitting church dedicated to his memory. The first figure to begin to dream big again with regard to St Peter's was Pope Nicholas V. He was elected at a crucial moment: not only had the Papacy just returned to Rome, but the eyes of Europe had now become firmly fixed on Italy and her classical heritage as "new"—for which read "old"—ideas of beauty became fashionable. Nicholas realized that the city of Rome needed no longer to be an embarrassment to the Papacy, but was, in fact, a treasure trove of ancient artifacts and an inspiration for new art as well. Alongside his cultural predilections, Nicholas had navigated a successful career as a diplomat and politician prior to ascending to the throne of Peter. He brought the skills honed managing the courts of Europe to managing the people of Rome. One of his first declarations was of a "Jubilee," essentially inviting all Europe to the city. Ostensibly this was for remission of their sins; however, others suspected that Nicholas had an ulterior motive. The Croatian humanist Janus Pannonius wrote: "All rush to Rome, all of the world flow into Town, / with all of those people not a free place remains. / Will this credulity be of use to them? I do not know, / but I know that the Pope will benefit enough."[29]

"Not a free place remaining" was exactly what Nicholas wanted. Not only would it showcase the urgent need for improvements to beautify the Holy City, but it would provide him with the financial resources to do so. It was estimated that at one point 40,000 people arrived in the city every day. Nicholas wasn't one of them: he chose to spend most of the Jubilee outside Rome in a hill town, free from the constant threat of bubonic plague. Deaths from overcrowding and disease aside, the plan worked, and by the end of 1450, Nicholas had the money to begin his grand project. He commissioned the architect Leon Battista Alberti to formally review the state of the basilica for the first time in its over-a-thousand-year history. Unsurprisingly, Alberti found the architectural integrity of the building wanting and recommended immediate building work.[30] Nicholas was not a man to begin a project without the proper degree of comfort in place for the initiator—and so the Pope started with an expansion of the papal residential apartments, which he formally moved to the Vatican for the first time.

Alas, Nicholas would not be able to see even the first part of his plan through, dying just five years after the success of his Jubilee, depressed by his political failure to unite Christians in an attempt to save Constantinople from conquest by the armies of the Ottoman Empire. Power, or lack of it, would trump beauty for the moment. However, the wave of attention to St Peter's begun by the wily old diplomat did not dissipate. The renewed quest for beauty spurned on by the Renaissance had only just begun.

"The smell of gunpowder is sweeter to me than all the perfumes of Arabia." It's the sort of quote you might imagine being attributed to one of the more psychotic generals of the Early Modern period, perhaps to a particularly militarily successful monarch. Well, in a sense you'd be right; the man who is often assumed to have said this was both of those things. However, he was also the successor of Peter, Bishop of Rome and leader of the Catholic Faith.[31] Julius II—a man who chose his papal name not in emulation of a saint or martyr but to honor his real hero, Julius Caesar—was perhaps the least likely bringer of beauty that Rome had known since Nero.

Julius's great love for violence and impetuous nature earned him enemies across the European continent. He spent his Papacy engaged in military campaigns, trying to force his great enemy, the King of France, out of Italy, visibly demonstrating that he was more at home in a suit of armor than in papal vestments. Erasmus of Rotterdam suggested that his default attitude to seeing the pearly gates would be to attempt to lay siege to Heaven itself.[32] He was referred to in contemporary publications as "a sly old stag," "a bearded moor," a syphilitic, a homosexual, a crab, and, perhaps most tellingly, he was compared to the Emperor Nero himself.[33]

Such a man might be thought of as having a uniquely perverse idea of what was beautiful. However, it was Julius, despite or perhaps because of his bombastic nature, who was the Pope who finally had the wherewithal to set out what it was he thought Catholic beauty could and should be. The process begun by Nicholas, continued by Julius's own uncle, Pope Sixtus IV, then bogged down by the corruption of Alexander VI, the infamous Borgia Pope, whose reign still managed to produce the very symbol of Roman Renaissance beauty, the Pietà, was finally reaching something approaching a coherent plan. The extended, haphazard attempt to make Rome beautiful again finally found its champion in the blood-soaked general-turned-pontiff. For Julius had decided that the only way to finally establish beauty at the heart of Christian Rome was to start again. He was not a man for tinkering here and there or for half measures and so, on hearing that there were issues with the basilica, he simply ordered St Peter's to be knocked down.

What was to replace it was a church worthy of the prince of the Apostles. It was to be beautiful, yes, but its beauty would be imposing, make a statement, invoke awe. It was to be the largest Church in the world. Gold was to feature heavily in its furnishings, its walls, even in the form of a great golden ball on the top of its dome. At Easter 1506, Julius, with much ceremony, laid the foundation stone of this vast new project and, somewhere, the ghost of Nero either laughed or wept.

For the task ahead, Julius co-opted two men who hated each other: Donato Bramante and Michelangelo. Bramante was a stolid, reliable, older figure, obsessed with symmetry and proportion. He had worked with Julius—and with previous Popes—for years on various building projects across Italy. By contrast, Michelangelo, as we have already heard, was renowned among his contemporaries for his mania. He was a full thirty years younger than Bramante. The older man viewed the younger as impetuous, untried, and unreliable. The younger man viewed himself as a genius and didn't care what anyone else thought. Julius's marriage of the two could have been a disaster, but it wasn't. He subtly pitched the two against one another and played to their strengths— Bramante dealt with the proportions and the structural rebuild, while Michelangelo, alongside designing Julius's own tomb, although untried as a painter, began the decoration of the Sistine Chapel, which would become perhaps the most iconic painted space in the world. There was a reason why Machiavelli grudgingly admitted that Julius had two attributes all rulers could do with: a touch of rashness and a lot of luck.[34]

Of course, as every figure who had a grand vision for Rome, from Nero to Nicholas, had known, such a project was going to cost money. The sort of stop-and-stare beauty that Julius, Bramante, and Michelangelo had in mind did not come cheap. Julius's other great hobby—war— was already putting quite the strain on the Papal coffers. It also had the side effect of making travel conditions across the Italian peninsula, which Julius had helped turn into an enormous battlefield, suboptimal, which ruled out a repeat of Nicholas's ploy of 1450.

To call the economics of medieval and Early Modern Catholicism complicated would be an understatement. Any institution covering every inch of land in Western, Northern, and Central Europe and operating at every level, from the hamlet to the nation state, is bound to be. That the Church had the potential to become an economic powerhouse as the only even faintly multinational and organizationally unified institution in the West was clear. Much of the direct and most easily sourced income came from the lands owned and managed directly by the Papacy in Italy itself, as well as through easy access to the substantial sources of credit via the developed banking systems of the peninsula.[35] However, when these revenue streams proved insufficient, there were options available to pontiffs who were strapped for cash, involving calling in taxes and favors from across the Western Christian world. This was rarely a simple process, involving negotiations and bureaucracy at every level of medieval society. For instance, when, in the late thirteenth century, some poor benighted Papal pen-pusher was tasked with squeezing money from the farthest reaches of Christendom, it involved enquiries via the French Abbey at Cluny, then via the Abbey at Reading, to find out, via its direct owners, a small monastic house on the Scottish Isle of May, the possible revenue from a piece of land suitable for the grazing of "10 sows" somewhere on the coast of Fife in Scotland.[36] Unsurprisingly, this form of trickle-up economics rarely resulted in quick and easy cash.

By the Renaissance, however, the Papacy had realized that its greatest economic asset was not its land or its influence or even its sources of credit, but its doctrine. The concept of doing penance—an act of charity or saying particular prayers or visiting a particular shrine or church—as an outward sign of a forgiven sin had been part of Christian doctrine since its very earliest times. At the high point of the Middle Ages, just as the Papacy's temporal power was beginning to expand, a French theologian, Hugh of St Cher, put forward the idea that the Church's capacity for dispensing forgiveness ought to be seen as "a treasury"; after all, to be in receipt of saving grace was the greatest treasure imaginable.[37] The theological imagery was a coherent one, building on Jesus's own comparisons to "a pearl of great price." However, it also set some bells ringing in the heads of the Church's more financially engaged leaders. If grace was a limitless treasury, surely it could be monetized. By the Renaissance, multiple bishops, religious houses, and other ecclesiastical institutions were no longer asking for direct penances of pilgrimages or acts of contrition and were instead accepting cold, hard cash in return for what became known as an "indulgence," the assurance of sins forgiven and less time spent in Purgatory, the place where Catholics believed you would be purged of your sins before going to Heaven.

Anything could be turned into a medium for the saving of souls and, thereby, for making money. Take, for example, the image in Rome, at Santa Croce in Gerusalemme, one of Constantine's great basilicas on Rome's outskirts. It depicted St Gregory the Great's vision of Christ while he celebrated Mass. The image proved so popular with pilgrims that it was copied and prayers were written out beneath it. These copied images became indulgences in and of themselves, offering those who prayed looking at them time off Purgatory. At first the image offered 20,000 years remit. However, as the earning potential of indulgences increased, some enterprising speculator doctored some of the images to offer 45,000 years instead, a 125% mark-up.[38] Unsurprisingly, given their popularity and profitability, at some point in the decade immediately after 1500, the practice of selling indulgences specifically to aid the building of St Peter's began.[39] After all, an indulgence from the Pope came with a cast-iron assurance. As costs rose along with the scaffolding around the Vatican, Julius seized on the scheme and began to issue indulgences at an incredible rate. He would finance the rebuilding of St Peter's with specific indulgences—complete with special Papal certificates—that would assure the possessor of the Pope's prayers, and make a tidy profit to boot.

It was just as the very first of those profitable prayers were beginning to ascend that Julius died. By the year 1513 he was worn out by endless fighting and by his pursuit of a perfect St Peter's. Given the weight of the financial and administrative task ahead of the Church, it made sense that the Curia selected a banker to succeed him. Leo X was a member of the Medici family, the hugely influential banking dynasty from Florence. More diplomatic than Julius, he is said to have exclaimed on his election, "God has given us the Papacy: now let us enjoy it!" And enjoy it he did, while also using his carefully cultivated Florentine eye for art and sculpture to take on Julius's mammoth task at St Peter's. As work continued, more and more money was required; Leo decided to push the indulgences campaign even further and began to dispatch specific preachers around Catholic Europe with the specific task of raising money for the greatest and most beautiful church on earth. It was an inspired piece of advertising. However, the nakedness of its intent began to rankle, and in further parts of Europe people once again began to ask that awkward question: Was this a price worth paying for beauty?

We don't usually associate advertising jingles with the quest for beauty. Few people would put "Autoglass Repair: Autoglass Replace," "Washing Machines Live Longer with Calgon," or McDonald's "I'm loving it" in a category alongside Mahler's 9th Symphony. Yet, it was the quest to rebuild a beautiful St Peter's that resulted in perhaps the most important advertising jingle of all time. In another age, Johann Tetzel would have been a sensational *Mad Men*–style advertising executive. However, fate was such that he was born in an age where his natural ability to sell things was best served as a Dominican friar. Tetzel toured Germany selling indulgences to fund the rebuilding of St Peter's with the catchy slogan: "Wenn das Geld im Kasten klingt / die Seele in den Himmel springt!", which roughly translated as, "When the coin in the coffer rings, then the soul from purgatory springs!"

Tetzel's all-singing-and-dancing indulgence jamboree reached North Eastern Germany in early 1517. He gave a particularly stirring, and profitable, rendition of his schtick at Jüterbog, a squat town of Gothic brick not far from the university town of Wittenberg. It was there that word of Tetzel's practices reached the ears of a monk and professor of theology, one Martin Luther. Luther had been spending a lot of time reading St Paul's Epistle to the Romans, with its emphasis that salvation didn't come through works but by God's grace alone. The thought of people giving their money on the understanding that it would save their souls, when in fact it was going to build the great big beautiful church of Michelangelo's dreams, riled Luther. He struggled with it over the course of 1517 until, on October 31, he went to central Wittenberg and nailed a document on the door of All Saints, the castle church. It was formally entitled "A Disputation on the Power and Efficacy of Indulgences," but would become known, due to the number of its arguments, as the *Ninety-Five Theses*.

Amid all the Biblical quotes, the philosophy, and the theory that make up the thrust of Luther's arguments, only one physical place is actually named in the *Ninety-Five Theses*. It is, of course, St Peter's Basilica in Rome. Thesis number fifty states that it should be taught that, if the Pope knew what it was the indulgence preachers like Tetzel were extracting from the ordinary people of God, "he would rather that the basilica of St Peter's were burned to ashes than built up with the skin, flesh and bones of his sheep."[40] For Luther, St Peter's wasn't a symbol of great beauty at all; it was rather a great monument to the ugliness of human corruption and to the rapaciousness of the Church. No amount of gold or marble could make it beautiful. It was, to him, as monstrous as any building planned by Nero. For Luther, the true beauty of the Church was "the grace of God," but, crucially, this beauty would always appear to the world to be odious, as "it makes the first to be last."[41] Luther's argument was that Christianity made that which appeared to the world to be beautiful, ugly, and what appeared to the world ugly, beautiful. It was, in reality, the opposite of what Julius had been trying to achieve. This wasn't just a debate about the economics or fairness of the practice of indulgences: it was a battle about the nature of Christianity—and of beauty—itself.

Counter-theses were published, denunciations were made, and, as the furor grew uglier, Luther claimed that the theology behind indulgences came from people who "hadn't even smelled a Bible," let alone read one.[42] A number of people, especially secular rulers, suspected that the Pope had been taking money and tax income that was more properly theirs for some time. They gave Luther shelter, support, and resources to continue his campaign. Soon, other thinkers and writers began to pitch in, some even more extreme than Luther. The debate raged: Could the quest for earthly beauty ever be the correct way to reach the Divine? Or was the human desire for the beautiful in fact a distraction from the desire to know God? Soon, the war ceased to be one of words and theses and became one of battles and massacres. Such was the strength of feeling that scenes that both sides would find indisputably ugly—massacres, burnings, and destruction—ensued across the European continent. Even Rome herself was sacked in 1527, in part by Protestant mercenaries who delighted in vandalizing the Holy City. Finally, Europe's tolerance for Papal power had reached its breaking point: what Nicholas had pulled off by charm, and Julius by sheer force, Leo and his nephew, Pope Clement VII, who reaped the full fury of the Reformation in the 1520s and 1530s, failed to pull off by Medici cunning. The quest for beauty would mean that Christianity would never be the same again.

Fun though it is to imagine it as purely a fight over an irritating jingle, in truth, the Reformation was an inordinately complex thing. Seldom, among all its manifestations in the various countries it touched in Europe, did it have a sole unifying cause. Politics mixed with religion and the immense societal and technological changes of the Early Modern period to make for a "perfect storm" of theological discord. In among those causes and factors stood St Peter's. How did a church on the wrong side of the river Tiber end up sparking perhaps the most important sociological shift in Europe since the fall of the Roman Empire? The answer is, in part, due to the obsessive search for the beautiful.

There is another Rome, on the other side of the world from Italy. Rome, Georgia, lies in the foothills of Appalachia, that long strip of land that once represented the hinterland of America's imagination. Unlike its namesake, this Rome is not a place much visited for its beauty or fame or history. Perhaps its most famous monument is a replica of the ancient Etruscan statue of Romulus and Remus, the mythical founders of Ancient Rome, which was gifted to the American city by Benito Mussolini after a joint Italian-American venture in building a chemical dye plant nearby. Just off the main north road out of the city itself, at the end of a path into the woodlands, there lies the Mountain Springs Church. It is a little clapboard building, whitewashed inside and out in order to be as simple as possible. Simplicity was the watchword of those who lived here, in small farming communities, going through a cycle of sustenance and service on what probably felt like the edge of the world. As it was with their livelihoods, so it was with their faith. The people who built this gospel hall in the nineteenth century were Lutheran Methodists, and based on the principles that evolved from Luther and his successors, men like Calvin, Zwingli, and Knox, they decided that their ideal of Christian beauty wasn't found in embellishment, but in simplicity.[43]

To these Romans, less was more. While the community for whom it was founded now lie, awaiting the resurrection, in the Georgian dust and soil that surrounds the church, there is a new community who come to maintain this little acre because the beauty of its isolation speaks to their faith. True, the Mountain Springs Church does not attract the millions who flock to gaze at St Peter's Dome, but there is little doubt that there is a beauty present in the church in the Appalachian foothills that is missing from the greatest basilica on earth.

Back in old Rome, beauty lingered, but did so sadly. Christendom couldn't be the same after the fractures of the Reformation, and so Rome couldn't be either. Undoubtedly, the grand old vision flared up from time to time. Perhaps the most influential man to dream of a Rome made beautiful by his own efforts was not a Roman at all, but a Neapolitan. Gian Lorenzo Bernini had first come to the attention of Pope Paul V, the man who finally completed the great basilica which had cost so much in terms of both blood and gold. Paul was a rather prickly lawyer, who is now primarily remembered in the Sussex town of Lewes, where his image is burned every November 5 due to his misfortune in having been the Pope at the time of the Gunpowder Plot. However, he recognized talent when he saw it and called the teenage Bernini "the Michelangelo of our age." And just as Julius II had sought to reshape and rebeautify Rome using Michelangelo at the start of the rebuilding of St Peter's, so Paul V planned to do the same now that the great church was finally finished.

Under Paul and then several of his successors, Bernini was to have a free hand to shape the site of St Peter's and, indeed, the whole city of Rome as he wished. First he turned to the interior of the cathedral, ensuring its ornamentation matched the impressiveness of the vision outside. It was the exterior, however, that would prove to be Bernini's downfall. Like many men before, from Nero to Nicholas to Michelangelo, his quest to beautify would end up consuming him. Despite the façade of the great church finally being completed, to Bernini there was still something missing. The greatest church in the world had domes and aisles and chancels and columns, but it did not have a bell tower.

48   *Twelve Churches*

Bernini—along with successive Popes, who hung upon his every piece of architectural advice—believed that it needed more than just a bell tower; it needed two of them, and they needed to be the most ornate and impressive on the face of the earth.[44] In 1638, with the enthusiastic backing of the then Pope, Urban VIII, Bernini began his construction. The south tower was to be built first, initially in wood, and later finished in stone.

All went well until one morning in the summer of 1641. The south tower was structurally complete and work was soon to begin on the north one. However, as the sun began to rise over the façade of the basilica, it became clear that cracks were beginning to appear in the stone. Undeterred, Bernini somehow persuaded the Pope to continue and began work on the second tower. However, by the spring of 1642, nervousness over the state of St Peter's had gotten the better of the Vatican authorities and Bernini was ordered to stop his work indefinitely. Urban died in 1644 and was replaced by Innocent X, who, as a cardinal, had been the leading voice against Bernini's influence. He was clear: Bernini would receive no more Papal commissions and the towers were to be torn down. It would later be proved that the fault was not Bernini's at all but was due to a miscalculation in the strength of the foundations some years earlier. However, for all the influence he was still to have on the rest of the city, Bernini's dreams for St Peter's were now over.

Bernini's were not the only dreams to die a death in Rome. As the centuries wore on, the city became less a living place for the invocation of beauty and more a museum. Rather than being the artistic center where young, ambitious purveyors of beauty came to find fame and fortune, it began to attract those whose ambitions and beauty was long behind them. Her palazzos were haunted by made-up, ghostly figures, becoming a city of has-beens and failures, who found it the perfect place to paper over the reality of their human ugliness with makeup and marble. In particular, ex-monarchs made the city their home.

Perhaps the most infamous of these monarchs without a kingdom was Queen Christina of Sweden. Having come to the throne of the Scandinavian nation—at this point the Protestant military superpower of Europe—as a child, by her mid-twenties she was fed up. Fed up with the ministers who patronized her, fed up with the endless questions about whether she would get married, and, increasingly, fed up with the Lutheran faith in which she had been raised. In 1654 she made the announcement that not only would she be abdicating her throne, but she would be converting to Catholicism as well. Christina was fascinated by theater, art, and by the quest for beauty: Sweden, she felt, was not the place whereby these could be pursued adequately, and so she set off, at the invitation of the Pope, to go and live in Rome. The truculent queen serves as a reminder that, for all the conviction of Luther's appeal to simplicity over ornament in the quest for Christian beauty, plenty made the journey in the other direction, compelled by the tangible reality of a beauty expressed by gold and marble, as opposed to the almost oppressive, cold beauty of the whitewashed Protestant mind.

For all that Rome's beauty was alluring to her, Christina certainly didn't conform to contemporary ideas about what made a woman beautiful. When she arrived in the city, Roman men were scandalized by her mode of dress, her bad language, and, most shockingly of all, the way that she sat on chairs. One commentator on life in the Eternal City expressed the general bemusement thus: "while many said for certain that she was a hermaphrodite, she professed to be a woman."[45] While she was initially welcomed by Pope Alexander VII—who even invited her to live in the Vatican in apartments designed by Bernini himself—it soon became clear that there was going to be a personality clash.

Alexander was a gloomy individual who described the day that he was elected Pope as "one he would always mark with bitterness" and slept with a coffin next to his bed to remind him of his mortality.[46] Having hoped that Christina would be a good advert for conversion, spending her life in Rome in quiet contemplation, he was sorely disappointed as it became clear that she was interested more in the fun side of the faith: amassing art, patronizing the theater, and surrounding herself with beautiful and profoundly inappropriate people. Christina's continued meddling in politics and religion was another annoyance, and her plotting to invade Naples in conjunction with the louche, card-playing, and woman-seducing French First Minister, Cardinal Mazarin, proved a step too far. In exasperation, the Pope evicted her and made her go and

50   *Twelve Churches*

live in the Palazzo Farnese, describing her as "a queen without a realm, a Christian without faith, and a woman without shame."

As she grew older, she became an eccentric figure in Rome. With the strains of age, her quest for beauty intensified: she commissioned music and art at an ever-increasing rate, always signing her orders as "The Queen." It was whispered that quantity had become her watchword over quality. There was one area, however, where Christina undoubtedly did make Rome more beautiful, or at least, less ugly. Since medieval times, the period of Carnival, the lead-up to the solemn days of Lent, had been a moment of abject terror for Rome's Jews. With the connivance of the Papal authorities, Romans chased them through the streets, harassing and jeering their attempts to escape. It was Christina's hectoring of successive Popes that eventually saw the practice banned in 1686. For all the terror she brought to Peter's successors, they clearly had some sort of soft spot for her: when she died, they granted her the rare honor of burial in the Papal vault. Her memorial is in the basilica to this day, directly opposite the Pietà. Finally, she had succeeded in her quest for beauty.

Other monarchical exiles followed Christina's example. In the eighteenth century, the once long-hoped-for Stuart claimant to the English throne, whose good looks and charm had earned him the epithet "Bonnie Prince Charlie," saw out his days of failure in Rome as "an elderly alcoholic of indeterminate nationality."[47] Charlie was an even more depressing figure than Christina had been, not even focused on maintaining his own beauty but instead being carried round Rome and displaying "a self-centeredness of the most graceless kind." To him, not even his faith especially mattered, as he entered last-ditch negotiations to convert to Anglicanism in order to gain a throne. By the time a stroke finally carried him off, nobody would have described him as beautiful. Still, he was buried in St Peter's too, more out of pity than affection. Others followed, from Napoleon II to Mohammed Zahir Shah, the last King of Afghanistan, who saw out his days in a flat near the Rome ring road. Rome was the place for remembering past glories, not making new ones.

By the start of the nineteenth century, this reputation was widespread: the English poet Shelley would write "Go thou to Rome—at once the Paradise, / The grave, the city, and the wilderness."[48] Soon, it wouldn't only be foreign monarchs who made Rome their beautiful prison. By the early 1870s, with the rest of Italy now a unified nation, only Rome remained under Papal control. On September 20, 1870, as Italian armies surrounded the city, Pope Pius IX—to show the world his stubbornness—ordered that a brief, token resistance be shown at the Porta Pia, a gate to the city's northeast, but that Rome and her beauty should be spared bombardment. Pius, who had once been known as a jovial, outward-looking Pope with a much-photographed grin and a penchant for snuff, retreated and made himself "the prisoner of the Vatican," refusing to leave the complex.[49] Its beauty became a reminder of the world as it had been and a defense against the world as it was.

Almost exactly sixty years after Pius's prolonged strop, the building itself, the very stones of St Peter's, became a separate state once more. The Lateran Treaty signed in 1929 between the then Pope and Benito Mussolini gave the Vatican its independence back and created the smallest state in the world. It would become a little island of beauty in an increasingly ugly world. It would be in the Vatican that another Pope Pius, the XII of his name, would sit, surrounded by the beautiful, while the Second World War made the continent for which he sought to speak and pray a living Hell.

The question of the price of the beautiful is never far from the surface in the home of Popes. In St Peter's a memorial might speak of a deposed monarch or a frieze of a poisoned cardinal, but the stones themselves speak too, of an ongoing tussle between the beauty of Heaven and the realities of earth. It remains a conversation in stone about the question of how the beauty of God and the ugliness of history might converse.

The Principal of Rome's English College—the academic and religious institution where would-be Roman Catholic priests from England come to be trained and prepare for the full extent of the duties of ordained life—returned to the institution's palazzo early one summer's afternoon. Said principal, Cormac Murphy O'Connor—who would one day become the Cardinal Archbishop of Westminster—found the entire body of students gathered on a balcony at the rear of the college building, overlooking the garden. Earlier on in the summer, an unfortunate technical issue had rendered unusable the usual swimming pool used by the Swiss Guard. The Guard is the collection of young, scenically shaped Swiss men first recruited as the Pope's personal bodyguards by Julius II and Michelangelo, and who continue to serve the Pope to this day. In the spirit of Christian charity, the English College had offered, with the full knowledge of the Principal, the use of its own pool to enable the Guard to cool off in the height of the Roman summer. What the Principal hadn't realized was that the Guard would continue in the traditional Swiss practice of swimming naked. On seeing his entire student body observing this spectacle, the Principal, perhaps reasonably, asked what it was they thought they were doing. Without diverting their eyes for a minute, a reply came from one of the students: "Oh Father, we're merely admiring the beauty of God's creation."[50]

The story perhaps best sums up the story of beauty in Rome: it is steeped in history, resonance, and undertones, but it is at its best when it raises an eyebrow, and reveals the beauty not of the abstract, but of the human. When I visited the Pietà, that great symbol of Renaissance beauty, there was a gaggle of tourists, snapping photos that will doubtless be lost to the ether of the "cloud," a set of bored schoolboys and a nun whose face revealed that she had seen the sculpture plenty of times before. At the side of this not totally prepossessing group, I noticed an older woman quietly crying by the edge of the rail that skirts the front edge of the altar. Even behind the bulletproof glass, installed after Toth's vandalism, the beauty of the statue evoked something within her that produced one of the most visceral emotional reactions possible: tears. Yet, the sculpture doesn't portray a beautiful thing, but rather a terrible one. A mother cradles her murdered child, his body mutilated and broken. It is not just a terrible thing but one of the most awful things it is possible to imagine within the realm of human relationships. And yet the statue conveys this beautifully.

I do not know what the story of the weeping woman was or which pains had made their mark on her life. I do know that her silent tears demonstrated the power of the beautiful to speak of the true, even in ways that seem unexpected, even when surrounded by the mundane. The quest for beauty, then, in the context of Christian history, might well be muddled in with the vain and the foolish and the superfluous, but it has at its heart an acknowledgment that the beautiful has a redemptive power. Beauty can redeem even crucifixion.

This was to become the theme across Christian places of worship. As communities sought to dedicate specific places to worship, naturally the question of what they should look like arose again and again. Christianity found a way to express things as beautiful—the painful, the human— which the Ancient Romans would have found bizarre. This unlikeliness of Christian beauty is perhaps its strongest attribute. In contrast to the expectations of Ancient Rome, what Christianity sought to suggest was that beauty might be found not in the monumentally perfect, but in the cracks, the broken, the unlikely. Rome is at its most compelling when it hints at the truth that there is beauty found in all things, just not necessarily in the way that Nero or Julius or Bernini or Christina of Sweden thought.

This truth is perhaps best demonstrated back where we began, by the cracked pavement that leads to the site of the Domus Aurea. Just opposite is the Basilica of San Clemente. It is not as well visited as the Vatican and certainly not as grand. Weeds poke out from its pavements; its courtyard is a simple one. It is calm enough when I visit for sparrows to drink undisturbed from the fountain in its center. For all its seemingly sleepy unimportance, San Clemente is a treasure trove. Beneath the current basilica are centuries of Roman history. First, the pre-medieval church, complete with aisles and wall paintings, then, underneath that, a temple to Mithras, the cultic bull deity beloved by Roman soldiers; beneath that is a Roman house.

San Clemente is a reminder that Christian worship in Rome began in houses like the one that lies beneath it. The beauty of the Gospel was expounded quietly, secretly, in the ordinary homes of men and women. It was from homes like this one that the first martyrs of Christianity were dragged, by Nero and by later Emperors. One such figure who may have lived nearby was St Agnes. She was a young Roman girl, aged about twelve, and as punishment for her refusal to submit to pagan worship she was dragged to a brothel and there the order was given for her to be gang-raped. After this she was stabbed to death. The site of her martyrdom, a short walk away, is now a great Baroque church, one of Rome's most beautiful. As ever, across Rome, the beautiful and the ugly, the heights of Divine beauty and the depths of human behavior, are more interwoven than we might like to think.

As we make our journey through the various churches, the theme of what they look like will arise again and again. Rome illustrates that, in Christianity, from its earliest times, the beautiful has never been simple. Indeed, it has often been cheek by jowl with that which is unmistakably not so. Yet, what the establishment of the Church in its earliest days shows—from as soon as communities committed to Christ began to meet together—is that Christianity had a remarkable ability to subsume and subvert that which had come before. Roman standards of beauty, Roman buildings and styles, even the city of Rome itself became Christianized. And not just Christianized but totally synonymous with Christianity. St Peter's is therefore symbolic of much more than just beauty or aesthetics but of the wider encompassing of culture in Europe, North Africa, and much of Asia by that which had begun as a small faith in Judea. Indeed, standards of beauty themselves became symbolic of the conquest of Rome by Bethlehem.

Back to San Clemente. To my mind the most beautiful part of the church is not its mosaics or even the best-preserved paintings but a barely preserved fresco corner of the pre-medieval basilica. Just along from the rare and carefully crafted depiction of Christ is an inscription that is barely legible. It instructs the reader to pray for the man who commissioned this painting, "Unworthy John." We don't know who John was, or what he did to render himself unworthy. However, we do have, over a thousand years since he felt the urge to atone for his sins, the remnants of his attempt to bring beauty into the world and thereby make right what he had made wrong. The story of Rome is very often the story of the cost of beauty, seen in the gold and gilt of St Peter's. In the crypt of San Clemente, there is a faded but still beautiful reminder of the benefits of it as well.

Chapter Three

Hagia Sophia, Istanbul, Turkey

(Completion: 537 AD)

Having established itself in communities, in particular places, the Church now faced a bigger challenge. How would it deal with the state? It might have won an aesthetic victory over Rome but now the challenge of the political—the life of the *polis*, the public sphere—loomed. As the new faith grew in numbers and influence, inevitably the question of its relation to power became a pressing one. As Christianity began to engage, not only with secular empires, but also with the nascent faith of Islam and the extant faiths of Judaism and European paganisms, the stage was set for a power struggle in the truest sense. Hagia Sophia in modern-day Istanbul tells the story of Christianity's strange and complicated dance with secular power better than any other building in the world.

In central Istanbul, a tortoiseshell cat wriggles awake in the midday sun and proceeds to clean herself. Sitting on the paving slabs in front of an audience of hundreds of people, this procedure hardly sings of dignity. The crowd want to be on the other side of the chain-link fence, behind which the feline lies; the cat doesn't much care, I suspect, for fences at all. Still, while her ablutions provide a momentary diversion, nobody has come to this specific place, at this specific time, to look at *her*.

It was a hot and sticky Friday in May 2022, and I was a member of that crowd. It was a mixed group: elderly couples who had bussed in for many hours from Antalya with bags of bread and apples with which they'd fortified themselves; young men, ribbing one another with jokes I didn't know the words to but could understand nonetheless; shy honeymooners, swiftly getting used to one another's company; and tourists, masked and anxious, darting glances between the floor, the sky, and one another.

All of us loomed in a disorganized mass, a polite scrum roughly where the gate in the fence was. And on the other side, uninterested,

58 *Twelve Churches*

lay the cat. We were each there, lovers, tourists, and pilgrims all, to gain entry to the enormous building standing on the other side of those railings. Specifically, many of the crowd were there to pray in it, as crowds of citizens in the city we now call Istanbul have done since the year 537.

The building itself is vast and domed; noticeably so, even in a place where vast and domed buildings scatter the cityscape with a regularity perhaps unmatched anywhere else in the world. It is Hagia Sophia, or the Church of the Holy Wisdom in the original Greek.

Or at least, it was. This ancient centerpiece of modern Istanbul is now a mosque, under the name Ayasofya Camii.[1] This is a relatively new development, and at least some of the group of would-be worshippers that gently surged toward the gates on that Friday were, I think, as much stimulated by curiosity as piety. The building's reconversion to an Islamic place of worship after nearly a century as a museum had only occurred a year or so prior to my visit, and for most of that time the general population of the city, in common with much of the world, had been avoiding exactly the sort of crowd they now found themselves in due to the prevalence of disease. Now, however, they were here to see how the return to regular worship had affected the centuries-old building. Despite this evident contemporary curiosity around the building's new (or, rather, old) identity, changes of use are the norm for the site. One constant has been, of course, the cats of Istanbul, who have long sunned themselves in its environs; they, in good feline style, care nothing about the building's flip-flopping religious loyalties, being advocates of flexible loyalty themselves.

This place, so Byzantine chroniclers insisted, began as a pagan shrine, given over to the worship of the old gods of the Roman Empire; gods which themselves had been adapted from the pantheon of divinities adopted by many in Ancient Greece.[2] That a promontory sticking out at the confluence of a river and sea channel should be a city's focal point is, from a geographical perspective, unsurprising. The promontory that Hagia Sophia stands upon looks across the main channel of the Bosphorus and the tributary known as "The Golden Horn," as well as the three chunks of landmass that border them. Thus, it grants sight from land over those arriving by sea; and, more importantly, vice versa—the first thing people saw upon arrival to the city by boat was a place of worship and, more importantly, a sign of Divine blessing upon the city. This is power by sightline.

In the year 312, a vision of the cross, shining brightly over the sun, with the words "IN THIS SIGN CONQUER" emblazoned beneath it, appeared to the Roman Emperor Constantine at the Battle of the Milvian Bridge.[3] The engagement, just north of Rome, was to be the moment when Constantine finally secured his earthly power, defeating a rival for the imperial throne and winning a long and bloody civil war. He would later tell of the cross appearing before him at the very moment the battle turned in his favor. In his mind, the link between his power on earth and the power of God, and specifically the power of Christ— "made perfect," as St Paul had written, in the moment of the cross—was clear.[4]

Such was the debt Constantine felt he owed to the cross of Christ that he issued the Edict of Milan the following year, legalizing Christian worship across the Empire. Other edicts, both in Christianity's favor and to suppress the previous pagan religion, soon followed, and within scant few years the faith which had been preached to just a few fishermen on the shores of Galilee some 300 years earlier found itself the state religion of the mighty Roman Empire.

This was quite the turnaround: while Christianity had started being in some form or other among small numbers of the general populace almost immediately after the period of Christ, it had suffered active persecution, including attacks from pagan and Jewish writers, as well as economic and legal sanctions. It persisted, but in the manner, many historians would argue, that all sorts of cults persisted around the Mediterranean of the time—hushed, behind closed doors, and with followers barely scraping the thousands. Suddenly, this once-despised sect was catapulted to become the state religion of the greatest Empire on the face of the earth. The moment is known as the "Constantinian Shift": the decision of one powerful man, changing faith, Empire, power, and himself, forever.

That Rome would adopt Christianity specifically, over and above

60   *Twelve Churches*

any other sect proliferating at the time, seemed even more unlikely, given its belief system. Not only had the Empire crucified the main figure of this religion on the grounds that he was an irritating upstart in one of their grottier and further off provinces, but almost everything that Jesus Christ was recorded as saying—about power, about who or what was important, about what Heaven would be like, about whom God preferred in the wider scheme of things, about worldly goods, and about the actual Roman Emperor himself—seemed to suggest that faith in Christ and the power of Rome were incompatible. Yet, in the person of Constantine, compatible they became.

The Constantinian Shift is often viewed simply as a moment of historiographical importance. But, as I wandered around the few remnants of the Emperor's eponymous city of Constantinople, now modern Istanbul, poking at the distinct collations of bricks that jut out of walls or cellars, marveling at seemingly randomly placed columns or milestones, and ducking down into cisterns, I wondered how this decision, which even today is viewed as about the most important choice you can make—to accept the power of Christ—had affected Constantine the man, as opposed to merely Constantine the cipher for power.

Perhaps to distinguish between the two is foolish. He certainly would not have appreciated it, I'm sure. For all his power—and for as much as he is indubitably a pivotal figure in the history of the world, not just at the site of Hagia Sophia or the city it sits in—Constantine remains a slightly enigmatic figure. We don't even know with any real certainty where his body is, or whether the enormous head in the Capitoline Museum of Rome, reputed to be his likeness, is actually based on him. In truth, we're even unsure when exactly he was baptized and formally became a Christian. It is rumored that he feared the power of the Nazarene so much that he waited until he was on his deathbed for his baptism, in order to avoid committing any sin while a member of the elect, a sin which would rain the judgment of Christ down upon him.[5]

Around the back of the Hagia Eirene, the smaller sister church to Hagia Sophia, there is a cloister which can be glimpsed through possibly the grubbiest glass window in the northern hemisphere. Through the fly corpses one can just make out a large, squat, purplish chunk of marble. This, it is said, is the great Emperor's coffin, lying abandoned and anonymous in the center of a never-ending building project. One of the main things that Christ taught about the nature of earthly power was that it was transitory.

For all his contradictions, there is no denying that the radical conversion of Constantine and his Empire changed the relationship between Christianity and power forever. To mark his commitment, Constantine ordered a whole range of churches to be built at the heart of his new capital, a city named after himself and intended to be a second Rome. Many of these were dedicated to holy aspects of his newfound faith. Two were built in close proximity to the great palace on that self-same hill that curves around from the channel of the Golden Horn: one was dedicated to the concept of Holy Peace, Hagia Eirene in Greek; the other to Holy Wisdom, Hagia Sophia.

Exactly when the latter building, already known as "the great church," was begun is unknown, but we know it was finished and consecrated under Constantine's son, also Constantine. He ordered the statues of the gods that his ancestors had worshipped be removed; they still littered corners of the site, awkward ghosts from that cruel and crucifying era now past. As it had been with the first Rome, so it became with the second, and the scourge of fire soon visited the city, claiming the two Constantines' original wooden church in the year 404 AD. Emperor Theodosius II saw a chance to stake his claim as the successor of the great Constantine, and so set about building a new, ornately decorated church on the site, described by contemporaries as a riot of both color and carved detail.[6]

Remnants of these early churches can still be seen there, hopped over and slept on by the cats which, like that tortoiseshell in May 2022, occupy much of Istanbul's space and attention. They speak of buildings of grandiose scale and profound complexity of detail. During a slow circumnavigation of the current church, I imagine these ruins painted with vibrant color and adorned with mosaics. The representation of faith in images is a central part of Orthodox faith to this day; and, indeed, the latter Byzantines became so obsessed with the role of images that they ended up debating, then fighting, then killing one another over them. Why? Well, they had learned well from the two Constantines and Theodosius II: they knew that the symbols of power, and the power of symbols, mattered very much indeed.

It may no longer be one, and it may not be the same one that those emperors thought would stand the test of time, but there is no denying that the current building was built as a church and decorated accordingly. And a church that was both decorated and built with a very specific purpose at that.

The first time I visited Hagia Sophia, some years earlier, it was still a museum. Its mosaics were still in place. Now, they are covered by a pair of sheets, to protect Islamic sensibilities about the representation of living things in places of worship. Under the sheets, they are truly astonishing testaments to both the faith and the skill of those who made them. Eyes pierce out from across the centuries, monumental hands gesticulate across apses and arches. The idea of "the living God" is tangible, even if these representations are made of colored ceramic. The great mosaic of Christ—known as the Pantokrator, meaning "all powerful" in Greek—is perhaps the best known and most impressive of them all. On that first visit, the face of Christ still stared down on the crowds, an astonishing Byzantine survival.

If you angle yourself at a particular southwestern corner of the central space today, you can still make out some features of the great mosaic in the apse. I position myself there on my May visit, amid the sweating crowds taking photos and distanced discreetly from those there to pray rather than gawp. The hands dispensing blessing and the main body of the stern face are obscured, but as I crane my head to an odd angle, a single eye just about pokes out from behind its covering. After all these years, all these changes, the Pantokrator is still there.

It is, I think, appropriate that it is so. Its very name speaks of the shaping purpose behind the entire enterprise of the interior and exterior views of the Hagia Sophia, then and now: power.

Emperors came and went, some strong, some weak, some good, some wicked, some loved, some hated, much as Emperors always are.

Hagia Sophia, Istanbul, Turkey 63

Eventually, though, through the cut-throat violence of Byzantine politics, coup and counter coup, a curly-haired son of Balkan peasants found his way to the throne of the Eastern Roman Empire. He meant to make the most of it. As Justinian I first entered the great church he had commissioned, he did so with head bowed. Slowly, ever so slowly, he raised his head, thick with his famed black curls, until his eyes were transfixed on the dome above him. Finally, he exhaled and spoke a line which has echoed down the centuries—at once the words of a man awe-struck into humility, and those which echo with the hubris only someone who considered themselves Emperor of the known world could possess: "Solomon, I have surpassed thee."[7]

Why did he need to show his power with a building? Surely a man who controlled such vast swathes of the earth had plenty of signs of his dominion already? Well, yes and no. Though the Emperors of Byzantium held the Mediterranean in their grip, the one place where they routinely lost control was, awkwardly, the capital, Constantinople itself. Around the year 530, the city's population was around half a million, considerably larger than that of contemporary Rome, the city it had supplanted. It was by a margin the greatest city in the region. The pulsating horde of inhabitants was split into factions based around various competing teams, whose names—green, blue, white, and red—reflected the colors in which those teams raced. These races took place in the hippodrome, the city's horse-racing arena, a short distance from Hagia Sophia and still present in the street layout to this day. Hooliganism was a constant blight upon the city as fights spilled out into the narrow streets after races. The authorities generally sought to crack down and, at the tail end of the year 531, they had condemned two notorious offenders—one from the green faction and one from the blue faction—to death.

Early in the year 532, on January 10, the two escaped and claimed sanctuary in a local church. Justinian, eager to diffuse the situation, announced not only that they would be pardoned, but that three days later, of all things, a horse race would be held to mark his magnanimity. To say this proved a strategic error would be an understatement. Quite what Justinian expected to happen when he gathered several thousand of Constantinople's angriest sporting hooligans in a confined space right

64 *Twelve Churches*

next door to the seat of political power, we will never know. But what occurred very nearly brought down the entire Byzantine Empire.[8]

Rather than being grateful for the party Justinian had thrown for them, the Blues and Greens forgot their enmity and the combined crowd began demanding the release of their hooligan heroes. They settled on a unified chant and began screaming *nika*, meaning "victory" or "conquest." The unrest soon blossomed into a full-scale riot and, five days later, vast swathes of the city lay in burning ruins. The violence only ceased when Justinian ordered gold coins to be thrown to the baying mob in a not-very-subtle act of bribery. Retribution followed and, by the end of the chaos, 30,000 people were dead, the authority of the Empire was shaken, and Hagia Sophia—along with most of Constantinople—had been destroyed. Consequently, for Justinian, rebuilding Hagia Sophia wasn't just an aesthetic choice: it was a necessity. A necessity with which he was determined to send a message to the city, to the world, even to God.

And so he did. On completion, the new Hagia Sophia which we see today—its third iteration, after the original wooden church and subsequent Theodosian edifice—was the biggest church in the world. It was to remain so—though by then it was technically a mosque—until 1520, when the cathedral at Seville was completed, marking a religio-political conquest which was the reverse of the one that was to affect Constantinople. To have built the single largest space dedicated to the worship of the Christian God said something about the ambitions of Justinian: as Rome had been to the pagan empire, so Constantinople would be to the new Christian one. Despite the small hiccup of the *Nika* incident, Constantine finally had a worthy successor, and the Nazarene had well and truly triumphed.

As Solomon had built for the Jews the first Temple to the God of Israel in Jerusalem, Justinian now claimed to build for the Christians the great Church of the new faith. But not just for them. As befitted the Emperor of Byzantium, he presumed to build it for the whole world. At that point, his domains stretched from the pillars of Hercules at the far Western edge of the Mediterranean to the interior of modern-day Iraq, bordered north to south by the Alps and the Sahara. As far as the majority of people who lived around the edges of Europe's great inland sea knew, Justinian indeed *did* rule the world, and so his presumption to build for it was, to their minds and his, only natural, the reality of his power.

And where did that power come from? Well, God of course. More specifically, the God of that strange and radical sect, the Christians, who had brought such blessing to the eastern Empire's founder, the Emperor Constantine. So it was that the man who believed himself king of the world sought to build a shrine fitting for the worship of the king of Heaven. Certainly, there was no shortage of ambition, an ambition more than matched by the casting of that power and presumption into marble and stone.

Finally, the crowd and I are allowed to surge past the cat's cleaning place and enter Hagia Sophia via its southwestern door. Justinian would have entered via the great imperial door, at the center of the western edge of the building—reserved only for the Emperor, a sign that his entry, like his power, was unlike anyone else's—just along from the smaller entrance through which we shuffled. Above this marble archway stands a mosaic featuring one of Justinian's successors, Leo the Wise, kneeling, begging for blessing from an enthroned Christ. Therein lies the paradox of the Christianity embodied by Hagia Sophia: this entrance speaks both of power *and* of humility. Entrance through this great gate affords the finest view of the central space; but from whichever angle you first encounter Hagia Sophia's interior, you are certain to be struck by awe.

There is the basic level of awe that infuses all old buildings, an inherent wonder at something that has stood for so long when impermanence is the normal fate for most human endeavor. Present, too, is that particular sense of astonishment when confronted with a building that is both old and monumental: as clichéd as it may seem, it's impossible to gaze at the building and not marvel that a thing of such scale, of such structural enormity, was completed without the aid of cranes, or cement mixers, or electricity, or any of the other paraphernalia of modern construction. It is all the more impressive when one considers that the present Hagia Sophia was built in a mere six years, a fraction of the time that many modern infrastructure projects take.

Merely surveying the exterior, even at a distance, will inspire such awe, but, as Justinian discovered, it is magnified within. The walls rise ever upward, drawing the eye of the visitor inexorably to the great dome. In the time of the Byzantines, the smoke of burning incense would have risen from the ground level, dissipating into the space above before ever reaching the dome's ceiling. Such scale was deliberate, to give the impression of its own atmospheric system, to infer that the worshipper might be in a place above the clouds, in Heaven itself.

Quite the lofty aim, to put Heaven upon earth, but Justinian had reasons beyond the purely pious. The primary purpose of the great church was to act as a symbol of his power.

So, from its start, power and its projection shaped Hagia Sophia, in a way that would become a pattern for Church elsewhere. It was designed to be a global church, not just a local one. It may have been intended as a church for the whole world, but, as is so often the case, the whole world had other ideas. It used to be that you could make your way up to the galleries at Hagia Sophia. One clergyman I knew used to make a concerted waddle up to the gallery on the southwest side of the church. There, when nobody was looking, he would aim a perfectly formed globule of spit onto the slab that lies in a corner there, marked with the name "HENRICUS DANDOLO." Now, he, and any other committed Byzantinists who might wish to do the same, are robbed of the opportunity. The galleries, which also contain astonishing mosaics of emperors, empresses, and the Virgin Mary, are currently closed, ostensibly for restoration, but, perhaps, as one Istanbul resident suggested to me that May after I'd found access to them blocked, as part of the reconversion to mosque status. There are, I suppose, only so many sheets available to cover the faces of long-dead dignitaries.

Why might a robust Anglican cleric seek to spit on a paving slab in far-off Istanbul? As ever with Hagia Sophia, the story contained in one piece of stone has a thousand strands leading all over the world. The carved letters, beautiful despite their crude shakiness, mark the fact that at one time the church held the tomb of Enrico Dandolo, a blind, geriatric sometime ruler of the Republic of Venice, and a man who reduced much of Constantinople to blood and ash.

Hagia Sophia, Istanbul, Turkey 67

Six hundred years after Justinian's triumphant entry to Hagia Sophia, the shape of the Empire he had ruled was very different indeed. Approximately thirty-three years after the church's completion, a boy was born in Arabia, on the frontiers of the Empire, who would become the prophet Muhammad. The rise of Islam took the extant powers in the Middle East almost totally unawares, and the speed with which newly converted Muslim Arabs conquered cities shook the Byzantine Empire to its core. By the early medieval period, the situation on the Empire's eastern border had reached such a point that the Byzantines asked the Church of the West—which had sought a deliberately different center of power in Papal Rome, and with whom the Church of the East had fallen out over both teaching about the nature of Jesus's identity and, inevitably, power—for help.

From the year 1096, successive waves of soldiers, pilgrims, camp followers, marauders, priests, and madmen from Western Europe surged into the Middle East on Crusade; ostensibly to win back under Christian control the places where Jesus had spent his earthly life, but, just as often, to make money, escape justice or poverty at home, fulfill obligations made in return for the Church's backing, and sometimes, even, just because they were bored. Almost all of them made the journey via Constantinople. By the early 1200s, the situation in the Middle East had flared up once again: the Crusader states established by the victories of the late 1090s—and a convenient buffer zone for the Byzantines—were now threatened by a resurgent Caliphate buoyed by the successes of late Sultan Saladin, who, before his death in 1193, dealt successive Crusader armies a series of major blows. Most of the kingdoms of Europe decided something had to be done, and began to assemble their forces and plan a journey to the Holy Land.

Most, as opposed to all, of the kingdoms is a deliberate distinction, because one—the Most Serene Republic of Venice—planned on making a profit. Despite the city having some of the most beautiful churches in Christendom, the Venetians, who spent prolonged periods of time with their entire home region excommunicated by the Pope, were not famed for their particular interest in religion. What they *were* famed for was their particular interest in *money*; and a Crusade represented the perfect opportunity to make some. Hordes of pious and opportunistic would-be warriors had crowded the shores of the Mediterranean, needing a way to get to Jerusalem. Fortunately, the Venetians had plenty of ships. They just had a *tiny* little condition in exchange for using them: after using the Crusader army to defeat the Croatian pirates who were harrying their trade in the Adriatic sea, the Venetians, under their Doge, the elderly but charismatic Dandolo, steered the fleet on a small detour to Constantinople.[9]

A massacre of Roman Catholics living in Constantinople in 1182 had not done wonders for relations between the people of the East (loyal to the Patriarch in Constantinople) and those of the West, or "Latins" (loyal to the Pope in Rome). During the orgy of violence, the decapitated head of the Pope's personal representative in the city had been tied to the tail of a dog and dragged around the city, and the Latin-born dowager Empress Maria of Antioch was, depending on the account one reads, either strangled on a beach by a eunuch or sewn into a sack and hurled into the sea.[10] Tellingly, modern-day denizens of Istanbul are blasé about the sites that saw such monumental violence: "Oh, that is where so-and-so was blinded," or, "there is the place where X and Y were massacred," they will say, with a faint gesture toward one historical building or ruin. Cities that become focal points for power invariably become focal points for bloodshed as well, and with so much of it drenching the city's history, it is hardly surprising that exact details or a sense of the individual tragedies get lost in the torrent. One such detail, however, which later chroniclers claimed—quite dubiously—to have dug up from the massacre of 1182 was the torture and blinding by a Byzantine mob of a Venetian merchant by the name of Enrico Dandolo.[11]

Even if the legend is partially true and Dandolo had been in the city during the massacre, the Venetians weren't simply motivated by revenge. Determined to secure commercial privileges in the Eastern Mediterranean, they had brought with them a pretender to the Byzantine throne. The feckless Alexios Angelos had spent his exiled adolescence hawking himself around the courts of Europe, promising vast rewards to anyone who helped him regain his throne. That he would never be in a position to pay his debts meant he got short shrift everywhere, with the exception of Venice, where a much darker plan was being hatched.

Hagia Sophia, Istanbul, Turkey 69

The installation of Alexios was pretty simple—he and his blinded father, Isaac II, were installed as co-emperors in mid-1203 after a relatively short siege, the might of the Crusader army being more than a match for the increasingly bankrupt Byzantine state. Of course, while Constantinople's money troubles won Alexios the throne, they also made it impossible for him to keep it. By February 1204, he was dead, and his own court chamberlain—also called Alexios—had been made Emperor. This new Alexios had no intention of paying the Crusaders anything and so, with barely disguised glee, the Venetians besieged and captured the city once more, intent on getting what they were owed.

If you wanted to quickly assess, and then shamelessly rob, the greatest treasures Constantinople had to offer, there was only one place you would need to go: Hagia Sophia. Later Byzantine chroniclers described the appalling destruction the Crusaders unleashed on the city: rape, murder, acts of wanton vandalism. But they saved their most trauma-ridden accounts for their descriptions of how the pillaging armies of Europe treated the great church Justinian had built for the whole world. Having made their way to the central symbol of Byzantine political and religious power, the Crusaders stole everything that wasn't nailed down. The pulpit, coated in silver, was stripped bare of its precious coating in a matter of minutes. The high altar—considered a masterpiece of craftmanship even by the standards of the church's ornate furnishings, and the very holiest part of the church—was smashed up, with soldiers fighting over gold-clad pieces in the place from which communion was usually administered.

It wasn't just material desecration that occurred. After all, Hagia Sophia's power was never purely found in her awesome physical scale; the spiritual dimension of her power required breaking down too. The Crusaders installed a prostitute in the semicircular row of seats, who sang ribald songs while the destruction unfolded around her, bringing in other women too, who began to dance around the holiest part of the church in "unnatural ways."[12] The inference the chronicles want to make is, of course, that those looting the great church had sex in all sorts of different contortions, in the place where the most dignified clergy of the Eastern church had traditionally sat.

70 *Twelve Churches*

Animals were brought in specifically to defecate, covering the marble floors with their urine and manure. This rendered them so slippery that one marauder, his arms filled with looted church plate, slipped and fell on his sword in such a way that it ripped his guts open at the bowel, his own blood and feces mixing with that of the animals. At this his fellow looters, rather than help, howled with laughter. Justinian had sought to make a building which could be mistaken for Heaven on earth: now it had been transformed into Hell.[13]

If Hagia Sophia's consecration had been the high point of Byzantine power, its desecration was to mark the Empire's lowest ebb. Yet, for all the desire to defile the great church, when the ancient trickster Dandolo finally died, it was there that he was buried. Of course, it was a no-brainer that, when the Latins came to crown a new Emperor of their own—who was, in an especially brutal insult to the proud and ancestry-obsessed Greeks, a minor nobleman from Belgium—they would do so in Hagia Sophia. Cleaned up, converted over to Catholic worship, it became, once again, a symbol of power.

And when the Byzantines finally regained the city some years later, where was it that they headed straight for, to give thanks that the great *polis* was finally under their power again? Hagia Sophia, of course.

The year 1204 was by no means the last radical change to the appearance, purpose, and existential identity of Hagia Sophia. Nowadays, just outside the building, what was previously an outdoor museum appears, to the untrained eye, to be just a random collection of old stones. Much of this scree is the remnants of interiors from Justinian's church, or the dumped remains from that of Theodosius. There are ancient coffins, long denuded of their contents, and bits of a former pulpit, which look a little like a child's water slide rendered in marble tracery. Columns and stones and other debris of past civilization, now worn down by time and the Bosphorus's salt spray, lie in jumbled piles. Many of them have inscriptions. Some have letters inscribed, but more often than not there's only a single symbol upon the detritus. It is perhaps the most widespread symbol in the world, and certainly the most powerful in Christianity: the cross.

It is precisely for that reason that they now lie scattered on a little patch

Hagia Sophia, Istanbul, Turkey 71

of grass to the building's west. The time was to come when no cross at all, Latin or Greek, Catholic or Orthodox, Venetian or Byzantine, would be found in what was once the church. That's the problem with power, even for a religion: it can be lost as well as gained.

Indeed, it was another day in May when Hagia Sophia's fate was to be changed forever. On the 28th of that month in the year 1453, the Emperor Constantine XI Palaeologus entered the great church, in much the same way that his predecessor Justinian had done nearly nine centuries before. His head, however, was bowed not with faux humility, but in deep and earnest prayer. There, he had united Western and Eastern Christians, Greeks and Franks, peoples from all over the world; for perhaps the first time in its existence, Hagia Sophia was exerting the power which Justinian had always intended it to have. Yet, the power of the city and Empire which the church had come to symbolize was at its lowest ebb. At the walls of Constantinople, the Ottoman Turks, having chipped away at Byzantine power for centuries, were preparing their final assault.

It was not in triumph that these nations and previously opposed coreligionists now united, but in fear. Even the notoriously slippery Cardinal Isidore, who had changed sides in the religious battles of the age more times than anyone could remember, was present. He would escape the coming onslaught by dressing a corpse in his rich cardinal's robe, and slinking away from the city in a slave ship while Turkish soldiers paraded the unfortunate corpse's skull, crowned with a cardinal's hat. But we have jumped ahead: back to Hagia Sophia, where the multinational citizens of Constantine's second Rome implored God for deliverance from the legions of Ottoman Turks under the command of Sultan Mehmet, soon to be known as "The Conqueror."

Beneath the dome, so familiar to nearly a millennia's worth of Christian worshippers, people prayed in all languages. The edifice that once had been testament to the Empire's reach and the city's prowess now seemed to stand vainly against the imminent destruction of both. What was an expression of power was now the epicenter of fatal, final weakness. Through the midst of the terrified crowd of worshippers moved the Emperor himself, subdued but majestically pacific. His prayer was not for deliverance: he knew that was futile. Some days earlier he had made up his mind to die defending the city, and the church at her heart: "God forbid," he said, "that I should live as an Emperor without an Empire. As the city falls, I will fall with it." Hagia Sophia had always been intended to be totally intertwined with the power of Byzantium and its Emperor. Now, as they fell, the fate of the church, the city, and the man were all tied up as one.

Such was the chaos of Constantinople's fall to the Turks that very little is known of the final hours of the man who claimed to be the last Roman Emperor. Some say he charged headlong on a suicide mission into the oncoming Turkish column as it finally made a breach in the defenses, his body being cut to pieces; others that he threw off his golden armor and fought as an ordinary soldier, until his unfortunate decapitation by a Turkish warrior.[14] Most accounts agree he was killed, and specifically that that same head which had bowed reverently in the hope of receiving the power of divine assistance was struck from its shoulders.

The belief that the head was the central physiological point of a person's power was widespread, hence the tendency to cut off the heads of the once great or powerful while dispatching the supposedly unimportant by more prosaic means. Now, the Byzantine Empire had been decapitated in real terms. Constantine Palaeologus's head was taken outside the city walls and presented to the expectant Sultan, who mocked it.[15] His body was dumped outside in a ditch. Some chroniclers vainly maintained that he escaped via a boat in the confusion of the city's fall, living out the rest of his days in anonymous shame elsewhere.[16] Either way, the Emperor, in both physical and spiritual form, had left the city.

Or had he? Some say he is still in modern-day Istanbul. There is a legend that he is merely sleeping, awaiting the chance to return the city, and his church, to Christian control. Proponents of this legend maintain that his body lies in another converted church, now the Gül Camii or Rose Mosque, but once the Church of St Theodosia. It is very much off the tourist trail, down a side street in a conservative neighborhood toward the ruins of Constantinople's great walls, far from the bars and clubs of westernized Taksim and Beyoğlu. The ill-fated Emperor stopped in here having left Hagia Sophia on his way to inspect the walls that final day.

Hagia Sophia, Istanbul, Turkey 73

I visit there as well, during that May of the cat and the crowd as opposed to the May of the conquest, after my own trip to Hagia Sophia. Though it is difficult to find, once stumbled upon, Gül Camii is unmistakable. The building rises suddenly out of a side street; its approach, as quirky and irregular as Hagia Sophia's, is grand and planned. It is a textbook array of Byzantine brick, arches, and domes; even as the small minaret on the side gives away its current purpose, and the satellite dish crudely attached to a corner of the eastern wall hints at the presence of modernity, you feel, even more so than at Hagia Sophia, that you could have stood in the same place some thousand years earlier and seen essentially the same thing.

The elderly caretaker, bearded and bespectacled, seems both confused and pleased that any tourist might have made their way to see the treasure for which he was now responsible. He speaks to us in Turkish, smiling and gesticulating, guiding us through the modern entrance hall—all 1970s paneling and stopped clocks—before leading us through into the main space of the mosque. The red carpet smells strongly of damp and the peeling paint gives an atmosphere of studied decay. Still, there is a strange thrill in being there. Hagia Sophia is now managed, curated, its narrative controlled, whereas there is a visceral spirituality to the Rose Mosque, a more tangible link to its past.

The caretaker leads us just behind the *minbar*—the equivalent of a pulpit from where the mosque's imam will preach. In the far southeastern corner, to the right-hand side of where the altar of the Byzantine church would have been, the upper-floor gallery was filled in, creating a small chamber. Nearby is an elaborate sign, written in the old Ottoman Turkish script, which says, "Tomb of the disciple of Jesus, peace be upon him." We ask if we might go up into the chamber, but the elderly caretaker shakes his head and deploys his one piece of English, presumably well-honed from other requests: "Muslims only."

The mosque maintains that the body in the tomb is that of Gül Baba, an early Ottoman holy man. Others say that the allusion to Christ is no coincidence and, in fact, it was here that the body of the unfortunate last Emperor was brought after his death on the walls. Legend is added to this conjecture: it is said he is merely resting, waiting for the opportune moment to spring from his marble bed and march back into Hagia Sophia, head bowed in prayer once more.

However Constantine XI ended his final twenty-four hours, what we do know is that he started them in Hagia Sophia, praying for a miracle that never came. Those prayers were to be the last official Christian ones to take place there. Hagia Sophia's near-thousand years of use as a church came to an end that day, its last service as much a testament to the Empire's lack of power as its first had been to its abundance.

Naturally, when Mehmet the Conqueror finally rode through the gap in the walls to the west of the city the following day, a hole blasted by his cannon and siege machines, he too made a beeline to the city's spiritual heart. As the old Empire had ended with Constantine's final, desperate prayers in that church, so too the new one would begin there, with Mehmet's thanks to Allah. As he arrived at the doors of the church, he picked up two handfuls of dust—rubble and earth from the debris-strewn ground next to the building. He proceeded to sprinkle this onto his turban before entering the sacred space. He did so as a sign of humility, to show that even he, conqueror of conquerors, a Muslim monarch at the doors of a despoiled Christian place of worship, feared the greatness of the God worshipped therein. Such was the power of Hagia Sophia.

For many years after the great siege of 1453, considerable swathes of the city remained abandoned. One of the problems with power is that not only do individuals like to show it off, but they also like to cling on to it, with violence if need be. On surveying the destruction from the ruins of the imperial palace, Sultan Mehmet recited a verse of Persian poetry: "The spider weaves the curtains in the palace of the Caesars; The owl calls the watches in the towers of Afrasiab."[17]

Desolation was the order of the day in the second Rome.

The process of rebuilding and converting buildings to new uses across the once-sprawling metropolis—especially the conversion of churches into mosques—was a slow one, taking many decades in some parts of the city. Hagia Sophia was the exception. One of Mehmet's very first actions was to ensure that this church, the great symbol of Byzantine power, ambition, and faith, became his personal possession as

Hagia Sophia, Istanbul, Turkey 75

Sultan. It would remain so until the fall of another Empire, this one the Ottoman Caliphate founded by Mehmet, 469 years later. Mehmet spent his own money turning it into a mosque, covering much of its Christian decoration and inserting all those furnishings necessary for Islamic worship. This was not just a run-of-the-mill conversion project: this was a pact between the Sultan and God. Just as they had for Justinian, the changes wrought at Hagia Sophia represented the seal of Heaven upon a ruler's earthly power.

Yet, earthly power is a transient thing. As unassailable as Mehmet must have felt surveying the largest church in Christendom, now his personal property, there was, perhaps, an echo at the back of his mind: that Justinian, great scion of the Empire which now lay in ruins, had once felt exactly the same way, in exactly the same place. Perhaps the key to success, to triumph, to power, was Hagia Sophia itself? If that was the case, any ruler worth his salt would do anything to preserve the sanctity of the building.

Hagia Sophia, then, was to be the seal on Mehmet's new power as it had been on Justinian's. On a sixty-six-meter-long piece of antelope skin, he had a new charter prepared for the mosque. So concerned was the Conqueror to ensure this part of his conquest that it ends with the following curse on anyone who sought to, as he had, change the purpose of Hagia Sophia:

"Let the curse of Allah and the angels and all mankind be upon them. Let them dwell in hell forever and their punishment shall not be eased. No mercy for them forever. Whoever changes it after hearing it and seeing it, his sin shall be upon those who change it. Indeed, he is the hearing, the knowing."[18]

Mehmet knew better than anyone that empires could be conquered, and earthly power lost, as easily as it had been gained. The power of faith, however, was quite another thing.

So it was that Hagia Sophia became a symbol of a new Empire. Its arches reverberated with prayers honoring the final prophet of Islam and so it became a symbol of a newer religion too. It remained as a mosque as the long years of Ottoman rule stretched out, with their regular violent interludes of palace coups and pogroms. Even as the Ottomans slipped into decadence and decline and their eventual deposition became inevitable with the First World War, still Hagia Sophia stood. A symbol to outlast the passing politics of man.

The man who did eventually conquer Mehmet's Empire was the vigorous, sly, and charming Mustapha Kemal, known as Ataturk, a soubriquet, which means "father of Turks." The name reflected his ambition. And, just like Justinian, Constantine, and Mehmet, he made change at Hagia Sophia a seal of his personal power too. Ataturk had come to dominate the modern Turkish state just as all the principles and presumptions on which the Empire that Mehmet had founded were crumbling.

A successful military career in the First World War left him in a position whereby he could march his armies across the corpse of the old Empire, which collapsed under the weight of external military defeat, lack of internal political will, genocidal violence, extrajudicial killing, and plain old decadence. As the colossus who emerged from the ruins, Ataturk viewed the nation and, in particular its historic capital, as decadent, idle, riddled with internal enemies, and strangled by the obscurantist and retrograde influences of religion.

Having become president of the new republic of Turkey in 1923 through a combination of guile and military power, Ataturk spent the following years on a radical nationalistic reform program. He had all aspects of Ottoman culture in his sights: the complex Turkish script used in writing, the segregation of women and men, whirling dervishes, the name "Constantinople," and Hagia Sophia. Modernization was his watchword: in particular he was determined to show to the West, and especially the emergent superpower of the United States, that his nation was no longer "the sick man of Europe," as it had been for much of the previous century, but a progressive and, crucially, secular state. A new form of power had arrived in what in 1930 officially became known as Istanbul. As with all the forms of power that had swept through before, reckoning had to be done with the great building that had become the physical manifestation of the city's soul.

The center of modern, secular Istanbul is the İstiklal, a long, broad boulevard with a riparian curvature to it, linking the huge square at Taksim with the still dominant Genoese medieval guard tower at Galata. Just as it bends around by the Galatasaray tram stop, there is a monumental building, recently restored and now hosting shops, some selling cheap designer clothing, others, kilos of nougat. Once, it was the Tokatliyan, one of the glorious decadent hotels of the Pera district, each lodging a heady orientalist trove of heavy furnishings and luxury available at the snap of a finger. Only two remain now: the Pera Palace, a grim identikit haven of overpriced drinks and muzak, and the gloriously chaotic Grand Hotel de Londres, complete with a bar staffed by a sexually inappropriate parrot, and a room full of Harley-Davidsons.

It was at the Tokatliyan Hotel on June 12, 1929, that the American archaeologist Thomas Whittemore hosted a dinner with a "who's who" of socialites who had floated through America and Europe to the ancient city. The attendees were ready, willing, and financially able to explore—and exploit—Ataturk's new Turkey. Whittemore was many things: a committed homosexual, a devout Christian, a dedicated vegetarian, and a man on close personal terms with Matisse and Gertrude Stein, as well as, perhaps surprisingly given his other traits, Mustapha Kemal Ataturk.[19]

Whittemore was also obsessed with Hagia Sophia, specifically its mosaics, which had been "restored" out of existence behind plain plastering in the previous century. He was determined to bring them back into public view, a renovation which would involve the end of the building's status as a mosque, where depictions of the human form are forbidden. This would require power and its two closest handmaids: luck and money. So it was that evening in June that Whittemore and his guests founded—or rather, *he* founded, and they paid for—the Byzantine Institute of America, a body dedicated to the preservation of the ancient heritage of the former Empire's capital, and now Whittemore's chosen vehicle for change. Backed by cash, he began the process of charming Ataturk.

While Turkey's new warrior prince had done a great deal to undermine the role of Islam in Turkish political and social life, he had hitherto avoided confronting the status of Hagia Sophia. Perhaps he was waiting for the exact right moment to consolidate his power. Perhaps he was unsure of the popular backlash. Perhaps he simply feared the old Sultan's curse. Whatever had been the cause of Ataturk's delay, Whittemore's combination of charm and cold hard money worked, and just under two years after Whittemore's luxury dinner, on June 7, 1931, Ataturk's cabinet agreed to his proposal that Hagia Sophia be converted into a museum. Whittemore's work could begin.

As worshippers arrived for morning prayers the next day, a sign was affixed to the building's door, written in Ataturk's own hand: "THE MUSEUM IS CLOSED FOR REPAIRS." Earthly power had built the church, had made it a mosque, and now, with one stroke of a pen, had made it a museum. Once again, the building had become a cipher for the power of a single great figure, and once again, the nature of its purpose was to change.

As we seek to trace how one building might serve as a lesson in the relationship between faith and power, let us jump forward again, to the very recent past. Hagia Sophia has been at the center of a power struggle once more: the building, its status, its purpose, and the claims it makes for itself and the city it has come to represent mean too much, both as symbol and as structural reality, to be left alone. Just as the great church acted as a seal on the power of leaders past, so it has proved to be for the dominating force in early twenty-first-century Turkey—Recep Tayyip Erdoğan. He was president the first time I visited the city and its church in 2018, but, at that time, raw evidence of his power—the propaganda and posters, the armed presence, the hardening of rules on dress and behavior—were subtler and had to be sought out, noticed only by those who were looking.

On my subsequent visit that May in 2022, the situation had changed enormously. A supposed attempted coup, the opportunities given to authoritarianism by the Covid pandemic, and the sheer longevity of his political career had combined to make Erdoğan ubiquitous in Turkey. Even on the liberal avenue of the İstiklal in Western Istanbul, where, in contrast to the conservative neighborhood around the Gül Camii, bars sell beer, men hold hands with other men, and young women dress with enthusiasm in the styles of the West, Erdoğan's pouty and mustachioed face stares down blankly from vast posters and billboards.

The Turkish president (for, it seems likely, life) has, in a sort of reverse of Ataturk, long sought to appeal to his base of supporters, who are broadly speaking conservative and religious dwellers of every part of Turkey *except* Istanbul. As well as frequent invocation of the Ottoman Empire, he has made a particular mission to reverse much of Ataturk's secularization agenda and reintroduce Islam to the center of Turkish politics. To his critics, he is both a reactionary and an opportunist, cynically utilizing the everyday faith of millions to consolidate his own power. To his supporters, he is simply reflecting the country he leads, reversing the actions of the last, much mistaken century. At the end of one trip to Istanbul, I plucked up the courage to ask my taxi driver what he thought. He shrugged and then gestured to the smooth road and shiny terminal in front of us: "New road, new airport, new Turkey." If Constantine XI ever does return, his first task will be to get the trains running on time.

For many years, Erdoğan floated, hinted at, even made promises about the reconversion of Hagia Sophia into a mosque. For the president of the new Turkey, the presence of a secular Hagia Sophia represented a threat to his power, just as a pagan site had to Constantine's, a Christian site to Mehmet's, and a Muslim site to Ataturk's. In July 2020, Erdoğan got his wish, and indeed personally led the first Islamic prayer service in the space for nearly ninety years.[20] In his speech afterwards, he specifically invoked the curse of Mehmet: now it was lifted and now, the implication went, God would restore the power of Turkey once again.

Despite the myriad changes it has undergone, despite the differences in the activities that now occur there—despite, even, the clumsily placed signs guiding visitors on the specific tourist route around the central space—perhaps the most astonishing thing about the building today is that it still forces the head, eyes, heart, and soul upwards. I must have been in the building six or seven times in total; each time, I have felt overwhelmed. It is perhaps the only place where one can still feel the ghosts of Byzantium, can really imagine what life in the Second Rome was like. More importantly, it is a place that tells a story of a deeper meaning, of a higher yearning, of an attempt—however vain or politicized it may have been—to express in living stone the enormity of the emotions people have felt while trying to contemplate the Divine. It is a building that sings, wholly and absolutely, of the greatness—the power—of the concept which generations have labeled, be it in Greek, Latin, or Arabic, "GOD."

Hagia Sophia's story is the story of power. Of the power of symbol, of the power of place, the power of an idea. It is the story of how something—a place, a symbol, an idea—can *mean*. Mean so deeply and so greatly that empires can fall trying to protect it and new ones can rise with the specific intention of seizing or using it. Yet, it was also built—and now is once more—as a place of worship: somewhere people might find escape from the oppressions of the secular powers of the world, where they might see fit to commune with a power on high.

Christianity's relationship with power has always been a complex one, as Hagia Sophia's potted history shows. The building isn't alone in that regard: the fabric and the very name of the city in which it stands are tied up with the interaction between it and faith.

Political power, military power, civil power: call it what you will, it is a reality of every human society. Just as Jesus had things to say on those other stalwarts of human action—purity, judgment, forgiveness and love—so he had things to say about power. Specifically, his teaching was that his power was "not of this world." While the limitations of human power were evident, with God, "nothing is impossible."

Much is written in the Gospels about the reversal of human power which Christ's coming heralds: his mother Mary sings at the start of Luke's Gospel "he hath put down the mighty from their seat, and hath exulted the humble and meek." Quite clearly, this hardly provides an obvious endorsement of human power. Quite, it seems, the opposite: it hardly even looks like the kind of manifesto which might deliver the fancy roads and sparkly airports people like to see from their practitioners of power.

Jesus Christ was not born a powerful man, and he died an even less powerful one. The journey from manger and no-room-at-the-inn to the death of a criminal on a cross was not one filled with the usual signs and symbols of earthly power. The only times he would have ever entered a building even slightly similar to Hagia Sophia would have been as he entered the Temple of Solomon in Jerusalem (which Justinian claimed he had surpassed), or the court of Pontius Pilate.

The Latin for judgment house—the sort in which Pilate might have passed judgment on criminals—is *basilica*. After the Constantinian shift, Christians realized they no longer had to meet in catacombs or cellars or the back rooms of hidden houses, but could build their own grand, formal places of worship. Naturally, they looked about them for inspiration and so chose the layout and architecture of the most important buildings they knew: the Roman courts. So it was that the layout of churches—including, of course, Hagia Sophia—were based upon the same floorplan as the very building in which the fate of the religion's central figure was sealed. This transition, this redemption even, of a Roman house of power and authority into a place of worship dedicated to someone who was put to death by the power of that same Roman Empire is perhaps the most striking display of power of them all.

In truth, the faith changed the Empire and, in many ways, the Empire changed the faith. Arguments continue to rage about whether that was a good thing, or an inevitable thing, or even a deliberate thing. But that they were now bound in a symbiotic relationship was undeniable.

The crux of that relationship—often awkward, sometimes heretical, sometimes dangerous, always interesting, and, perhaps most importantly of all, *inevitable*—is played out in stone at Hagia Sophia. More than any other church in the world, it speaks of the sacrifices made in both directions, of the compromises, and of the contradictions inherent to the interplay between power and faith. One can view this as a theological statement in and of itself: that there is nothing beyond the redemption offered by Jesus Christ. Even power—that blood-soaked dynamic that rears its ugly head whenever one human encounters another—even that can be redeemed and exercised in a way that points to God and to the good.

Indeed, "nothing being beyond redemption" is a particularly important narrative for the Hagia Sophia. The ups and downs of the building's history have been such that it's almost a necessary doctrine for the place's continued existence. Take, for example, the things which hold the entire edifice up: the pillars. Such is the scale of the dome, and such is that natural instinct to look up, that it is easy to forget the structural supports when one stands inside the church. They are much more than just scaffolding, however. Within the Hagia Sophia are eight columns of a very deep green-gray marble. They're easy to walk past, but, once noticed, they draw the visitor's eye: the stone has a mesmerizing, enigmatic quality, like the iris of an eye.

That is, of course, deliberate. Originally, the eight green columns stood in one of the wonders of the ancient world: the Temple of Diana in Ephesus. Indeed, since the destruction of that temple, they are now its most substantive remains. Justinian was something of a magpie and so ordered architectural detail and material to be transported from across his dominions to underline the idea that Hagia Sophia would be *the* church for the whole Empire.

Istanbul remains filled with treasure from across its old Empire; although it tends to be of the monumental sort, columns, obelisks, and the like, largely because the Venetians pilfered anything that wasn't nailed down or too big to transport. The columns of the Temple of Diana are different to these, however.[21] They are testament not just to Justinian's earthly power, but to the power of Christ: these great cylinders of stone which once held up the most famed place of worship in the pagan world were now co-opted and used to support the place of worship of the Christian God. They were testimonies in stone not only to power, but to redemption and fresh purpose.

There is another pillar, toward the northwestern corner of the building, just on the far side of the imperial door. I make my way toward its site that May day, only to find it cordoned off, outside the prescribed route for worshippers and tourists. Strange to choose a specific column to render inaccessible, you might think, but what looks like an ordinary pillar has been at the center of numerous myths about the current church at Hagia Sophia since its very construction.

It is a pillar which, many people believe, has power. It is known by many names: the weeping, the wishing, or, my personal favorite, the sweating column. Toward its base are two rectangles of slightly grubby metal. In the center of the upper rectangle lies a worn-down, shinier circle of metal, in the middle of which there is a hole. It used to be that you could poke a finger or thumb into it. When you did so, it would come out wet.

Hagia Sophia, Istanbul, Turkey   83

So far, so simple, we might say: a case of damp or poor drainage or any of a million other dull and prosaic explanations. Not so; for marvelous stories are told of the column and the effect its moisture has on the faithful. One says that the dampness is caused by the tears of the Virgin Mary, whose house the rock adorned before it was brought to the edifice by Justinian's builders; it was against this pillar that she wept when Jesus told her he was destined to die, and such was the power of the moment that now the very rock imitates the Virgin and sheds tears.

Another says that the Emperor Justinian suffered from chronic headaches and, having called every doctor in his Empire to him to no avail, went one night to vent his frustration within his great masterpiece. In frustration he banged his head against this pillar and suddenly, miraculously, he was cured. Still another legend claims an angel blessed the pillar with healing properties, in order to make up for a broken promise made to a boy working in the building's construction. Different narratives, contradictory even, but all insist upon a fundamental truth about the pillar: it does not have a defect at all. It has been chosen as a vessel of Divine power.

The idea that the purpose of power is not to crush or to rule, but instead to transform the flawed into the beautiful, is central to Christian teaching. St Paul, the apostle also put to death by the Roman Empire, writes endlessly about power, particularly the power of God over death. We will, he writes, be changed and our bodies be made "like unto His glorious body."[22] That is, of course, the body of Christ; the same Christ whose power was, Paul wrote, "made perfect in weakness." Here is the paradox at the heart of Christian power: the weak is the one who is truly strong, the dead is the one truly alive.

When one begins to see things this way, the idea that a defective pillar might be, in fact, the most important part of a building, makes absolute sense. It demonstrates, in physical form, a constant theme in the history of Christian belief: to expect the unexpected. In the early days of the Church, the convert St Paul's message to new Christians in Corinth, a prosperous outpost of the first Roman Empire, was that true strength, true power, found its perfection through weakness. In other words, a key tenet of Christianity is that true power—the power of God, no less—expresses itself through what looks like defeat, through vulnerability. In that sense, you might argue that Hagia Sophia came closest to being a bastion of true Christian power when it sheltered the terrified and helpless at the end of its time as a church, as opposed to its stint as a glorious temple of Constantine's imagination, or as Justinian's reality. Redemption of power, then, is something that Christianity has always done; just sometimes not in the way that its followers think.

Did Christianity's redemptive message always make itself known and felt through the centuries of blood and power? Perhaps not. Does Hagia Sophia continue to encourage people to bow their heads in humility at the power of something greater than themselves and then, cautiously, like Justinian all those years ago, to raise those same heads in the faint but oh-so-powerful hope that they might somehow be a part of that greater story? Undoubtedly, yes. Therein is the essence of Christianity's particular power, that we will see again and again on our journey: its ability to take the ways of the world, subvert and subsume them, and then make them its own. In no area was this truer than of political power itself.

Contra Justinian himself, I'm of the opinion that the Bosphorus ferry affords perhaps the most impressive view of his great church. From the sea, you can see exactly why it was that the site at the top of the peninsula that pokes between the straits and the Golden Horn was so fought after, as the orange-pink of her thick buttresses sternly guard the entrance to the Bosphorus straits and Black Sea beyond. Later that week in May, it is from that ferry that I fix my eyes once more on Hagia Sophia.

Justinian believed his power could be—perhaps even would be—without end. He sealed that belief with a great building dedicated to the God whom he believed had given him such power. Constantine XI went there having submitted to the loss of power, knowing that his Empire and his life were both about to be lost forever. Mehmet the Conqueror sought to bind a higher power through spells and curses, so aware was he of earthly limitations. Ataturk believed so strongly in the power of progress and of capital that he thought the building's mysticism could be tamed and rationalized. Erdoğan has so closely identified it with his

Hagia Sophia, Istanbul, Turkey

own power as to make this nearly fifteen-hundred-year-old building a live geopolitical issue again. One might say, in all these endless twists and turns, Hagia Sophia has been nothing more than a passive actor, a victim even. Perhaps so, but then St Paul is adamant about the Divine reality in that regard: "strength is made perfect in weakness."

Constantinople is no more. Istanbul is changed, unrecognizably, from what she was. But Hagia Sophia has, almost inconceivably, remained. True power, Divine power, as Christ said, is the performance of the seemingly impossible.

As the sun set on that Friday evening in May, I stood on the rear deck of the ferry, looking back at the retreating metropolis. I did so through a shower of stale bread, thrown by an old man for the gulls, which littered first the air then the water. The tea man did his noisy rounds while couples clung closely to one another and watched Europe slip into the distance.

As one makes this journey, the old city—*the* City, as the Greeks still call it—slowly disappears from view. The Blue Mosque slips behind a bend in the Golden Horn, the Galata Tower becomes just another roof among a mass of roofs. Eventually, even the High Gate of the Topkapi Palace shrinks to doll's house size.

What remains, as it has remained for nearly two millennia, an unbowed testament to its own particular power throughout history, is the great church, the high mosque, the once museum. Hagia Sophia.

Chapter Four

Canterbury Cathedral, England

(Founded 597 AD)

Inevitably, as states and political entities that had an explicitly Christian nature began to be established, other issues began to arise for Christianity. As the Church became more than just a gathering of the faithful and accrued very real power to itself, the defense of that power became a priority. While the Church benefitted from the collapse of Roman authority and the sometimes oppressive power of its Empire, it also now faced a world less secure and more violent than before. As the exertion of violence became the primary means of demonstrating worldly power, the Church had to begin to address its own relationship with the violent. As we saw in Bethlehem and Rome, violence has been present in the Christian story from the very beginning. As we trace the Church's development, however, especially into an age where violence was the norm, the relationship between the faith of the Prince of Peace and a world that was far from peaceful became more complicated. It was in a church on the then edge of Christendom, at Canterbury Cathedral in England, where the story of Christianity and violence would play out in a way so dramatic that it shocked even Medieval Europe.

One of the first things the monks did was to scoop up the blood and the brains. Retrospectively, this was framed as an act of reverence, an acknowledgment of the viscera made holy by martyrdom. In reality, it was more likely to have been a grimly practical act. The brothers of Canterbury did not expect their murdered Archbishop to become a saint. It is, in fact, likely that they were rather relieved to be rid of him. Like good Christians, the monks had hated the Archbishop and, in return, the Archbishop hadn't been enormously keen on the monks either. Thomas Becket had been a quarrelsome man; prone to violence of speech and action. Now, he had suffered a violent death, hacked to pieces by a gang of knights just as he was on his way to one of the few religious services which he deigned to attend. Whatever is the equivalent of "a long time coming" in Middle English or Latin was doubtless whispered cowl to cowl in the hours that followed, as shock dissipated and a level-headed reality began to take over.

Canterbury had known violence before, of course. The Romans, people for whom the violent was not something to recoil from but rather their primary source of entertainment, had built an arena in the city they called Durovernum.[1] Plays were performed there alongside torture of both people and animals.[2] The Vikings, too, had paid a visit to Canterbury. In 1011 they had laid siege and then sacked it, kidnapping the then Archbishop, a former hermit named Alphege. They took him up the Thames to Greenwich and tried to extract a ransom for him. The Archbishop refused, knowing that his already ravished city would starve if it tried to pay the ransom. Irritated, the Vikings pelted him with ox bones until an impatient Norseman put Alphege out of his misery with a single axe blow to the head.

Alongside the city's history of bloodletting, there was medieval society itself, where, despite the efforts of Christian teaching, life was still short and of little value, and justice, law, and order were most effectively enforced by the sharp end of a sword. As the most obvious figures representing Christianity, you might imagine that the clergy were immune from this. However, the clergy were very much part of the medieval economy of violence, both on the receiving end and in committing violent acts themselves. Even at their lowest ebb, after the Black Death, by which they were disproportionately affected, priests and monks represented roughly 3% of the total population of medieval England.[3] Their role in violent incidents corresponded almost exactly to their population. As such, they were just as likely—or in some parts of Europe, more likely—to be murdered as anyone else. Priests being on the receiving end of popular violence became something of a trope, from the robbery of the abbot in the stories of Robin Hood to the French folk tale *Sacristain II*, which involves an elderly landlady at a tavern mistaking the corpse of a murdered monk—which has been concealed in her pantry—for bacon, which she proceeds to cut and serve to her clientele, despite complaints about its toughness. It ends with the punchline, "By St Leonard! I think this bacon is wearing shoes."[4] The medieval punters presumably found this hilarious.

The main reason why the clergy were often considered fair game for violence was because of a general sense of their hypocrisy in this area. Indeed, the university towns of Europe were plagued by violence perpetrated by priests and clergy in training. Some scholars suggest that the reason why trainee priests were so violent is that they were the only group of young men in society with easy access to a dangerous trio: lots of free time, a modest income, and copious amounts of alcohol. Bar brawls in Oxford and Cambridge fill the medieval court rolls and invariably clerks training for holy orders could be found to have provoked them. However, clerical participation in violence wasn't even limited to that most obvious class of perpetrator: bored, drunk young men in urban settings. Religious women occasionally took part in acts of violence too. One such example, in late medieval Ireland, was Elicia Butler, abbess of Kilculliheen, who, to enforce discipline, used to beat up her nuns. The sisters successfully complained on account of the fact that she had drawn blood in some instances, which corrective punishment, and specifically the clergy, were not supposed to do.[5] It had its own set of particular rules, but violence, undoubtedly, was everywhere, even in the Church.

Despite this context, the events at Canterbury were different. Even in a society much more violent than our own, the murder of Thomas Becket, Archbishop of Canterbury, on the way to vespers, the monastic service of evening prayer, in his own cathedral in December 1170, shocked and appalled. An eyewitness, a monk who was visiting from Cambridge, one Edward Grim, related how it happened. It began with a misheard—or misinterpreted—moan by King Henry II. He and Becket, who had once been best friends, were at loggerheads over the legal statuses of Church and state. The old power problem rearing its head again. Henry, stewing in his lands in Normandy, expressed irritation that the "drones and traitors" of his household would allow him "to be treated with such shameful contempt by a low born cleric!" This, at least, was Grim's record of things, though later, of course, the line mutated to the famous "Will no one rid me of this turbulent priest!" Whatever Henry actually said, it prompted a group of knights to hop on a boat and make their way to Canterbury with the express intention of murdering Becket.

Having surprised the Archbishop in the cathedral, the knights demanded that he forgive them for what they were about to do. Becket, not one for compromise, refused. So they, "laying sacrilegious hands on him," tried to drag him out of the cathedral, which caused Becket to cling to a pillar. They were going to have to butcher him there, or not at all. Each of the four knights there inflicted blows, specifically aiming for his head, where he had been anointed with holy oil when ordained. The final blow sliced off the very top of Becket's skull, exposing his brain to the view of the horrified monks. The final accomplice, not a knight but, even more shockingly, a clerk—a literate man and probably one of those trainee priests about whom we read so much in the crime records—stamped on the Archbishop's neck with such force that brain and blood spurted out of the hole in the top of his head.[6] Grim wrote that this final detail was particularly horrible to relate, doubtless as flashbacks haunted his mind. Amid all the violence of previous years, the cathedral had stood above the chaos, an oasis of peace among the day-to-day aggression and murder; it was, in religious and legal terms, a sanctuary from blood. Now, the brains and skull fragments of the nation's most senior priest were daubed on one of the side altars; violence had broken through the hallowed doors, thrust into the center of the cathedral itself.

As Bethlehem showed us, Christianity had been about making people and places holy from the very beginning. What happened when the holiness of a place became compromised—by violence or sex or greed or any other form of flawed human activity—became an area of major concern to Christians in the medieval period, when flawed human activity was going into overdrive. What made murder at Canterbury so shocking was that it had a claim to be *the* holiest spot in England. Not just any church but the church from which the English-speaking world was evangelized. Not just symbolic as a place of holiness but the definitive symbol of Christianity in England. The shockwaves traveled far and they traveled fast. The earliest depiction of Becket's braining isn't in England at all, but at Monreale on the Mediterranean island of Sicily. One of the most famous carvings showing the murder is on the font of the tiny church at Lyngsjö in central Sweden. Across Europe, the sheer violence of Becket's death—and, of course, its redemptive consequences—proved to be a complete sensation. Overnight, Becket became a saintly superstar. Why? Well, the Becket story had it all: betrayal, friendship, miraculous healing, and, above all, shocking violence. The current Dean of Canterbury described the murder to me as being like "The twin towers of the twelfth century." Everything was defined as before and after the event.

However, as always in history, while the weighty concepts float ethereally above any great moment in time, there are ordinary people on the ground getting on with the irritating practicalities that great moments and great men always seem to leave in their wake. The next job for those grumbling monks in Canterbury, as the mist and blood cleared, was to dispose of the Archbishop's clothing. Had there been a reasonable expectation of sainthood for the murdered Archbishop, they would have kept any scrap they could. Relics were big business and a cloak worn by a saint, torn into enough pieces, might feasibly keep a monastery or cathedral in food and wine for months. Tellingly, they instead began to give away his clothes to the poor and needy of Canterbury. Within days, strange stories began to circulate around the city. Those who had received the clothing claimed to have been cured of illnesses and ailments. Soon, people from all over the local area were beginning to gather at the cathedral, wanting to visit the grave of Becket in the crypt.

The monks tried to get control of the situation: they attempted to gather back as many would-be relics as possible. One enterprising monk even claimed to have got hold of some of the Archbishop's spattered blood and brains. These were diluted with water to make what was held to be a healing remedy, sort of like the world's most horrible version of orange squash. The monks also began to take testimonies from all those who came to the cathedral. They followed them up as well, so as to see which miracles were genuine. What was produced was one of the most complete records of the voices of ordinary people in the medieval world. Because of this, we know the names of blind leprous beggars, of criminals and cripples who might otherwise have been lost to history. An ironic outworking for a high political spat between a prince and a prelate.

94

Twelve Churches

The stories are wonderful: in the truest sense of being amazing not only in the deeds described and the healings attested to but also in their powerful conveyance of personalities across the centuries. Perhaps one of the most graphic was that of Eilward of Westoning, a man, presumably of a Saxon family and so unlikely to be wealthy or powerful in Norman England, who was accused of stealing clothing as part of an ongoing feud with his next-door neighbor and who, in an excellent illustration of just how day-to-day violence could be in medieval times, was blinded and castrated by way of punishment. He prayed to St Thomas and, miraculously, after a vision of the murdered Archbishop, those parts of Eilward which had been so violently taken away were restored to their full functionality. After this, Eilward became something of a celebrity in his local Bedfordshire, even generously allowing local people to feel his genitalia for themselves so as to ensure that his testicles really had grown back. Eventually, he made a pilgrimage of thanks to Canterbury, where a monk, Benedict of Peterborough, recorded his tale for posterity.[7] The whole story is now, with all of its gory detail, depicted in the stained-glass windows of Canterbury Cathedral, quite literally part of the fabric.

In the window next to Eilward is told the story of the two sisters of Boxley, a village near Maidstone on the other side of the county. Their legend stated that they sought Becket's intercession for their lameness.[8] After a night of prayer, one sister was healed. The other, however, remained unable to walk properly and so hauled herself to the shrine, where she proceeded to chastise the saint aggressively for his failure to treat the siblings fairly. The next day, the martyred Archbishop, clearly receptive to a bit of berating—which had, after all been his modus operandi in life—had healed her as well. Whether they were from Westoning or Boxley, or much further afield, by the end of the following century, ordinary people were flocking to the spot where Becket's blood and brains had spattered the stone floor.

By February 1173, Becket had been canonized as a saint. This attracted a swell of pilgrims, who brought money as well as prayers. This, and a series of fires—disastrous at the time, but ultimately quite convenient—allowed for a massive redecoration and expansion of the cathedral. The centerpiece was to be the shrine of Becket himself, adorned with marble and precious stones and surrounded by vast windows of stained glass. Not only were the stories of Eilward and the sisters written down, but they were also immortalized in the glass, now set in the windows of the east end of the cathedral.[9] These figures had moved from the very margins of medieval society into permanent places in the physical fabric of the institution at its very heart. That, truly, was a miracle. And a miracle made possible by the bloody and gritty reality of Becket's death.

What had begun as an act of violence became legend and passed into that realm rather than the world of the painful or visceral. In the excitement, even details of the murder—the very things you'd expect to become *most* important—were lost. Even exactly where Becket had been when he was killed was wrapped in time's shroud and forgotten. My guide posited the steps to the choir as the most likely location, but we are unlikely to ever know. Nor, really, does it matter. The actual act of violence and all its grisly specifics were subsumed. Violence became healing. Death, as St Paul wrote, was swallowed up in victory.[10] Even the blood and brains ceased to be things of horror and instead became effective instruments of healing in their own right. In the case of Hugh of Jervaulx, the cellarer (a monk in charge of catering at a monastery) of Jervaulx Abbey in Yorkshire, was confined to bed with appalling headaches, to the despair of his doctors. After drinking a solution of water mixed with traces of Becket's blood and brains—which, in fairness, was only marginally more horrible than other cures posited by the medieval medical mind—Hugh suffered an enormous nosebleed. After this, depicted in glorious technicolor in the Canterbury glass, Hugh recovered, despite being almost 300 miles from Becket's tomb itself. For the monks, who made a big deal of the event, the message of the miracle was clear: nothing earthly, not medicine, not physical distance, not even violent acts, could get in the way of the purposes of God. Once again, Christianity had turned something ostensibly horrific, indisputably gory, and with its roots in violence, into a point of unity, a show of faith, something holy.

Becket's murder was shocking and is interesting precisely because it gives us an insight into what "too far" looked like for a society as generically violent as medieval England's. However, it's primarily interesting as one of the best case studies of how Christianity was capable of turning anything into holiness, even the violent.

Of course, Canterbury's road to redemption was not unique. Violence and redemption had danced across the scene of Christianity from its very beginning. The faith had, after all, been born of a violent act: the crucifixion. Early Christian history, from the crucifixion itself onwards, is a litany of it. There were the martyrdoms in Rome and Jerusalem of the earliest saints and apostles, and while these ended in the West after the period of its initial persecution, the Church's accruing of power and wealth made it a target for violence by all sorts, from ordinary robbers to rulers of empires. In many parts of the world, in particular those affected by the Arab conquests in the wake of the rise of Islam, the brief moment of the Constantinian Shift was merely a short period of respite before the resumption of the norm of persecution. Yet, like any idea sincerely believed, Christianity was capable of inspiring violence as well as being on the receiving end of it. From roughly the end of the second century onwards, when Mileto, the eunuch Bishop of Sardis, asked in his Easter sermon, "By whom was He [meaning Jesus] put to death?" and then gave the answer, "By Israel," there had been a growing sense among Christians that it was the Jewish people, not the Roman Empire, who were really to blame for the death of Christ.[11] As the power of Christianity grew, so its followers began acts of violence, in particular against Jews. By the medieval period, acts of mob violence against Jews, often around times of major religious significance, such as Easter, were regular occurrences across Europe.

To say that this inheritance of both suffering and perpetrating bred a mixed attitude to violence within Christianity would be an understatement. The Bible, as is the case with its teaching on so many ethical topics, offers mixed advice. It isn't even as simple as there being an "old" Jewish version of the teaching which Jesus replaced. Christ himself appears to say totally contradictory things about violence. Famously, he instructs his followers by saying, "Whosoever shall smite thee on thy right cheek, turn to him the other also," seemingly an endorsement of a particularly extreme form of non-resistant pacifism.[12] A few chapters later, however, in the same Gospel—that of Matthew—Jesus corrects his disciples saying, "Think not that I am come to send peace on earth: I came not to send peace, but a sword."[13] In short, the Bible has plenty of violence, acknowledging it as a fact of fallen human nature—Cain, after all, commits the first murder pretty early on in the story arc of Genesis—and it often looks forward to a time, in the coming Kingdom of God, when it will be no more; but on what happens in between, it is less clear.

Unsurprisingly, this resulted in a quandary for the Church, especially at the time of Becket when violence was the norm. There were later medieval thinkers who were close to being what we might understand as "pacifists": the fourteenth-century English theologian John Wycliffe was adamant that Christians ought to prefer the *lex caritatis*, the law of absolute charity; by contrast were the vengeful instructions more frequently, but not exclusively, present in the Old Testament. Indeed, Wycliffe went as far as to argue that the instructions of Christ were so clear as to make any act of violence—even in resistance or on behalf of the vulnerable—wrong.[14] Unsurprisingly, late medieval society wasn't too keen on Wycliffe's views about this, or a number of other subjects, and some thirty years after his death, his bones were dug up and burned on the direct orders of the Pope. An act of violence re-establishing the cycle over the physical remains of one who'd tried very hard to break it. However, at the time of Becket's death, even Wycliffe's attempted pacifism was a very long way away. So deep was the medieval understanding of justice, contrition, and revenge as being rooted in an "eye-for-an-eye" model of the Biblical books of Exodus, Leviticus, and Deuteronomy, that the only possible retribution that could be conceived for the murder was more violence.

So it was that, after Becket's death, yet more blood flowed in Canterbury Cathedral. Blood of penance. The blood not of a bishop but of a king. As it became clear that the murder of his one-time friend and political rival was to be the catastrophe of his career, a weeping and horror-struck Henry II made pilgrimage to the tomb to show the world that he was sorry. There, he stripped, lay prostrate, and allowed the assembled clergy to whip him: five strokes of the whip from each of the bishops present, and then three lashes from each of the eighty monks.[15] Henry's act was deeply symbolic: of the limits of kingly power, of the ability of the church to make a king crawl on his knees, but also of the transformative power of a good story, even over the cruder powers of death and violence. Canterbury was not unique, but it encapsulated that transformative power of Christianity over the violent act better than almost anywhere else. No wonder a society as violent as that of the Middle Ages was so drawn to it; to many, the miraculous must have seemed like almost the only way out of the cycle.

On my visit to Canterbury, on a damp and still autumn day, the world of blood and gore seemed distant imaginings. It is a fairly sleepy English city these days. The cathedral close—the little gated community immediately under the great church's shadow—was quiet, perfect for an unobtrusive wander. This I did, as the odd schoolchild hurried past. Just beyond the east end, a smart Georgian frontage peeped out from between ruined arches. It is now a boarding house for the school but it is said, in the house's less salubrious past, that Lady Hamilton danced on a table there for Admiral Nelson while he was on shore leave. A moment of levity before returning to the violent life of the high seas. The Gothic remains that frame it look as if they have gone through a war. In many ways they have.

As the Reformation seized Europe, another wave of violence broke out. The changes wrought by Luther in sixteenth-century Germany inspired numerous others, from the fastidious, exacting figure of Jean Calvin in Switzerland to Scotland's reforming whirlwind, the bombastic John Knox, who famously referred to women as "a monstrous regiment." Churches and priests were targeted. Blood and treasure were spilled. In England, the Reformation found itself in more delicate hands. Thomas Cranmer was the charming, faintly cynical man whom King Henry VIII had installed as Archbishop of Canterbury in 1533, just as he was attempting to persuade the then Pope of the merits of his divorce from Catherine of Aragon, his first wife, who could not give him an heir. Cranmer's own sympathies were with the reformers, but he was acutely aware of the political eggshells on which he trod. He had been part of the delegation who went to Rome on Henry's behalf in 1530, only to have their entire efforts stymied when a spaniel, the pet of the Earl of Wiltshire, one of Cranmer's colleagues, rushed forward and bit Pope Clement VII on his big toe.[16]

Knowing that he had been appointed for reasons of political utility, Cranmer was particularly keen not to tread in the footsteps of his predecessor, Becket. Consequently, he actively welcomed it when Henry and his chief minister, Thomas Cromwell, drew up a piece of legislation decrying Becket as "a rebel ... who shall no longer be named a saint" and that "his pictures throughout the realm are to be plucked down and his festivals shall no longer be kept, and the services in his name shall be razed out of all books."[17] Henry justified this by claiming that Becket's death had not in fact been a martyrdom at all, rather a totally reasonable consequence of his actions. His proclamation of November 1538 specifically drew attention to the fact that Becket was reported to have acted violently toward the knights who were merely trying to reason with him, until "in the throng, Becket was slain."[18] Violence, then, was still important as a means of apportioning blame.

Henry, of course, was a man of violence himself. His particular loathing of Becket's legacy was because he had himself ordered the death of his own former friend, advisor, and defender of the rights of the Church, Thomas More. He had been beheaded in July 1535, just as Henry's embrace of the Reformation stepped up a gear with his insistence on royal supremacy over the Church. Since then, their shared first name and the similar circumstances of their deaths had made devotion to Becket a covert way of supporting the cause of More and, implicitly, opposing Henry. For a king who sought control over all, this would not do. The cult of Becket had to go, with violence if necessary.

Bonfires were lit in Canterbury as once again it became the place where the kingdoms of this world clashed against the kingdoms of the next. Onto them were tossed the ornate structure of Becket's tomb—after, of course, the King's men had stripped their valuable decorations for safe deposit in the royal treasury—and, most shockingly, the bones of the saint himself. The comfort that Becket's afterlife had brought was over, for now, scattered to the wind in a flurry of ash and flame. Now on the site of the tomb there is a simple candle, that burns night and day, a sign of light in darkness. In many ways, it is more powerful than any ornamented tomb might have been.

In the end, Cranmer would follow Becket and suffer a violent death on the orders of a monarch. Both men were politicians, both gambled, and both, in the end, lost. On the accession of Henry's Catholic daughter, Mary I, in 1553, a campaign of vengeance against those who had led the Reformation in England was begun, with Cranmer a key target. After some vacillation, including signing a recantation of his past beliefs, Cranmer realized the game was up. Condemned to be burned in Oxford, he thrust his right hand into the flame before the rest of him was consumed, as punishment for its offence of signing his false confession. The fires of the Reformation may have brought light to some, but, like many a flame, once lit and deployed, they brought pain and destruction as well.

These flames spread all around the world. Far, far away from Canterbury, on the Plaza Mayor of Lima in Spanish Peru in April 1592, flames lapped at writhing limbs in another act of holy violence. Unlike the murder of Becket, though, this was not violence retrospectively and subversively made holy; this was violence inflicted in an attempt to ensure that holiness was not compromised. On the dusty ground of colonial Lima, Christianity was being used as the justification for an execution of horrific violence. Five people were strapped to stakes erected on the Plaza and then burned to death. The explicit reason was their religion: two were Spanish subjects who were accused of transgressing the strict religious law of the colony by being secret or "crypto" Jews and the other three, Englishmen, had been captured as pirates but, rather than hang them for piracy, it was decided to burn them for the much more dangerous crime of being Protestants.[19]

This was over 400 years since the events at Canterbury and almost one hundred years since Columbus had first set foot on the shores of the Americas. Of those events we will learn more in coming chapters; however, one of the many things that Europe had brought to the New World was its religious violence. In the Spanish possessions in South America, the institution of the Inquisition had been granted sweeping powers to police the thoughts, actions, and beliefs of the residents of the New World by the Spanish Crown. The Inquisition had been a long-standing organization within the Catholic Church. Originally it had been a subdivision of the Papacy, instructed with ensuring that the doctrines of the Catholic faith were correct and were being properly taught. However, as Church and state began to grow in their scope and in their interests in the lives and beliefs of their members, the Inquisitions of Catholic Europe correspondingly began to become useful instruments to weed out dissent. Particularly in the hands of the rulers of the ethnically and religiously complex new kingdoms of the Iberian peninsula, the Inquisition began to become agents of violence in the name of religion.[20] The unity that Christianity at least theoretically provided, and the need to police its parameters, became even more important as Europeans crossed the Atlantic.

As we shall see in the following chapter, these new, fragile societies, far from the sources of authority of the Old World, insecure in every sense of the word, were at pains to protect their boundaries, both physical ones and ones of thought and belief. Violence was the ultimate safeguard to protect from threats to beliefs that were necessary to maintain cohesion. For many in the New World, Christianity was a driving force behind their presence there, whether they were ambitious Spanish friars climbing the hierarchy of the institutions of New Spain, or English Puritans seeking a purer new Jerusalem in the wilds of Massachusetts. For these Christians, protecting that faith—or more specifically their version of it—became essential, and if violence was needed to do so, then so be it.

From the pogroms of Europe in the twelfth century—when, as part of Mileto of Sardis's legacy, just two decades after the violence that had so shocked in Canterbury, terrified Jews in York, led by Josce, their Rabbi, chose to slit the throats of their own families rather than face the Christian mob outside—to the last man executed by the Inquisition, a school teacher in Spain, hanged and then placed in a barrel painted with flames—as, by 1826, burning at the stake was considered a step too far—that Christians were capable of violence despite the teaching of their founder was rarely in doubt.[21, 22] Yet, in Canterbury, in the midst of what its Dean called "the soup of history," there is a lingering sense

102 *Twelve Churches*

that things aren't quite as simple as a tale of cyclical violence and human tragedy.

Some 800 years after the murder that so defined the place, two men knelt and prayed on the spot where Becket had supposedly died. Archbishop Robert Runcie, the successor of Cranmer, and Pope John Paul II, the successor of Clement VII, of the bitten toe, spent time together praying in the side chapel of Canterbury Cathedral known as "The Martyrdom." They did so while acknowledging their differences, and in full knowledge of the enormous history of violence between Catholics and Protestants. It might seem normal for Christians to pray together, but, given the context of such historic violence between those who adhered to different churches, Runcie and John Paul were committing a radical act. It is no coincidence, of course, that they chose to do so at the site of Becket's death: if anywhere symbolized the ability of Christianity to transfigure past violence into a point of unity and piety, it was there.

Still, however, there were those who clung then, and still cling now, to the old violent acts of thought, word, and deed, justified by their faith. When Runcie was in Liverpool that year, preaching at the parish church, he found himself picketed and pelted by the Protestant Orange Order, who screamed "traitor" at him for his willingness to engage with the Pope.[23] Yet, it was a visible symbol of how far mainstream Western Christianity had come in its relationship with violence and the direction of travel in which it was seeking, despite continued differences, to go.

The irony is, of course, that for all the times Christianity led the way in inflicting or at least justifying violence, it also played a pivotal role in making the West less violent over the years. Wycliffe proved to be not quite the outlier that the medieval world imagined him to be and successive priests, nuns, monks, and ordinary Christians made enormous leaps, both through great arcs and acts and through little personal endeavors. The teachings of Jesus—the Prince of Peace—about turning the other cheek and about loving our enemies were considered insane in the ancient world, where might was right. Indeed, the very founding principle of Christianity, the idea of a crucified savior, one who overcame violence with death were, in the words of St Paul, "a stumbling block to some and folly to others."[24] Yet, they slowly became the accepted gold standard—if not the permanent practice—of the Western world, even long after it lied to itself that it had shed the specific bonds of Christianity. As with the monks cleaning up Becket's brains, the stories of individuals and the great sweep of movements are often closer than we like to think. In no sphere is that truer than when it comes to violence.

There is another aspect at play, of course, in the particularities of Christianity and violence. Perhaps a place, perhaps a people, perhaps a faith, all need to have gone through some sense of what it is to know pain in order to heal. A place that has suffered the reality of violence is necessarily more convincing as a scene of peace and reconciliation. Of course, this mirrors the life of Christ. God—in Christian teaching—draws humanity closer by knowing what it is to die, and dying violently himself. Is it paradoxical? Perhaps. Has it echoed in the hearts of men and women for centuries since? Undoubtedly.

It is another example of that strange magic of Christianity, that ability to turn something so ostensibly opposed to the purposes of God into something which draws people *to* God. That the violence it was capable of inflicting was supremely wicked is in no doubt, but that sits alongside its capacity to bring about the end of violence, and to use the violence of the past to forge reconciliation in the present and future. That those things sit uncomfortably alongside one another is true, especially in an age that demands clear-cut ethical judgments on the past. However, the truth is that this discomfort and complexity is much closer to the realities of how violence operates—and, crucially, to how Christianity teaches that God operates—than anything more simple and more comforting.

However, Christianity is not just a faith of the past, nor is violence a thing of it. For many, the particular discomfort of the way of the cross is not just theology, it is reality. It is part of the faith of today as much as it was of yesterday.

One place where Christianity has been shaped by violence of late is Cairo. Ain Shams is part of the great sprawl of houses, shops, and endless, noisy roads to the northeast of New Cairo. Once, in the days long before

Christianity, it was the site of the city of Heliopolis, an Egyptian settlement dedicated to the worship of the sun. The Old Testament prophet Isaiah proclaimed that, one day, the inhabitants of this city, despite it being a symbol of Egyptian pagan religion, would swear allegiance to the Lord.[25] He was right, after a fashion. Ain Shams is now something of a mixed neighborhood, with a sizeable Coptic Eastern Christian population living alongside the majority Muslim one.

Both communities are ancient ones: the very earliest areas to come under the sway of Islam were in Egypt and some of the very oldest documentary evidence we have of the Bible come from somewhere nearby.[26] Outbreaks of tension, and sometimes bloodshed, have been unhappy, though in the scheme of things only occasional, parts of life in Ain Shams, with religion invariably serving as the easy justification for violence.

One outbreak, horrific in its levels of violence, took place on Friday, March 28, 2014. In the midst of political unrest in Egypt surrounding the status of the Muslim Brotherhood Party, a protest after Friday prayers spilled over into violence targeting Christians. Near to the little Church of the Virgin Mary and the Archangel Michael, a young Christian woman, Mary Sameh George, was driving her car. She was on an errand to deliver medicine and financial support to those in need within the Coptic community. As with so many cars in Cairo, hers was adorned with little trinkets and art representing the things the driver loves. When I visited in 2022, I saw decorations as varied as the Arabic name of the Prophet Muhammed, branding for Coca-Cola, and the bizarre American twentieth-century sex symbol, Betty Boop. All harmless; fun, even. Mary Sameh George's symbol, the sign that she loved and had wrapped around her rearview mirror, was a cross. This symbol, on that day, in that place, was not harmless at all. Rather, it marked her out as a target for the most appalling violence.

It appears that Mary was initially badly wounded by a spray of gunfire, which brought her car to a halt. Such violence on account of what was dangling from her car mirror is appalling enough, but the eyewitness account of what happened next, after the mob had spotted her, is particularly shocking, but bears repeating:

"Once they saw that she was a Christian [because of the cross hanging on her rearview mirror], they jumped on top of the car, to the point that the vehicle was no longer visible. The roof of the car collapsed in. When they realized that she was starting to die, they pulled her out of the car and started pounding on her and pulling her hair—to the point that portions of her hair and scalp came off. They kept beating her, kicking her, stabbing her with any object or weapon they could find . . . Throughout [her ordeal] she tried to protect her face, giving her back to the attackers, till one of them came and stabbed her right in the back, near the heart, finishing her off. Then another came and grabbed her by the hair, shaking her head, and with the other hand slit her throat. Another pulled her underpants off, to the point that she was totally naked."[27]

This is not the sanitized violence of the video game or even of modern drone warfare. What happened to Mary Sameh George was as brutal as any medieval massacre or Reformation persecution. Her tragic case is a reminder that, while many Western Christians can afford to theorize about violence, comforted by the easy distance of time, for many of their Eastern brothers and sisters, violence is a reality, and a risk, of their faith.

In the same book of Isaiah that prophesied that the people of Ain Shams would one day follow the Lord, there is another, even more radical prediction.[28] It predicted that the Messiah, the Chosen One of Israel, the figure promised by that same Lord to bring about all those seemingly impossible prophecies, including an end to violence itself, would in fact have to suffer. Indeed, it would not be through strength or power that his aims would be fulfilled but by making himself subject to violence. The specifics of how this would happen, how strength might be shown in weakness, were predicted, and have obvious resonances: "I gave my back to the smiters, and my cheeks to them that plucked off the hair: I hid not my face from shame and spitting."[29]

When Christ was crucified, the accounts in the Gospels are clear in their sense that this specific prophecy had been fulfilled. To his murderers, Christ presented his back, they tore his hair, they lashed his cheeks. Almost 2,000 or so years later, Mary Sameh George's murderers did the same. The Coptic Bishop whose care and jurisdiction the attacked church fell under said, "Mary, you who are beloved of Christ. They tore your body because of the Cross."[30]

This is where Christian interpretations of violence are at their most radical and most difficult.

To read of the details of the death of Mary Sameh George is to immediately—as a fellow human let alone as a Christian—ask a series of questions. Was there any logic? Any positive aspect? It's very hard to see one, to understand any way that looks on the event as positive or redeemable. Christianity views such events as a symptom of violent, fallen humanity being not as it should be, and needing something beyond simply good wishes or human schemes to change it. Yet at the same time it also says that this is not the whole or the only story; a violent, horrible death does not define Mary Sameh George, but rather the hope of the cross does.

That is why the Bishop chose to emphasize the role of the cross in her fate. The cross was both the cause of death and the hope that made death no longer fearful, the seal by which a belief could be held that death and violence would not, in the end, win. Such a belief is not an easy one to hold. Doubtless it is a stumbling block to some and pure folly to others. But there is no denying that it robs even the most extreme acts of violence of their emotive power. And that is a radical thing indeed.

What, then, is the future relationship between Christianity and violence? An age is dawning where the secular world has followed the Christians of the past and reconfigured definitions of violence to, once again, include thoughts and words as well as deeds. In parts of the West, especially in its academic centers where thought is shaped for future generations to come, the former distinction of violent deeds as somehow more worthy of punishment than violent words is fading away. Of course, this is nothing new—from Lima to Oxford, this chapter has been as filled with the violent power of thoughts and words as much as the violent power of deeds. However, this occurs now without Christianity having the power or the influence to define what those thoughts and words are. And it also comes in the context of violence itself being no longer the norm that it was in, say, the medieval period, but more subject to condemnation than perhaps ever before.

However, that is not to say that we now live in a violence-free society. In the circular logic of morality, the absolute condemnation of violence means that, ironically, violence can be justified, providing it's against the right target: i.e. someone who themselves is committing violence against the innocent. There are occasions where especially younger people seem very willing to justify violence. A poll conducted by Harvard University in late 2023 found that 51% of Americans aged eighteen to twenty-four felt that political, national, and ethnic grievances justified violence.[31] We are once again in a situation where violence of action actually becomes justifiable in some quarters by way of correcting violence of thought. A revolution is under way: the question of who is seen as justified in committing violence is shifting away from the monopoly once held by the state and toward individuals.

Of course, this state of affairs has not arisen in a vacuum. Undoubtedly, in certain modern circles, the nineteenth- and twentieth-century specters of Communism and Fascism have a role to play: after all, as Marx wrote, "when our turn comes, we shall not make excuses for the terror."[32] However, the truth is that even Christianity, for all its opposition to those two creeds, is capable of an intellectual outcome whereby violence of thought (i.e. beliefs so wrong as to threaten the sense of security of those who disagree with you) is worthy of violence of action. Indeed, in the past, religious revolutions were defined by claiming a Divine mandate to bypass the state's monopoly on violence and allow individuals and groups to inflict it in the name of God.[33]

The words of Henry II which so quickly resulted in Becket's blood being shed, the Reformers' zeal that so rapidly spiraled from arguments about ideas into flames of destruction, the brutal murder of an innocent woman for displaying a cross; none of these are as far away from the hands and hearts of humans as we sometimes like to think. Violence bubbles under the surface as an ever-possible reality, regardless of the ideology which co-opts it.

On one level, Christianity functions in exactly the same way as any other thing which people believe passionately. There are times when belief in its principles can lead those who hold them to commit acts of uninhibited violence, so convinced are they that certain ideas or places or

108   *Twelve Churches*

people need punishment or protection from thoughts, words, or deeds which might harm them. However, Christianity, by being born of the radical idea that God himself, in the form of Christ, suffered violence and rose above violence, perhaps has a unique potential among all of the ideologies to have inflicted violence on the world to reconcile the violent and the painful.

Perhaps the best illustration of this strange potential is found in a final return to Canterbury.

Back in Canterbury, in the 1180s, and the woman writhed and thrashed as they finally dragged her to the tomb. The other pilgrims stepped back in horror as they saw her. She made eye contact with some of them, in particular children. She would fix her maniacal glare at one of them and, lying still for just one terrifying moment, she would then lurch out toward them and her hands, all marked skin, gaunt bones, and uncut fingernails, would try to find their way around the child's neck. It is only violence that can contain her from such acts; she is constrained, is heaved by burly men whose task it is to render her less of a threat; often she is beaten.

Mad Matilda, as she was known, spoke only in ravings. They sounded close to English but never quite made the leap into being comprehensible. How she had ended up in Canterbury was anyone's guess. The city and its cathedral attracted countless people, from all over the country, in search of healing at Becket's tomb. Many of them were desperate, a trip to the shrine a last resort when all other prayers or cures had proved useless. Many had suffered grievous injury or were in the advanced stages of diseases, which made their physical form scary for the ordinary citizens to look upon. None, however, elicited quite as much fear as Matilda.

One day, however, a piece of her puzzle fell into place. A monk, who found himself in Canterbury having been born in the east of the County of Flanders on the borders of modern-day Belgium and Germany, happened to overhear Matilda's ravings. Except they weren't ravings at all. They were deep, heartfelt lamentations spoken not in the English of a madwoman, but in the distinct dialect of Cologne and its environs,

Canterbury Cathedral, England 109

known as Franconian. It was close enough to the monk's native Flemish for him to begin to discern Matilda's real story. She was not mad at all, but grieving. Matilda had loved, deeply loved, a man back in Cologne. She even bore him a child, despite their not being married due to the opposition of her family, who thought him unsuitable. Not long after the baby was born, Matilda's brother ambushed her love and murdered him. The loss affected her hugely. She found herself alone with her child, bereft of its father. Driven wild by grief, with a single shake or a slap, she killed the child. Violence, not for the first time, begat violence.

Driven mad by grief, for her lover, for her child, for the life she might have had, Matilda roamed Western Europe. On her way, she paid particular attention to children, terrifying them. Fears that she might harm them, either physically or by some deep magic, abounded. Events, or perhaps that same desperate desire for healing that compelled so many to visit Becket's shrine, brought her to Canterbury. There she became known as Mad Matilda. An outcast, a danger, a bringer of violence. Violent deeds were done to her and violent words spat at her. Finally, after days spent in the environs making, frankly, as the monks perceived it, a nuisance of herself, Matilda was dragged to the space directly in front of Becket's shrine and collapsed on the floor. For four hours she stayed there, contorting herself on the marble and screaming at God for the violence inflicted on her and for the violence she herself had done. At about the fourth hour, suddenly a wave of peace came over Matilda. Her rantings ceased; her face became calm. She no longer sought to harm the children she encountered. The cycle, and power, of violence had been broken.

What had done it? What had enabled this person, so broken by the violence of the world, to find a sense of peace? The monks naturally put it down to the miraculous intervention of Becket, adding mental illness to the list of things they could claim their shrine was efficacious for. However, their successors, the Dean and Chapter at Canterbury today, have a different theory. The cathedral is, the Dean told me, "thick like soup." In it are contained hopes and fears from generations long past. Those stones had known the kind of violence and pain that Matilda knew. It was the fact that it too had suffered that meant it could be the

110   *Twelve Churches*

place where she could finally put her suffering aside. The fact it had known violence helped to break the cycle of violence in the life of one who knew it too well.

Unlike some other belief systems, Christianity doesn't teach that the abolition of violence by human means is possible. It is not that it doesn't seek to mitigate it—and some of the most effective institutors of non-violent change, from John Wycliffe to Dr. Martin Luther King Jr., have done so from Christian principles—however, there is a stark realism in the acknowledgment that it will take nothing short of Divine intervention to remove violence from the cycle of human existence. Indeed, even the final abolition of violence, associated with the second coming of Jesus, the Son of Man, that is to say Christ—predicted by the Book of Revelation and riffed on by Christians, science fiction authors, and occasionally serial killers ever since—suggests he will come carrying not something sweet and cuddly but a "sharp sickle."[34] Even the abolition of humanity's violent ways seems to involve aspects of the violent as inherent to its healing. In the meantime, until the final age comes around when "nation shall not lift up sword against nation, neither shall they learn war any more," Christians have shown the most remarkable ability to hold violence alongside holiness and to refuse to allow cycles of violence to predominate and continue, instead looking to redemption of even the most violent acts to become symbols instead of healing and hope.[35]

In fact, it takes it a step further: the places that have known the most extreme violence are therefore capable of healing in a way that those that have not known it can never be. Mad Matilda had doubtless been in many churches and to many shrines, but it was Becket's, with its history of blood, that proved to be the place where she could finally have her soul healed. Of course, Christianity is not unique in knowing this to be true—from the violent carved imagery of Buddhist temples in South East Asia to modern-day trauma psychology, the concept of needing to have violence acknowledged to overcome its power is well established. However, theologically speaking, Canterbury seeks to root this healing in not just violence against humanity but against the Divine. Such a theology is, as the Dean told me, to make those places and their people "memetic of the cross." The site that has a claim to be one of the very first holy places in Christianity is Golgotha. The place of the skull, a place of violence, the site of the cross.

The cross is, after all, for Christians at least, both a place of extreme violence, and a place of healing. Christian history doesn't make a case that violence done to hearts, minds, or bodies is a good or a holy thing—despite the attempts to make it so in that complicated past—but it does quite simply make the argument that the world, despite the continued presence of horrific violence, can't be beyond redemption. Violence, then, whether it be done to Christ on the cross or Becket in the cathedral or Matilda at the tomb or Mary in her car, doesn't get the final word. However difficult it might seem, the final word goes to redemption.

So, as with so many of the themes in this book, to explain Christianity's development and progression, we have to keep in mind its origins. The cross is, along with the manger and the empty tomb, one of the transformative moments in the original story of the faith. It transformed its specific moment, but—and here is the secret of Christianity's ability to subvert and subsume the ways of the world—to Christians it continues to transform. It is not so much that Christianity made accommodation with violence as the medieval period progressed, but rather that throughout all ages—including in those places where violence is a daily reality in our age—Christians necessarily see things through the lens of faith and in the context of past, present, and future, rather than simply as a horror of a particular place, and time. Nowhere better illustrates that refraction of history through faith than Canterbury Cathedral.

The sun set slowly on that autumn day in Canterbury, sinking at its own gentle rate beneath the horizon. I left the precincts with David, my kindly guide, with the same sense that I always get there: one of calm and peace.[36] As a place, it is living proof of one of the strangest Christian ideas: that through a thing of violence, peace might come. The Dean quoted Seamus Heaney to me during our meeting, saying that Canterbury, like Troy, was a place "where hope and history rhyme."[37] The hope of the cross is a strange but powerful thing, bringing light in darkness. As we passed through the great gate and back into the world beyond the precincts, the sun finally set. And Becket's candle still burned.

Chapter Five

Mount Athos, Greece

(Organized monastic life can be traced to 963 AD)

As the Church found itself subverting the political powers of the world, it began to find itself in a position to change society in other ways as well. Having changed how people saw the roots of state power and begun a degree of regulation of the violence required to enforce it, it also found itself in a position to begin to change the way ordinary people lived their lives. In some cases, this was even more radical than Christianity's effect on politics. It certainly affected more lives directly. Of no aspect of human society was this truer than sex. From the very earliest days of the apostle Paul, the Church began teaching on how humans related to each other in contexts outside the church: their relationships and their sexual activity. In the earliest days, celibacy was advocated; however, its adoption as a permanent and universal doctrine would have made the continuation of the new faith very difficult indeed. Instead, the Church adapted: a clear example of how the subversion and subsuming could be a two-way process as well.

Yet celibacy did continue, in East and West, even as the Church itself split politically. However, for all the Church's idealism about sex, a certain realism or rather turning of a blind eye began to creep in. How, then, did Christianity effect a sexual revolution and how effective has it actually been? What do we still owe to Christianity in our approach to sex today? As even Mount Athos in Greece—the home of Eastern monastic celibacy since the high Middle Ages—shows, the story of Christianity and sex would prove to be very complicated. Indeed, the truth is that Christianity and sex have always had a relationship much more complex than advocates of any particular pathway or theology or practice would care to admit.

Brother Cassianos was an old monk, tall and with eyes that worked in perfect tandem with his oft-smiling mouth. "It has been so many years,

116 *Twelve Churches*

that I cannot remember," he told me, when I asked him in the courtyard of the Pantokrator Monastery how long it was that he had been there. I suppose he was not being entirely truthful. His command of English, specifically a spoken English of that considered, old-fashioned type, and the little upward dance that the corners of his mouth would do when particular places in the far beyond were mentioned, suggested he had known a life away from Mount Athos, where the Pantokrator clings to a rocky headland. That said, Athos has a tendency toward timelessness. It is perfectly possible that Cassianos didn't know how long he had been at the monastery. Certainly, he wasn't born there. Nobody is. Because on the whole of Mount Athos, there are no women.

Athos is a peninsula at the northern end of Greece, about three hours' journey from Thessaloniki. At the end of it is a mountain, long considered holy. It rises out of the sea with such indisputable presence and beauty that on sight even the most skeptical of tourists can identify it as a, or rather, *the* Holy Mountain. It is said that the Blessed Virgin Mary landed there after being blown off course on a journey from the island of Patmos. After Christ's own instruction from the cross that she "behold her son" in the person of St John, she had been visiting or living with him on that other isle for some time but, after their unscheduled stop, found Athos to be much more to her taste. So it was that she made intercession to her Son to "make the mountain her domain" and the mountain became known as the "Garden of the All Holy."[1] Whether the story is based on historical events, a corruption of a pagan legend about Aphrodite or Athena, or just corroborative detail designed to add some color to the fact that the location is an easily defended one, remains open for debate. Regardless, it is clear that, from the later centuries of the first Christian millennium, religious people were coming to live in communities on Athos.

Well, not *all* people; men. The particular holiness of the place brought communities of men who had taken vows as monks, and the desire to preserve its monastic character led to the various monasteries agreeing a rule that only one woman was allowed onto the sacred mountain, and that was the Blessed Virgin Mary herself. Now, at the little port of Ouranoupoli at the edge of the mountain's peninsula, the women stay on the

Mount Athos, Greece 117

quayside by the tavernas and the shops hawking cheap icons while the ferry is boarded by men only. Male pilgrims make their way to Athos for its tangible holiness. It is not just the Blessed Virgin's visit which is said to have given the mountain this quality, but the men themselves who now live there. Brother Moses the Athonite expressed it thus: "the Holy Mountain was called 'Holy' because of the holiness of its monks."[2] Or, put another way, the monks first went to Athos because it was holy; now Athos is holy because of the monks.

At the heart of the concept of monasticism was, and still is, the idea of a call to holiness of the spirit, the idea that the purpose of the Christian life was to seek as close a union with the purposes of God here and now as possible. It requires an absolute dedication and, naturally, the removal of parts of life that might get in the way or distract from the search for the Divine. Specifically, monks take vows of obedience, poverty, and chastity. That is to say, they give up personal possessions, freedom of movement and association, and sex. The desire to keep to the latter vow is the reasoning behind Athos's drastic measures around the banning of women, which dates from at least 539 AD and the New Constitutions of the Emperor Justinian: "women shall not enter a monastery for men."[3] At the heart of this isn't so much the women themselves—they aren't considered less holy and, as per Justinian's decree, nunneries have the same rules against men—merely that they are the most likely targets for male sexual desire. As someone once observed, heterosexuality isn't normal, it's just common. Consequently, the *typikon* (a Byzantine foundation document reaffirming Justinian's rules) of 1045, issued by the Emperor Constantine IX Monomachos, forbade the entry of eunuchs or teenage boys as well.[4] Clearly, for those who formalized the rules for monastic life on Athos, lust was a temptation of the most dangerous order; and it wasn't just caused by women.

Where did this fixation come from? Unlike other issues—such as power or violence—which we have encountered so far, a return to origins is not as helpful as it might seem. In the Gospels, Jesus Christ famously says very little directly about sex. Later Christian writers, however, came to view it as particularly important, as the most obvious manifestation of

118   *Twelve Churches*

the life of "the flesh," which stood in direct competition with the life of "the spirit" to which people of faith were called. Central in the development of this, as he was with many doctrines and ways of Christian living that emerged in the years immediately after Christ, was St Paul. In the first letter he wrote to the new group of Christians in the Greek city of Corinth, he addressed this conflict directly. They would have been a gathering much like those small churches we encountered beneath the pavements of Rome. However, even more so than in other places, where early Christians were mostly Jews who had come to believe the claims of Jesus, Corinth had a community of believers made up of both Jews and those who had once worshipped the pagan gods.

The community had some particular problems: the continued offering of meat to pagan idols and, in particular, the continued presence of all sorts of sexual behavior that didn't sit right with those preaching a new life in Christ. While Judaism, with its strict purity laws, had a relatively constricted attitude to sex, ancient paganism was less picky. In the sixth and seventh chapters of his letter advising the community on how best to live as followers of Jesus, Paul goes above and beyond the direct teaching of Christ in order to prevent discord in the community which might arise from this contrast of attitudes. In chapter six, he sets out the idea that our bodies are in fact temples. By this he didn't mean that they ought to become, as per the modern understanding, chiseled edifices that might be made of marble or, indeed, ruined, overgrown testaments to the excess of the past; rather he meant they ought to be living places of the Holy Spirit. Paul claims that such a state of the body is threatened by fornication. "Fornication" is a tricky term. Some say it refers to heterosexual pre-marital sex, some to all sex, some specifically to sex outside a perceived heterosexual norm. Paul himself seems to qualify what he means later on in chapter seven, when he concedes that, despite believing that absolute sexual abstinence is the best way to avoid the defilement of these holy bodies we have been given, for some people it is "better to marry than to burn."[5] The burning he refers to is that of desire rather than immolation, but by Paul's advice, later included by Church councils as part of the Bible, the underlying principles for much Christian thinking on how "ordinary" believers should live their

Mount Athos, Greece 119

lives were set. Celibacy is best, but if you can't manage that, then a single marriage to someone of the opposite sex would do.

As Christianity spread from the fringes into the general population of the Roman Empire and its neighboring states in the early centuries of the second millennium, the distinction between the two ways of living became clearer. Some believers chose to be set aside in "holy orders" to live the life as initially advocated by Paul: one of sharing possessions in common, regular worship, and complete sexual abstinence. Monks and nuns could be livers of a "consecrated" life—praying and abstaining from the life of the flesh—while other Christians, including initially priests, got on with family life. The question then arose, how would these monks live? And what were they going to do about sex?

Brother Cassianos's namesake, St John Cassian, was a writer and proponent of monasticism who was particularly concerned with sexual urges. To the point that he is "on occasion," wrote the cleric and scholar Owen Chadwick, "boring" due to his "spend[ing] more time than is reasonable on sexuality."[6] He believed that monks were defined by "a life marked by such rigorous abstinence that even to those of another creed the exalted character of their life was a standing marvel."[7] However, to achieve such a character required the removal of distractions. Cassian dedicates the sixth book of his *Institutes*—guides to monastic life—to the question of sex, specifically the dangerous, distracting sex he calls fornication. For Cassian, "spiritual knowledge cannot be had without integral chastity"; i.e. people cannot be fully spiritually enlightened without being totally free from sexual desire.[8] What's the best way to ensure this, to defeat temptation? Well, to remove the temptation altogether. When the monk who took his name from Cassian came to Athos is not clear; why he did is a little easier to discern.

John Cassian was born in 360 AD, in a region now somewhere lost between the borders of Romania and Bulgaria. As a young man he traveled to Palestine, to visit those places most associated with the life, death, and resurrection of Christ. He did so just as the religion in which he had been brought up was becoming the official religion of the entire Roman Empire, courtesy of the Edict of Thessalonica by the Emperor Theodosius in 380. In the Holy Land he saw the extreme asceticism of

120   *Twelve Churches*

the monks who had honed their holiness in the deserts of Egypt. He was impressed and joined them for some time. The experience stayed with him, even as he was called by the Church to make use of his skills as a linguist, back in the imperial capital of Constantinople.

Coupled with his respect for the hard discipline of the monks in Palestine, Cassian's experience of Constantinople shaped his view of sex in a profoundly negative way. The city teemed not just with sexual acts of every kind but with sex's consequences. Cassian didn't see people healthily acting on their natural desires, he saw abandoned babies, murdered prostitutes, men forcibly made eunuchs against their will, and children of both sexes forced into sexual relationships by the powerful. Indeed, a contemporary writer observed the regularity of accidental incest in the Byzantine world, due to fathers "unknowingly having intercourse with a son or daughter who has become a prostitute."[9] This reality was not in accordance with that vision of holiness which he felt was the proper destiny of humans, and so he prescribed "rigorous abstinence" to those, like the men who made their way to Athos, so as to become more closely attuned to the purposes of God. Specifically, Cassian advocated abstinence from sex not as "virtuous in itself" but because of its positive effects on the soul. He said that it could only be achieved by humility and self-knowledge—good things in themselves—and that it would result in a heavenly reward far better than the pleasure any orgasm might grant on earth.[10]

All this might sound very conceptually lofty and far removed from ordinary life, but Cassian was not a sort of isolated husk, repressed to the point of inhumanity. In fact, he was all too human. One of the reasons why he thought sex was such a particular problem was that he felt the lure of it all too well. In particular, multiple chapters of his *Institutes* deal with the feelings of guilt after a "nocturnal emission" or "wet dream." He says such an incident is "a manifestation of a hidden interior fault."[11] Sexual doings of the body were utterly related to the state of the soul. On Athos, even solo, involuntary, uncontrolled sexual activity is considered to be a violation of one's vows. Rigorous abstinence indeed. Eventually, in both the East and West of the Mediterranean, Cassian's statutes became the central pillars for communities seeking to set rules for monastic life. He wasn't alone in his advocation of rigor.

Mount Athos, Greece 121

St Augustine, a thinker more associated with the West of the Empire and the Church than Cassian's East, despite his origins in Africa, had rather a lot to say on this. He believed the world to be a fallen, wicked place. Few people looking at the world of the fifth century could disagree with his diagnosis of brokenness; indeed, one might say the same for our own fractious era. What Augustine set out, though, was a very clear cause for this state of affairs: people. In many ways he was one of the great misanthropes: his view on humanity was not a high one. As such, Augustine came to the conclusion that it was by sex that humans had become broken. After all, it was that which perpetuated humanity. That sex was linked to sin was obvious to Augustine: Jesus was born without sexual intercourse and had only been a feature of human existence *after* Adam and Eve had eaten the apple in Eden.[12] Like Cassian, Augustine's own life, feelings, and experiences undoubtedly shaped his teaching. Not only was political stability seemingly fracturing all around him as the Roman Empire fell, but he himself knew what it was to experience uncontrollable lust—what he referred to as a "whirlpool."[13] He used prostitutes, had relationships, possibly even experienced same-sex attraction, and, in the midst of his sexually adventurous youth, famously prayed: "God make me chaste, but not yet."[14] When the time of "yet" came, and Augustine became "good," he made the link between the obvious wickedness and evil that he saw around him and the burning lust which he knew all too well. Other authors established the same logic; and in a world of rape, incest, the sexual exploitation of children and the vulnerable, it is easy to see why. Sex, for Christians, had become a problem.

It wasn't always thus. Indeed, Athos was once a place where the sexual would have been very much present. In Ancient times, prior to the birth of Christ, there was a temple there dedicated to Zeus, a god renowned for his promiscuity. More importantly, perhaps, the peninsula is covered in clearings and little woodland dens, places once synonymous with a world very far from the celibacy which the brothers at the Pantokrator take so seriously. Sex once ruled in the groves of Greece. It was there that the ancient god Pan was believed to dwell.

Pan was a busy deity, with plenty of ancient patronages. From shepherds

122 *Twelve Churches*

to improvised music, uncultivated land to al fresco sex, all of Pan's areas of interest were related to the wild and disordered, those areas outside the safe and clear boundaries of ancient society. In Greek myth, he is often seen as an agent of the feral and anarchic, characteristics which his particularly devoted followers sought to mimic. Indeed, such was the frenzy that Pan could invoke—especially when awoken accidentally—that the Greeks gave the name πανικός (*panikos*), meaning "that which relates to Pan," to any feeling of sudden overwhelming emotion or fear.[15]

Pan was known to indulge in rape, bestiality, and incest.[16] His sexual influences were all-pervasive: ancient myths suggested masturbation entered the human world via Pan, who taught it to the shepherds of Arcadia, having learned it from his father, Hermes, as a consolation prize for not being able to rape the nymph Echo.[17] It's in this context—the association of sex with frenzied disorder and the blurring of boundaries between young and old, animals and humans, consenting and not consenting—that the Christian understanding of sex came to its most explicit understanding. Such was the world that St Paul and the Corinthians inhabited and in which he began to write those epistles. Combined with the Jewish law's clear prohibitions of all sorts of sex found in the Old Testament, a consensus among writers in the early centuries after the main events of Jesus's ministry began to emerge and become popular among Jews and pagans alike.

Across the Mediterranean world, a slow change crept into being. Communities like the one in Corinth began to attract larger numbers of people who had once been pagan worshippers of gods like Zeus or Pan. In the later years of the first century, Plutarch, one of the last great pagan philosophers, writers, and priests, wrote of a sailor rounding the coast of Paxos, a small island which today lies a few nautical miles south of the party strip of Kavos on Corfu. As this ancient mariner, Thamus by name, sailed by, a voice cried out to him with a set of instructions: "When you arrive at Palodes, take care to make it known that the Great God Pan is dead!"[18] It was with this story that Plutarch predicted the beginnings of the death of ancient paganism and the rise of a new faith. Pan was the perfect symbol of the mores of the past, pagan world. And now he was dead. Subsequent Christian writers and apologists obviously seized on this and it became a rallying cry for the triumph of Christian moral values over those of the "Panic"-stricken pagan world. Yet, while worship of Pan might have died out, many of the practices associated with him continued. Despite the best efforts of some in the Church—such as the teacher Origen, who is said to have castrated himself to remove the problem of sexual urges altogether—sex remained.[19] And Christians seemed just as capable of doing all those things Augustine and Cassian had been so shocked by as those who worshipped Pan. While it officially censured such acts and even punished them on occasion, Christian Byzantium had as many instances of sex that fell outside of Paul's limits as pagan Rome. For a number of Christians, especially pubescent boys from poorer backgrounds and women eager to avoid the possible oppression of marriage to the wrong man, the life of a monastic, with no sex at all, seemed more attractive than the sort of sex being offered by the secular world.

So it was that Cassian's vision won out, the strictness of his rules not an example of off-putting rigidity but an understandable rock to which to cling in a chaotic world. As violence, rape, and political instability seemed to reign all about—as if Pan was not, in fact, dead after all—shelter could be found under the cross and under the monastic cowl. In order to maintain their integrity, such communities necessarily needed to retreat from the world, needed custom-built centers of life; they needed monasteries.

The Monastery of the Pantokrator looks like a castle at a distance. Even more than just a castle, it is a fantasy in stone, a mass of towers, balconies, and ramparts which seem to hover between rock and sea. It has been there since its foundation in 1360 by two Byzantine politicians. The name Pantokrator means "all powerful," and is an epithet given to Christ in the Eastern Church to emphasize that he was and is not just an ordinary man, with ordinary capabilities or urges, but rather that he is the second part of the Trinity. That he is God. The best Western approximation would be "the Almighty." We have encountered it before, hidden behind cloths at Hagia Sophia, designed to echo the great political power of Justinian. Here at the monastery, the emphasis is on power of a subtly different nature. It is a dedication that seems to suit the monastery: a fortress dedicated to the all-powerful Christ, defying the world's ways as much as it appears to defy its geography. Part of that defiance was necessary for protection against pirates or Ottoman warlords or occasionally other monks, but much of it is symbolic.

In actual fact, several women—twelve it is said—have managed to make the trip up the rocky precipices on the peninsula. Some came as a result of their rank. The Empress of Serbia, Helena, managed to land upon the mountain in 1346, but was refused entrance even to the great Serbian national monastery of Hilandar. She later became a nun herself and much of the information about her later life now lies in manuscripts in the library of the very monastery that wouldn't let her in. One woman who was allowed onto the mountain—and then given a full guided tour—was Eliza, the Viscountess Stratford de Redcliffe. She visited in 1850 when her husband was the British Ambassador to the Sublime Porte at Constantinople. Mindful that, earlier that year, the British Foreign Secretary, Lord Palmerston—a man as pugnacious as he was randy—had sent battleships to Athens over the mistreatment of a British merchant, the monks decided that her ladyship might be allowed a little trip after all. They got a very stern letter from the Patriarch of Constantinople, under whose nominal authority they still fall, but they did avoid bombardment by a British gunboat. Of course, the woman of highest rank who is purported to have visited a monastery on Athos is the Blessed Virgin Mary herself, said to have appeared in a photograph of 1903 among a gathering of the very poorest hermits associated with the monastery of St Panteleimon.

However, plenty of women have arrived without high-ranking invites. From shepherd families in the earliest years to partisans in the Second World War. The exactness of Athos's wilder land border is not all that clearly defined even now and the drifting across of at least the odd contravener of monastic exactitude was an inevitability. There is, perhaps, a metaphor there for the way in which churches of almost all shades have allowed a degree of osmosis across the strict technical boundaries of its sexual mores. However, as with the attitudes of some to Christian rules about sex, some have even taken the extension of

Justinian and Cassian's rules to a whole geographical area rather than just a single monastery as a personal challenge to overturn.

Two of those in particular among the list of women who braved the trip solo stand out. Aliki Diplarakou had won in 1930 first the title of "Miss Greece" and then, after being told by the Greek Premier that it was her duty to represent Hellene womanhood, that year's "Miss Europe" competition as well. Invariably a whirlwind of social prestige followed and so it was, in 1932, that she found herself on a yacht just off the coast of Ierissos, the beach town that represents the final place women can access on the north side of the Athos peninsula. Reports vary quite how she got from there to the holy mountain: some say it was an impromptu, cocktail-fueled expedition courtesy of an enamored sailor with whom she swapped clothes. Others suggest that a monk, struck by her beauty, aided and abetted her transgression.[20] Either way, the story didn't take long to get out, some say due to the Virgin Mary striking Diplarakou with a nasty tummy bug. The more practical result was the banning of future beauty contests after outrage by the Church—a ban which was to last for twenty-one years—and a declaration of those who breached Athos's rules as "anathema" (i.e. cursed) by the Patriarch of Constantinople, Photius II.

The vehement reaction to the beauty queen's prank is perhaps explained by a visit by a woman just three years earlier. While Diplarakou only managed a brief trip, a French journalist called Maryse Choisy claimed to have spent an entire month there before being detected. The exact configuration of her sexual organs aside, Maryse Choisy was not the most obvious candidate for the religious life. As she wrote, understatedly, in one later article, "I have the habit of taking the bull by the horns."[21] Brought up by her eccentric aunts in a remote castle, by the mid-1920s she was a subject of Sigmund Freud, who converted her to an interest in psychoanalysis. She had come to Athens in the late 1920s specifically to meet and study the minds of lesbians, observing that "in Athens ... this lesbianism ... has its origins in the woman who works."[22] Whether inspired by her Athenian encounters or simply by her love of mischief, we will never know, but latterly Choisy decided to disguise herself as a man and spend as long as she could on the holy mountain.

Choisy's own testimony is, admittedly and perhaps unsurprisingly, somewhat varied and unreliable but it seems she went to drastic measures to ensure the success of her plan, even claiming to have undergone a mastectomy to avoid her sex being discovered.

The result of her escapade was a book, published in 1929 and titled *Un Mois Chez les Hommes* [*A Month among the Men*]. Given that it was part of a pair of books, alongside *Un Mois Chez les Filles* [*A Month among the Girls*], in which she lived in a Paris brothel, the inference was clear: that sex was not as absent from Athos as the rule by which the monks lived would suggest. Choisy claimed to have had prolonged conversations with sexually suggestive brothers in one of the monasteries, who talked at length about desire, temptations, and guilt. Eventually—whether due to her probing questions about sex or natural femininity it is unclear—she was ejected from the mountain and sent packing. Although the experience clearly didn't have an initial spiritual effect on her—she spent the mid-1930s editing three separate occultist journals—she did eventually convert to Roman Catholicism on the eve of the Second World War. When her book about life on Athos came out, it caused a sensation and some monks took the unusual step of speaking to reporters from the Greek newspaper Μακεδονία: "How is it possible for a young and pretty girl, prone to adventures, to have remained, even for a day ... among five thousand stout and lively monks and not bring any of them to temptation?"[23] The latter statement did not have the calming effect on the rumors that the monks presumably expected.

Given this history of intrusions, you'd be forgiven for imagining that the monasteries are hostile places for visitors. Despite its forbidding exterior, the interior life of the Pantokrator is friendly and welcoming. And despite the studied absence of women, there is a sort of charmed domesticity to its inner courts. Beneath the orange tree below the decorated galleries a monk sits mending something small and unimportant. Two kittens scamper about along a little stone wall that leads to the church. There in the sun I sit and wait until Father Nikitos, a monk in perhaps his forties, appears. He is the community's guest master: his English, Russian, French, and various other languages are good. He is also a

Mount Athos, Greece

127

tennis fan, asking me in great detail during my July visit about my take on recent events at Wimbledon.

Unlike Cassianos, Nikitos can remember where he came from. The distance from Athens to Athos is not quite as far as some of the other monks have come to find their spiritual homes, but, as he points out behind a wry smile, Athens is not a city known for calm contemplation. The isolation and beauty of the Pantokrator had especially called to him. I asked him whether he would consider going to another monastery and he answers me with another question. All clergy, in my experience, have a tendency toward the gnomic, but the monks of Athos, who drink the wisdom of ages for breakfast and are experts at silence, take this to a superior level. In the face of my stupidity, they are positively sphinx-like. "When you are at a wedding, do you ask the bridegroom—'When will you marry someone else?' No! Of course not! Now, a marriage it can break down, divorces can happen, but you hope, on entering a marriage, that it will be for life. So it is with a monastery."

The simile is not unique to Nikitos, of course—there is a reason why nuns are known as "brides of Christ"—but the reminder of the analogy—that being a monk is like a traditional marriage—is a salient one. And, of course, exactly how St Paul conceived of things when he wrote to the Corinthians. At the heart of both lies an idea of holding one's material possessions and physical space in common, foreswearing all others, and being in the agreement for life. Both institutions are intended to make the individual grow into something more than themselves. The difference, of course, being that a marriage is between two people, not between a person and Christ, via the mediating body of a community. And, as St Paul makes clear, marriages are places for sex, while monasteries, as St John Cassian makes even clearer, are not.

Despite the analogy with marriage, even in the Orthodox world, the monastic route is increasingly unusual. So, seeing how this life of absolute dedication, this foreswearing of the material, the worldly, and, yes, the sexual, works for the monks, attracts pilgrims. Thousands of men, Orthodox and other denominations, visit Athos every year, drawn by the way of life. Christianity is very good at overturning preconceptions and Athos is a reminder that the asexual, or anti-sexual even, can be just as attractive as the overtly sexed. There is a special wing for these visitors at the Pantokrator, simply furnished. The monks ask for no charge, seeing unquestioning hospitality as much a part of their ministry as celibacy or prayers. Somewhat ironically, almost everyone in the guest quarters has to sleep naked to achieve any form of comfort, such is the overwhelming heat of the Athonite summer.

In a metaphor for Christianity more generally, for all the strictness of the rules, there are multiple other reminders of intimacy on the mountain. Some are evocative of the transgressive, some simply intimations of the need for human closeness, which Christianity has almost always sought to bless and promote.

It might seem odd for a celibate community, but kissing is at the center of life on Athos. Unlike many people in conventual marriages, the residents of the Pantokrator kiss many times every day. Monks grasp one another's shoulders and kiss the air each side of their bearded cheeks by way of greeting. Devout pilgrims kiss the hands of Father Nikitos as he welcomes them into the monastery. In the prayers that pepper the day, monks kiss the Holy Scriptures from which they read, intone, and sing. One eager young convert, there with me during those hot July days, bounded into the evening vespers. It is the custom of all who enter the monastic church to kiss the icons in a particular order, beginning with various saints and ending with the two final holy images of Virgin Mary and Christ as Pantokrator. This pilgrim, in his eagerness to get to Christ, missed out the Virgin only to be gently reprimanded by an old monk who was standing praying in the stalls—"Don't forget to kiss your mother!" The man—perhaps twenty-one at the oldest, and French— made his way back to the icon of the Virgin and kissed her reverently. Afterwards the monks gained much humorous mileage in the thought that it was Greeks who had taught a Frenchman how to kiss. Finally, before they go to bed each evening, the monks and their guests are invited to kiss the relics the monastery possesses, shards of bone and wood and blood encased in silver and gold. The relics represent the transformation the monks are seeking to effect; indeed, which all Christians ought to be aiming for. The transformation of that which is obviously frail and

Mount Athos, Greece 129

fallible and human into a precious offering worthy of the Divine. Sex is the awkward reminder of grubby physicality.

Yet whether it's naked pilgrims, regular kissing, or female intruders, sex is present if you want to look for it on Athos, just as it is everywhere. The monastery can keep at bay many of the world's more egregious or offensive manifestations or, indeed, its modern excesses, but it can't get rid of sexual desire completely. The challenge for the monks mirrors the challenge that many Christians believe they face in the wider world: How does a believer ensure that sex (or for that matter money or power or any other facet of human existence) is not getting in the way of their relationship with God? How does it not become a God in itself, with devotions of time and effort? Put another way, were sex to become a regular feature of life behind the Pantokrator's walls, the fundamental reasons behind the existence of the community would be compromised, and, in the monastery, the needs of the community are paramount.

The very design of the monastic building is predicated around this theory. Unlike plenty of buildings designed for beauty or vanity, the Pantokrator is built in such a way that it might best serve the needs of the community. At its heart, as you'd expect, is the church. It is around worship that the life of the community revolves. The first service is at 4:30 a.m., when a monk makes a tour of the courtyard, banging an ornate wooden board with a hammer by way of an alarm. The monks then have three hours or so of worship. Mostly it consists of the chanting of passages of the Bible and of specific prayers written for the season and the day and the hour. As with all church services there are rules about standing up and sitting down and saying "Amen" that are only learnable through years of practice. Some of the monks seem to do them in their sleep. The actual singing is in the hands, or rather mouths, of two monks who stand at reading desks on each side of the church. On the south side where I am sitting the monk chants in an almost poppy tenor, which catches me and a number of others unawares. We look up as he begins and I see that he is almost certainly a little younger than me; born into a world of Big Macs and Super Mario and free internet porn, and yet here chanting liturgy composed in an age before even Augustine was born. He is aware of the attention and his matinee-idol eyes glint through the candlelit gloom of the early morning. People go in and out with a degree of nonchalance, but despite these random egresses, the atmosphere remains tangibly holy. I take the briefest of breaks just before the dawn and, outside, the sky is clearer than I have ever seen it, as if Heaven is somehow closer. Which is, I suppose, the point.

After this comes breakfast, which is eaten close to the church in the refectory, a long hall decorated with frescos of Biblical scenes. Passages from the lives of the saints are read to the monks as they eat their meals. The abbot sits alone on a table at the top and, when he finishes, everyone finishes, regardless of how far they are through their meal. Then the monks go to their cells, arrayed on corridors and balconies that wrap around the monastery's exterior. There are kitchens and, of course, the guest quarters: not there for their own sake but to enable the ministries of hospitality and learning to take place alongside more formalized prayer. There is also the monastery's library, containing ancient fragments of manuscripts. One of the oldest consists of scraps of the Book of Revelation dating from the tenth century or so. The final line of the surviving text is Revelation, chapter twenty-two, verse fourteen, which, when translated, reads: "Blessed are they that do his commandments, that they may have right to the tree of life, and may enter in through the gates into the city." If anything summed up why the monks believe that their pattern of life and foreswearing of certain things was so important, it is this: for them it is literally the direct command of God, by which they might hope to enter Heaven. The work of the day varies until the sun begins to dip beneath the edge of the sea and then worship begins again. The monks occasionally have cause to go to Karyes, the strange all-male town in the middle of the peninsula, but generally the monastery is their world and the routine is the same.

But this design and the way of life it is designed to sustain isn't unique to the Pantokrator monastery; it isn't even unique to Athos or to the monastic centers of Eastern Orthodoxy. Such a blueprint was the norm across Eastern and Western monasteries for centuries, as millions of men and women sought to put Cassian's theories about the very best way to serve Almighty God into practice.

•   •   •

Mount Athos, Greece 131

Coming from Britain, a country where a signpost to a monastery or abbey will lead you to bucolic ruins nestled in a valley, it is hard to imagine monasteries as powerhouses. Even in the nominally Catholic nations of Southern or Eastern Europe, the influence of those in monastic life is not what it was, though more of their buildings remain. The rise of the nation state, a greater variety of economic opportunities, and a greater elasticity in Christian teaching on how it is Christians are supposed to approach sex—in almost all denominations—has led to a decline in the numbers of people being monks and nuns and in the general social utility of monastic life. Where once those whose lives were consecrated to Christ ran schools and hospitals across Europe, now they often have less prominent roles in such institutions, if any at all.

Persecution has played its part in this slow diminuendo. The thing about people giving up money, sex, and power is that it, theoretically, makes them very difficult to flatter, cajole, or persuade. From medieval monarchs to French revolutionaries and the totalitarian regimes of the twentieth century, secular powers have found monks and nuns to be the most awkward obstacles in their visions of absolute power. Consequently, they have more often been targeted, by propaganda and by persecution, than almost any group, other than people of the Jewish faith. Conversely, monasticism has also suffered through genuine issues of its own making. Not every tale of corruption was made up by a Henrician commissioner or a Marxist commissar. The recent collapse of both the power of the Church and of the faith of individual Roman Catholics in the once devout island of Ireland was largely brought about as the crimes of clergy—and monks and nuns in particular—were brought to light. The problem with claiming such high ideals as those set out all those years ago by John Cassian—be they about sex or anything else—is that you really do have to follow through on them to be convincing. The occasional lapse will be forgiven; massive systematic hypocrisy and abuse will not. Both factors have combined to give us a Europe today which is less monastic than it has ever been since the death of the Great God Pan. Only in very particular parts of Sub-Saharan Africa—and, of course, on Athos—is it possible to see what a society shaped by Christian monasticism looks like in the here and now.

132   *Twelve Churches*

Yet, as much as Athos seems a mystical outlier even to many Christians in the twenty-first century, it remains true that much of the Christian faith, indeed much of the life of the West, as received and practiced in this day and age was shaped by communities like it.[24] Far from Athos, on the islands that pepper the fringe of the Atlantic, at one point the very edge of the Christian world, monks set up communities to try and live to a similar rule. At Skellig Michael, a seemingly forsaken rock off the coast of County Kerry in the far southwest of Ireland, a group of men, committed to following a rule of life set up by St Augustine, built a series of little domed cells and a church. As with monastic life at Athos, the exact date of the arrival of the monks is unclear. Legend has it that the founder was Finnian, who lived at the end of the fifth and beginning of the sixth centuries. Finnian was a dynamo of energy who, in between founding monasteries and preaching, found time to give his name to a "penitential"—a guide to the various punishments and penances to be assigned to those who strayed from Christian morals. There is a focus on sex—clerics who find themselves "continually in lust and unable to quench their desire" are singled out for particular penances. What is abundantly clear is that Finnian was very much acquainted with the writings of none other than John Cassian. Skellig Michael is a long way from Palestine, or Athos for that matter, but the night-time preoccupations remained the same.

As the wind and sea, and occasionally the Vikings, launched their frenzied assaults on Skellig Michael, the monks remained convinced they were in the right place to seek and know God. Isolated locations have always attracted those seeking to live a simpler, holier life and, at Skellig Michael, nature provides a fortification against the world that, at the Pantokrator, is afforded by man-made ramparts and towers. Skellig Michael might look different to the Pantokrator on Athos, and it might have been on the other side of Europe, but the motivations of its inhabitants were the same. Much of monasticism may seem about being alone, or at least separate, from the rest of the world, but the fact that, in an age before mass communication, Skellig Michael knew of the ways of Athos and vice versa, that they lived according to similar rules and crafted their long days according to the same pattern, is a reminder of the unifying power of the seemingly countercultural. For the men who lived thus, to be a monk was to be connected to others and to God in a deeper way than the conventional, physical ways of the world.

The patterns of life, the physical structures and the sets of rules found in Skellig Michael and the Pantokrator were repeated across Christian Europe, Asia, and Africa. By the medieval age, monastic life was a center point for much of society. A rough estimate of the English monastic population around the time of the Black Death puts it at about 2% of the whole. Yet, the power of the monasteries vastly outweighed that proportion of the population. Again, people were drawn to the safety of monasteries as the wider world teemed with violence, chaos, and sex. As they accrued land, they became economic centers responsible for the production and distribution of goods. The network of contacts and shared principles as evinced by Finnian's book of punishments for sexually incontinent monastics also provided the perfect web from which to build a dominance in international production and trade. Monks were granted charters to run fairs and markets and, in many parts of Europe, managed to corner particular areas of economic activity, be that beer in Belgium or wool in Wales. As they accrued the wealth that came with this economic power, the monasteries became centers for learning as well, as monks had the time, resources, and predilections to pursue study. It is no coincidence that the layout of the monastic refectory at Athos—a top table with rows leading out—can still be found in the dining halls at Oxford and Cambridge today. Monks were the midwives of the university in the West, their legacy lingering more recently than we might think. The last college to abolish its single-sex statutes—modeled after those given out by the Emperor Justinian—and admit both men and women at the University of Oxford did so in the year 2015.

The monasteries may have been conceived of as refuges for many from violence, chaos, and sex, but, often, violence, chaos, and even sex had the Church's blessing. The crusading forces who rampaged across Europe and into the Holy Land were often spurred on by clergy in their attendant violence, especially toward the Jewish communities they encountered on their way. Generally, these rabble-rousers were itinerant, populist preachers, but some were monks with clear political aims. The deeply unattractive figure of Sigebert of Gembloux—a lifelong monk—is one such example. When not toadying to the Holy Roman Emperor (a pastime which often involved him having to be fantastically rude about his other boss, the Pope), he was often found castigating the Jews and lauding the pogroms committed by the early Crusaders, specifically stating that, before the war in the Holy Land could be conducted, Jews needed to either convert or be killed.[25] While there were bishops, priests, and monks who sought to stop the massacres, the image of crowds whipped into a murderous frenzy by clergy lingered long.

As it was with violence, so too with sex. The clergy's foolish mistakes or active hypocrisies linger longer in the collective memory than the times when they followed the rules. Today, on the junction of Redcross Way at Union Street in London, two unprepossessing back roads bisected by the great brick arches of the main railway line out of London Bridge station, is a patch of scrubby garden. It is strange enough that, in the midst of one of the world's most expensive patches of real estate, this should remain undeveloped, but to compound the oddness of the place, the gates to it are covered in ribbons and trinkets. Little statues of the Virgin Mary hang next to plastic flowers woven through the iron railings. This is the Crossbones Graveyard. It was here during the medieval period that the prostitutes who worked for London's most successful pimp were buried when they died. The Church refused to consecrate the ground due to their lives of notorious sexual sin. The problem was that the pimp who earned money from their perceived failure to live up to Christian sexual mores was none other than the Bishop of Winchester, one of the most powerful clerics in England. The Bishop held personal control over the "Liberty of the Clink," and used its unique legal status to promote various activities which the authorities in the rest of the city would have clamped down upon. It meant that theater and playhouses flourished on the south bank of the River Thames, and that sex work did too.

Ironically, at the center of the Liberty of the Clink was a large monastic house, the Priory of St Mary Overie. Its monks were accorded particular privileges by the Bishop and lived, in comparative comfort, according to the rule of none other than St Augustine. In 2015, the senior cleric of that church's successor institution, the Dean of Southwark Cathedral, came to Crossbones and prayed over the ground, finally giving the blessing of the church to those it had used. A much-delayed gift of dignity for the souls who lay there. For all the truth in the vision of monasteries as refuges from a world where people treated one another as a means to an end, the side of human nature that is flawed—evil, even— was just as likely to be found in monks and nuns as it was in soldiers or prostitutes.

Monastic hypocrisy had its lighter side too. The supposed sexlessness of monks and nuns was the butt of endless jokes and dirty stories. Not far from the Crossbones Graveyard is the site of the Tabard Inn, where the pilgrims in Chaucer's *Canterbury Tales* departed for Canterbury. The Monk in Chaucer's work is a heavy-drinking, good-living bundle of gut. Quite a long way from the emaciated ascetics who so appealed to John Cassian. Meanwhile, in the library at the Pantokrator, among the scrolls and carefully bound works, there is Codex 234, which contains a delicate gold illustration of an elderly cleric lecturing a young man. The latter is Emperor Michael VII Doukas, while the older man is one Michael Psellus—or Michael the Stammerer—a monk himself but a great author of castigating satires on monastic hypocrisy.[26] Perhaps his most forceful work, in *Iacobum Monachum* or "Against the Monk Jacob," deals with another particularly infamous flouter of the way set out by John Cassian. Psellos addresses the monk as a "shameless catamite, who conceals his doings" and an "abomination of all hidden carnal pleasure."[27] If only he'd told us what he *really* thought. There is the argument that these stories were funny to the medieval mind because of their absurdist incongruity. The sex-crazed monk attracted attention not only because of the inbuilt hypocrisy of his situation but also because he was, necessarily, an outlier. It was the monks who kept—or at least appeared to keep to—the rules who became the norm and who attained positions of power in economics, religion, politics, and learning. It was those monks who arguably contributed most to the formation of our world today.

•   •   •

Of course, the call to monastic life—whether played out in Oxford or Ireland or Greece or anywhere else beyond or between—was always about more than the vow of chastity, but it has been, for centuries, the part of the monastic life—much more than poverty and obedience—that has intrigued the rest of the world. Perhaps because, by the late medieval period, the power of the monks meant that poverty and obedience more often fell by the wayside. Even Christian societies where the keeping to Paul's teaching was ostensibly the legal norm it attracted much comment. In case we fall into the trap of thinking this to have been the far and distant past, it is worth briefly reminding ourselves how recently—or indeed how currently—this description of "secular" society could reasonably apply in matters of sex. Adultery remained under the direct legal jurisdiction of the Church in England until 1857 and still stands as a reason for the granting of a divorce in English civil law. In the United States it is a crime in fifteen states and the Commonwealth of Puerto Rico. Paul's teaching is manifestly engrained still in Western sexual and legal mores. So it was that these sexless islands of piety shaped much which we take as read today: from university statutes to divorce laws.

Almost nowhere is this truer than of our view of sex itself, however different it might initially appear to be. Some secular Western societies like to think that their particular attitudes about sex and the individual sprung fully formed in the late twentieth century. This is not the case. The reason why the particular hypocrisy of the Crossbones Graveyard or Jacob the Monk anger us today is rooted in the sense that people ought to be treated with dignity—a concept alien to Roman society but in fact an outworking of Paul and Augustine's ideas of the individual. The fact that we still view many of the sexual practices that shocked Cassian—incest, child prostitution, rape—as taboo is testament to the convincing nature of the arguments he made, even if we now have a slightly tamer attitude to wet dreams.

Even where there is a manifest difference between the attitudes now associated with Christianity and the sexual norm, the situation is still cloudy. After all, one can convincingly argue that the language of the sexual rights of the individual goes back to Paul.[28] To many Christians it seems abhorrent, but the pro-abortion slogan of "My body, my choice"

Mount Athos, Greece

has its origins not in the models of the ancient world that viewed the body either as prison or pleasure palace, nor in the world of paganism, where individual agency was routinely subordinated to the dynamics of power, violence, or communal need, but rather in Paul's idea that the body was a temple and worthy of consideration over what was done with or to it. It owes much, too, to his strong defense of individual faith being necessary in order for a person to be saved. From that comes much of the idea at the heart of Western economic, political, and, yes, sexual identity of the individual having agency over their beliefs and actions. Perhaps this is why the West appears to struggle so much with its wars around culture: both sides are arguing from the same initial Pauline premises, but with radically different results. In some ways, this is nothing new, as per Rome or Byzantium or the British Isles, and now, as then, some have always sought simply to remove themselves to quiet, sexless contemplation.

Back on Athos, I made my way to one of the little wooden balconies that intersect the cells and guest quarters. They were originally used as lookout points, affording as they do views of the sea and anyone seeking to use it as a means of approaching the holy mountain. The Pantokrator is on the north side of the peninsula and, if you point out from one of the balustrades you are drawing an invisible line more or less directly to Istanbul, where the only person with nominal authority over the peninsula, the Patriarch of Constantinople, still resides, despite his lack of authority over Hagia Sophia. Now, these balconies are used not to check for raiding Saracens or incoming Patriarchs but as incredibly scenic smoking terraces. Most of the pilgrims are, after all, Greeks. It was on one of these that I met Michael, who was studiously rolling more cigarettes than he could possibly smoke in an evening. I asked him what brought him to Athos. Father Nikitos was, it transpired, his spiritual confessor, providing him with much-needed support. Things, he said with a sad smile, had been a little difficult recently, a fact corroborated by the bandages on his wrists. At Athos, he said, he could find peace, be separate from the world. His presence was a reminder that, for many, the world is not just a sweet shop from whence we might pick the choicest delights. That things that bring joy can also bring hurt, and that sometimes, in order

138   *Twelve Churches*

to be put back together again, we need time away from the world and its ways. Michael alone was a convincing argument for the continuation of a monastic life away from the ways of the world.

It is easy, in the twenty-first century, to look at communities like Athos as gatherings of the foolish or vulnerable or credulous. In particular, to view their attitude to sex as wrong. Perhaps it is because they are celibate for the "wrong" reasons. It is not something done as a fulfillment of their own identity but a sacrifice deemed necessary to reach a sense of the more profound whole. "Being who you want to be" is a common mantra that, as we have seen, in part evolves from St Paul's emphasis on the individual being saved by their faith alone.[29] For Paul, there is neither "Jew nor Greek, slave nor free, male nor female: all are one in Christ"; i.e. who we were doesn't matter, we can be who we want to be, and who we're meant to be free of established identities in Jesus Christ.[30] Modernity has simply removed those final three words of caveat.

However, if denial or even repression becomes part of who we want to be then that seemingly simplistic moralizing instruction becomes much murkier. Deluded by our own rationality, we find it very difficult to cope with the idea that we might have contradictory or conflicting desires or identities or even that one might have to give way to another. A community that faces up to these potential pitfalls, names these conflicts, and puts in processes and rules in order to seek to manage them is not a relic of the past but rather a long-standing attempt to deal with inherent human issues which we still face in the present.

It bears repeating that which we established at the start of this chapter: Christianity and sex have always had a relationship much more complex than advocates of any particular pathway would care to admit. St Gregory of Nyssa—another thinker of the Byzantine period—seems to suggest that sex and gender as we understand them only seem to enter the world after the Fall and that there is a sort of transcendence of gender in the person of God. In his great anthropological treatise, *On the Making of Man*, he writes that "male and female created he them— a thing that is alien from our conceptions of God."[31] He continues "in such a being [as God] there is no male or female." Not the doctoral writings of a gender studies graduate, but the theological postulations

Mount Athos, Greece 139

of one of the most orthodox thinkers in Christian history, to whom we owe much of our understanding of the Trinity. Thinking about sex in Christianity has never been simple.

Alongside the theoretical, the actual lives of Christians, from the ordinary day-to-day lay people who sought to follow Jesus to the most elevated ecclesiastics, reflected a broad range of practice as well. Plenty of monks fathered children, still more had concubines and other encounters very far from their vows of celibacy. Even the Papacy was not immune from sexual acts very far from the Pauline ideal. Pope Paul II, it is said, died while being sodomized by his page boy in 1471. At the very height of the Reformation, Innocenzo Ciocchi del Monte was a devastatingly handsome street boy, whose first contact with the Church was when he was spotted begging by Cardinal Giovanni del Monte, who employed him as a carer for his beloved pet monkey. In return, the cardinal gave him his name and a roof over his head. Soon it became clear that the young man was taking care of more than the monkey. The cardinal was then unexpectedly elected Pope Julius III—the major candidates all vetoed one another, leaving del Monte, who was notoriously not interested in ecclesiastical affairs, as the last one standing. On his lover's election, Innocenzo moved into the Papal apartments, and bed, with him. Julius III also made him abbot in charge of monastic communities in Rome, Normandy, and Verona. The Protestant Reformers seized on this as evidence of Roman Catholic corruption, although, in truth, Protestants stood accused of similar or worse flouting of sexual norms.

The Reformation undoubtedly changed sex. Whether Martin Luther would have been able to fathom quite how one draws a line from his restatement of Paul's doctrine of salvation by faith alone and the importance of the individual to Monty Python's "Every Sperm is Sacred" song, highlighting the differing views on contraception between Roman Catholicism and Anglosphere Protestantism, we'll never know. What is clear is that, be it theological defenses of Divine gender fluidity in Orthodoxy, the triumph of the individual conscience with regard to Protestant prophylactics, or good old-fashioned clerical sodomy, thinking about God and the practice of sex are intertwined in ways more surprising than might appear from a cursory reading of Cassian.

None of these historical examples change the existence of certain Biblical passages; none of it changes the historic teaching of many Churches; none of them disprove the arguments of Cassian or Augustine. Many believers simply say it shows how many hypocrites have been drawn to ecclesiastical offices. But it does paint a picture that shows interpretation—and that which is even more important, practical living—as varying from the very earliest days of the faith. The fact is that, despite the best efforts of innumerable monks, bishops, philosophers, and ordinary people since, sex that happened outside the married limits conceived by Paul has always been part of Christian lives. Recently, official attitudes in some churches have begun to change: gay sex might have always happened in Christian circles, but gay marriages are a newer development.

Gender, too, alongside sex, has been subject to the most monumental changes in Christianity over the last few decades. In many Christian circles the role of women has changed enormously from those we encountered at the start of the chapter. It is now unusual for them to be viewed solely as distractions by which holy men might be turned from the path of righteousness. This isn't only in the Protestant sphere, but even in the world of monastic discipline. Indeed, in many Churches, the number of nuns is now outstripping the number of monks by an enormous degree. In the Roman Catholic Church, there were, as of 2019, only 50,295 monks compared to 630,099 nuns.[32] If there is going to be a revival in the religious life, it seems statistically more likely to be led by women than by men. But, again, such phenomena are not as new as we moderns like to think. As with sexuality, the history of women and Christianity is not clear-cut. One of the reasons why early Christianity spread in the way it did was due to its domesticity and appeal to women. In some ways Augustine and Cassian, in their tendency to view women as agents of sexual temptation, were already fighting a rearguard action. After all, Augustine himself admitted he was converted to Christianity by the prayers of his mother.

Where does that leave the future? In the contemporary West, the role of Christianity in the formation of mores seems to be slowly abating, but so, too, does the full-blooded hedonism associated with the reaction against Christianity in previous centuries. Poor copies of the monastic patterns are emerging once more: mindfulness, making time for ourselves, mental health apps. Then there is the statistical fact that young people in the West are likely to be more celibate than they have been for centuries. It is very possible that this chapter's description of monasticism as a minority pursuit among the Western societies it once shaped will look preposterously short-sighted.

The thing about sex is that it is done—*almost* always—by people with other people. And people are imperfect, with a capacity to hurt one another and misuse things that can be good to cause serious harm. Put another way, in sexual relations, "I am no longer in charge of what I am."[33] They involve mutuality and interdependence, both innately risky and dangerous things. Whether implanted by God or as a result of evolution, whether it's between partners of the same or the opposite sex, the sexual and the emotional are inherently tied together in the human psyche. So sex does matter, not just because of its biological or physiological consequences, but because of its emotional impact as well. Giving humans absolute freedom is almost never a recipe for treating one another in a way that maximizes the fulfillment and well-being of all—so it should not be a surprise that religion, which seeks the betterment of people through union with the Divine, should place a high level of importance on sex. Indeed, that it should sometimes view sex as a barrier to a proper sense of self, because, quite simply, it sometimes is.

In an age where it no longer appears that the Great God Pan is dead, it isn't surprising that men like Nikitos and Cassianos and the monk with the matinee-idol eyes should seek a place where a connection to God might be explored away from the overtly sexual.

Sailing away from Athos, as the little bars and the bathers of Ouranoupoli hove into view, there is a sense of a return to normality. On the short strip of beach, couples hold one another and happy, healthy sex is back after a tenure in a world where it is banned. As much as this feels refreshing, there is also a sense of something left behind. Father Nikitos was right when he said that the atmosphere was different on Athos. The mountain existed as a fortress to protect against the world and its different ways.

Sometimes the only way to appreciate things is to be deprived of them. Things that I would have paid no attention to, little ordinary aspects of summer life in a beach town on the Mediterranean—from the ubiquity of Coca-Cola to the wearing of shorts in the heat—these I now noticed and I appreciated their presence. But their presence undoubtedly drew my attention away from contemplation and toward the quotidian. That instinct to wonder, that space for thought, I suppose, was what was lost.

The most noticeable difference, however, was the return of women. The world that Athos was trying to keep at bay was, undoubtedly, one associated with the comfort of modern clothing or the commercialization of American sodas, but it was first and foremost the world associated with the sexual, with secular freedom and, yes, distraction represented by the bikinis on the beach. Perhaps Father Nikitos was right again. Perhaps life is like a marriage: we only have room for one focus of our love.

Yet, at Ouranoupoli, it was clear that the world had been changed by the ways of Athos as well. Christianity's impact on how humans relate to each other in intimate, personal terms remains just as considerable as its influence on politics or violence. This no longer looks like the cold, hard delineation between the celibate and the sexual; rather, it is as a conversation, between body and spirit, between aspiration and day-to-day reality, between Ouranoupoli and Athos. As I looked around, it occurred to me that there was more talking that went on between the two places than either the beaches and bathers or the walls and towers would suggest. Sometimes this dialogue was full-on shouting matches between Church and world, sometimes the sly whisper of innuendo, occasionally charming sweet nothings, but most often a conversation where neither appeared to be listening, but in fact both had subtly changed their patterns of speech to match their interlocutor.

Along from the beach, just beyond the little terrace where single women sat and waited for their husbands to reappear on the ferry to and from the monasteries, there was a little bit of woodland. An anonymous enough sort of a place, with a little clearing, separate enough from the beach to afford some cover and a sense of mystery. It was, really, the classic Grecian grove. As I sat letting the condensation drip off a glass of beer—another post-Athos luxury—I noticed a couple slink to the grove.

Mount Athos, Greece

Perhaps it was to be another example of sex in the secular, a showcase of exactly what the monks feared? No, the pair used the cover of the grove as a natural changing room before emerging onto the beach, thus preserving their modesty and thoughtfully not tempting any of the clergy who strolled on the upper part of the promenade—or me—into an unwitting sexual sin. Cassian would have been proud.

I thought of his namesake and his knowing twinkle and said, under my breath, "The Great God Pan is dead."

Chapter Six

Bete Golgotha, Lalibela, Ethiopia

(Built *c.* 1200 AD)

As the Church entered the medieval era, it wasn't only in the fields of sex and violence that it found the sands shifting and its teaching developing accordingly. Perhaps the most significant development of the era was the rise of the nation state. Having taken over the Roman Empire and then coped with its collapse, the Church developed into a supranational institution, almost a replacement for the Empire in the arbitration and management of everything from high politics to ordinary people's lives. In the West, at least, this mirroring was deliberate. The Church making a power base of Rome was no coincidence. Yet, politically, the void filled by the collapse of Rome was such that the Church alone could not fill it. Groups of peoples began delineating themselves in terms of language, culture, geography, and raw power. Having dealt with Rome, the Church now had to deal with the successor powers of England, France, Spain, and so on. This was not confined to Europe but across the Christian world, including those parts of Africa which had not fallen to the Muslim conquests. This is where we must travel next to see the full outworking of church and nation, working both together and in opposition.

The churches of Lalibela are symbols of Ethiopian nationhood, indeed specifically of its survival against external conquest, to this day. Yet they also remain churches, places that speak of the universality of the Christian faith. As such, they perfectly demonstrate the complex relationship between the specificities of nationhood and the universality of the faith which spoke of all nations being called to a new Jerusalem.

Where is Jerusalem? Even the obvious answer to that question is fraught with complexities, with assumptions, with implicit political statements. Specifically, statements about nationhood; about which people possess which land. About what it is to be a nation.

That is before we even get to the idea of *what* Jerusalem is. Jerusalem has long been a symbol, *the* symbol. The heart of the city of the original Jerusalem, Mount Zion, was, in Judaism, the symbolic dwelling place of God. It became a cipher, a synonym for anywhere where God was thought to be, and, specifically, a symbol for where his chosen people, his nation, were thought to be as well. Jerusalem became a shorthand, a byword for a nation special to God.

Christianity was crucial in the wider development of Jerusalem as not just a symbol for the ancient people of God—the Jews—but as a global metaphor for a place inhabited by a chosen people. Indeed, as we shall see, it was the Christian concepts about how authority and individuals might interact that led to the development of the nation state as we understand it today. And yet, this all occurred as inspired by the teaching of Christ, whose final commandment to his followers was to go "and make disciples of *all* nations," not just a particular or special one.[1] Not for the first or last time in this book, we will see Christianity's astonishing ability to hold paradoxes together when it comes to the idea of the nation. The people involved in that process vary from presidents to princes, God-emperors to ape-people, traitors to saints. Specifically, we will see how Christians have managed, or failed, to reconcile the call to be part of the "Kingdom of God"—higher and greater than any nation—while also dwelling in particular places, with particular customs. At the heart of the story of this aspect of Christianity is how the idea of the perfect vision of a heavenly country—the heavenly Jerusalem—brushed up against nationhood as a human, political reality.

For Christians, reconciling the reality of place and nation with a faith that necessarily puts its claims above those things and asserts that Jesus came for the *whole* world and not just one people has been the project of millennia.[2] As we will see, theological, practical, and political answers abounded to the question of what is the relationship between faith and nation, from theocracies to total separation. Wherever the Christian faith spread, so too did attempts to reconcile it to the national particularities of place. Eventually, peoples all over the world began to have an answer to the question: Where is Jerusalem? The answer, very often, was "here."

•   •   •

One such "here" was carved into the hard red rock of Ethiopia. It is a part of the world that can claim to have been the very oldest place that humanity first stopped and called a place home. It was at Hadar, in the Afar region of northeastern Ethiopia, that the skeleton of "Lucy," a hominin of the extinct species *Australopithecus afarensis*, was excavated. Lucy is considered one of the earliest examples of a skeleton showing markedly human characteristics. In this part of Ethiopia, the history of people—or what were almost people—goes back a very long time indeed.

It is no surprise, therefore, that the nation which arose there millions of years later had a very deep sense of history and of their nation's place in it. These senses were instrumental in the building of a very particular Jerusalem. Just over a hundred or so miles away from where Lucy was found, a good three and a bit million years after she died, a small town was utterly transformed by one man's vision. One day in the late twelfth century, the King of Ethiopia, Gebre Mesqel Lalibela, passed into a state of ecstasy. For three days, he was entranced, to the fear and fascination of his court.[3] When he finally came back to his senses, he announced that he had received a vision. God himself had shown him the city he was supposed to build.

Of course, Lalibela's vision was not without context. The Emperors of Ethiopia were not exactly modest men. From the time of King Sembrouthes—known only by a single ancient Greek inscription on a coin of the third century—to the reign of the last Emperor, Haile Selassie, whose name became one of the most well-known on earth—they claimed the title "Negusa Nagast," which means "King of Kings."[4] In fairness, they had some justification, tracing their lineage as they did to Menelik I, a figure who claimed to be the child of the union between the Biblical King Solomon and the mysterious and alluring figure of the Queen of Sheba, mentioned as visiting the great King of Israel in the Old Testament.[5]

It was said that Menelik hid the Ark of the Covenant in Ethiopia, making it, in fact, the true Israel, the real nation chosen by God, the real Jerusalem. Despite—or perhaps because of—this goodly Jewish heritage, Christianity came early to Ethiopia, and continues to be proudly maintained there. Indeed, it had such a special link that places were allocated

150   *Twelve Churches*

in the Jerusalem of Solomon for Ethiopians, ones which survived multiple changes of ruler, including after the Islamic reconquest of Saladin.[6] It was not long after returning from a pilgrimage to this shrine in the actual Jerusalem that Lalibela had seized the throne. Via a convenient extension of Menelik's myth, whereby Solomon not only lavished his attention on the Queen of Sheba but on one of her maids as well, Lalibela's usurping Zagwe dynasty made a claim that they too were direct descendants of the man who built the Temple in Jerusalem.[7] So when he decided that he would build a new, appropriate Jerusalem in Ethiopia, he was simply repeating the works of his many times great-grandfather and establishing a proper capital for God's *real* chosen nation.

The place he chose was not especially auspicious, being a great, dry clump of basaltic rock in the Ethiopian Highlands, occupied by what were ungenerously described as "troglodytic dwellings" in archaeological reports from the early twentieth century.[8] Here, though, by chiseling into the rock, great monoliths were made, each representing a church of the old Jerusalem recast in basalt for the people of Ethiopia. This was not a case of imposing new buildings upon ancient foundations but recasting and carving the very landscape itself into a place made for the glory of God. The site adopted a new name, Lalibela, after the Emperor whose vision it had been, and it became a site of pilgrimage for Orthodox Christians across the Ethiopian Empire. Contemporary chroniclers were keen to emphasize the almost miraculous nature of the site. Not only had Lalibela done "nothing but that which God had showed him," but his workers had not been humans but angels.[9] As we saw in Canterbury, so often Christian history is a strange mix of the lofty exalting narratives and the ordinary practical work of men and women through the ages. A mix of the doggedly human and the aspirationally divine.

At the heart of this new city would be churches. They were very deliberately designed to mimic places in Jerusalem. The holiest and most important of these was to be the Bete Golgotha—"the House of the Place of the Skull." The Place of the Skull—Golgotha—was, of course, where Christ was crucified. It was also supposed to be where Adam, the first man, was buried. On the face of it, Bete Golgotha doesn't particularly evoke the idea of death and the grave. True, it is carved out of rock, but it feels as alive as any church built from more conventional materials. As you approach it, via a trench hewn from the southwestern end of the Bete Maryam, the Church of Mary, light dances on the orangey-pink stone. It is linked by a trench to the Bete Mikael, another church, and both rise out of the rock—at one in color and material with the landscape that once held Lucy. They are not particularly monumental in scale: the fact that they are hewn into the rock and so are below the usual ground level makes them perhaps the most impressive of the churches we will visit on this search. There's a crumbly vulnerability to them, patches are missing, green slime lurks on the side of Golgotha. Yet it astonishes: it does feel like a Jerusalem, a place where the mystic infinity of God might yet be encountered.

As astonishing as the exterior of the Bete Golgotha is, the interior is, if anything, more so. Bright carpets and curtains shroud almost every surface, with the distinct stone just occasionally peeping through. Carvings of all sorts of designs adorn the interior, from crosses to images of saints to swastikas, an emblem long considered lucky or blessed in Africa and the East before its more unfortunate modern Western connotations. Part of the church interior is entirely closed off, hidden behind lavish gold hangings—a holy of holies. This is the tomb of Lalibela himself. Solomon was renowned for the glory of his raiment and his dress—something Christ himself remarks upon in the Bible. Clearly his self-appointed Ethiopian descendant wasn't going to be outdone. There is, however, as you arrive at the complex, a point of contrast to this power and glory. At the end of a trench, up some uneven steps, stands a giant, hollowed-out piece of stone, which appears gray and grim where the rest of the church is bright and colorful. It is another, very different, grave.

This stone is called "The Tomb of Adam." It dates from the construction of the church, by angels or Ethiopians or Lalibela or God. What its presence says is significant. The message was that this city was the true Jerusalem, the true home of the nation of God. But, it said more: it said that this place is the cradle of humanity itself. No ordinary land, but the very home of Adam, the first man created by God.[10] I wonder if Lucy, still in the ground a short journey away, was capable of smiling?

•　　•　　•

152 *Twelve Churches*

Lalibela remains an astonishing sight today; to plenty of visitors in the past it was, literally, unbelievable. Francisco Alvarez was a Portuguese priest, diplomat, explorer, and spy who accompanied a mission sent by the King of Portugal in the 1520s to Ethiopia. The rumors of a Christian nation in Africa, rich and strong and with links going back to the Kings of Israel in the Bible itself, had long been repeated in Europe. Marco Polo had written in the 1290s of a powerful and vastly wealthy figure called "Prester John," who was a Christian and the only leader strong enough to challenge the might of the Mongol Khans.[11] The Christian Kings and Emperors of Europe imagined that such a monarch might prove to be a useful ally against the dominant power of Islam in north Africa and the Middle East. The problem was, for all the tall stories of merchants or adventurers, from Polo onwards, very few people could provide evidence for what they saw to be a mystic nation. Alvarez was keenly aware of this issue. He wrote awestruck chapters on the buildings he saw at Lalibela, concluding with this sad note:

"[I]t seems to me that they will not believe me if I write more, and because as to what I have already written they may accuse me of untruth, therefore I swear by God, in whose power I am, that all that is written is the truth, and there is much more than what I have written, and I have left it that they may not tax me with its being falsehood."[12]

But unlike Marco Polo's tales of Prester John or of unicorns or of men with dogs' heads, Alvarez's account of Lalibela was true. Alvarez's account subverts many of the ways we imagine Europeans viewed Africa in the Early Modern period. Far from seeking to represent what he saw as primitive or barbaric, the Portuguese priest was at pains to mention quite how astonishing he found the entire experience and how impressed he was with the piety of the Ethiopians. He was particularly struck by the Bete Golgotha: it could almost have been Jerusalem itself, for it seemed to Alvarez that "miracles are done there."[13]

What was the purpose of this new Jerusalem? What—three-day vision aside—had inspired Lalibela to make, well, Lalibela? In part it was an attempt to make a statement about his own legitimacy and the all-important idea that he was descended from Solomon. By repeating what his purported ancestor had done in building a dwelling place for God, he showed himself to be his true and worthy successor, even if that was through a very dubious link via a chambermaid. In rock and stone, Lalibela was establishing forever the legitimizing link to the Kings of Israel for him and his dynasty, which, by blood, was a little more questionable.

However, as a statement, Lalibela went beyond the ambitions and insecurities of one man. This was about a people being marked out as special, as holy. It was a statement not just of the king's link to Solomon but Ethiopia's link to Israel. They were, it said, the real chosen people. The real nation of God.

The attempt to establish this claim for the Ethiopian nation was as sophisticated as any modern-day PR campaign. It was not only in rock that this was written, but in ink as well. Contemporary chronicles suggested that, by making a new Jerusalem, King Lalibela now ranked above Moses and Aaron, because he had built the place to which Jesus would return. The churches were nothing less than "the Lamb's bridal chambers, none of which are done by other peoples."[14] Lalibela was unlike anywhere else because the Ethiopian people were unlike anyone else.

The problem is, however, that Lalibela is one of many attempts to build Jerusalem. From Turkey to Connecticut to Yorkshire, wanting to say that a particular people were blessed by God in their national life was not unique to the Ethiopians. Of course, there have always been visions of the new Jerusalem which don't suggest it can be built on earth, but rather that it will arrive, ready made from Heaven, in a specific place. Candidates for this Divine landing spot vary, from Pepuza in modern-day Turkey, where the Montanist sect in the fifth and sixth centuries believed that the heavenly Jerusalem would physically descend and plonk itself above a cave network in Asia Minor, to the Irvingites, a group adjacent to the Church of England, who believed that the first stop of the returned Christ would be Gordon Square, in London's Fitzrovia, and so built there a vast church complete with a special, very glamorous outfit for Jesus to wear when he celebrated Holy Communion for them.[15]

However, the problem with such specificity is that people get a little bored of waiting: both the Montanists and the Irvingites have now died out. Generally, the visions of an earthly Jerusalem that have stuck around—both physically and in the consciousnesses of various nations—have been those

154   *Twelve Churches*

that sought to link the special blessing of God to a particular people. To invoke the Christian God in political expressions of nation has been the norm for almost all nation states with a Christian majority population. This is not even particularly archaic; of the nearly fifty nations who choose to mention God in their constitutions—including those who profess to have a separation of Church and state—the vast majority did so in the twentieth or twenty-first centuries. To understand this, we have to go back to someone who tried to build, not a second Jerusalem, but a second Rome. We have to go back to Constantine.

The Constantinian Shift—that acceptance of power which we saw Christianity manage in the first few centuries of its existence—was soon followed by another shift, if anything, a more important one. Empires like Constantine's were held together along the lines set by ancient Rome: a combination of complex bureaucracy and infrastructure, military might, and, often, the sheer charisma of one person: the Emperor or, occasionally, Empress. However, as Rome's authority fractured, on the edges of its maps, older, more primal ways of setting up, consolidating and expressing political authority were re-emerging. Tribes, groups joined together by language, genetic links, and a limited, rather than expansive, geographical spread, were beginning to defeat Rome's legions. These would be the nascent forms of the European nation states that still exist today.

Franks, Saxons, Jutes, Goths, Visigoths, Slavs, and Vandals: they picked apart the corpse of the Roman Empire and then settled, making little nations of their own. Slowly but surely, these groups were Christianized. The figures who did so—from the irrepressibly ardent St Boniface, who cut down the great oak of Jupiter at Graesmere in modern Germany, to the quieter and more scholarly brothers, Saints Cyril and Methodius, who evangelized the Slavs by codifying their language—invariably brought not only Christ but also a sense of national cohesion.[16] Christianity became another marker by which these nascent national groups delineated themselves. Little Jerusalems sprang up everywhere as tribes settled and became nations and sought, in that particular place, to make good their claims to be particularly blessed by God.

The extent to which chroniclers sought to demonstrate this necessarily depended on the extent to which a people had genuinely embraced Christianity, whether that had occurred before or after their cohesion as a nation and the extant national myths which had already grown up in pre-Christian times and to which plenty of nations were already very happily attached. Pity poor Cosmas of Prague, the national chronicler of the Czech people in the eleventh century. His *Chronica Boemorum* sought to tell the story of the Czechs and how it was they had a particular, divinely ordained claim to the much contested part of central Europe where they found themselves.

The problem was that the foundation story of the Czech people was already well established before Christianity had arrived. Whereas countries such as Spain, France, and even England had evidence of Roman Christian worship from the first centuries of the faith, the legions had always struggled north and east of the Alps. Cyril and Methodius hadn't managed to evangelize them until the ninth century, by which point Christian Constantinople had already stood for over 500 years. And of all the foundation stories the Czechs could have chosen, the story of Libuše and Přemysl was about as obviously distant from Christianity as you could get. It even makes the tale of King Solomon and the chambermaid from Ethiopia look tame.

Princess Libuše was a pagan prophetess who, having gotten fed up with the "pitiable, boorish men" who constituted her father's tribal council, set out to find a new and permanent homeland for them all.[17] The place she chose just happened to be where a Dark Age hunk called Přemysl was ploughing the land. She told Přemysl to take off his peasant's garment (and, presumably, a fair bit else besides), as he was now a "dux" or leader of the Bohemians. And it was in a suitably Bohemian way that they celebrated the new Czech homeland: "having fortified their bodies with Ceres and Bacchus (the gods of grain and wine) they gave themselves over to a whole night's worth of Venus and Hymen" (the goddesses of love and virginity: in this case the loss of it).[18] It is not a tale exactly brimming over with obvious Christian allegories.

Still, Cosmas had a go. Firstly, he blamed the whole situation on the Great Flood of Noah and the incident of the Tower of Babel in Genesis 11, where God, annoyed at humanity's attempts to build a massive tower into Heaven, confused their plans by having them all speak different languages and scattering them over the face of the earth. It is an interesting story as it seems to suggest that one of the key distinctions of nation—that of language—is in fact a result of human hubris and sin. Cosmas doesn't dispute this, and the sort of free love commune fed on acorns which he describes, though "simple in its mores," was a less-than-ideal setup, he infers, for a complex modern society.[19] Cosmas also reminds his readers that pagan prophets weren't all bad; after all, those of ancient Greece— who cried, if you remember, that "the Great God Pan is dead"—and the Wise Men of Matthew's Gospel both foresaw the birth of Christ despite not then being Christians.

He also pointed out that the military success of the descendants of Libuše and Přemysl had largely occurred *after* they'd been baptized, evidence for him of the chosen nature of the Czech people. Even Cosmas, however, had his limits as a creative historian. As he finally got to the part of his epic story which dealt with more recent and quantifiable events, he remarked that he would leave it up to his readers to discern "what was fact and what was fiction."[20] In truth, the foundation stories of nations have always blended the two, as the stones of Lalibela bear witness. Cosmas was, in this sense, considerably more honest than the modern historian who presents history as solely comprising of the former.

The Czechs and the Ethiopians weren't alone in finding a need to blend inauspicious origins with a sense of vocation to be a Christian people and it wasn't only the contortions of the chroniclers which varied in scale when it came to invoking the particular blessing of God on a particular people. In Europe, the Holy Roman Empire, a confederation of central European kingdoms, was an attempt to re-create the strong central European power of Rome. At its first capital, Aachen, its founder and greatest leader Charlemagne sought to imitate not only Rome, but, more importantly, Jerusalem. Lalibela, it seems, was not alone in his vision. Charlemagne's polygonal designs for his personal chapel were like Lalibela's plans for his city, deliberate imitations of the presumed layout of the original Temple back in Jerusalem.[21]

Bete Golgotha, Lalibela, Ethiopia 157

Unfortunately for Charlemagne, his vision did not last long. Partly because plenty of individual nations within his grand conglomeration of small states fancied building their own Jerusalems. His successors' power diminished until they became figureheads of a fractious conglomeration, dragged in various religious and political directions. Some 900 years later, Voltaire could quite accurately state that Charlemagne's creation was a misnomer: "it was neither holy, Roman, nor an Empire."[22] But, Aachen remained, and however small or successful they were, as with Lalibela, physical re-creations of Jerusalem were statements of both existing power and intent: this place was and would continue to be the dwelling place of the chosen people of God. From the grand palaces of Europe to little shrines in the pre-Muslim conquest communities in the deserts of north Africa, as post-imperial states formed, they sought the imitation of Jerusalem and the protection of God.

As these states formalized, with the rise of medieval dynasties who sought to centralize power away from local leaders, barons, or warlords and into the hands of an individual or family, the question of legitimacy became even more important. As we have seen, this process was a bloody one. Borders shifted, blood flowed, nations rose and fell. As this violent process took its course, the Church became the sole bestower of the blessings of God, not only to individuals but to states as well; and so national legitimacy was no longer simply aided by Christian narratives, but became dependent on Christian blessing. As the Papacy had been the one institution to continue during these torrid times, the particular approval or disapproval of the Pope mattered.

In fact, the idea that the legitimacy of a nation state's political apparatus was dependent on the blessing of God—or rather of his representatives in the Church—became quite a useful tool for keeping the ever-warring nations of Europe in line. Functioning like a sort of predecessor to the United Nations, the ultimate sanctions that the Pope had at his disposal to pull misbehaving nations and their monarchs into line were excommunication and interdict. These essentially put the individual ruler and then the whole country they represented outside of the boundaries of the Church, and therefore of salvation.

Examples of this conflict between Church and nation abound. On

158   *Twelve Churches*

Passion Sunday, two weeks before Easter in the year 1208, parish priests across England announced that they were, effectively, going on strike. The refusal of the unfortunate King John to accept Pope Innocent III's choice for Archbishop of Canterbury, the fiercely political Simon Langton, had led to the King being excommunicated and, by extension, his whole realm being placed under interdict, which would last a chaotic six years.[23] All of it added to the general sense that John was cursed. In fact, it dented John's authority to such an extent that it was only lifted when he backed down and admitted Langton, fearful of an impending civil war against his own barons in which he would need to appeal to the idea that he had the legitimacy of God in Heaven in order to enforce a semblance of his own authority on earth. Unfortunately for John, the opposite view had become quite considerably entrenched and it arguably precipitated the move to force him to sign the Magna Carta, thereby limiting his powers and establishing the idea that states were governed by the rule of law as much as individuals were.

The Church's threat of a withdrawal of legitimacy most obviously affected monarchs—individuals who were the human representations of the state. However, it could be used against republics as well. In 1604 the Most Serene Republic of Venice found itself on the wrong end of an interdict after an argument between Church and state about who got to enforce standards and discipline on the clergy. Indeed, the use of that interdict could also be hyper-localized. In 1289, the people of San Gimignano, the hill town in Tuscany famed for its fantastical cityscape of medieval towers, were placed under an interdict that suspended all church activity there for nearly four years. The reason? Essentially nothing more than a planning decision, as the local clergy and the town council bickered over who was going to pay for a new town hall.[24] Once again, the affairs of nations showed themselves to be issues of human pettiness but painted onto a global canvas.

However, not unlike the United Nations, the Church's interventions weren't always particularly effective. Lalibela was a prime example of the power of an individual monarch to shape narrative and give himself a lineage—in this case to the Queen of Sheba—that gave him a dominance over the Church. European states were not shy of doing this either. The

Venetians, in particular, maintained they had inherited the prerogatives of the Byzantine Empire and so continued their "conspicuously" different celebration of Catholicism—in particular their encouragement of "lax standards" when it came to the behavior of the nuns of The Most Serene Republic—despite the Pope's official protest.[25] From Ethiopia to Italy, some nations thought they were *so* blessed by God that the views of his purported representatives on earth were, at best, a footnote when it came to their decision-making.

Of course, as Lalibela shows, it wasn't only in Europe that the link between God and nation was being utilized to build a state. Sometimes, indeed, the link became too close and became fractious. One such example might be found in Russia. In 1655, on the edge of Moscow, a city which had been built to be a "third Rome" after the capture of the second by the forces of Islam, like many before and since, one man decided to build Jerusalem. This man was Nikon, born the son of peasants during "The Time of Troubles," when in some places up to 50% of the population of the states of Muscovy and Novgorod were killed in an orgy of violence.[26] Nikon rose through raw talent to become the Patriarch of Moscow and All Rus. Like Lalibela had been determined to rebuild Ethiopia in his image, Nikon was determined to remake Russia, both its Church and its State.

Nikon's reforms varied from a modernization of the practices of the Church to seizing political authority, even going so far as to state that he, as "supreme bishop," was necessarily above the authority of the Tsar.[27] The crowning glory of Nikon's new Russia would be a new monastery named "New Jerusalem." No previous Russian ruler had dared to invoke the Holy City and the specific sense of Russians as the people of God, preferring to defer to Constantinople. Nikon didn't just invoke Jerusalem, he built it. The landscape around the monastery was renamed and reshaped. The river became the Jordan, parts of the complex became Cana and Capernaum. The message, as at Lalibela, was clear: this new regime had the blessing of God; this was the new Holy City.[28]

However, the monastery and the man became too much of a oneness for some in the new Russia. Constantly bickering with the Tsar,

Nikon eventually resigned his patriarchal role in an attempt to force an issue and make the monarch back down, retreating to his New Jerusalem. The move backfired and eventually Nikon was exiled to the North. Twenty years later, as it became clear that he was dying, he was allowed to return to the New Jerusalem but died before he could arrive. His monastery, however, became the symbol of the Great Russia that he intended. Even after the collapse of the system that Nikon helped create with the Revolution of 1917, the monastery was considered too important a symbol to destroy. It became a museum of Russian culture, continuing its role as a place where the myth of the chosen nation was propagated. Even in its darkest hour, when in 1941 retreating Nazi troops blew up the great bell tower, it became a symbol of national resistance. Just as the Bete Golgotha outlasted the Ethiopian monarchy that built it and became a symbol of the Ethiopian nation, so too did Nikon's own attempt at a local Jerusalem. The link between Christianity and nation, and specifically the idea of a new Jerusalem, could survive even the official suppression of religion.

While Lalibela and those other attempts by rulers to "build Jerusalem" might suggest Church and nation necessarily danced closely together, in fact, the opposite was often true. Conflict as much as harmony defined the relationship between Church and nation. By the time the Reformation careered toward its denouement, the intertwined nature of Christianity and the nation, now in their forms of Church and state, was as complicated as ever. Yet even ostensible areas of conflict, like Protestant Reform, found ways to reinvent the Church–state relationship. While Protestantism dispensed with the power of the Pope, the idea of a Church body that had a role in legitimizing the state did not. To this day, at eight o'clock every Sunday morning, I wander to my little church in the Cotswolds and say prayers for the King as part of a service of Holy Communion. These words were controversial enough to get our old friend Thomas Cranmer sent to the stake, such was their assumed usurpation of the proper relationship between nation and Church, but now they are well worn and well loved, little vignettes of deep England— part of the nation's story in a different, subtler, gentler way.

The Reformation conflicts, which were simultaneously national and

Bete Golgotha, Lalibela, Ethiopia 161

religious, raise the question which we constantly encounter as we consider our unlikely history of Christianity: Who were the people driving this? It wasn't only the princes and popes, archbishops and kings, doges, tsars, or patriarchs. Plenty of ordinary people enthusiastically took part in this politico-religious nation-building as well. Lalibela might have been the project of one king, but it took plenty of workers who carved the rock, plenty of priests who said the prayers, and plenty of ordinary subjects who bought into the vision, too, in order to make it viable.

As it was at Lalibela, so it was across the Christian world. The vision of a nation state shaped by religious principles wasn't just the preserve of a ruling class, but was put into action by ordinary people too. Though geographically far from the efforts of ordinary Ethiopians, there were English, Russians, French, Greeks, and Dutch who were building nations that they believed were part of the vision of God. Albeit, sometimes, in much more violent ways.

It was in June 1572 that the "Sea Beggars," a ragtag group of former nobles, sailors, and chancers, stormed into the small Dutch town of Gorkum. They were committed to two aims: the independence of the Netherlands from Spain and the propagation of Calvinist Protestantism. For them, the issues of Church and nationhood were utterly intertwined: to be Dutch meant being anti-Catholic, so much so that they adopted the slogan "Liever Turks dan Paaps" ("rather a Turk than the Pope").[29] On arrival in Gorkum, despite the specific instructions of William the Silent, leader of the Dutch national cause, not to harass those of a different confession, they rounded up Catholic clergy as enemies of the new Dutch nation. Nineteen of them were transferred to the Sea Beggar stronghold of Brielle, nearer the coast. One of those rounded up was a parish priest called Andries Wouters. Wouters was not known as a particularly pious priest. Aged about thirty and blessed with dark good looks, he mostly used his position to indulge in a campaign of rigorous womanizing. He was clearly virile as well, fathering numerous children around Gorkum. Still, being a bad priest didn't make any difference and, on July 9, Wouters, along with his more conventionally holy colleagues, was taken to a turf shed just outside Brielle. Wouters was given a chance to recant and

162   *Twelve Churches*

deny his faith and commit to the new Dutch state. He refused, saying, "Fornicator I always was, but heretic I will never be." He and his fellow priests were then hanged. For much of Europe in the era of the Reformation, building a Jerusalem meant knocking down any existing opposition.

Even far away from the extreme violence that necessarily radicalized ordinary people, the relationship between Church and state, and the subtler, more nuanced relationship between Church and Nation, continued to be played out on a local level. Like Wouters, Sir Christopher Trychay was just an ordinary parish priest. Unlike Wouters, he was known as a paradigm of quiet and holy living in the small Devon village of Morebath, where he became vicar in 1520. He would remain so for fifty-four years, dutifully recording all the changes that convulsed the English nation and her Church in that time. He bought new Bibles, swore new oaths, knocked down statues when required. Much of his account gives a sense of his deep sadness in doing so but still, cautiously, gently even, he complies, wishing perhaps to spare his people the ire and violence which religio-national conflict was so adept at causing elsewhere. Sir Christopher was just one example of the millions who lived the reality of the fraught, tightrope-like relationship between Church and state for much of the era of the nation state. And as with many, trying to live through the conflict didn't mean that he loved one more or less, but rather that the conflicting visions of it which he had to navigate were all the more powerful precisely because ordinary people did care about—and in Sir Christopher's case, love—both.[30] Unlike Lalibela, Sir Christopher couldn't build his own Jerusalem according to his own perfect vision. In this he is much more representative of the billions of ordinary Christians through the ages who have sought to make the best of things in imperfect churches and imperfect states. Not everyone can construct their own Bete Golgotha, but, instead, have to find their place in someone else's.

There were examples, however, where ordinary people did not just put up with the visions of Lalibelas and Nikons and Cranmers. Let us return to the Czechs, who, perhaps still replete with the spirit of Libuše from their raunchy origin myth, chose to flip the Church–state relationship on its head. In the early fifteenth century, inspired by the teachings and subsequent execution by burning of Jan Hus, a scholar at Prague's University, a group of radical thinkers, priests, and military figures began to put forward a very radical idea indeed. They began to agitate for a nation formed entirely by God, without any intermediary relationship via a king or even a state. Far from the ordered vision of the Bete Golgotha, a church whose construction was dictated by a monarch, the new Jerusalem being built in Prague was to be an experiment in something approaching Christian Anarchism.

In the years 1418–20, Prague became a hotbed of anti-monarchical rhetoric. Inspired by Biblical teaching against those Kings of Israel who had proved wicked or just plain useless, sermons began to be preached against the idea of monarchy—or even conventional republican rule—altogether. God would soon judge the world, and so it was incumbent on devout Czechs to form radical new egalitarian communities—*real* Jerusalems—in order to be pure and ready for the Last Judgment. Radical pamphleteers like Vavřinec z Březnové pioneered an idea of "anti-majesty."[31] All the trappings of their enemy King Sigismund were in fact evidence that he was a monster, murderous, inhuman, even—the horror—effeminate![32] Inspired by this and similar messages, the radicals scored a string of astonishing military victories against a variety of regional foes. At one point their prowess was so great that opponents who even heard their atmospheric battle hymn "Ktož jsú boží bojovníci" ("Those who are God's warriors") would flee in terror.

Yet in the end the problem with this new Jerusalem was the same as the problems of the others, from Lalibela onwards: not everyone really wanted to live there. The idea of shared property, radical egalitarianism, and endless holy singing was actually quite a tough sell to plenty of people who lived in Bohemia—both those who had a vested interest in the status quo and those for whom simply living a quiet life, with their old faith, in a functional state, was a more attractive proposition. For the radicals, victories weren't enough and a group of moderates joined with Catholic and traditionalists to outmaneuver them. Eventually, they trapped them at Lipany, east of Prague, cutting down their leader, the priest-general Prokop the Great, and thousands of his men.

164   *Twelve Churches*

However, the dream of a radical Christian nation didn't die on a hillside outside Prague. Equivalent sects and groups continued to spring up across Christendom wherever faith and nation or Church and state seemed to align too closely. As Britain's failure to work out exactly what the relationship between Church and nation would be descended from an issue of high politics into an issue of Civil War, there were those who, seeing the violence that the question had caused, chose to opt out of the debate altogether.

One such figure was a seventeenth-century Englishwoman called Katherine Chidley. It's not really known when Chidley was born, nor when she died. She certainly spent part of her early life in Shrewsbury, a town on the English/Welsh border. We know she was there because she appears in legal records, endlessly getting in trouble in the period leading up to the English Civil War for the specific crime of not going to Church, or at least not the official services of the Church of England.[33] Eventually, she moved to London and there made contact with other likeminded men and women who sought freedom from the constraints of the state and her Church. Relations between the two were fraught, as Parliament made war with the King, in part over religious direction. By the time Chidley came to publish her pamphlets, the Puritan Parliament had just executed William Laud, the Archbishop of Canterbury.

It might sound as if Chidley was a nice, reasonable woman, a precursor to the civilized tolerance we like to imagine predominates in our time. Not, alas, so. One of Chidley's favorite metaphors was from a story in the Bible, of Jael and Sisera, where Jael, the wife of Heber, secures a victory for the righteous people of God in Israel by driving a tent peg through the head of the Hazorite general Sisera.[34] The significance of her quoting a woman inflicting a head injury on a godless enemy in the year that the Archbishop of Canterbury had been beheaded would not have been lost on readers of the time. For Katherine Chidley, a looser relationship between Church and state wasn't desirable in order to allow people to be free in their beliefs but to make it easier for the true inhabitants of Jerusalem—the *real* Church—to purge themselves from the people around them, the latter day Siseras. These people were "godlesse in their lives . . . and yet one with the land" and it was necessary to "separate the precious from the vile."[35]

These radical reinterpretations might seem a very long way from the rocky dignity of Lalibela. But in the immense latitude between the stone of the Bete Golgotha or in the ink spilt by Chidley and her fellow radicals, we can see just how broad, how complex, and how important the relationship between the two concepts of Church and nation was.

However, as nation states evolved, there were those in which the idea of state and nation having any relation was rejected. The successors of Chidley gave birth to the United States, which included a separation of Church and state in its constitution. Yet it also referred to itself as "one nation under God" and generations of its political leaders drew inspiration from a sermon by another English religious radical, John Winthrop, who described the colony he was about to found as "A shining city on a hill." They often left out the following sentence from Winthrop's oration: "So that if we shall deal falsely with our God in this work we have undertaken and so cause him to withdraw his present help from us, we shall be made a story and a byword through the world." The inference of Winthrop's words is clear: America as a political entity was one that was entirely dependent on the good purposes of the Divine. Even where it had been officially rejected in a structural sense, the pervasive idea of Jerusalem continued.

Even with Church and state technically separated, the age-old problem, which had stalked Christianity's relationship with the nation from Lalibela to Prague to Gorkum, made its way to the New World as well. Fundamentally, even in a nation barely a few decades old, people cared enough about both their faith and their nation to seek a relationship between the two. Specifically, they sought a special relationship of blessing of one by the other. It proved impossible to stop Lalibelas from springing up everywhere.

Just as the Bete Golgotha was designed as the place where the Ethiopian people expressed their particular covenant with God, so it was that many Americans began to yearn for their own version of Lalibela. Multiple plans came and went for a national church for the United States

166   *Twelve Churches*

until the late half of the nineteenth century, when, finally, Washington National Cathedral was proposed.

On approaching it, you can immediately see why it provoked opposition. Its soaring English Gothic central tower evokes Canterbury Cathedral, while its double towers at the west end of the church and sandy stone coloring evokes Westminster Abbey. The decision to base it on the two English churches with closest links to the state was deliberate, not least because its first bishop, the redoubtable and elaborately mustachioed Henry Yates Satterlee, was of the opinion that English Gothic was "God's preferred building style."[36] As such, it looks very different to Lalibela, yet it is just as significant an attempt at building Jerusalem.

However, the cathedral's existence was much more about a longstanding crisis in the nation as it was about an attempt to enforce the Church on the state. Thirty years before building began, the young United States had been plunged into a Civil War. Both sides believed that it was the will of God that their vision for the city shining on a hill should prevail, one involving the ownership of other human beings as a right, the other forbidding it. Union soldiers marched into battle, sat around campfires, and even rotted away in prisoner-of-war camps to the strains of "The Battle Hymn of the Republic," a song which explicitly linked their campaign to the aims of Jesus and the building of a new Jerusalem worthy of his promises:

> In the beauty of the lilies Christ was born across the sea
> With a glory in His bosom that transfigures you and me
> As He died to make men holy, let us die to make men free
> While God is marching on

While the Union was explicitly linking their, initially unsuccessful, military campaigns to the direct blessing and purposes of God, their opponents in the Confederacy went a step further. Whole dioceses of the Episcopal Church broke away from their Northern brethren, seeking to become a state Church for the Southern states. In Louisiana, Bishop Leonidas Polk, who would later become, and be killed fighting as, a Confederate General, described the situation in the following terms:

"Our separation from our brethren in the Protestant Episcopal Church in the United States has been effected, because we must follow our nationality."[37]

For Polk and many others on both sides of the war, their Christian identity and their state identity were entirely bound up together. We might well wonder how it was that a bishop could have so twisted the teaching of Jesus about the dignity of those in need and the love of God so as to back slavery, but for Polk it was quite simply the case that to be a Christian and to be a Louisianian were inseparable parts of the same calling. Nation and Christianity being intertwined was always complicated; in Polk's case it led to first his rebellion and then his death.

Part of the purpose of the national cathedral—a church of that reunified the Episcopal Church which Polk had left in 1861—was to act as a physical reminder of reconciliation after such a bloody internal conflict. Like the Bete Golgotha, it was to be a statement as political and national as it was religious. The question of how a nation can keep its coherence when there are those within it who seek its destruction or seek the exclusion or denigration of others within its borders is a question which faces a number of nations today, as it has done through history. Faith's role in this is complex, not least when one thinks back to John Winthrop and his reasons for seeking that city on a hill in the first place. The fact that today a Christian view of the nation can inspire both sides of a seemingly impossibly polarized debate only deepens that complexity.

Perhaps, in truth, Christianity is, like the idea of the nation, too broad and too open a concept to hold all the multitudes it might seek to. Then again, nowhere in the Bible does it suggest that Jerusalem can be built without sacrifices of one sort or another.

As the twentieth century wore on, Christianity and nation continued to find ways to dance together—and ways to drift apart. Toward the end of that century, sometime after Katherine Chidley, another radical Englishwoman, the daughter of a preacher, strode on stage to the sound of a poem set to music. William Blake's "Jerusalem" is thought by many scholars to be intended as a bitterly ironic denunciation of the state of his nation at the time of writing. Yet it ends with the age-old evocation of Jerusalem brought to a specific place at a specific time:

> I will not cease from mental fight,
> Nor shall my sword sleep in my hand,
> Till we have built Jerusalem
> in England's green and pleasant land.

Blake's "Jerusalem" was the vision of a better, more equitable nation, closer to the principles of Christ. It proved to be a rallying cry—for socialists and conservatives—ever since it was set to stirring music by C. H. H. Parry, an Edwardian humanist who had little truck with religion.[38] The woman who walked on stage to its strains was Margaret Thatcher, a prime minister determined to re-create her nation in the image of the world she had learned from her Methodist preacher father: one of economic prosperity, individualism, and, yes, faith. That vision brought her into conflict with a number of institutions, not least the Church of England, whose then primate, Archbishop Robert Runcie, once laconically referred to her as "not my sort of girl."[39] The other body with which Mrs. Thatcher clashed in her vision was the European Community. Arguably, her reasons for both fallings out were the same: neither could support her personal vision of British particularity.

"You cannot build Jerusalem in Brussels," Thatcher told a conference of political candidates in 1992.[40] In doing so she did not mean to cast doubt on the suitability of Belgium as a promised land—though she may have wished to do that too. Rather, she was suggesting that the vision of the state as it should be, the vision of a nation as God would have it be, couldn't be based on multinational or supranational theory but the actualities of countries as they were. It must have borders and limits and opportunities that are unique to it. In this she was merely stating what King Lalibela was presumed to have stated with the Bete Golgotha 600 or so years previously: Jerusalem is a somewhere, not a nowhere. Specifically, it is "here."

Herein lies perhaps the great tension at the heart of the question of where Jerusalem is, of what is the relationship between Christianity and the concept of the nation: Is it in a specific place or is it more a general state of mind, or action, or belief? For Mrs. Thatcher, as it had been for King Lalibela and Sir Christopher Trychay, it was a particular place, where it was their duty to show the particular blessing of God. For others, from Vavřinec z Březnové to William Blake, it was not about physical place but about actions, about giving evidence through word and faith and deed that you were a citizen of the real Jerusalem. Tellingly, such distinctions have spread to other ideas, ones which we imagine as secular, be they about citizenship or rights or moral rectitude: Does one simply come from geographical location or political adherence or must they be earned by other means? The question of what Jerusalem is might rarely be posed as an exclusively religious one these days, but it hasn't gone away.

There was, however, a third way. For many Christians their true nation has been somewhere else altogether. For many, Jerusalem wasn't a human place at all.

To some scholars, even Lalibela, about as rock solid an attempt to build Jerusalem in, well, rock as you could want to find, is in fact more about theology than actual practical architecture. There is an argument that it represents a Utopian vision of the ideal rather than a statement about the location of God's chosen people in a particular place.[41] Making your way around those tunnels and passages that lead to the Bete Golgotha and the other churches is a physical representation of the journey the soul must undertake to become one with God. In other words, it is a metaphor for Christian life more generally: a labyrinth around which the individual must walk in order to reach the *real* Jerusalem, that is to say Heaven.

Wrapped up in this is an idea which Christianity and its most intelligent advocates had discerned as central to the message of Jesus, although it had, in reality, been around long before the events in Bethlehem. Put simply, it states that what we see and experience here in this world is, in fact, just a likeness, merely a pale imitation of the more real world that lies beyond. The idea dates back to Plato, the Greek philosopher of the fourth century BC. Such philosophy seemed to have direct parallels to the words of Jesus. In the Gospel of John, when confronted by Pontius Pilate—the representative of a great pagan Empire—about why his own "nation" had handed him over to be executed, Christ replies: "My kingdom is not of this world."[42] The idea that the kingdom about which Jesus taught so much was, in fact, a reference to a truer reality, rather than a geopolitical entity like Ethiopia, or Rome, or England, seemed obvious.

One figure who sought to put this in Christian terms was Thomas Aquinas. In many ways, Aquinas was about as obvious a manifestation of the explicitly earthly as you could imagine. The son of the Count of Aquino, a local aristocrat and warlord and already destined for a clerical career as a younger son, Thomas's brothers were determined to force him to take an easy job at a rich abbey. Thomas was having none of it, already having determined that he would join a group of preaching, teaching friars (who were, crucially, without vast property), the Dominican order. In response, his brothers kidnapped him and imprisoned him in their father's castle at Monte di San Giovanni Campano. There they tried bribing, abusing, and cajoling Thomas into giving in. He always refused. Eventually, his brother Raynaldo had reached the end of his patience and so burst into Thomas's room with a famously attractive prostitute, in the expectation that he, like his brothers, would give in. Instead, Aquinas grabbed a poker from the fire and chased her out of the room, before drawing a cross on the floor in the embers and then returning to his books.[43] His family, eventually, admitted defeat.

Aquinas's ordeal certainly didn't calm him down: he was known for his temper and continued to indulge his enormous appetites, becoming one of the few saints to be recognizable purely by the size of his belly. Amid all these symptoms of his very fleshly humanity, Aquinas was also perhaps the most impressive theoretical theologian ever to put pen to paper in the Christian West. Today, the cell where he was kept is a tiny stone chapel at the base of the tall, square tower and, as you climb a set of higgledy-piggledy steps and look upward, you see a fresco of Thomas, double-chinned and unsmiling, looking down at you.

At some point in the 1260s, Aquinas composed a series of hymns to be sung during the benediction of the blessed sacrament. This ritual, still a regular part of Roman Catholic and High Anglican worship, involves the consecrating of bread as per Holy Communion but, rather than eating the host—as the wafer is known—it is used to bless a congregation. Its efficacy comes from the belief that this bread has, by its consecration,

Bete Golgotha, Lalibela, Ethiopia 171

become the body of Christ. Aquinas's most famous hymn, to be used at the moment where the host is venerated, goes thus:

> Tantum ergo sacramentum
> Veneremur cernui,
> et antiquum documentum
> novo cedat ritui.
> Præstet fides supplementum
> sensuum defectui.

In English—when it's used in worship—it's often translated thus:

> Therefore we, before him bending,
> this great Sacrament revere;
> types and shadows have their ending,
> for the newer rite is here;
> faith, our outward sense befriending,
> makes our inward vision clear.

Aquinas's debt to Plato is obvious. The world as we know it now, the nations that people fought so hard to establish, the churches they sought to make so concrete, the Lalibelas, are merely "types and shadows."

Aquinas—like many since—looked beyond the nations being forged in his own time and toward what he believed was the real "homeland," the true nation yet to come. In another of his hymns designed for and still used at the same service, Aquinas wrote:

> O salutaris Hostia,
> Quae caeli pandis ostium:
> Bella premunt hostilia,
> Da robur, fer auxilium.
> Uni trinoque Domino
> Sit sempiterna gloria,
> Qui vitam sine termino
> Nobis donet in patria.

172 *Twelve Churches*

Normally this is set to music and sung with the following English translation:

> O saving Victim, opening wide
> The gate of Heaven to man below;
> Our foes press hard on every side;
> Thine aid supply; thy strength bestow.
> To thy great name be endless praise,
> Immortal Godhead, One in Three.
> Oh, grant us endless length of days,
> In our true native land with thee.

Our "true native land" is therefore not anywhere where we were born. The nation which we ultimately have to choose to belong to would, of course, not be one predicated by the things that shaped nationhood on earth below, but rather by something much more radical. By Christ himself. That the gate is "open wide" to "men" (meaning here all humanity) is radical too. This is not just for one nation—Jews or Ethiopians or Venetians or Englishmen or particularly holy Czechs or Americans—but to all.

Such a vision puts Christianity in direct conflict with nation and nationalism. It explains why some churches remain targets for nationalism today. One such example happened recently in India. In the Mahim neighborhood of Mumbai, the parishioners of St Michael's arrived one morning in January 2023 to find almost every cross in the little cemetery there smashed. It was a small-scale incident—but then St Michael's is only really a small-scale church. It lies right on the Lady Jamshedji Road, an artery that links the new wealth of North Mumbai with the more warren-like South Bombay. It is a popular church, even among non-Christians; however, in recent years there has been an increased sense of unease there. Across India, groups of angry young men, largely supporters of the ruling government of Narendra Modi, have taken to attacking churches like St Michael's. Modi swept to and maintained power with the simple equation that to be Indian, *truly* Indian, is to be a Hindu.

Bete Golgotha, Lalibela, Ethiopia 173

Consequently, the presence of not only the cross but also the Muslim crescent in public places has become a source of ire to supporters of the regime. For many, nation and faith are one: and that faith is not Christianity. The police sought to blame a local man with mental health issues, an explanation that was treated with caution by Christians.[44] Here, the conflicting requirements of faith and nation are leading to violence once more.

Of course, Christian nationalism exists too—many of those who hallow the memory of Leonidas Polk would proudly describe themselves as believing in such. Yet not every Christian is a nationalist; nor, for that matter, is every Hindu. And not every person who loves either their country or cares about their faith believes that a violent exclusion of others is the only possible way that it can be expressed properly. More typically, Christianity's relationship with nation in the lives of ordinary people across the world is merely another continuation of a natural meeting of two things which matter to most people in working out who they are—what they believe and where they live. We return once more to those ordinary people we encountered at the Bete Golgotha, people for whom it was a place of both national pride and of religious devotion.

For very many millions of believers, like those visitors to Lalibela, Christianity is entirely bound up with the relationship they have with their nation in a way less vicious or violent, less complicated or confrontational, than the examples discussed. Fruitful expressions of faith and nationality vary, from Pope Francis and Pope Benedict XVI both cheering for their respective national teams in the 2014 Football World Cup final, to the England epitomized by "the old maids biking to Holy Communion through the mists of the autumn mornings" in the visions of George Orwell and John Major.[45] In many cases, love of nation and love of faith inspire people not to violent acts but acts in service of humanity as a whole.

That a particular form of Christianity has been experienced by a person in a particular place, and therefore has an association in the mind, or, more importantly, the heart of their belief does not make either their national identity nor their Christianity less valid or untrue. Indeed, it is the whole point of this book. Places matter. And so do the people—from Lucy onwards—who live in them.

Lalibela still stands as a symbol of all those complexities, of the paradox of building Jerusalem on earth, from Ethiopia to the Arctic, as the Church found itself coming into an accommodation with the nascent nations around it, and developing structures, both architectural and metaphorical, around them. From the medieval period onwards, to tell the story of any nation with a Christian population became also the story of the Church, and vice versa. Even as nation became an important motivator in the actions of individuals and political entities, faith remained one too. Aquinas's assertion that our true home is the heavenly Jerusalem might well be true; but that might not, indeed ought not, stop people trying to build Jerusalems—our own little Lalibelas—here in the meantime.

Chapter Seven

Templo de las Américas, Dominican Republic

(Originally founded 1494 AD)

One of the things about these nation states was that they didn't stay still. Borders shifted, conquest and counter conquest continued to scar Europe, the Middle and Near East, and Africa as those nations sought to dominate or subjugate one another. Indeed, for some of the nations on Europe's western and eastern edges, there was a long-running belief that expansion could and should involve whole new continents altogether. From tales of Irish monks and of Viking raiders to the wares brought from the East by Venetian and Genoese merchants, the idea of worlds and nations beyond those that were "known" by Christian nations was an inspiration to explorers and thinkers alike. Soon, men were sailing across the great sea, landing there and settling there too. With them came priests and behind them were a thousand theological justifications for their enterprise. In front of them lay just as many theological challenges. With the rise of European expansion in Africa, Asia, and the Americas, Christianity was involved at every level.

Yet as with so many of the themes we have seen so far, while Christianity was instrumental in shaping the theory and realities of expansion, it did so in a huge variety of ways, sometimes complementary and sometimes conflicting. With Christianity's role in the expansion of the West, in exploration, in colonialism, and in the parallel movements that both supported and challenged it, the faith's role was almost always central. What it never proved to be was simple. Once again, the picture that will appear of Christianity in the ages of expansion is one that frustrates crude attempts to bend it to one narrative or another. Indeed, we will see the shadowing of the tropes of violence from Canterbury or power from Hagia Sophia or beauty from Rome in the New World. This mixed picture was evident from the very first confirmed Christian place of worship in the continents of the Americas, the church to which we will make our way next, now known as the Templo de las Américas. Most critically,

178   *Twelve Churches*

it shows how, while Christianity might have set out to shape a new world, the story of the Church in the age of exploration and expansion, is as much one of the New World shaping it as vice versa.

"The beginning and the end of the Enterprise [of the Indies] was the increase and glory of the Christian religion and that no one should come to these parts who was not a good Christian."[1]

So wrote Christopher Columbus on November 27, 1492, in his *Diario*, the account of his famous voyages which resulted in continued European contact with the Americas and the creation, one could argue, of the modern world. There can be no doubt that the expansion of European nations into the Americas represented a significant shift in the history of global development in any number of areas, from art and culture to slavery and disease. It is often a tragic and rapacious tale, with episodes of heartbreaking exploitation and violence. Yet in the midst of it were laid the foundations of world-changing ideas—from global trade to individual rights. What role, in the midst of such a sea change for humanity, did the Christian faith play?

Well, as the man responsible for the first successful permanent European settlement made clear in that diary entry, it was everything. Those first ships arrived with crosses emblazoned on their sails, not as a design choice, but as a statement of missional intent. Yet, as we have found so often before, the picture is mixed. Christianity both inspired conquest and checked its excesses, was both a force moving the navies of kingdoms across mighty oceans and also a movement in the hearts of unlikely individuals. It affected every possible angle or side that we could draw when telling the stories of expansion, empire, and colonialism, from the forces that shaped them to those that opposed them. Perhaps most importantly of all, global expansion may well have been caused, in part, by the Christian faith, but there is no doubting at all that the same process radically changed that faith forever. This chapter is the story of how those changes came about.

Inevitably, Columbus's writings are all an exercise in self-justification. The extent to which he realized he was doing this is debated by historians. Some believe Columbus really was trying to bring about a great theological change as much as an economic or political one. In his *Libro de las*

Profecías or "Book of Prophecies," Columbus maintained that his voyage represented an attempt to fulfill Biblical predictions and therefore bring about the Second Coming of Christ. Specifically, having landed on the islands of the Caribbean, Columbus maintained that these were the "people of the isles" spoken of in, among other Old Testament sources, the Book of the Prophet Ezekiel.[2] There are those who maintain that these were retrospective attempts to justify his behavior in the light of a Divine mission which was, by the fact of it being from God, above reproach.[3] There were those who sailed with Columbus who thought it was a characteristic exercise in toadying behavior, invoking God so as to try to secure the protection of the emerging Inquisition under Tomás de Torquemada or, more likely, that of the devout Queen Isabela, who had been his primary backer at the Spanish court.

Perhaps more interestingly, and contrary to the idea that everyone in Europe was chomping at the bit to expand over the Atlantic, plenty of people didn't think that his voyage had been about the glory of God at all, or even the glory of Spain, the country under whose flag he was flying. Rather, an official investigation into Columbus's behavior in the New World, the *Pesquisa de Bobadilla*, alleged that Columbus had used the "enterprise of the Indies" for his own personal enrichment and was intent on murdering and mistreating almost anyone who got in his way.[4] Many of the allegations came from how he had controlled life in the first permanent European settlement in the Americas, a small town with a fort and a church on the north coast of Hispaniola. It was not the first place that he tried to found a European base in the New World: the lost fort of La Navidad in what is today Haiti was established in 1492 after that first voyage. However, by the time Columbus returned, he found the site abandoned and those he had left there missing or dead. So it was that he needed a new, permanent town. He chose a spot, more easily defensible, further down the coast of the island. Like all good toadies, Columbus kept one eye on the important folk back home and named his settlement after the woman who had made his voyage possible.

A Catholic mass in Isabela, Columbus's first settlement in the New World, was celebrated on January 6, the Feast of the Epiphany, 1494,

180   *Twelve Churches*

almost certainly in the open air. It was the first celebration of the Eucharist of a new era, in a new world. The date is a significant one. Epiphany is the moment in the Christian year marking "the manifestation of Christ to the Gentiles." Whereas all those originally at the first Nativity—oxen and asses aside—were Jewish, the three wise men from Matthew's Gospel were not.[5] Their arrival was seen as the sign that Christianity was set to be a global faith. Not limited by familial ties or tribal inheritance as Judaism had been, but one that would seek out converts from every tribe and tongue, just as the Old Testament prophets like Ezekiel had said. As the Spaniards listened to the familiar words of the Mass, the unfamiliar sounds of the island rumbled around them, and so they took comfort in those rhythms of worship so well known. Undoubtedly they would have been scared; though perhaps most terrified of one another and of their leader. In the remains of La Navidad it was not entirely clear if the Spaniards had been killed by the Taino or Carib people at random or because they had shown weakness by squabbling with one another.[6] At Isabela, the same could have happened again.

The men who made up the Spanish population of Isabela—and they were all men—were in a sorry state. Those who had made the voyage had almost invariably contracted scurvy, the supply of fresh fruit and vegetables running out fairly rapidly as they crossed the great sea. Alongside bleeding gums and rotting teeth, dysentery and other diseases associated with the long journey and substandard conditions, they were plagued, too, by diseases relating to their new environment. Mosquitos plagued the men. Malaria killed them. Storms lashed the coast. Life was short. The vast majority of those found buried in Isabela died before they reached the age of forty.[7]

In addition, the general character of the men was such that fights, theft, and plenty of old-fashioned grumbling were the norm. Settled, successful family types were unlikely to be the first to follow an egomaniacal adventurer across a sea previously thought to be uncrossable. Columbus's claim that "nobody should come to these parts who was not a good Christian" would have been open to challenge even in his own day. This was a band of adventurers, criminals, and men with nothing to lose. The settlement at Isabela is often euphemistically referred to as the first example of

Templo de las Américas, Dominican Republic   181

"inter-continental encounter." What that actually looked like in the lives of individuals from the indigenous communities probably meant murder and rape. Many Spaniards took sexual partners from the community—among the human remains found there are those of Taino women and some of infants, presumably born from those "encounters." Faith and fortune might have brought the Spaniards there, but sex, sickness, and violence were their daily bread once they'd arrived. There is a sense, even in Columbus's own apologetics, that the entire enterprise was invariably one disagreement away from bubbling over into full-blown anarchy.

To avoid a repeat of La Navidad, a focal point was needed. The focal point that had brought them across the sea was, theoretically, the Christian faith. That manifested itself physically in the need for a church. We don't know exactly what the original chapel at Isabela would have looked like but it was almost certainly a very modest building. It was about fifteen meters long and five meters wide, with a single aisle. It was made of earth rammed between wooden frames and then dressed with a stone covering, a simple and fast construction technique known as *tapia pisada*, which was used for all the public buildings in Columbus's colony. We know the church was built first as it was the only building to have a roof made of wood and palm thatch rather than clay tile, meaning it predated the kiln, probably the second public building to be completed. There was a small tower on the north side, on the top of which would most likely have been that symbol with which Columbus sought to conquer, the cross. We know, from fragments of paint on archaeological remains, that there were rudimentary attempts to decorate its interior, to evoke the great colorful cathedrals of the Old World. Despite these efforts, it would have been a dingy building; smoky and draughty too. But to the scared and sickly men of Isabela, it was, quite literally, the only thing keeping them going.[8]

The church was deliberately located close to Columbus's own residence, the building which has the most considerable remains present today, creating a deliberate "political-religious axis" to the settlement.[9] These two buildings stood between the main body of the settlement— a ragtag gaggle of thatched huts—and the ceaseless roar of the Atlantic Ocean. The orientation of the Church, eastward, is not unusual.

182 *Twelve Churches*

However, the altar facing back toward the Old World—both a link back and a barrier to return—necessarily provided a focal point that made a statement: political and religious authority would be coming from Spain. Even the bodies in the church's graveyard—and, such was the rate of death from disease and misadventure in Isabela, there were many—were oriented with the head at the west end of the grave and the feet at the east, so that, at the resurrection, they would be facing the right way, toward Jerusalem and the Old World.[10]

As the first year of Spanish settlement neared its end, Isabela began to fall apart—from disease, lack of supplies, attacks from the originally friendly Taino people who had grown fed up with Spanish rapaciousness, the effects of the hurricanes which battered the Dominican coast, and, most invidious of all, from internal disagreement. Columbus had left the settlement to fetch more supplies and guns and men from Spain, leaving his feckless brother in charge. Many, including the settlement's leading priest, Father Bernardo Buil, were unhappy with the way the Columbus family ran the little town and with the behavior they exhibited. Buil and other public figures abandoned the colony, either returning to Spain or starting their own settlements free of Columbus's rule. Despite further Masses—mostly for the ever-increasing piles of the dead—even the power of the cross could not prevent Isabela's collapse. First the huts, kiln, and castle gave way to the elements and soon the church fell down as well, becoming merely a ruin surrounded by the graves of those whom the New World had claimed. On top of each was a cross, the symbol that had heralded their arrival in the New World also marking their departure from it.

Yet what began in La Isabela did expand. Just ten years after the final abandonment of the miserable little town and its decrepit church, the oldest surviving stone church in the Americas was built at the new capital of what was now known as Hispaniola, Santo Domingo. There, the friars began missionary work. Mexico was conquered by 1521 and the rest of the South American continent—with the exception of Brazil, which the Pope had allocated to Portugal in the Treaty of Tordesillas in 1494—followed. Some 500 years after the first mass at Isabela, a group of Catholics—now numbering a billion or so adherents worldwide, over

Templo de las Américas, Dominican Republic 183

40% of them in what was to become known as Latin America—returned to Isabela and built a new church atop the ruins of Columbus's one. They called it "The Temple of the Americas."

The present church on the site of Isabela is also a modest one. The Templo de Las Américas stands on its own, surrounded by lawns. The odd dusty path wends its way through them, allowing the visitor to tread gently over those former residents who rest there. The body of the church is up a short flight of steps which lead to a Gothic-style doorway. The aping of the Old World is conspicuous: the arches of the door, the pointed roof of the bell tower, the window over the entrance with shapely frames, and a little Juliet balcony. All things which the original population of Isabela might only have dreamed of in half-remembered evocations of their homes. It is a sweet, almost twee, building, designed to evoke a world that never was, a comforting, Mexican restaurant–style vision of early Spanish America. It made me think of the wooden church in Isabela, where scant comfort would have been available for the angry and scared men who sought to maintain something of their faith there.

However, while there are these little nods to the Gothicism of medieval Europe, both the exterior—largely in the very distinct Spanish colonial style—and the interior bear hallmarks of a different story. The decoration, from the coral pulpit to the indigenous-inspired stained-glass windows, all speak much more of the New World than the Old. The space is designed for worship that those Spanish sailors, soldiers, and friars would barely recognize. Instead of the Mass of the medieval, that worship which would have provided comfort on Epiphany 1494, this is a church designed for the worship set out by the Second Vatican Council in the 1960s, where the liturgy was changed to a less formal, more folksy style, in part to specifically reflect the fact that Catholicism's strongholds were now in places like South America rather than Europe.

Columbus may have envisaged a situation whereby Catholicism changed the New World; in reality what happened was that Catholicism—and Christianity as a whole—were just as much changed by the experience of global expansion themselves.

The people whom Columbus and his sponsors envisaged evangelizing

184   *Twelve Churches*

this new continent were, of course, Catholic priests. Catholicism and the Spanish state were involved in about the closest dance of any of the European powers. Ferdinand and Isabella, the joint monarchs of the newly united kingdoms of Aragon and Castile, were both devout (although she notably more so than he) and had, in 1478, allowed Torquemada to establish the Inquisition, which patrolled every area of Spanish social, cultural, religious, and even economic life in order to ensure that Catholic orthodoxy was upheld and that "crypto" enemies of the state, in particular converted Muslims and Jews who were thought to be only feigning adherence to their new faith, were flushed out. Even more than was the case in the rest of late medieval Europe, in 1490s Spain, the Catholic faith was everywhere and was everything.

One of those brought over at the very earliest stages was Fray Ramon Pané. A member of the missionary order of St Jerome, he painstakingly recorded the native beliefs of the Taino people whom the Spanish encountered on Hispaniola. Not that his research necessarily made him hugely sympathetic to them: he described their idols as "properly speaking, demons."[11] He recounted how religion became an early source of tension on the islands, with the Taino chief Guarionex sending a gang of youths into the little chapel at Isabela to steal the images of the saints therein and then urinate on them. Even Pané acknowledges that this unfortunate incident was preferable to the original plan of Guarionex, which was to have all the Spaniards killed. He also notes that Bartholomew Columbus, Christopher's deputy and brother, whom he had left in charge, had the four young men burned for their efforts. Tellingly, however, the people who handed them over to the younger Columbus were not the Spaniards, but the Tainos themselves, a group of whom had become catechumens, that is to say those preparing for baptism.[12] The incident, which must have occurred in the mid-1490s at the very latest, illustrates two things: firstly, that Christianity was set to spread rapidly across the New World and, secondly, that bloodshed was going to spread even more quickly.

That the settlement at Isabela was a less than ideal advert for Christianity has already been established. And yet, it appears that, the urination incident aside, there was genuine initial enthusiasm for the faith. Pané even gives us the name of the first Taino to become a Christian.

Templo de las Américas, Dominican Republic 185

Guaticabanu was an important figure among the indigenous population of the island. In September 1496 he was the first native Amerindian to receive baptism, taking the name "Juan Mateo." Much of that enthusiasm may have come from the fact that in the very early days of Spanish colonialism, it was often the friars and priests who treated the people they found living in the New World with even an iota of respect.

While Bartholomew Columbus was beginning the burning, rape, and exploitation of the indigenous people of the Caribbean, a young man—also called Bartholomew—was standing transfixed outside a church, staring at the elder Columbus and the men he had brought with him to Seville. San Nicolas de Bari is not a particularly ornate church, which itself is worthy of comment in Seville, where the dominance of decorated Spanish Gothic catches the eye around almost every street corner. Its frontage is plain plaster, as it would have been in 1494, within which are set two religious images. One is of St Nicholas himself, who is the patron saint of seafarers and actually from Myra, not Bari. He was an obvious choice of saint to pray for in this part of Spain: life in Seville was defined by the sea. The estuary of the Guadalquivir river, on which Seville sits, would become the departure point for most Spanish voyages to the New World as well as for Spain's commercial enterprises. It was by this archway with an image of the saint that Bartholomew de las Casas first saw someone who had been born across the great sea, the sea which would so shape the city of his birth.[13]

The gold belts, the rhinestone jewelry, and the parrots which they had with them captivated Las Casas, then a man of barely eighteen. Within eight years, the sight of such people was no longer just a captivating oddity but part of Bartholomew's daily life. He arrived on Hispaniola, at the new capital of Santo Domingo, in 1502, the same year it was rebuilt after a devastating hurricane.[14] From there he took advantage of the *encomienda* system, which powered Spanish territorial and economic expansion in the Caribbean. The initial theory behind the *encomienda* was one which had the writings of Christian social teaching—the work of thinkers like Augustine and Thomas Aquinas—behind it. A Spaniard would have rights to ask indigenous people for goods and labor in return for protecting their homes and livelihoods, defending the area from encroachment by more hostile native peoples or, more likely, other Spaniards, and by instructing them in the Catholic faith.[15] From this the Spanish crown extracted a small tax to continue contact and relations with the Old World. Theoretically this provided indigenous people with some, albeit limited, rights and protections and prevented any individual Spaniard from becoming too mighty or powerful in the manner in which a certain Genoese Admiral might have done.

However, the theory and practice were very different. Generally, the Spaniards viewed their duties toward the indigenous peoples as entirely superfluous. Even the man who had instituted the system, the Governor Nicolás de Ovando, who had been brought in as a compromise between Columbus and his enemy, Bobadilla, routinely committed acts of monumental cruelty under its auspices. Perhaps most infamous was the Xaragua Massacre, an incident where the mass slaughter of indigenous people was conducted under the false auspices of a local festival.[16] Exploitation and violence became the de facto means of treatment toward the indigenous inhabitants of the Caribbean under the *encomienda*, a system which spread to Cuba with its conquest in 1511 and Mexico with the defeat of the Aztecs in 1521. As Portugal came to conquer modern-day Brazil and set up its own Empire, its leaders looked on the *encomienda* system as needlessly complex. They instead opted to introduce a system which they felt would end up with much the same result without the attendant complications: slavery.

The one duty toward the indigenous people that was taken with a degree of seriousness was the spreading of Catholicism. Few of the Spaniards who directly profited from the *encomienda* system did this themselves, leaving the task to missionaries of the Catholic Church. The Dominican Friars, an order of preachers especially powerful and numerous in Spain, had followed the Order of St Jerome to the New World. They were known for their sermons and persuasiveness in argument: Thomas Aquinas had been one of their number, after all. The Dominicans had noticed that the treatment of the indigenous people not only fell short of the agreements implicit in the theory of the *encomienda*, but that they fell short of the basic duty of a Christian.

Templo de las Américas, Dominican Republic 187

On the fourth Sunday in Advent, the time in the Church's year where the attention of preachers traditionally turns to weighty themes of judgment, death, Heaven, and Hell, the Dominican Father Antonio Montesinos ascended the pulpit in the modest church of Santo Domingo.

Through the thin light of the candles, he scowled down at the congregation of Spanish notables. He drew himself up to his full height and began to ask them a series of questions.

Montesinos's original text is in Spanish, but clearly was deemed important enough to go through multiple disseminations and translations. The text is wide ranging but the most important part, where Montesinos contrasts the treatment of the indigenous peoples by the colonizers to the obligations demanded by Christianity, is worth repeating in full. In part because its rhetorical force remains compelling over five hundred years later.

"Tell me by what right of justice do you hold these Indians in such a cruel and horrible servitude? On what authority have you waged such detestable wars against these people who dwelt quietly and peacefully on their own lands? Wars in which you have destroyed such an infinite number of them by homicides and slaughters never heard of before. Why do you keep them so oppressed and exhausted, without giving them enough to eat? Or curing them of the sicknesses they incur from the excessive labor you give them, and they die, or rather you kill them, in order to extract and acquire gold every day? And what care do you take that they receive religious instruction and come to know their God and creator, or that they be baptized, hear mass, or observe holidays and Sundays? Are they not men? Do they not have rational souls? Are you not bound to love them as you love yourselves?"[17]

The congregation were outraged. The first movement against the situation in the New World had begun and at its heart was Jesus Christ's summary of the law of God in the Gospel of Matthew: "love thy neighbor as thyself."[18] Among those listening was Las Casas. Faith had become an increasingly important part of his life and, in 1507, he had been ordained a priest. This hadn't stopped him from taking part in raids to expand the *encomienda* system, however, or taking part in the invasion of

188 *Twelve Churches*

Cuba. In fact, he initially became an opponent of the Dominicans, trying to justify the status quo against Montesinos's critique.

In the end, it was the Bible that changed him. In 1514, as part of his efforts to justify the regime he had worked under, Las Casas was studying the Book of Ecclesiasticus, part of the Wisdom literature which is in the Apocrypha for many Protestants but part of Scripture for Catholics.[19] A phrase leapt out at him:

"The most High is not pleased with the offerings of the wicked; neither is he pacified for sin by the multitude of sacrifices ... He that taketh away his neighbor's living slayeth him; and he that defraudeth the laborer of his hire is a bloodshedder."[20]

Las Casas made immediate arrangements to return to Spain as an advocate for the indigenous people in the New World. He arrived in 1516 as King Ferdinand, the man who had, alongside his wife, commissioned Columbus in the first place, lay on his deathbed. By lobbying the regents for his successor, Charles V, Las Casas secured the appointment of a royal commission to investigate the way in which the *encomienda* was being administered. He also secured a title for himself, *Protectoria de Los Indios*: The Protector of the Indians. With sweeping powers, he was to ensure that, in his own words, the Spaniards did not fall into "mortal sin" by treating their Amerindian brothers and sisters in the Christian faith as anything less than equals in Jesus Christ.[21] Over the next fifty years of his life, he went back and forth between Spain and her colonies, reporting, advocating, preaching, and fighting the corner to which he believed God had called him. Primarily, though, he produced endless writing. A cross between civil service reports and theology, in works like the *History of the Indies* and the *Destruction of the Indies*, he drew attention to mistreatment and atrocities that shocked Europe.

As ever, though, Las Casas's writings are complex. For some modern thinkers his characterization of the indigenous peoples of South America as "the simplest people in the world" represents an indication that he thought of them as intellectually inferior, even if the primary thrust of his argument was that they were "brothers."[22] Some scholars believe that Las Casas was instrumental in the creation of the very concept of race as a means of identification and of identity.[23] Then there is the fact, now more contentious than at any time since that of Las Casas himself, that he was in favor of the principle of a Spanish Empire, even if he abhorred the conduct of it in practice. Amid it all, he maintained that "the Admiral," whom he had first seen in Seville parading indigenous people as plunder all those years ago, was a good man.

For all this necessary nuance, it is clear that Las Casas was instrumental in shifting the story that was told about the Indies to financers and political and religious leaders back in Spain and in the rest of Europe. For all his efforts to claim that Columbus himself was fundamentally decent, it was in the accounts of Las Casas that the seeds of the Admiral's less-than-rosy posthumous reputation would be sown. Ironically—and just to underline how complex and intertwined the history of Christianity's expansion is—the only reason we have a copy of Christopher Columbus's apologetic *Diario* is because it was transcribed by a priest in the 1530s, in part, no doubt, to try to work out the motivations behind the original voyage and track quite where it was that things had gone so wrong. That priest was one Bartholomew de las Casas.

If the life and career of Las Casas demonstrates anything, it is that, as ever with the history of Christianity, simple pictures are rarely complete ones. Plenty of priests like Las Casas worked exceptionally hard to advocate for better treatment but there were doubtless many who shared the view of the conqueror of Mexico, Hernán Cortés, who wrote that the specific duty of Christians was to "punish the enemies of the faith."[24]

Yet it would be wrong to characterize the story of Christianity's expansion as merely the story of "good" or "bad" Europeans engaging with the New World and its peoples in light of their faith—or not, as the case might have been. Indeed, much recent scholarship is challenging the idea that Spain itself had the capacity to act as anything more than a nominal overlord. Much of what is characterized as Spanish rule occurred not from Madrid or Seville but on the ground, with relationships between indigenous and colonial stakeholders varied and complex.[25] From Guaticabanu onwards, millions of indigenous people became Christians or were born into families which were now Christian. Invariably, these men and women began to make the faith their own.

190 *Twelve Churches*

While this would eventually spread to and shape every flavor of Christianity, this process began with Catholicism in particular. What can be said of Catholicism in the Spanish colonies is that it gave a degree of agency, a sphere for expression that the colonial authorities would otherwise deny to the indigenous peoples whom they had conquered. Perhaps the most astonishing figure in the early days of Global Catholicism was a man who had been born not in Europe or even under the rule of the Catholic Spanish Empire but instead in a subordinate state of the mighty Aztec Empire, the same Empire which Cortés would so effectively punish in 1521.

The world in which Juan Diego Cuauhtlatoatzin spent most of his existence is almost impossible for us to imagine. His home at Tlacopan was on the shores of the great lake on which the Aztec capital of Tenochtitlan was built. It was a maze of canals, smallholdings, palaces, ball courts, and, towering above them all, temples. Life under Aztec rule had at its heart a cycle of sacrifice and bloodshed centered on these temples. The Empire engaged in a near endless cycle of conquest and warfare on the surrounding peoples in order to supply victims for these sacrifices. Aztec religion was not simply a set of beliefs around what would make the sun rise or please particular gods at particular times; it was also a tool of political repression.[26] In part because of the writings of Las Casas and even Columbus, who were keen to show parts of the New World as a sort of prelapsarian paradise, there can be a tendency to think of all pre-Columbian societies in terms of a romanticized ideal. In fact, as even a cursory look at Aztec society shows, violence was not invented by the Spanish, nor were they even necessarily the most enthusiastic advocates of it. There was a reason why many indigenous people flocked to Cortés, unattractive and rapacious a figure as he undoubtedly was, as a potential ally against the bloodthirst of the Aztecs. There was a reason why, on surveying the "naked and bloodied corpses" of sacrifice victims, the pyramids of skulls, and the gore-soaked idols, that Cortés identified the Aztecs with "the enemy," that is to say the Devil.[27]

This was the world which a peasant farmer, one Cuauhtlatoatzin, was born into sometime around 1474. It was also the world he saw destroyed by Cortés over a few brief years, culminating in a bloody denouement in Tenochtitlan itself in 1521. One of the first things he did was to construct great crosses on the tops of the temples where so much blood had been spilled. Cuauhtlatoatzin's own town of Cuautitlán had, nearby, a hilltop shrine dedicated to one of the many goddesses of death, life, and destruction, whose cults peppered the valleys and mounts around the Aztec capital, most likely Tonantzin, a harvest deity.[28] It is not known exactly when Cuauhtlatoatzin converted to Christianity but we do know that he took the baptismal name Juan Diego and that he developed a particular devotion to the Blessed Virgin Mary.

On December 8, 1531, a full decade after the collapse of institutional Aztec religion, Juan Diego Cuauhtlatoatzin was walking on that hill. Around him were the remnants of the past cult still strewn there, toppled stones slowly being returned to the domain of the jungle. Suddenly, he was dazzled by a vision of a young woman, speaking in the Nahuatl language, which was all that her hearer could understand. She announced that she was "the Mother of the true God."[29]

There was an obvious person to recount this vision to: the Protector of the Indians. Bishop Juan de Zumárraga was the direct successor to Las Casas. He had found himself dumped into the deep end of ecclesiastical-political management. If the Caribbean had been a hot bed of poor treatment of indigenous people, then the former Aztec Empire was a whole new sphere of horror. The Bishop arrived as the first Bishop of Mexico to mass outbreaks of disease among the ordinary people, to tales of murder and massacres, and to even his own priests being harassed and killed by the *oidores*—the secular figures with nominal authority over the new lands of Central America—every time they tried to stand in the way of maltreatment of the indigenous peoples. It's hard to escape the impression that poor Zumárraga wished he was anywhere else but Mexico. The one silver lining to his time in the New World was the innovation of drinking chocolate, which a group of nuns from Oaxaca, who felt sorry for their beleaguered bishop, made specially for him one miserable Mexican evening.[30]

It was unsurprising that, on hearing the story of the apparition, Zumárraga's first response wasn't to jump for joy. An appearance of the Blessed Virgin in such a benighted place and speaking such a guttural tongue seemed, frankly, unlikely to the bishop. He had developed a reputation back in Spain of being profoundly skeptical of supernatural matters, dismissing a number of acts of witchcraft in the notoriously retrograde Basque country as merely hallucinations. There were also the inevitable political ramifications of the appearances: protecting the Indians was one thing; giving their visions credence, especially on the site of pagan worship, was quite another. The bishop set the enthusiastic Juan Diego Cuauhtlatoatzin a series of challenges for the apparition. He was to go back and ask her for a miracle.

A few days later, Juan Diego Cuauhtlatoatzin's uncle was, it seemed miraculously, cured of an illness which had left him on the point of death. Cuauhtlatoatzin returned and spoke directly with the apparition. He was guided to a spot on the other side of the hill where he found growing a group of Castilian roses, not a flower native to the shores of Lake Texacoco. He gathered them into his *ayate*, a particular cloak worn by the indigenous people, and ran with them to the cynical bishop as proof of the Virgin's appearance. When he arrived in front of the bishop, he threw open the folds of the cloak, expecting the flowers to fall down. Instead, they had transmorphed into a miraculous image of the Virgin herself. Even the world-weary Zumárraga sat up and paid attention. This Virgin had told Juan Diego Cuauhtlatoatzin she was to be known as "Our Lady of Guadalupe." The New World had its very first apparition of a saint.

Was this a fusion of Aztec and Christian religion? Perhaps. But it is worth noting the cynicism of the bishop and institutional Church who had exactly the same thought, initially mistrusting the vision because Cuauhtlatoatzin was indigenous. It is also worth noting his own insistence on the validity of his vision and the specific devotion it engendered to the Blessed Virgin Mary.

This Mary was a distinctly American Mary. From the fact she was printed on a traditional indigenous cloak to the significance of her title "Guadalupe," probably a corruption of a Nahuatl title, this vision didn't need to be a syncretic mishmash, an Aztec goddess "in disguise," if you will, to be significant. Tellingly, the main primary source we have for the apparitions is also one of the first and most complete written renderings of the Nahuatl language: *Huei Tlamahuiçoltica*, which, roughly

Templo de las Américas, Dominican Republic   193

translated, means "The Great Event." Our Lady of Guadalupe marked a new moment for Catholicism and for Christianity more widely. All the power of place which had so characterized Christianity in the Old World, from the incarnation at Bethlehem to the concept of building Jerusalem, would be just as present in the New World. Christianity could no longer be said to merely be an imported religion, but was beginning to tell, as it always seems to manage to tell, stories specific to and shaped by a certain place and time. Put another way, it was now as much the faith of and for people who had once been subjects of the Aztecs as it was of the Pope in Rome or the King of Spain. Mary, and the faith of and in her son, were now, unequivocally, for everyone.

It wasn't only to indigenous people that these new expressions of South American Christianity gave a degree of agency and power. As we know from those graves in the ruins of Isabela, the early Spanish Empire was a man's world. Catholic institutions were one of the few places where women could find themselves a degree of autonomy, the protection of the Church being, as with the indigenous people, one of the few refuges in a world where Spanish men were able to do more or less as they wished. One such figure was to become nothing short of an international Catholic superstar.

Isabel Flores de Oliva was born into a family of well-to-do Spanish colonists in Lima, the new capital of Peru, where just a decade or so earlier Francisco Pizarro had conquered the Inca Empire with much the same tactics as Cortés had defeated the Aztecs. She was devout even as a child, wanting to imitate the great medieval mystic and ascetic, St Catherine of Siena. However, her beauty was also famed—hence the nickname "Rose"—and her parents wanted her to marry. In defiance she made her fasting even more rigorous—resorting to "miraculous levels of abstinence"—retreated to a "recluse's cell" and put herself under the patronage of the Dominican order. From wearing a crown of thorns to inflaming her face with peppers if men looked at her lasciviously, her disciplines grew more and more extreme until, eventually, she died aged thirty-one.[31]

By the time of her death, all Peru was talking about her famed piety.

The Dominicans, with whom she lived at the end, had a phenomenal public relations program and her story was spread from almost every pulpit in Peru. In Lima itself she became the must-see attraction, due to a mix of genuine faith, all too human curiosity at her acts of devotion, and the fact that there was not a great deal much else to do in the colonial capital. While we might look on such extreme acts as those practiced by Rose as signs of some form of illness or social disorder, in a time and a place where life was brutal and short, such concerns were hardly worth mentioning in the wider litany of issues of the day. To the Early Modern mind, Rose was clearly "touched by God" and showed particular holiness in her devotion to living as closely to Christ as possible. Her ecstasy was extreme, but then she was from a place of extremes, a new world of extremes. As a new form of Catholicism began to emerge after the Reformation, this South American girl, with her passion and her devotion, became more and more popular. Soon news spread to Spain and to Rome.

Tales of Rose's sanctity were rushed into print and published by the Vatican, for distribution in particular in places like England and Germany, in the hope that stories of such devotion would be effective in reconverting those who had strayed from the Roman Catholic Church and embraced Protestantism.[32] People began praying to Rose and, fifty years after her death, the quickest time possible, she was put on the road to being declared a saint. The New World had had its first apparition; now it had its first native saint. Both, tellingly, were women and both were distinctly American. Something was changing. Rose had been born in 1586, ninety-two years after that first Mass in Isabela where the Spaniards had prayed for the conversion of the Americas. In that short time, the reverse of that process had begun, and the Americas were returning to convert Europe.

Of course, it wasn't only in what was to become known as the Latin or Hispanic world that this sort of exchange happened. The Templo de las Américas presents itself deliberately as totemic of the whole process by which all types of Christianity came to the New World. For some, the New World acted as a place where freedom of worship could be sought. Expansion was not just about economic activity or a lust for more land and power: plenty of ordinary Christians saw the simple fact of greater physical space and minimal ecclesial power as a chance for them to practice their faith as they wished, rather than as they were told to by authorities. For others, the relationship was more complex. One such person was John Wesley.

John Wesley was educated at the University of Oxford in the eighteenth century. It was a place about as far from the cut and thrust of life in Isabela as it was possible to be. The historian Edward Gibbon described his time there as "the most idle and unprofitable [months] of my whole life." In contrast to the prevailing attitude at the university, Wesley and his brother Charles decided to embark on an active religion. They met with students and read the Bible together. Such actions were met initially with scorn: academics and students alike at the ancient university referred to them as "Bible Moths."[33]

Given such attitudes, it is no surprise that, like many before and since, Wesley felt he needed a bigger, freer canvas. In late 1735 he set sail for Georgia. Interestingly, he set out from Gravesend, where the most famous North American convert to Anglicanism found her final resting place. Looking over the departure pier at Gravesend stands the church of St George. In its yard, in a grave now lost, lie the mortal remains of Mantoaka, known to many in history as Pocahontas. Her experience of the "exchange" that began at the Templo de las Américas between Christianity and indigenous peoples was not a happy one: it involved interracial warfare, kidnap, and, eventually, death on the banks of the Thames. It was perhaps a portent of Wesley's own journey.

Wesley's faith was challenged early. En route to America, Wesley sailed with a group of Moravians—a sect of Christians who focused strongly on the relationship of the individual to Christ. As the ship on which Wesley sailed lost a mast, other types of Christians panicked, whereas the Moravians stood firm, prayed, and sang hymns until the danger passed. Such profound faith deeply affected Wesley and made him question his own response.[34] When he finally arrived in Georgia the following February, he encountered disappointment after disappointment. He had set out believing that it would be the indigenous Native Americans who would be most receptive to his teaching. But he was wrong, and later said that he had not "as yet found or heard of any Indians on the continent of America who had the least desire of being instructed."[35] The colonists found him just as annoying: it isn't an episode of Wesley's ministry in which he, as a man, comes across very well.

Wesley returned from America changed. Less naïve, undoubtedly, but more determined than ever. The movement he would begin, inspired by those principles and practices which he saw en route to America, and in light of what he had failed to do while there, would become known as Methodism. Those inspired by Wesley went back to America and then to Africa and Asia until Methodism became a branch of Christianity which now numbers 80 million adherents worldwide. Now it is by far stronger in Africa than it is back in Britain.[36] Like the story of the Templo de las Américas, the story of Methodism in the wider world is one of two-way traffic from the very beginning.

It wasn't just in the West and the New World that this exchange was occurring. In 1784, among the many petitions over which the Russian Empress, Catherine the Great, cast her eye was a petition from one Grigorii Shelikhov, a fur trader from Siberia. Shelikhov proposed that he set up a permanent settlement in Alaska in return, of course, for a monopoly on trading rights. As Russia had expanded rapidly across Siberia and the rest of Asia, Catherine and her courtiers formalized a system of government which will sound familiar: the central state—that is to say Catherine herself as Empress—owned the land, but this was managed by Russians whose job it was to extract a "ясак" (*yasak*) or tribute from the indigenous peoples they found there. The Church's job was to ensure the good treatment and education of those peoples, in return for them becoming good members of Holy Orthodoxy.[37] Sometimes this even worked.

Shelikhov proposed the expansion of this system permanently to Alaska and founded there the first permanent settlement on the Aleutian islands. As in the Caribbean 300 or so years earlier, the process of expansion was bloody and replete with acts of injustice, but theologically speaking it was indisputably multidimensional. The theory of participation by God in all things—that we can "give thanks to God in all things," as put forward all those years ago by John Chrysostom from his pulpit in Hagia Sophia—struck a particular chord with the Aleut and Alutiiq peoples, whose native beliefs of shamanism spoke in not dissimilar terms.[38] In return, it helped Orthodoxy discover an expression of itself not linked to an "ethnocentric" understanding of faith, which its expressions in Russia, where it was linked to the Tsar, and under the Ottomans, where it was the formal representative of the Greek "millet" (a community within the Ottoman Empire designated as separate for tax purposes), had made necessary.[39] Such an expression, and the writings and lives of the priests who advanced it, like Metropolitan Innocent and Herman, the Wonderworker of All America, would prove invaluable as both those regimes dissolved in the early twentieth century, taking with them the religio-political norm that had defined Orthodoxy since Constantine.

All over the world the process which began at the Templo de las Américas was repeated. I have stood in countless churches where the mix of worlds and the exchange that occurred between them has not been historical theory but the reality of people's lives. It would be naïve to think that this was always a process desired by the people of the time, nor would it be right to suggest that, because it often ended up with exchange and mutual learning, the violence which it came in the wake of was justified. Whether in Argentina or India or Siberia, the presence of my brothers and sisters in Christ was always edifying, always educational, and always brought me a great and profound joy. But it was never simple.

This was perhaps expressed best in the Afghan Memorial Church in Mumbai. The whole edifice was designed as a monument to the excesses and hubris of Empire. Britain lost thousands of men in the doomed Afghan expeditions of the 1840s, often leaving their bodies to freeze or to be baked into oblivion in the Afghan mountain passes. The Anglican incumbent there, the Reverend Joel Vedamrutharaj, was good enough to show me around when it was under scaffolding, part of a long-term renovation process. As we looked up at the stained-glass windows, filled with the classic Victorian images of saints, white-skinned, bearded, and scowling, he chuckled and said, "They look like you." Yet it was not my

198   *Twelve Churches*

church, but his. His to show me around, his to gently mock the presumptions of, but also his in which to encounter the living God.

This expansion in reverse affected global Christianity in two main ways. The first, and perhaps most important for the long-term history of the faith, is about theology. Or rather theologies. The list of theological movements which have arisen out of the fact that Christianity is now a global rather than an explicitly Western creed is enormous. So, too, has been the extent of their influence on it as a faith. Liberation Theology of South America has been a major force in shaping much of popular Catholic social teaching since the Second World War. Black theology informed by the sufferings of slavery continues to shape Christian responses to Empire in the twenty-first century and countless innovations in the way Christians worship, from the widespread popularity of Gospel music to the changes wrought by the Second Vatican Council in response to perceived Catholic needs in Africa, Asia, and Latin America; the areas of influence are broad, wide, and deep.

Secondly, the individuals who now make up the group of people we call Christians have changed as a result of the process begun at the Templo de las Américas: leadership in plenty of denominations is no longer de facto in the hands of people from Europe. Perhaps the most significant example of this trend was the figure of Pope Francis: the first Pope to be from what was once "the New World." The election of the Argentine pontiff in 2013 represented a pivotal moment in the two-way history of Christian expansion, in particular in the Spanish-speaking Americas. In some ways it was the ultimate fulfillment of the story of Rose and Las Casas and Juan Diego Cuauhtlatoatzin.

As always, there is complexity lurking: plenty accuse Francis of having acted as if he were fully cognizant of the worst excesses of "the Old World," and he was on record as rejecting some of the Marxist excesses of Liberation Theology. He could be high-handed and dictatorial in a way which would have made his Renaissance predecessors blush. Yet, with appointments and sackings, pronouncements and sermons, he reshaped undoubtedly the future of global Catholicism in a more South American image. Whether that proves to be a "good" thing is almost moot.

Yet, that story itself, of good and bad, is still affecting our world to this day. The point where these two effects of Christian expansion—theology and people—meet is one of demographic fact. In a speech in the summer of 2023, in response to criticisms about the relevance of the Church in the West, then Archbishop of Canterbury, Justin Welby, pointed out that the average demographic profile of an Anglican was a woman in her thirties in sub-Saharan Africa.[40] It is predicted that, by 2050, over 40% of the world's billion or so Roman Catholics will be from Latin America, with a median age of thirty-one.[41] Even Methodism grew in Africa in the 2010s by 329% in some regions.[42] By contrast, the average age of Christians in the West—indeed the average age of Westerners in general—is much higher. The changes affecting our world in terms of who actually lives in it means that the most likely places for Christianity's future center of gravity are all in the global South, in nations formerly colonized by a formerly Christian West. That will invariably mean changes for how Christianity is practiced and what Christians believe.

After such a necessarily wide-ranging trip around the world, let us go back to the Templo de las Américas. The atmosphere there is much better than in the days of Isabela, but still, it feels odd. An incoherent blend of a place, both commemorating the faith of the Old World and so obviously shaped by that of the New. But it is precisely because of its oddness and idiosyncrasies that it is the perfect symbol of Christianity's relationship with global expansion.

Put simply, Christianity inspired both the men who so cruelly subjected the indigenous inhabitants of this and other places, and the men who sought to stop them. It enabled the justification of violence in the name of expansion and it gave credence to attempts to stop that violence. It was co-opted to deny the dignity of the people whom its adherents encountered, who were different from them, and it also afforded that dignity in a way that no other movement or set of beliefs involved in European expansion did. Christianity is never simple, but its part in this aspect of history shows one thing quite clearly: that there are few things more awe-inspiring, and more terrifying, than the doctrine of God in the hands of mortal men.

In the same way that his church at Isabela can be seen as a symbol of this, so too did Columbus encapsulate this paradox with his claim that the "beginning and end of his enterprise" was the Christian religion. It is easy to dismiss such hubris and hypocrisy in light of his actions but, ironically, he was right. Just not in the way he thought he was. It was more a fulfillment of the prediction of Ezekiel than it was an act of closure as Columbus expected. In many ways his voyage and the evangelization of "the people of the isles" *did* bring about the end of the world. At least the world as many had known it. It brought about the end of pre-Columbian American civilizations, which gave way to swathes of dead, from smallpox and in silver mines. It brought about the end of the medieval age, for Europe itself could never be the same again after its expansion. It gave birth to a new world of global empire, global commerce, and global faith. Christianity would and could no longer be a religion limited to the former outposts of the Roman Empire. Instead, it would have Empires of its own: British, Spanish, French, Russian, and Dutch. In this sense, Columbus's moment was as significant as Constantine's. However, in time, it even brought about the end of that world it had created as well. In the seeds of the Gospel were sown, arguably, the roots of Empire's destruction.

For all this complexity and radical change, in many ways, the expansion of Christianity into being a worldwide religion was a case of it doing what it had always done, from St Paul and St Barnabas's missionary journeys around the Mediterranean onwards. Yet, it was more than the story of a religion being spread. It was a change that necessarily made Christianity more diverse, forced its practitioners to face up to parts of the Gospel involving human dignity and the claim of Christ to be a savior for *all* based on faith rather than race or country of origin, which had been easier in a smaller, older world. It necessarily led to an explosion of new ways of thinking about God and about worship. It raised issues about purity, it opened up new avenues of persecution, and, in plenty of places, it brought Christianity's tense relationship with other great movements of human motivation—like politics and profit—to a global stage.

Chapter Eight

Kirishitan Hokora, Kasuga, Japan

(Worship began at some point in the early seventeenth century)

Not every culture Christianity encountered during its expansion welcomed the arrival of a new faith. Often Christianity encountered sophisticated and complex belief systems of many millennia standing, beliefs that people were not prepared to give up quickly. While the commerce that Western expansion often brought might be adapted to the needs or even advantage of a local leader, Christianity, with its claims upon truth, its subversion of worldly power structures, and its focus on the individual, was less adaptable. Many rulers saw it as a threat and sought to eradicate it accordingly.

This meant that in many places, in some cases for the first time since the era of Constantine, Christians—often relatively recent converts—had to decide how much their faith meant to them. It meant they had to work out what they were prepared to sacrifice to keep it. In some places it became a "hidden faith"; the world of the "*kakure kirishitan*" or "hidden Christian communities" in Japan, for instance, developed on their own hidden and parallel trajectory to the rest of the faith as they necessarily worshipped in secret. As Christianity itself fractured violently and as it, in these fractured forms, encountered hostile faiths and rulers, the faith had to compete, no longer sure of protection or propagation and in many places actively persecuted. So it has continued to be, although now there are added pressures on faith alongside persecution: legal threats, competing ideologies, and, most threatening of all, pure indifference.

Perhaps the place most evocative of this tension, and of what the power of faith meant in practice to many believers as the global religious conflicts of the sixteenth and seventeenth centuries erupted, was Japan. It is to there that we must travel to work out what the faith meant in a world which viewed it as a matter of life and death and from there work out what it might mean in a world that thinks it is of little or no importance at all.

"It's just rocks." This was the incredulous response by a friend of mine who knew Japan well when I said I wanted to write about the shrine on Mount Yasumandake, a rural and, admittedly, very rocky part of Japan about two hours northwest of Nagasaki, on the nation's southeastern coast. The mountain rises over the great mass of green which is the countryside on the Hirado Island before undulating down toward the sea. The top of the mountain itself is made up of a flat, long ridge and then a sharper, more obvious peak. Slicing their way up to this rather underwhelming summit are a series of paths, some no more than faint outlines in the dirt but others, more established, made up of shallow steps, designed to help the ascendant. Beside these paths are shrines, the little marks of public religion that you see all over Japan. As a general rule, they are not elaborate edifices. Many are simply a collection of rocks beside which people leave offerings.

Someone had left a bottle of wine on the ledge at the Hakusan-hime shrine on Mount Yasumandake. It is something of an all-purpose shrine, hallowing both Buddhist deities thought to reside in or on the peak and also Shinto spirits of the ancestors of people who live there. Such an arrangement—a syncretic bringing together of the two dominant faiths in the island grouping—is not unusual. It's a sign of the remarkable mixed-mode toleration which Japan historically extended to a number of religions. Except, very notably, one. Hidden a little way from the Hakusan-hime shrine is another shrine, the one of special interest to us. It consists of little more than a short central column, now struck at an irregular angle, and a clearly carved stone acting as a pagoda-style roof. They might attract the eye's briefest scan of attention, but then again, in a nation where shrines are the norm, it might be mistaken for a misplaced bollard. To most passersby it appears to be simply a crude collection of stone—the "just rocks" my friend warned me about. This is the Kirishitan Hokora. The Christian Shrine.

It is very different from the other shrines and churches and cathedrals we have visited so far. Of course, there are those on this list—such as the Templo de las Américas—which are shadows of what they once were, mere theme park reconstructions of the original church. There are others, like Hagia Sophia, which no longer fulfill the purpose for which they were built. The Kirishitan Hokora is not like that. It was always supposed to be mistaken for "just rocks." What it has in common with those other churches, unlikely as it may seem, is that its form and its purpose are inherently tied to the people who used it to worship God and speak the name of Jesus Christ. It is inherently linked to their quest to keep their faith.

To "keep faith" in something is a phrase much bandied about. There are lots of things that purport to inspire faith in the modern world. The modern West is a cultural sphere where we profess faith all the time, just less often in the traditional repositories of faith that once dominated. As the Roman Catholic moralist and popular author G. K. Chesterton was purported to have remarked: "the first effect of not believing in God is to believe in anything."[1] We profess faith in celebrities, in abstract concepts, in processes, and in people. In everything from whether our football team is going to win to the much knottier concept of humanity itself. But do we really mean it? And what, really, does it mean in and of itself? The question reaches its sharpest point when a related question arises: How far would we go to prove that faith?

Establishing how we might simply define the Christian faith is, inevitably, a tricky task. At its center, though, is the belief in Jesus Christ as Son of God, in his incarnation, resurrection, and ascension. And that these truths about Christ have totally changed who humans are in the sight of God and how they engage in the world. Making that initial leap of faith is, for many, hard enough. However, allowing for that, the question then becomes one of how did Christians *keep* their faith, given the ups and downs of the history of the Church from the very earliest days? There have been many attempts to make followers of that faith renounce it: some by force and some by the temptation of easier or simpler or more immediately rewarding beliefs and practices. Some have worked, many haven't.

Of course, Christians were told that this would happen; a recurring theme in all the Gospels is a warning that belief would lead to persecution, even to death. However, Jesus also promised, alongside each prediction, that in being persecuted, his followers would, in fact, become

206   *Twelve Churches*

closer to him and become blessed.[2] We have already encountered Nero's human torches and Paul's and Peter's respective deaths. Yet we also have encountered Constantine, and the shift for much of the West to Christianity as a religion with power. However, that too would prove to be a threat to faith. Alongside his predictions of martyrdoms, Christ also warned of other forms of "falling away," other failures to "keep the faith." In the Parable of the Sower, Christ talked about those who will "fall away in temptation" or who are "choked with cares and riches and pleasures in this life."[3] Keeping the faith, then, is not just a story of how Christians coped in times of intense persecution, but in times of comfort as well, when people, as per Chesterton, felt they no longer needed a faith in God, such were the wealth of other options available.

By exploring the story of the Kirishitan Hokora, and by seeing how Christians across the world sought to hold true to their beliefs in varied circumstances and across continents and centuries, we might find out what "keeping the faith" really means in a Christian context and, by doing so, learn much about the faith itself, the places it has been practiced and the people who have done so.

Luis Frois was a fastidious man with an eye for detail. He noticed things of the most prosaic and, at times, unnecessarily close quarters kind. "In our latrines," he wrote, "we sit, whereas they squat."[4] Fois was from Portugal, the nation whose merchants had, at some point in the early 1540s, been the first documented Europeans to set foot in Japan.[5] Twenty years after that first contact, in July 1563, Frois arrived in the port town of Yokosora sponsored by the Society of Jesus, a Catholic Order more commonly known as the Jesuits.[6] He took part in missionary work but his real gift was in observation. Faced with a culture so vastly different from his own, Frois set about doing what, to him, was the most logical response and listing every possible way he could think of that Japanese daily life differed from the existence he had lived as a young man on the Iberian Peninsula. As well as an in-depth analysis of lavatorial habits, Frois wrote chapters on medicine, costumes, dress, music, and the use of horses. Strange and occasionally inaccurate though his observations might seem, they remain an extremely useful source for understanding ordinary life in seventeenth-century Japan; after all, cultures very rarely write about things which are to them normal day-to-day habits. What the Japanese thought of this Jesuit who wanted to watch and take notes while they relieved themselves is sadly not a matter of historic record.

Alongside these quirkier observations about their vastly different cultures, European and Japanese exchange was, initially, mutually profitable. Japan's politically fragile and militarily focused domestic situation made the importation of European weaponry a priority for its myriad local magnates. For the Europeans, Japan represented all that the age of exploration had sought to find: a wealthy trading power keen to do business with the West. It is worth remembering that Japan and her surrounding islands were the intended destination of Columbus's first voyages. As with Columbus, when Europeans finally did reach Japan, Christianity became inexorably linked to commerce and to the possibility of conquest. These links were to prove both an opportunity and, in this case, its undoing.

The Society of Jesus, of which Luis Frois was a member, was not any ordinary missionary organization. We might tend to think of the clergy as lovers of the quiet life, of gentle collectors of stamps or bees or good wine in those parts of the world with gentler patterns of life. Or, even if we think of urban (or urbane) clergy, ministering in the great metropolises of modernity, we still imagine them as people rooted in one place, and of passions which are governed, kept generally under control. Not so the Jesuits. The order was founded by Ignatius Loyola, a Spanish former soldier, who, while recovering from a wound, underwent an intense religious conversion. As a group they encouraged an intensity of piety and service which the older, more established orders balked at. Invariably, they attracted adventurous and strongly devout young men to their ranks who were more than willing to form the vanguard of missions to those parts of the world just coming into contact with Christianity in the aftermath of European exploration.

They were often astonishingly successful in these efforts, seeing rapid conversion rates in parts of the Portuguese and Spanish Empires.[7] However, such success earned them enemies both within and outside of the Roman Catholic Church. Indeed, the Jesuits still exist, though perhaps it is telling that, despite their energy, their undisputed global reach, and, at one point, their power, it took them until Pope Francis to finally secure the Papacy. They often became a byword for Catholic subversion—in Elizabethan England, for instance, "Jesuitical" became a word meaning sly or fundamentally dishonest.

As it was in England, so it became in Japan. Christianity was originally welcomed by the Japanese establishment, as well as proving incredibly popular among ordinary people. In particular, major trading ports, such as Nagasaki at the south of the Japanese mainland, became centers of missionary activity, with large numbers of local converts. Initially these were focused in the merchant community but, with remarkable speed, ordinary Japanese in rural and remote coastal areas came to be baptized and declare themselves to be Christians as well. However, the Jesuits knew they were playing a carefully balanced game. The Japanese authorities, disparate and unstable though they were in the sixteenth century, were acutely aware of Spanish colonial expansion in the Philippines to their south and the presence of Portuguese troops at the trading stations on the Chinese coast. By the late sixteenth century, Shinto advisors to the de facto ruler of Japan, the former peasant turned Regent and unifier, Toyotomi Hideyoshi (豊臣 秀吉), were alarmed by the rate of Christian conversion and sought to discourage it. In 1587, Hideyoshi issued an edict known as the "Bateran Tsuiho Rei" or "The Edict of the Padres," a reference to its warning it gave to missionaries to leave the country, because of their consistent broaching of "the free will" of Japanese people, which went against Buddhist law—that is to say their success in conversions.[8] With this warning in place, active persecution by the authorities was constantly one incident away.

All it took was the injured pride of one Spanish crew member to set the entire story of Christianity in Japan onto a different footing. Once again, an entirely personal story, or, rather, a deeply human reaction, led to monumental change. Christianity's constant dance between the great overarching narratives of the centuries and the individual foibles and actions of men and women continued even in a society which seemed as alien to them as Japan. Very little is known about Francisco de Olandia's origins. He was to become famous as the pilot of *San Felipe*, a merchant ship filled with Chinese silks and other such valuable cargo, which departed Manila in the autumn of 1596. Tasked with navigating the long voyage from the Spanish Philippines to the Empire in Mexico, some contemporary accounts suggest he was a cautious man, as would befit his task. When his ship began to founder, he was all in favor of limping to one of the designated enclaves at Nagasaki where the Japanese authorities allowed Western traders to act with a degree less suspicion. His passengers, however, were shattered and his cargo was in peril, and so, in the end, de Olandia agreed to weigh anchor at a nearer coast, in the province of Tosa.[9]

The local *Daiymo* or ruler was primarily interested in his cargo, specifically in the idea that the galleon might be carrying gold and silver, as Spanish ships were wont to do. De Olandia asserted his rights and asked that the case be escalated to Toyotomi Hideyoshi. Hideyoshi and the local ruler were not on the best of terms, and so it seemed as if the best way to ensure the safety of his cargo was to exploit the political weaknesses of the man who most obviously wanted it.

From Kyoto, the regent of Japan sent one of his most trusted advisors. Mashita Nagamori was an even more careful man than de Olandia. And he had a plan. Nagamori was first intensely civil to the Spanish men. He *was* on their side after all. They entertained him with displays of fencing and showed him their wares. He dined with them, engaging them in casual conversation. De Olandia in particular was keen to talk. The Spanish were there, he said, because of God. "Why," Nagamori asked, "did God want them to come to Japan?"[10] De Olandia, disarmed by the smoothness of the Japanese civil servant and, perhaps hoping to get better treatment by associating himself with the leader of the global superpower, then proceeded to explain that the King of Spain had come to rule half the world. This was partly due to the providence of God and the strength of his army and navy, but in part due to his habit of sending in missionaries first and armies later. Nagamori probed further, "Surely not all the missionaries were working for the Spanish King? What of the Portuguese?" De Olandia merrily exclaimed that the King of Spain was the same man as the King of Portugal: Felipe II and Filipe I were identical. For the sake of an "i" to an "e" and a single Roman numeral, the fate of Catholicism in Japan was sealed. This was the final straw: the Jesuits had always assured the Japanese that the Portuguese and Spanish were different powers who, along with the English and Dutch, could be carefully managed. Nagamori hurried back to Hideyoshi with his narrative prepared. These Christians were simply a vanguard for a Spanish Japan. Hideyoshi was apoplectic. It was as he had always feared.[11]

Indeed, in contemporary writings, the Spanish backed up this narrative. By contrast to the predominantly Portuguese Jesuits, who were chiefly interested in the battle for souls, the Spanish Franciscans were, as we saw from the events in South America, closely bound up with political and imperial expansion. Contemporary records seem to want to set up the idea that the *San Felipe* itself was a divine incident to "sustain the idea that divine providence wanted the intervention of Spain in the Japanese evangelisation."[12] Nation, expansion, and faith all bound up in one conversation between a shipwrecked sailor and a dubious bureaucrat. The sense was that the captain had given away the plan that the Spanish had been working to all along and that the Christian faith was merely a front for the expansion of Spanish imperial power.

Initially, the response was localized. Hideyoshi demanded blood from the most prominent Christian community in Japan in an attempt to dissuade Japanese from converting. In early 1597 a group of twenty-six men and boys, mostly, but not all, Franciscans, and mostly, but not all, European, were taken to a hill outside Nagasaki and nailed to crosses. The victims, some still children, were then pierced by spears and lances in a deliberate echoing of the events at Golgotha. Watching the grisly spectacle from the safety of a boat in the harbor was a Franciscan named Marcelo Ribadeneira. As he returned to Europe, he was determined to write an account, because it was "necessary to provide truthful information."[13] The scene he described shocked Europe, but it appeared to have the opposite effect to that which Hideyoshi had wanted. Rather than the stream of missionaries drying up, if anything, more volunteered for the mission, smuggling themselves in disguised as fishermen or hidden in boxes of goods.

The more Christians there were, the more intense the persecution became and the more the martyrdoms spread. By the second decade of the seventeenth century, the prosecution and execution of Christians, both European and Japanese, was widespread. Crucifixion remained a particularly favorite method of execution. As well as those killed in the manner of those outside Nagasaki, Christians who had previously been subject to torture at the hands of the state's Shinto and Buddhist inquisitors would be tied to crosses at low tide. The incoming spray and surf would lash them, filling their wounds and lacerations with salt water—a tactic deliberately designed to cause maximum pain. Eventually, their lungs would fill with that same water, or they would be ripped up from their crosses by the power of the tide and dashed against the rocks, and they would die—die for their faith.

It wasn't just crucifixion. Other methods were employed. Freezing to death in the mountain lakes that dotted the Japanese landscape, being covered with boiling water, being thrown off cliffs, being burned alive, being beheaded—although this was generally reserved for the newborn babies of Christian parents who were often given the arguably even more horrific punishment of having to watch.[14] There was even an entire new method of torture crossed with execution which was devised especially for Christians. *Ana-tsurushi* was a punishment by which the Christians were hung upside down, generally over a pit. To alleviate the pressure in their heads, and so keep them from passing out, sometimes cuts would be made in their foreheads. In the pit was rotting meat and offal, which would mix with the victim's blood and make a horrifying stench. Over a matter of days, the pit would be filled with water and, if they still had not recanted their Christian faith, the victim was lowered into it until they drowned.

One such victim was a young girl. Known simply as Magdalene after Mary Magdalene, she had been born to Christian parents in Nagasaki in 1611, when persecution was already well underway. Her parents were killed at some point in her early adolescence and so she put herself entirely at the service of the Dominican Order. Its priests and European brothers had fled to the immediate countryside around Nagasaki, favoring in particular mountainous areas like that of Mount Yasumandake. For contact with the outside world, they relied on Japanese

Christians, to whom they continued to give Holy Communion, preach the Gospel, and baptize converts. One such go-between was Magdalene who translated for them, and brought them food and supplies.[15] Soon she too withdrew to the mountains but felt that she was called to something even more. For some reason—whether to save those who sheltered her, or to hasten her own martyrdom—during a period of crackdown in the 1630s, aged only twenty-two, Magdalene went to the local judges on the island of Kyushu, where Nagasaki and Mount Yasumandake are both located, who were specifically tasked with finding female Christian leaders for execution, and volunteered herself as one of them.[16] She lasted thirteen days until she was drowned, all the while singing praises to God.

As it became clear that there would be no relief from the persecution, whole communities found their beliefs outlawed and punishable by these increasingly creative punishments. One such village was the tiny settlement of Kasuga on the Hirado island off the coast near Nagasaki. All of the residents of Kasuga had been converted to Christianity by 1561.[17] Some Christian graves on the Maruoyama hill just outside the village date back to 1550—barely seven years after those Portuguese merchants first came to Japan.[18] Many of its residents by the early to mid-seventeenth century had only ever known Christianity as their faith. Despite their rural location, which even today is about as far from the hyper-technological stereotype of Japan as it seems possible to be, the inquisitors still managed to make their way to Kasuga, and on the island of Nakaenoshima they put to death a number of local Christians using a variety of methods from crucifixion of adults to the beheading of infants, hurling their bodies into the sea to prevent their mangled corpses from being seen as martyrs who suffered as Christ did.[19] The persecution wasn't just designed to eradicate faith but to suppress hope as well.

In a number of cases this approach was successful. For some, their faith simply wasn't strong enough to continue in the face of such appalling torture. Often, the state's agents made the choice seem astonishingly simple. Images of Christ or Mary known as *fumi-e* were presented to suspected Christians and they were asked, calmly and simply, to tread on them. In the Japanese cultural norms so assiduously documented by Luis Frois, this represented an absolute rejection. It wasn't only some converts who recanted their faith. With the horrors of the alternative, some missionaries and priests did too. Perhaps the most famous example was Frois's fellow Jesuit—the Vice-Principal of the order in Japan, no less—one Christovão Ferreira.[20] After nearly twenty years as a missionary in Japan at the height of the persecution, during which he was tasked with writing about the martyrdoms of those killed by the state, Ferreira was captured. While being tortured by use of *ana-tsurushi*, Ferreira cracked and agreed to give up his Christian faith, even going so far as to marry a Japanese woman, take a Japanese name (and help write an anti-Christian tract entitled "Kengiroku" or "The Deception Revealed").[21] His case shocked the Jesuits, who prided themselves on the strength of their faith. But Ferreira serves as a reminder amid all the stories of strong faith and heroism that plenty of those who sought to try and keep their faith while under such intense pressure were simply, fraily human.[22]

However, there is another side to that frail humanity: in many cases, the torture and persecution didn't work. A whole group emerged that would later be identified as "the hidden Christians," "*kakure kirishitan.*" These communities sought to continue their worship but with the knowledge that they would never be able to do so in public, becoming little islands of the Christian faith, ever more separate from the rest of the world. One such group was the villagers of Kasuga. At some point in the early seventeenth century, probably not long after watching their co-religionists killed just over the water at Nakaenoshima, they went up the nearby mountain and built their shrine. It became the closest thing they had to a church for the next 250 or so years, until the ban was finally lifted with the arrival of an American naval squadron and the reopening of Japan in 1853. Unsurprisingly, many hidden Christians continued their practices and shrines like the one at Kasuga. Here they had come with their hopes and dreams, their half-remembered prayers, and their concealed objects of devotion—objects often disguised as household items. Here they had made offerings to carvings which appeared to be Buddhist or Shinto deities or demi-Gods but were, in fact, depictions of Christ or the Virgin Mary. Here, above all, they would seek to encounter

214 *Twelve Churches*

the God for whom their fellow believers were willing to die, such was the strength of their faith that *He* had died for *them*.

It was not just the Japanese state of the seventeenth century which felt threatened by Christianity. Persecution of Christians has continued through every age and on every continent. Indeed, today, Christianity remains the most persecuted religion on the face of the planet, with over 365 million Christians considered subject to "high levels of persecution and discrimination" in the year 2024.[23] Christians suffer at the hands of regimes on almost every continent. Some have suffered for years, such as those in North Korea, whose regime has persecuted them for nearly seventy years; others more recent, such as the sweep of persecution across the Middle East. What often ties these myriad examples together is a sense that it is a faith which, if enough pressure is applied upon its believers, will eventually give in to those who oppose its teachings.

In Uganda in the 1970s, the dictator Idi Amin fell out with churches who sought to oppose his totalitarian rule. It had not been the first time such a conflict had occurred. In the 1880s a number of Anglicans and Roman Catholics were killed in a number of violent ways, in an attempt to stop the Christian faith spreading in the kingdom of Buganda and thus challenging the rule of its kings. The bravery of the various clergy and laity in fact inspired mass conversions, challenging narratives around the incompatibility of traditional bravery and the Christian faith.[24]

Amin learned no lesson from this and when, in 1977, the Anglican Archbishop of Uganda publicly challenged him about the fact that he and his priests had "buried many who died as a result of being shot," despite the regime's claim that plenty of students and opposition activists had merely "disappeared," he decided to make an example of him.[25] Janani Luwum was arrested and then dragged in front of a rally of soldiers, where Amin laid out a rambling series of conspiracies, which he claimed that the Archbishop was involved in. To each accusation, Luwum shook his head. Amin appealed to the soldiers: "What do we do to traitors such as this?" "Shoot them," came the reply. Luwum was dragged away, but not before he had told the other bishops lined up there for humiliation that he "saw the hand of God in this." The next day Amin released a statement saying Luwum had died in a car crash overnight just outside the capital of Kampala. In fact, he had been shot to death, twice in the chest, almost certainly by Amin himself, after hours of violent torture.[26] Amin doubtless expected that to be that.

In fact, the murder of Luwum further crystallized opposition to a regime that was recognized as being dangerously out of control. Luwum was acclaimed as a martyr; Amin was forced out of power by a coup within two years as his support in the army crumbled away. Today, Luwum is considered a saint within the Anglican Communion, remembered at the same time as the martyrs of the 1880s, men killed for refusing to renounce their faith, a specific reminder of the power of faith even after persecution and death.

Once again, targeted persecution seemed to be designed to invoke a culture of silence. Public, violent murders of even those in powerful positions gave the impression that nobody was safe from Amin's wrath, that his power was absolute. Faith in anyone or anything other than him was, therefore, mistaken, and replaced, instead, with "a grave and ominous fear" in each Ugandan.[27] The problem was that, as we saw in Japan, very often faith is not suppressed by fear, but cures it. As the first Epistle of St John, written at a time of intense persecution and suffering for the Christian faith, observes, "there is no fear in love, and perfect love casts out fear."[28] The calculation that Amin made was that enough fear would destroy something that threatened his power. But that calculation was wrong.

Amin was not, however, alone in making it. Whether it was the Roman Empire or Tokugawa Japan or almost all of the totalitarian states of the twentieth century, Christianity was discerned as a threat. Why? Well, for as little as those contexts might appear to have in common, what is telling is that, in all of them, Christians were seen to pose a threat for two specific reasons: one, because they appear to hold allegiance to a power—that is to say, God—which is necessarily greater than the earthly power which is seeking to exert absolute control over a particular area. And, secondly, because they hold that allegiance, many of the coercive efforts, which said earthly powers seek to use on the rest of their populations in order to show their control, don't work. People keep their faith

216 *Twelve Churches*

in the face of the most astonishing levels of violence or deprivation or targeted dehumanization.

Indeed, even our brief trips to Japan and Uganda show that, for some, seeing the reactions of others to persecution even acted as a reason to adopt faith. Why? Well, the obvious conclusion is that those who are prepared to suffer for it believe that faith to be true. They believe that the promises of Christ are such that earthly persecution is but a blink of the eye compared to the promises of Jesus. The idea for suffering for what one believes is not necessarily unique to Christianity, of course. Some 450 years before the birth of Christ, the Prophet Malachi predicted that much of "the coming of the Lord" would involve pain and purification, that it would be like "refiner's fire and fuller's soap," and that those who underwent such trial would end up purer, just as silver and gold are put under heat to remove their impurities.[29] What is unique about Christianity is the idea that God himself, as Christ, has suffered as well. Keeping that faith when you believe you are going through an experience God also went through has proved to be something which, in multiple places in multiple generations, Christians have achieved, even when that experience is death itself. As far as Kampala and Nagasaki might seem from Golgotha, that such acts of faith proved compelling enough to make others do likewise is, sort of, the whole point of the Christian faith.

What, then, of keeping the faith in different circumstances? What of those places where believers do not find their faith proved as such, but rather find it gently sidelined or conveniently ignored? That adversity allows a believer to show their mettle and the power of their faith is indisputable, even if it is a challenge which very few believers would actually seek to undergo; but what happens when the key challenges to faith are not rigorous persecution, but the prevalence of comfort? What happens when places simply don't bother anymore? "Keeping the faith," then, means something very different indeed. Plenty of countries which formerly had a Christian majority suffered a falling away of "plausibility structures"—that is to say culturally normal behaviors—that have the Christian faith at their center.[30] Religion ceased to be something people constructed their lives around, let alone would die for. Keeping the faith in such circumstances, therefore, becomes difficult not because, as for those who came to worship at the Kirishitan Hokora, it is considered dangerous by the state but rather because it becomes so unusual that it seems unimportant.

The irony is that it is often in places where Christianity was at its strongest historically that such a phenomenon has been observed. Germany, France, Switzerland, and Britain reported some of the lowest numbers of people who were "certain" about their beliefs in God in the whole world, despite all four nations being utterly shaped by the Christian faith.[31] Although Britain had the highest faith of those four, it is in one of its constituent countries where the contrast is most stark.

Religion used to matter very much in Scotland. At around the time Christians were first coming to Japan, a Scottish preacher, John Knox, initiated a Reformed Church there that actively embraced a violent, judgmental vision of God. Of those who rejected this vision, Knox wrote: "such as continue obstinate in their impiety, have no portion of these promises. For them will God kill, them will he destroy, and them will he thrust, by the power of his word, into the fire which never shall be quenched."[32] By the time Knox died in 1572, Scotland had a reputation for clan-based violence, religious extremism, and intensely difficult living conditions, a sort of Afghanistan of Early Modern Europe. Other leaders followed Knox in their refutation of moderation. One such figure was a woman, Jenny Geddes. On July 23, 1637, the Dean of the Cathedral of St Giles in Edinburgh began reading from a new Book of Common Prayer authorized by King Charles I, the joint king of England and Scotland. To Jenny and multiple others, the words the Dean was speaking sounded worryingly similar to the Roman Catholic Mass of which John Knox had not been a fan, describing it as *inter alia*, "a diabolical profanation," "blasphemous to Christ," and, "like daily committing manslaughter."[33] Short of any other weaponry, Jenny picked up the portable stool she was sitting on and hurled it at the Dean's head, yelling, "Daur ye say Mass in ma lug?" ("How dare you say the Mass in my ear?").[34] Riots followed, then a Covenant to secure the independence of the Scottish Church, then over two decades of Civil War. Religion used to matter very much in Scotland.

218   Twelve Churches

Now the Church of Scotland is arguably one of the most liberal mainstream denominations in the West. It is also one of the fastest shrinking. The gap between Scots of faith and those of none was brought into sharp focus in 2023, when a young member of the Scottish Parliament, a woman called Kate Forbes, ran to be leader of the Scottish National Party. Forbes was a member of the "Free Church of Scotland," a group who split from the main church in the early nineteenth century over what they saw as liberal tendencies. Forbes's faith was not something many in modern Scotland felt comfortable with. "I want a Scotland where the only weeping and gnashing of teeth is over the performance of the national football team," wrote one commentator.[35] Faith was not something that had a part to play in modern Scottish life.

To see this in its physical form, let us go to another rocky place, far from the Kirishitan Hokora. As ever, stones are capable of telling this story in a way which mere graphs or pie charts cannot. Symbolic of the decline of Scottish faith is the "Mither Kirk" or mother church of the city of Aberdeen, St Nicholas. It is a very different church to the Kasuga shrine, designed to be visible. It is a tall, austere building, its gray-white stone rising above the quays and narrow streets which lie beneath its shadow. Surmounting it all is the great spire, an enormous pinnacle reaching to Heaven on behalf of its town. There has been a place of worship on the site of St Nicholas's since at least 1157, when it was mentioned in a Papal document of Pope Adrian IV.[36] Around the great kirk lie Aberdonians of varying degrees of earthly greatness. Perhaps my favorite of the burials is that of John Anderson, known as "the wizard of the north." Anderson was the first man to catch a bullet and is credited with introducing the now classic magician's trick of pulling a rabbit out of his hat. At the center of John Anderson's act was a suspension of belief. A suspension of belief is exactly what has now affected St Nicholas's. Now the dead are the only ones who expect the resurrection there.

Michael Gove looked wistfully at me over a glass of not-very-Presbyterian claret. He was remembering St Nicholas's as, well, a church. His adoptive parents had been married there, mourned their parents there, baptized children there. He had since gone far from Aberdeen, indeed had climbed the ranks of the British state. But

St Nicholas still meant something, or rather, a lot, to him. It was still his church. Except it wasn't one anymore. He described the plaque to relatives, described sitting in the pews as a boy, described what it had meant to the people he loved and, by extension, even many miles away and many years later, to him. "All gone," he said. "A tragedy." As an adoptee and as someone who rose from unlikely origins, I suspect roots were important to him. The place where those roots had found their most meaningful growth was now gone.

That's the thing when churches die: it isn't just faith that goes. Indeed, if polling is to be believed, faith in the sense of belief continues. But faith isn't just the theory, it's the practice too. It's the getting out of bed on a Sunday and going to a specific place at a specific time; it's paying for ornamentation and for memorials; it's shaping a place so that future generations can know the same connection with the Divine there. And humanity requires physical place for this practical faith—which is where churches come in. They aren't just repositories of memory, they are living organisms. But that requires a living faith. Faith that something matters more than just football.

Aberdeen is not, in many ways, an especially comfortable or hopeful place. It is a place which is currently experiencing falling life expectancy, rising dependency on drugs, and increasing unemployment.[37] However, it is not at all clear that practical faith is capable of making a comeback even in a context where the adversity which so crystallized belief in the past is making a comeback as well. Sometimes, it seems, the memories of faith are just too far away. The fact that faith still exists in this practical form on a mountainside in Japan, but not in a great kirk by the North Sea, is a strange twist in the tale of the Christian faith.

In the midst of such uncertainty, there may be a change coming. If our trip through Christian history tells us anything, it is to expect the unexpected. There were those who rejoiced in the West's seeming abandonment of Christianity. Christianity, like all religion, was, according to the New Atheists who became intellectually prominent in the English-speaking world in the late twentieth and early twenty-first centuries, merely an evolutionary staging post. Everything, for men like Professor Richard Dawkins in his book *The God Delusion* of 2006, necessarily evolves toward progressive morality married to hard materialist reasoning. The demise of faith should be rejoiced in as it is a sign of society moving toward being more rational. A lack of faith, the New Atheist argument goes, should be celebrated as it necessarily is replaced by reason and good common sense. According to such logic, those who kept going up the mountain in Japan should be pitied for their stubborn irrationality, not admired for their fortitude.

Almost twenty years later, and Dawkins has changed his mind. He describes himself now as a "cultural Christian."[38] He has come to the conclusion that the consequences of the Christian faith for culture and for society are too important to just jettison, and that many of his own presumptions about who humans are and how the individual functions are based as much on the ideas behind Christianity as they are on science. In particular, Dawkins is concerned about what might replace Christianity's role in the West, whether it be an identity politics that he feels violates biology or a more obscurantist version of Islam or, more likely, a sort of permanent pursuit of pleasure. Put another way, faith in things isn't going away. Quite what it is that will cause people to keep the power of faith in Christianity specifically in a new century remains to be seen. It might be Dawkins's fear of the irrational, it might be the power of AI; statistically, as all those hundreds of millions of Christians around the world know all too well, it may still be persecution. It might be all three.

Let us return to the "just rocks," that pile up on the side of a mountain on the other side of the world from Godless Aberdeen. Rocks have a good pedigree in the Gospels: in both Luke and Matthew, Jesus talks about those who keep the faith in the light of persecution or of doubt as being like the man "who built his house upon the rock."[39] "Just rocks" are a very firm foundation for a faith.

The Kirishitan Hokora is itself an answer to the question that we started with: How far would people go to keep their faith? In the context of Japanese Christianity, they went to the very top of a mountain and found themselves thrown to the bottom of pits. How people keep their faith in the context of great comfort is a slightly tougher question, but it may involve people realizing, in the manner of Dawkins, what it is they have lost by not paying attention to or believing that they have "outgrown" those "just rocks."

The Book of Hebrews was written at some point in Christianity's first hundred or so years to those Jews who were struggling with the implications of the new Christian faith. In it is found one of the most famous descriptions of what faith actually is: "Faith is the substance of things hoped for, the evidence of things not seen."[40] Put another way, for as long as the world remains imperfect, as long as there are things to hope for, to look forward to, there will be something that calls people in the deepest recesses of their soul to look to hope, and that hope will be held on to by people. That was, is, and in the future will continue to be what keeping the faith is.

In the specifically Christian context, it looks like holding on to an idea that human nature, with all its capacity for cruelty and persecution, for all its tendencies toward the comfortable and the inane, for all its flaws and fallenness, that same nature has been innately changed by the reality of Jesus's birth, death, and resurrection. And, for those who believe that article of faith to be true, it means they have to live in a certain way, proclaim certain truths, hold a certain faith, even if doing so means swimming against the popular tide, even if doing so means being put to death.

Indeed, as it looks like attempts to create a perfect world drive the human race further and further toward despair, keeping the faith may yet be more important than ever. Will equivalent hidden shrines exist in the future, when all the "mother kirks" are gone? Perhaps; perhaps not. But either way, never underestimate the power that can be found, the faith that can be maintained by "just rocks."

Chapter Nine

Site of the First Meeting House, Salem, Massachusetts, United States

(Built 1672 AD)

Spread in various forms to places from Japan to the Caribbean, it was clear now that the Church had become a global institution. It also became a fragmented one. From the simple facts of geography to cultural differences to encounters with hostile regimes, difference not unity was now the norm. The more fragmented it became the more its branches desired to differentiate themselves, to prove that their particular part of it was the "true Church." Many sought to do so by a return to the very beginning, to evoke and imitate the practices of the early Church in that first century after the manger. For Christians of all shades, as the world became more complex in the aftermath of the Reformation, a rise of new religious and political movements meant that the seventeenth and eighteenth centuries led to a renewed focus on purity.

Of course, a desire to set parameters to the faith had always been there: having a chosen people "inside" a church meant, at least implicitly, having those who were not chosen outside. The fact that, for all the influence that Christianity had achieved in the world, the ways of the world and of the Church were not one and the same was still a sore subject for some Christians. To them, the only solution was a pursuit of absolute purity, a rejection of any external worldliness in favor of a smaller but holier Church. The problem was that having claimed to have rejected the enemies without, they turned to the enemies within. In some ways this represented Christianity shaping society, in others it represented society, with all its tensions and insecurities, shaping Christianity. One church, as many readers will already know, became a byword for this process and for the dangers of the pursuit of purity. That church was in Salem.

The junction of Hobart Street and Forest Street in Danvers, Massachusetts, is about as stereotypical a slice of a particular sort of Americana as it's possible to imagine. Both of the suburban roads are lined with a row of houses, each decked in wooden plasterboard frontage, American flags, and little porches. The curtains don't quite twitch on cue but, as you walk past, you'd be forgiven for thinking they do. By turns it is comforting and slightly sinister, in a way that people from Washington Irving onwards knew only New England could be. There is now a sense of Disneyfication here in Danvers. I visited most recently at Halloween 2024, and the town was replete with fake cobwebs and plastic headstones on those immaculate lawns. There is a strange echo of Canterbury and its commercialization of gore—a very modern take on a much older phenomenon. In fact, the SUVs in driveways and wires overhead bely the fact that this is a very old part of American suburbia indeed. In fact, from its foundation in the year 1628 on the land the native Abenaki peoples knew as Naumkeag, it was a suburb, or rather a dependent farming community, of the main settlement of Salem Town, about five miles to its southeast.

Indeed, such was its relationship to Salem town proper that the village wasn't originally known as Danvers at all, but as Salem Village. A little Salem or, to those who lived there, just Salem. The name, of course, derives from Jerusalem. And, just like King Lalibela in Ethiopia or those Victorian industrialists in the North of England, a similitude of the heavenly Jerusalem, the community of the saved, is exactly what the settlement's founders intended to establish here. By the latter quarter of the seventeenth-century Salem Village had grown sufficiently to justify the construction of its own meeting house. This building was the focal point of the little community. In it, legal proceedings were conducted, community meetings were held, but, above all, it was the place where Christian—specifically Reformed—worship occurred. While those who made up the population of Salem, and indeed most of Massachusetts, had either personally left or were the children of those who had left England due to the influence of the Church of England on the state, the majority were not against the idea of an ordering of day-to-day life that was entirely predicated on religious rules.

Indeed, for most of the inhabitants of Salem, that was precisely what they were there for: to build a pure community of the faithful away from the corruption and wickedness of the world. Throughout

Site of the First Meeting House, Salem, Massachusetts, United States   227

Christian history, believers have sought to live authentic and devout lives by removing temptation, becoming pure, even at the cost of complete rejection of the world. The discovery of the New World provided an opportunity for those who believed that those distractions were so great that a completely fresh start was needed. The Meeting House was the heart of this whole vision. In it, the people would gather on Sundays—a day on which no other activity was allowed, in order to keep the purity of the Sabbath—and listen to Scripture and long sermons on its meaning and its centrality to their lives delivered by perhaps the most important person in the whole settlement: the minister. In his person and in that place, Church and state were essentially one; he was religious leader, community leader, legal figure, and political totem all rolled into one.

The building itself would have been bigger than the houses that surrounded it, although not by much. It was a plain wooden rectangle with a steep roof containing a wide single open room, with places to sit arrayed on its edges, and at its center at one end, serving as a focal point, was a reading desk and place from which to preach. The interior would have been fairly dark or, rather, just a little darker than would be comfortable to sit and read in. Undoubtedly, with the whole community gathered there, it would have been uncomfortable, everyone necessarily an inch or two closer to one another than they would have liked. As with so much in Danvers, much about the meeting house was just *slightly* out of place. The sinister power of small differences is something the place knows well.

While the original building is long gone, merely rotting remains of timbers under the earth and concrete of current American suburbia, we do have an idea of what the Meeting House would have looked like. A faithful replica from the original plans exists a fifteen-minute or so stroll southeast of its original location. It stands in the grounds of a real building from the seventeenth century, the Rebecca Nurse homestead, built meticulously in the 1980s as part of the set of a film.[1] Now, the building, as mentioned, was not of any great architectural value and New England has had many colonial-era buildings lost to fire or earth or concrete. Why was a Hollywood production team so keen to re-create this one and why specifically re-create it in this place? Well, Rebecca Nurse was, on March 24, 1692, brought to the original meeting house and there accused of being a witch in perhaps the most egregious miscarriage of justice in the whole sorry tale of the event that was to become known as the Salem Witch Trials. An event that would change America forever.

It was an event, too, that puts into sharp and painfully human focus one of the greatest challenges that Christian communities have faced from the very beginning: that of purity. In his earliest letters St Paul exhorted the first Christian communities to keep an eye on the moral character of their congregation and to "put away from themselves" wicked people within them.[2] Christians were, Paul said, called to be new people living according to the new rules of Christ. Consequently, it was necessary to "purge out the old leaven"; those parts of the community who, in little ways, like leaven or yeast affects bread, were affecting in an adverse manner the common life of the Christian community.[3] So it was from the very beginning that the issue presented itself of how both to welcome the stranger and the new convert and to keep a community living up to the standards set by God. It is not an issue that has ever been resolved since.

The quest for an ever-purer community of faith has affected not just church buildings like the deliberately plain and austere Meeting House at Salem Village but also, as Rebecca Nurse and nineteen others would discover, countless human lives and deaths. At the heart of what purity means in the context of a church (or rather, The Church), is a question of how a community functions, and how it deals with conflict, with dissension, and, explicitly, with things it cannot immediately explain. The tension of a faith whose founder said, "Come unto me all ye who are heavy laden," that seeks to embrace all those in need, and an all-too-human desire to seek a purer, safer community is ever-present in any church.[4] In an environment fraught by its own doubts and insecurities, where purity is all, sometimes little differences can prove fatal.

The first things that seemed to go awry in Salem in the early spring of 1692 were little ones.[5] A few of the young girls who lived with or near the Minister Samuel Parris's house—including his daughter Betty and niece Abigail Williams—went away from home for just a little longer than they should have done.[6] Pinpricks, little scrapes, and bite marks began to appear on the children's skin, all explainable rationally and yet occurring with a frequency that began to disturb. Eventually, the young girls, along with Elizabeth Hubbard and Ann Putnam, began to exhibit fits of disturbing similarity. They complained of more and more pain and exhibited it in more and more dramatic ways. Samuel Parris consulted some of his fellow residents and, on February 29, 1692, made an application to the magistrates and constable of the county to have three women arrested on the charge of witchcraft.

What it is absolutely crucial to understand is that, for Christians in this period of history, witchcraft was real. To believe that there were those who would seek to use the power of the devil or of evil spirits more generally to commit malicious acts that broke the laws of God and nature was not some cranky idea of a deranged few but one that was held—albeit with varying degrees of sincerity—by people in every stratum of society. Such belief goes back to pre-Christian times. In the Old Testament, witchcraft features as a recurring crime against God. In Exodus, as Moses is clarifying the laws by which the children of Israel are to govern themselves, there is one very clear instruction on witchcraft: "Thou shalt not suffer a witch to live."[7] This didn't stop witchcraft, of course, and even Israel's kings had recourse to witches, such was the belief in those who had "familiar spirits" and unusual powers. Tellingly, however, these figures often lived apart from the more established society of Israel—when King Saul sought to consult a witch, he did so at Endor, a Canaanite border village, and under the cover of darkness.[8] Even if witches were widely consulted in the days of the Old Testament, it was done so in such a way as to maintain religious purity.

The New Testament continued the Old's prohibition of witchcraft. In Galatians 5, one of Paul's earliest pieces of writing, he lists witchcraft as one of the "works of the flesh" that risks corrupting the early Church. His advice on dealing with it was clear: "I would," he wrote, "that they were cut off that trouble you."[9] Purity was, again, paramount. As time passed, and Christianity inevitably found itself either subsuming or suppressing aspects of folk belief, the scope of witchcraft in the Christian mind grew from its Biblical foundations. In the Netherlands witches were thought capable of extracting magical powder from the anus of a particular demon.[10] In Lorraine, they were considered to be capable of doing special dances due to their possession of cows' and goats' feet.[11] Beliefs of a similar nature continue to this day in places where ostensibly Christianity remains the dominant religion. In Zimbabwe, witches are believed to command goblins, which are responsible for, inter alia, stealing the panties of people while they sleep.[12]

Witchcraft was specifically associated, in the minds of both the secular and religious authorities, with an extreme collapse of order—the haunting of the popular imagination by the "Prince of Disorder, the Devil"—as systems and structures disintegrated.[13] In many Protestant nations it became a "political crime," implicitly treasonous and an attempt not only to subvert God's providence in a religious sense but in a political one too.[14] Witchcraft, therefore, became a crime as much to do with safeguarding the boundaries of society as it was about defying the commandment of God. This was particularly the case in those places where the Reformed faith sought to make churches that were assemblies of the elect—those chosen by God as pure enough for salvation.

The specific situation of the New World was therefore ripe for witchcraft crazes. Not only were royal, legal, and ecclesiastical authorities—which tended to insist on due process—distant or theoretical while ordinary life was prone to violence or disorder at any time, but the pervading religious motivation for settlement there was the preservation of purity and the ejection of those who compromised the religious integrity of the people of God. The smallest dissent from what was already a profoundly febrile societal setup could be thought to have spiritual implications. Witches, therefore, in the minds of the people of Salem, could be anywhere and anyone. A little pinprick or a child away for an extra hour were no small things at all.

However, it is important to note that while people did believe witchcraft to be "true" in the sense that it had power and an effect over their lives, they also believed that it was not a day-to-day occurrence. The idea that every slightly unusual event was explained as witchcraft is a crude parody of the Early Modern mind. The statistics bear this out: while there were witchcraft trials across colonial America between 1640 and 1670, in fact, convictions were rare and executions were even rarer.

Site of the First Meeting House, Salem, Massachusetts, United States 231

Indeed, there was only one event that could be described as a "craze"— in Hartford, Connecticut, in 1662.[15] What saw such a dramatic increase in witchcraft trials in the late seventeenth century in America is unclear. Indeed, the last confirmed trial ending in executions back in England— from whence most of the protagonists traced their ancestry—had taken place in 1682 in the rural West Country town of Bideford, and even then it had been considered to be a barbarous outlier by men like the Lord Chief Justice of England, Sir John Holt.[16] One theory behind the sudden increase in America is that Puritanism was at a moment of inexorable decline. Between the restored anti-Puritan monarchy in England and increasing disquiet at the excesses of those European witch trials, a situation had arisen where the Puritan vision of a community committed to purity at all costs seemed somewhat out of date and under threat. In Europe a "critical mass of leaders" had "lost their certainty" in the "prevalence ... if not the existence of a diabolical conspiracy; and the practicality of identifying and punishing those involved."[17]

It's therefore even more notable that the events at Salem in this period became such a byword for witch trials more generally. They were, in fact, a last hurrah for a more superstitious, purity-driven Christianity and for a popular belief in the supernatural more generally. Yet, despite the fact that it was at the tail end of wider witchcraft hysteria, in many ways it had all of the classic hallmarks of the ultimate trial. It began with small incidents which then escalated into bigger, more shocking ones. The initial accusations were not of a necessarily supernatural nature, but soon escalated into being so. Equally important was the role of children. The Puritan denizens of Salem would have taken very seriously Jesus's instruction that "except ye be converted, and become as little children, ye shall not enter into the kingdom of Heaven." Children were considered to be pure and therefore their accusations—assumed to be free of malice or agenda—bore a weight which those of adults often did not. Finally, those who were initially accused had one very clear thing in common: the violation of purity.

The three women accused of practicing witchcraft in Salem were, when judged superficially, disparate in the extreme. However, all had been named by the girls as instrumental to their torment and all had, in other ways, violated the intended purity of Salem's social norms. The first to be arrested was Tituba, the slave, possibly of mixed African and Native American descent, who worked in the Parris household. She corroborated the accusation that she was co-conspirator with Sarah Good, a woman in her thirties of limited resources and a notably difficult temper, and Sarah Osborne, a wealthier woman possibly in her fifties, who had scandalized the village by her relationship with an indentured laborer and her consistent refusal to attend church.

To the villagers of Salem there was only one logical place for the trial to take place: the Meeting House. Tituba was the first to be interrogated. A large portion of the community gathered there; the atmosphere was exceptionally febrile. For the people present, the threat of witchcraft was absolutely real. One of the two magistrates tasked with overseeing proceedings, Jonathan Corwin, began to question her, albeit with perhaps one of the broadest opening questions ever admitted in a court of law:[18]

"Do you never see something appear in some shape?" he asked.

Tituba replied very clearly that she had never seen such a shape, responding, "No never see anything."

Within a couple of questions, however, Tituba had begun to backtrack on her initial denials and began to construct a very detailed picture of supernatural phenomena that shocked the court and the assembled villagers. Having admitted that a "man in black" came to her, whom she presumed was the devil, she then detailed how it was that he engaged in the harm of the girls.

Corwin asked, "How doth he appear when he hurts them, with what shape or what is he like that hurts them?"

Tituba replied, "Like a man, I think yesterday I being in the Lentoe Chamber I saw a thing like a man, that told me [to] serve him."[19]

Interestingly, Tituba survived the trials, though she suffered appalling privations in prison with the other accused, eventually leaving Massachusetts with whomever it was who paid her bail some years later. She has become perhaps the most interesting and enigmatic figure in American religious and cultural history. The intense detail of her testimony and her pre-existent proximity to the Parris family has caused some to suggest more was at play. Undoubtedly Tituba mixed African, Native American, and older European concepts of witchcraft into her testimony—influences which reverberate to this day, from the concepts of witches flying on brooms to pacts and covenants with the Devil. Her role as the sole non-White protagonist is also significant, with concepts of racial "otherness" beginning to be formalized in the thought patterns of the Americas. Modern scholars point to the obvious power imbalance between her and even her juvenile accusers.

Perhaps most mysterious of all is her relationship with Parris himself: Had he briefed Tituba on what to say as some suspected, in order to settle scores in the community which he sought to lead? Undoubtedly he had beaten her for her behavior and yet he also allowed her considerable access to the children in his care. Was the reference to the Devil as a man dressed in black who gave her instructions, who featured so prominently in Tituba's testimony, in fact a veiled reference to Parris himself?[20]

The arrival of Good and Osborne into the dark atmosphere of the Meeting House turned it from a place of religious trial to being itself a center of supernatural phenomena. On seeing the two women, the girls who had accused them began to writhe and cry out in pain. As the contemporary court record put it, when Good arrived in the room: "the abovesaid children then present accused her face to face, upon which they were all dreadfully tortured & tormented for a short space of time."[21]

Good protested, but it was to no avail. The girls' apparent pain had sealed her fate. She, Osborne, and Tituba were found guilty and taken to Boston.

Regardless of motivation, there were doubtless those in Salem who thought that the arrest of the three women would mark the end of the episode; that it would be a troubling footnote in the godly little community. But it was not to be so. As March progressed, things got stranger. A former minister who returned to visit the town, Deodat Lawson, described what he saw when he visited the Minister's house on March 19, 1692:

"When I was there, his Kinswoman, Abigail Williams, (about 12 years of age) had a grievous fit; she was at first hurried with violence to and fro in the room (though Mrs. Ingersol endeavored to hold her) sometimes making as if she would fly, stretching up her arms as high as she could, and crying 'Whish, Whish, Whish!' several times; presently after she said there was Goodwife Nurse and said, 'Do you not see her? Why there she stands!' And she said Goodwife Nurse offered her 'THE BOOK,' but she was resolved she would not take it, saying often, 'I won't, I won't, I won't take it, I do not know what Book it is: I am sure it is none of God's Book, it is the Devil's Book, for ought I know.'"[22]

Goodwife Nurse was Rebecca. She had been known as one of the most pious and pure members of the community; a "good wife" in every sense of the term. She kept a good house, tidy and clean and so well built that it still, as we know, stands today. The accusation against such a respected member of the church and community, one known for her regular attendance at worship and adherence to the teachings and practices of Christianity as Salem understood it, marked a turning point in the quest for purity. It was no longer simply a purge of the obvious transgressors but a complete turning inside out of the community. Now nobody was beyond suspicion, everybody could be harboring an evil spirit or seeking liaison with the devil no matter how externally pious they might seem. Dorcas Good was interrogated despite only being four years old. The Reverend George Burroughs, who had been the community's minister ten years previously, was accused and convicted of being a witch, despite his former position. The craze proper had begun.

Some members of the community began to feel uneasy. Many of the accusations that were spreading through the community came from those who had confessed to witchcraft themselves. This was thought to be conclusive by multiple Salem residents, and evidence of just how deep the coven went in the village. Thomas Brattle recorded that, "The great cry of many of our neighbors now is, 'What, will you not believe the confessors?'"[23] However, Brattle and others felt that such a system had a flaw: surely those who were making the accusations were under the influence of evil spirits; how, then could their testimony be accepted? One person who raised such objections was John Proctor, a prosperous farmer in Salem. When his wife was accused of witchcraft, Proctor rigorously defended her. He believed that the accusations were "lies" and that the whole process was tantamount to "the spilling of innocent blood."[24]

It didn't take long for him to be accused and brought for interrogation at the place which had once been a place of worship. On his arrival, Abigail, one of the girls, cried out that he was here to pinch her and then had a fit. To the assembly, Proctor's fate was sealed. The Meeting House, where once the community had come to express their faith in God and their hope and trust in his good providences, now became a dark place of superstition, mistrust, and, above all else, fear, as a community so obsessed with purity and its limits began to lose control of every other aspect of their lives.

None of this is to say that what happened at Salem was purely mob violence. Indeed, the courtesies and specifics of the legal system were rigidly adhered to even from the start: the very first documents of the trial refer to the crimes as being "done, at Salem Village contrary to the peace of our Sovereign Lord and Lady William & Mary, King & Queen of England."[25] One wonders what the notoriously dry and rationalistic William and Mary would have made of it all, in the comfortable, witch-free surroundings of Hampton Court just outside London. Despite the legal formalities being adhered to, even on the wilder side of the Atlantic, there were those who were uneasy about the trials. Specifically, there was a debate about the nature of the evidence presented: How, contemporary legal and theological minds asked, could people be denounced as impure or as afflicted with demons when the accusers themselves were affected by evil spirits? Increase Mather, the President of Harvard and scion of one of the most dedicated Protestant ministerial families in America, wrote a detailed account of his very specific concerns about how accusations had been made:

"This then I Declare and Testify, that to take away the life of any one; merely because a Spectre or Devil, in a Bewitched or Possessed person does accuse them, will bring the Guilt of Innocent Blood on the Land, where such a thing shall be done. Mercy forbid that it should, (and I trust that as it has not, it never will be so) in New-England."[26]

Even in the attempts to rid the community of those who were believed to have so sorely troubled it, new cracks emerged in the fabric of society in Salem and new doubts crept in. Families were pitted against families, neighbors against neighbors. Even Increase Mather's own son repudiated his father's statement of doubts: Cotton Mather, whom history would record as one of the great villains of the trials, was instrumental in pushing for the death sentence for those accused. In trying to make things purer and more unified under God, those who initiated the trials in fact further exposed the cracks and divisions that affected New England society. Counter accusation followed accusation, and nobody was safe. The example of John Proctor was not an isolated one. Nor were the paroxysms of fear limited to Salem Village itself. John Hale, a minister from Beverley, an even smaller settlement just over the river from Salem, arrived in mid-1692 to assist with the questioning of the accused. By November of that year his own wife was on the receiving end of an accusation of witchcraft.[27]

Mather's treatise embodies all that was going on at Salem: a heady mix of legal and religious concerns, of little, petty community hatreds fused with a lofty and spiritualized understanding of evil. The very natural and the supernatural, the deeply irrational and the cold systematics of legality all clashed together in a heady brew which became a byword, both then and since, for a community turning itself inside out in the quest to be pure.

About a fifteen-minute drive into the modern town of Salem proper, just down the unremarkable Pope Street, itself seemingly only serving as a rear entry point for the carpark of a Walgreens, is Proctor's Ledge. It was here that the afflictions which had so taken hold of Salem finally ended—at the end of a rope. Nineteen people were executed in what is now such an unassuming place. Among those who died there were Sarah Good, John Proctor, George Burroughs, and Goodwife Rebecca Nurse. One other victim, eighty-one-year-old Giles Corey, was crushed to death during torture as he refused to enter a plea as either guilty or innocent. Multiple others, including Sarah Osborne, died in horrible conditions in prison.

Eventually, the craze came to its end. It was never destined to remain merely a localized horror in the dark room of the Meeting House, but as accusations of witchcraft spread across Massachusetts, inevitably those authorities of Crown and Church, which the Puritans had been so

Site of the First Meeting House, Salem, Massachusetts, United States 237

eager to escape, began to take notice. While personally dubious about the legal legitimacy of the trials and of the actual efficacy of witchcraft, the new governor of the state, Sir William Phips, feared the power of men like Cotton Mather, who were zealous for the trials to continue. He began by accepting the accusations but by insisting that proceedings were transferred from the febrile atmosphere of the Meeting House to proper courts under direct royal jurisdiction. However, when accusations of witchcraft were directed at his wife, Phips decided that he had to crush the craze once and for all. He wrote to William and Mary, back in London, in October 1692:

"When I understood what danger some of their innocent subjects might be exposed to, if the evidence of the afflicted persons only did prevail either to the committing or trying any of them, I did before any application was made unto me about it put a stop to the proceedings of the Court and they are now stopped."[28]

And that was that. It had started with little things awry and now it ended with a simple letter. Strange whimpers rather than great bangs.

A mere four years later, official documents would describe the events thus: ". . . in the year of our Lord 1692, when many persons in Salem and in other towns there about were accused by some evilly disposed or strangely influenced persons . . ."[29]

It took barely four years for the community to repudiate the events as the work of a few bad-faith actors and to move their focus away from a quest for purity and toward trying to live together in unity. Legal settlement took a little longer: Elizabeth Johnson, the last victim of the witch trials in Salem to be cleared of the crime for which she was executed, was not formally pardoned by the State of Massachusetts until May 2022. The example of Salem continues to stand as a horrifying example of the ends to which a quest for purity of thought, belief, and action can drive a group of people who are ostensibly unified in other areas.

What role did Christianity play in all this? Well, on one level it was essential. Jesus's intrinsic call for people to follow good over evil, the later Biblical admonitions to pursue pure communities, free from those who would trouble them, the very particular Reformed interpretation of this and, of course, its basic metaphysical contention that there are powers which we cannot see and things which we cannot by ordinary means control, all were the soil in which the seed of the events of Salem were sown. Without Christianity's complex relationship to purity, Salem would never have happened.

Yet, there is something deeper going on. Christianity was undoubtedly the primary shaper of the way in which the people of Salem thought and acted. They would have said, and, indeed, in their court testimonies consistently did say, that they were good Christians. However, what broke through the illusions of their Christianity as the panic took hold was a raw, ugly human nature—accusations and confessions motivated by a brute desire to survive and, in some cases, a vindictive desire to punish. More than that, the paranoia, the cyclical violence and the triumph of fear seem to be antithetical to the core commandments of that same faith which the villagers professed. It is very hard to see the command of Christ to "love thy neighbor as thyself" in the pointed fingers and staged fits that caused people who had lived next to one another for decades to call for each other's violent deaths.[30] If anything, the witch trials seem to suggest that John Calvin—the theologian who inspired the same Reformed faith to which the people of Salem generally clung to so doggedly—was right in his reading of human nature as "corrupt and damnable" and "totally depraved."[31] Or, put another way, there is a strand of Christianity which states that even those who think they are doing right are bound to eventually do wrong. In this regard, the example of Salem is hard to refute.

Yet there is even further paradox, because those who tried to stop the trials or mitigate their effects *also* did so as a result of their Christian faith. From the lukewarm warnings of Increase Mather to the brave testimonies of Rebecca Nurse and John Proctor, even to the final decisive action of Sir William Phips—all acted, spoke, and were inspired by their Christianity as much as Cotton Mather or Abigail Williams or Samuel Parris were. Once again, we see the paradox of a faith capable of inspiring fear but also enormous bravery, of encouraging superstition and also of banishing it, of being the driver of a purer society and a part of a corrupting influence. Above all, perhaps, we see the paradox that faces any community seeking absolute purity: the purer they try to be, the more corruption they will inevitably find.

Site of the First Meeting House, Salem, Massachusetts, United States   239

. . .

Of course, it wasn't only in the New World that Christian communities found themselves concerned about keeping themselves holy and pure. It wasn't only witchcraft that presented itself as a representative of "the other" that threatened the integrity of the faith. And it wasn't just the purity of their own churches which have been long-standing matters of concern; Christians had been capable of constructing stories about those who were different from them for many years before the clear dividing lines of the Reformation were drawn.

In Lincolnshire, one of the sprawling, low counties of England's east coast, there are still places where they sing a very ancient, haunting folk song, which begins thus:

> The rain runs down through Merry Land town,
> The rivers swell and swell.[32]

Merry Land town is not a Never Never Land place, but rather the city of Lincoln itself. The ballad then goes on to tell a grisly story, terrifying even now, some 800 years after the events which inspired it. In the rain a group of young boys play with a ball until one of them knocks it over into the garden of some local Jews. One of the boys—Little Sir Hugh—goes to collect the ball but is enticed by a woman known as "The Jew's Daughter." She takes him to a quiet back room, binds his limbs, and bleeds the child to death before throwing his corpse down a well. The end of the ballad has Hugh trying to tell his mother where his body can be found and begging for a Christian funeral.

The song is not one easily forgotten: its central theme of a ritual killing of a child is disturbing enough, but its anti-Semitism, in a world where we know exactly where such sentiments can lead, is even more so. It becomes even more chilling when you realize that the death of Little Sir Hugh actually happened, that the narrative quickly arose about those responsible, and that it prompted one of the more chilling cycles of Christian zeal for societal purity ever to have taken place.

On August 29, 1255, the body of a young boy about eight years old, soon identified as one Hugh, who had gone missing a month or so

240 *Twelve Churches*

earlier, was fished out of a well in Lincoln. Very quickly, Hugh's death was blamed on the Jewish community: it was alleged that they had sacrificed Hugh by inviting other Jews to the town in order to witness an "insult and opprobrium against Jesus Christ" as they crucified the young boy and performed rituals with his blood.[33] The accusation was one of several that affected medieval Europe but England in particular. The Jewish presence in England began with the Norman Conquest, and the obvious outsider status of the Jewish people made them obvious targets for a population still tense and suspicious of foreign rule. The first accusations came in Norwich in the 1140s, with many that followed in cities with Jewish populations across the land. Invariably a child had actually been murdered but each of the communities, in their fear and in their desire to find a perpetrator who "fitted" the idea that such a horrific deed must have been perpetrated by someone outside the mainstream community, or, to make it more religiously explicit, that no Christian could have done such a horrific thing, blamed the Jews.

In previous cases, the authorities of the Church and state were initially very skeptical. Jewish contributions to the economy were essential for the functions of medieval kingship and local leaders, bishops included, were rightly fearful about large-scale social unrest among the majority peasant population. However, in the case of Hugh, a change occurred. A local Jew named Clopin confessed and the city's bishop considered his confession credible. The arrival of King Henry III in the city might have calmed the situation but instead made things worse: Henry's regime was heavily indebted to Jewish moneylenders and he was a king notoriously easily swayed. Soon, ninety members of the Jewish community were arrested, and a number of those hanged. Once again a community spiraled from one single traumatic event to a whole societal contortion, with much bloodshed on the way. And, once again, while such a panic is a mark of the darker side of human nature more generally, the specific horrors of the case would have been impossible without the particular beliefs and structures of Christianity.

Thirty-five years after the death of Sir Hugh, the entire Jewish community was expelled from England. The idea of those who were "other" being impure and therefore needing to be removed entirely had spread from a town reeling from a murder to a whole nation paralyzed by expensive wars. In the events of 1290, many Jews died, from those murdered in pogroms to those who killed themselves to those who were promised safe passage on a boat only to be led onto a sandbank to drown as the tide came in. The event was marked in Lincoln with a new shrine to the boy local people now called Little Saint Hugh. For the following two and a half centuries, people came there to pray and to worship, in part to ask for the purity of faith that they felt a child—and especially a murdered one—exhibited better than any other. Such sentiments seem perverse to us today, especially given that Hugh's death led not to justice but to more blood.

The Reformation marked the end of the cult of Little Sir Hugh, but the shrine's site remained undeveloped, a grim marker of memory which, as time moved and understanding of the horrors that such cycles of purity can bring changed, many would rather have forgotten. However, 700 years after the death of Hugh, and only ten years after the end of the conflict which saw anti-Semitism and an even darker, post-Christian drive for a society pure not in religious terms but in racial ones, the Dean of the cathedral ordered that a new plaque be placed over the site of the shrine of Little Sir Hugh. It read:

"Trumped up stories of 'ritual murders' of Christian boys by Jewish communities were common throughout Europe during the Middle Ages and even much later. These fictions cost many innocent Jews their lives. Lincoln had its own legend and the alleged victim was buried in the Cathedral in the year 1255. Such stories do not redound to the credit of Christendom, and so we pray:

Lord, forgive what we have been,
amend what we are,
and direct what we shall be."

Sometimes, attempts to drive purity have, albeit after many years and much horror, finally helped Christians see the truth which ought to be at the heart of their faith: that purity of heart is best achieved not by attempting to force external conformity on others, but by focusing on the failings which we exhibit ourselves.

242   *Twelve Churches*

• • •

This theological truth points to a wider historical one: that purity isn't only about the physical or societal demarcations or differences that define a community. Purity is a more complex thing in Christianity and perhaps the most serious disagreements—from the very start—were not about external matters of purity at all, but about purity of belief. Jesus in the Gospels is constantly fighting with those members of the Jewish establishment—in particular the sect of the Pharisees—who wanted to emphasize purity of outward action, such as keeping food and Sabbath laws and not mixing with sinners, as the most important aspect of faith. He routinely disparages them as "hypocrites."[34] For a whole chapter of Matthew's Gospel—the ninth one—he spends time with progressively less "pure" people in the sight of the Jewish law, from a man sick with palsy to a tax collector (Matthew himself), to a woman with menstrual hemorrhaging, to finally a man "possessed with a devil."[35] Throughout, the same point is made by Jesus: that it is faith that matters, not the external cleanliness or social status or health of the person involved.

In the very first two decades after Jesus, the debate raged. Initially, Peter and James, another disciple and probable blood relative of Jesus, sought to maintain Jewish purity standards, a battle in which they were opposed by Paul. Peter, however, changed his mind at some point before the Council of Jerusalem in 50 AD after receiving a vision in which a sheet covered in animals came down from Heaven and said, "What God has cleansed, do not call unclean."[36] It's gloriously trippy stuff, but critical in the history of Christian purity. Consequently, the root question for those who sought to follow Jesus in the centuries to come became a question of what were the limits of that faith? Where were its boundaries? The tale of Christian purity might well have taken twists and turns into very dark places—places like the Meeting House in Salem or the gallows in Lincoln—but the main thing Christians thought needed to be "pure" for much of their history was what they believed, not what they did.

More councils followed that of Jerusalem, all attempting to work out what proper Christian belief, and therefore purity of heart, was. Perhaps the most notable of these was the Council of Nicaea, in 325, which hosted fierce debates about who Jesus was and what his relation was with

Site of the First Meeting House, Salem, Massachusetts, United States   243

God the Father and with the Holy Spirit. One priest, Arius, advocated a concept of Jesus as being created by God and so not equal to the Father. In the end this was condemned by the Council as heretical and outside what it was possible for a real Christian to believe. Later chroniclers suggested that the person responsible for convincing the Council was our old friend St Nicholas of Myra, who slapped Arius on the face in order to try and hit the nonsense out of him.[37] As we know, violence and the quest for purity went hand in hand. Metaphor was a powerful weapon for those who sought to defend Christian purity, and when chroniclers, such as the Greek historian Socrates Scholasticus, heard that Arius had died after his bowels exploded, they could barely conceal their glee: here was a man who had spread theological shit while alive; now dead, he was covered in the physical stuff.[38]

While we might think of this as far-off stuff with no relevance to Christianity today, in reality, the process of seeking doctrinal purity has never ended. Even Anglicanism at the height of its nineteenth-century power, influence, and politeness had fierce fights over what was and wasn't real Christianity. Perhaps the most notable was the one involving Bishop Colenso of Natal in Southern Africa. Colenso had become Bishop of Natal in the Kingdom of the Zulus in 1853, after a fairly undistinguished career as a vicar in Norfolk. Having been appointed by the doughtily conservative Bishop Gray of Cape Town, he soon departed from his mentor's way of thinking. A year and a half after arriving in South Africa, he wrote his first controversial treatise, on the issue of polygamy. To say it was an area of tension between the Zulu people and the missionaries they were encountering, in some cases for the very first time, would be an understatement. Many missionaries sought to force apart Zulus who were in polygamous marriages and had converted; such a status was incompatible with being a Christian. Purity, once again, was at the forefront of Christian controversies.

After a year or so grappling with the issue, Colenso came to a different conclusion to his fellow Christians. He published a tract arguing that forcing the dissolution of such marriages would cause more pain, that in fact the more Christian thing would be to tolerate them.[39] The backlash was furious. Letters were written, articles published, Bishop

Gray in Cape Town began to get a sense of unease. More was to come; Colenso began debating with Zulu converts about whether their ancestors who couldn't have believed would be in Hell, about the nature of translating certain concepts into Zulu, about Biblical stories. Colenso published more, in particular on the Bible, which he had now come to believe contained some inaccuracies, or, to put it another way, was not purely true in a literal sense. His vast volume *The Pentateuch and the Book of Joshua Critically Examined* dealt with Biblical issues as varied as the etymology of some names which Colenso thought must be corruptions to the problem of the numbers of animals referenced at various points.[40]

The response was even more serious than the polygamy backlash. The poet Matthew Arnold mocked Colenso as "the supreme Pontiff of the Philistines."[41] Bishop Gray went one further and had him excommunicated and removed from his office as Bishop of Natal. Yet, the issues Colenso raised never went away; arguably, they went deeper even than just being questions for or of Christianity. As Church and state danced together, purity of doctrine became a social issue as well as one of conscience, as much a political demarcation as a religious one. Indeed, there are scholars who argue that Colenso represented a threat to the entire British Empire, as taking *him* seriously would have meant having to abandon the "underpinnings" of the whole project.[42] Even today, the question of whether the views of people in one corner of the Anglican Communion compromise the purity or integrity of people on the other side of it is a live issue, at once religious and political. While today the issues are more likely to be about homosexuality or the role of women, the fundamental drive for purity is the same.

There is a reason why, to understand purity in today's Christianity, it first is necessary to understand the effects of expansion and of faith under pressure. Inevitably, the bigger the faith got, the wider its borders and boundaries became and the more likely it was that the purity of the faith would be compromised. Tempting though it is to view Salem as a far-off exception, or Colenso as an outlier, the truth is that even today, purity of belief matters in Christianity and Christianity has transferred many of those preoccupations and that desire for purity to a secular world that has taken them on with gusto. It does not have to be in a claustrophobic meeting house in a Massachusetts village that such a cycle plays out. Now they can happen across whole continents, or over the internet, and all in the blink of an eye. It becomes very hard to judge those who are dead for their purity cycles when we are ourselves in the midst of our own.

Though, as an afterthought on poor Colenso, even very recently, his trial was continuing to cause controversy in South Africa. A diocesan report of 2004 asked the critical question "Can Colenso be re-tried?" For all the theoretical drives for purity, the answer was gloriously straightforward: "No, as he is dead a re-trial is not possible."[43]

For people of any faith, a focus on purity is not merely about moral superiority or a fussy attention to detail: if you believe that these matters pertain to God himself and, perhaps even more importantly, that the salvation of people depends on it, then you want to get things right. Acknowledging this also leads us to another tricky problem for any simplified narrative: that Christian purity is not just a simple tale of moral hypocrites taking their own failings out on people at the edge of society. As ever, it's more complicated than that, and always has been. Indeed, to return to Paul, in the same letters that instructed the early Church to cast out witches, he also informed them that they should "forbear one another, forgive one another."[44] A religion or any other belief set, for that matter, can be both absolutely egalitarian and welcoming and completely exclusive at the same time. Indeed, Christianity is and always has been necessarily both.

In some cases, the traditional understanding of Christianity as a calling to be against the world has won out in the midst of that paradox. Across the United States of America, evangelical Protestant Christianity has sought to promote "purity culture" among young people. As the world—or perhaps more explicitly, the state—has become less rigid in its policing of sexual morality, the refusal to engage with the "impure" sexual culture of the world becomes the main way in which a young Christian can mark themselves out as different. It is not just, of course, about faith. It speaks equally of the tensions inherent in the radical social changes of the twentieth century—those we saw in our visit to Mount

246   *Twelve Churches*

Athos—and to the tensions of a newish nation founded on the principles of "a shining city on a hill," as we saw at the Templo de las Américas. Even in this very tight and contrary world, however, there is room for what appears to be the sense of paradox. One of the figures held up as "the epitome of welcoming whiteness" and "a good Southern Christian girl" is the music artist Dolly Parton.[45] Yet, Parton is explicitly affirming of the gay community, has had hit songs about whorehouses, and had a stint as a feminist icon: she is, in short, one who contains "mountains of contradictions," yet she is still held up as a figure who epitomizes this culture, who is demonstrably "pure."

In others, however, the purity of Christianity is itself considered suspect by the morals which predominate today; even where those morals are largely or entirely informed by the teachings of Christianity itself. Multiple countries in the early 2000s—in particular Ireland and Australia—suffered from catastrophic revelations about priests who used their reputation for purity and for righteousness to commit appalling acts of sexual and physical abuse on those who were, according to Christ himself, the very purest of all: children. As more and more discoveries were made, and as it became clearer and clearer that the drive for purer morals was coming from outside the Church and not from within, more and more people began to see the Church's claims to be pure as hypocrisy at best, and as a cover for wickedness at worst. Between 2011 and 2022, the percentage of twenty-five to thirty-five-year-olds identifying as practicing Catholics in Ireland fell from 80% to under 5%.[46] It is less the case of the Church expelling the impure as envisioned by Paul and more the pure expelling the Church. The echoes of the above horrors are clear: the testimony of children and their harm being central to the events, the darkest aspects of human nature that they exposed, and the collapse in faith and trust which they engendered. Except, in this case, it wasn't conspiracy but reality and the quest for a purer, more honest Church resulted in the persecution not of the innocent but of the demonstrably guilty. For all the excesses of these historical examples, for all that we would want to sit here in judgment upon the villagers of Salem, and for as much as we would not put those of a contrary view to death, it is very hard to escape from the fact that for a faith or any other type of community to act in a way which honors—as per

Site of the First Meeting House, Salem, Massachusetts, United States   247

the direct command of Christ—the vulnerable, then certain barriers must be put in place, and certain exclusions of those who vaunt or threaten them have to happen.

Purity is not, therefore, necessarily always an unnatural or exclusionary urge in Christianity. There has to be a line, there have to be defining parameters, either of creed or of any of the other million ways in which human beings can and do seek to mark themselves out as different from others. And seeking purity is—or has been very often—an attempt to protect the vulnerable from evil.

Back to the Salem Meeting House, or rather the site of what was once the Salem Meeting House. The fact that it is now such a sleepy corner of suburbia, almost comatose in its respectability, tells us something, perhaps, about how purity is often an illusion. If we were to be able to enter the worshipping space that became the scene of such high drama, a paradox would still present itself. The interior was deliberately plain, the idea behind its design being that clutter or ornament distracted or corrupted the mind, drawing it away from the pure worship of God. In terms of Church buildings, if Salem tells us anything it is that the human mind doesn't need any external help when it comes to corruption, and that a place can be as pure and plain as it likes, but the darker side of human nature will always find a latch there. Indeed, we might go one further and say that a drive for purity in externals invariably drives these darker thoughts and instincts within, where they fester until bursting out in a paroxysm of retribution. Of course, while at this stage of our story we find ourselves in colonial America, it is inherent to the life of the Church everywhere, from medieval Lincoln to modern Ireland. Salem might have become synonymous with it, but there is a tension almost baked into Christianity and her churches. Indeed, this tension will always be present in the building of any community based on shared belief: between keeping the beliefs and practices that hold the community together coherently, while also welcoming in those from outside, and growing.

Christianity is just as likely to be seized upon and used to fulfill that dark human impulse to exclude and oppress the other as any other worldview. However, it is worth noting that for every Colenso, or Little Sir Hugh or Salem, there have been countless incidents—smaller, more personal, more *human*—when as a faith it has encouraged people to look honestly at their own failings in light of God and therefore welcome those who fall short of society's expectations of what is "pure." Christianity has in fact been remarkably successful at dealing with the tension, or rather embracing this paradox, that is inherent in all attempts at building a community of fellow believers. A faith that has at its heart the idea that God becomes man will necessarily have to be so. Perhaps in light of this, the last word should not go to Cotton Mather or Abigail Williams but to Dolly Parton. Parton perhaps best explained why, despite those well-publicized failings, Christianity has in fact been so effective at dealing with the paradox of purity on a human level: "If God can forgive, then we all should forgive."[47]

Chapter Ten

Christ Church, Zanzibar, Tanzania

(Built 1873 AD)

These attempts at enforcing purity, as we have seen, did not result in a smaller Christian faith but, if anything, an even bigger and broader one. As the Church emerged from the twin paroxysms of the Reformation and the great global expansion of Christianity, it found itself in uncharted waters. It was, in one sense, more powerful, of more global importance, and could claim more souls than ever before. Yet, as the eighteenth and nineteenth centuries progressed, its position faced greater threats than ever. Not only were there the issues of external persecution, both by other faiths and by secularism—the idea that the Church ought not to have *any* power—and the issue of vicious opposition between denominations, but also there were other major movements that began to make claims on aspects of society and common life that had previously been the presumed preserve of the Church. Perhaps preeminent among these, certainly in terms of claiming power over motivations and methods of both nations and individuals in a newly globalized world, was capitalism.

The Church had always had a complicated relationship with money. Despite early attempts, even at the height of its power as the arbiter of day-to-day life in Europe, it had never exerted the degree of control—even nominally—over money that it had managed over, for instance, sex. How people made money was obviously an ethical issue, fraught with potential mistreatments, and therefore of interest to the Church. However, it had often found hard cash to be an enemy—or at least a competitor—which was very hard to overcome when it came to claiming the loyalty of men. To explore how it was that the Church navigated these battles, especially in an age where capital seemed triumphant, we must make our way to Zanzibar and to a church built on the foundations of a market: the perfect symbol for the complex relationship between faith and profit which played out across the world as the eighteenth and nineteenth centuries progressed.

It was the Sunday before Pentecost 2024, and the then Archbishop of Canterbury squinted into the darkness. He is not an especially tall man, but even he had to stoop as he peered into the dank cellar. The basement of St Monica's Guest House in Zanzibar might seem to be a strange place for the Primate of All England, member of the House of Lords, senior non-royal in the order of precedence of Great Britain, et cetera, et cetera, to go on a foreign visit. He is, by nature of his office, used to engagement with things above, not things quite so literally below. The cellar is a room with a ceiling barely higher than five feet. Around its edge is a continuous slab of stone, while in its center is something of a trough. Tiny slits in its upper wall let in just the tiniest amount of light to see what went on there. What did go on there? Well, like many cellars, it was used for storage. Except what was stored here were not goods, but people. Or, rather, they were people who were considered to be goods. People who were bought and sold. Slaves.

The cellar was part of a wider complex of markets and stalls. By the mid-nineteenth century, Zanzibar was the largest slave market on the face of the planet. It is estimated that, by the end of the 1850s, 30,000 enslaved people were sold at Zanzibar every year. At any one time there were thought to be 200,000 enslaved people on the island.[1] Slavery maintained the profitability of the other industries—those of cloves and ivory. While it reached its peak in the late nineteenth century, as the economic demands of global trade reached their zenith and advancements in transportation made the mass marketing of human beings even more profitable, the trade in slaves at Zanzibar went back much further indeed. The island of Menuthias, or Menuthesias, was recorded by Greek traders as being due south from the Arabian gulf in the Periplus of the Arabian Sea.[2] *The Periplus of the Erythraean Sea*, a sort of guidebook for Greek traders from roughly the time of Christ, described the coastline as being the preserve of Arab pirates, men who would raid the coast for things to sell or use at their own desire. Things or people.[3]

Exactly 1,850 years later and the root cause of Zanzibar's wealth had not changed. It was still the case that thousands of Africans from the interior of what is now Tanzania would be shipped to that same island. There they would either be put to work or sold on for further demeaning, life-shortening labor. There were some differences from the time of the Ancient Greeks, though. Perhaps most crucial was that, by the heyday of the trade, the majority of the inhabitants belonged to the Islamic faith. Chattel slavery, the buying and selling of non-Muslims as slaves, was permitted by both the Qur'an and later Hadiths, the developmental traditions of Islam linked to Muhammed himself. There was, indisputably, less ambiguity than we will see was the case in Christianity. By the time of the nineteenth century, when Islam had become a political as much as a religious power, slavery, like most other practices which concerned interactions of Muslims and non-Muslims, was governed by a complex system of rules. Jews and Christians were regulated by the *dhimmi* system, which gave them limited rights in exchange for taxes. Indigenous Africans, considered pagan, however, had no rights whatsoever and could be bought, sold, raped, or killed, without any ramifications.[4]

By the nineteenth century, as other nations slowly abolished the trade in enslaved people, Zanzibar clung to the institution, its market becoming ever bigger and more profitable as it became more of a global anomaly. One of the central points of the market was perhaps the most terrible. At the complex's heart was a whipping post. It was a tall stump built into the ground to which enslaved people would be shackled and whipped until chunks of their flesh spattered the floor around. It had, by the late nineteenth century, become stained with blood. We cannot possibly know how many people were whipped into physical collapse there, nor how many died due to their treatment. The dehumanizing nature of the trade was such that it is almost impossible to find the names of those who were sold there. They exist in records merely as numbers, as sales figures, as profit.

There are some exceptions: in 1847, the British Royal Navy intercepted a slave ship coming across the Indian Ocean and, as per government orders in the Atlantic, seized the vessel. They took the people who had been sold as "cargo" to Bombay, where they were invited to give testimony about their ordeal. One, a young woman named Futaleh, related that she had been "playing in the garden one day when she was blinded, and dragged away into slavery." Her wish now was "to be free and return to her own country."[5] Given such testimony, it is easy to see why so many Victorians saw slavery as particularly symbolic of humanity's sin and departure from the Garden of Eden, and, by extension, that ending it was the work of God. However, while she was useful as a record of inhumanity for abolitionists, to view Futaleh as just a written record is its own form of inhumanity. The record we have relates her hopes, but not her fate. We will never know if Futaleh did get home. She has a voice briefly and then disappears into the anonymity of the past along with her fellow victims. Like their fates, whether any of these freed slaves passed through this specific cellar in Zanzibar is unknown.

Today, while that same cellar is preserved as a reminder of the past and her horrors, it is part of a very different complex indeed. Trade still happens on Zanzibar. You can wander around the narrow streets near to the center of Stone Town and still see that the hustle and bustle of the market is the dominant mode of human interaction there. Men with grins or grimaces will wave. The souk, selling everything from lobster pots to phone chargers, is still firmly present, as is the ancient spice market; but the slave market is gone. Its buildings have been repurposed. Slavery was abolished in Zanzibar in 1873, when the British representative, the imperial administrator Sir Bartle Frere, a man not now known for taking a "softly-softly" approach to anything, threatened the island's Sultan Sayyid Barghash bin Said al Bu-Said with a naval bombardment if he did not abolish the trade which had brought him so much of his wealth. Reluctantly, and mindful of British naval might, he agreed, although only if he got to sign a direct agreement with Queen Victoria herself. Much of the pressure for the British government to act in Zanzibar—a full forty years after they had abolished the trade in its own colonies—came from the Church, in particular the Scottish missionary Dr. Livingstone. He had initially favored an attempt to stop the trade "at source" by attempts to convert those who were enslaved in the interior, giving them *dhimmi* status and, in Livingstone's opinion, also having the beneficial side effect of saving their souls.

However, the nature of the climate, the difficulty of sourcing appropriate bases for missionary operations, and the general opposition of both the traders who controlled much of the navigation into the interior and many of the would-be converts themselves, meant that the scheme to focus attempts at evangelism was moved to Zanzibar.[6] Consequently, the group of enthusiastic young Christian men who made up the Universities Mission Society made their base on the island, and felt there was no better place to put their headquarters than on the site of the slave market itself. What had been a place of torture and lack of dignity became a place where humans would be called to the ultimate dignity: redemption itself. The idea of a "redeemer" comes from the era of the Roman slave market. It was a person who would buy a slave and then immediately free them, with no expectation of return or recompense. St Paul, in his letter to the Colossian church, explains that this is the model which Christ offers too. A freedom from our sins at a price paid entirely by him, leading us, and the whole universe, into reconciliation with God their creator.[7] What stands where once people had been bought and sold is the Cathedral Church of Christ, Zanzibar, and there is preached redemption, of both bodies and souls.

The presence of the cathedral in the middle of a market, and a former slave market at that, raises a number of questions: How did Christianity treat the issue of slavery, how does it treat the making of money more generally, and the question of whether anyone ever did find a way to serve both God and Mammon? Though to find the answers to those questions, we will need to travel from Zanzibar to places as diverse as the Caribbean, Alexandria, Liverpool, and Monte Carlo; for all the incongruity of its location, Christ Church, Zanzibar, goes some way to telling the story of how Christianity and profit came to coexist.

It might seem strange that an Anglican cathedral would lie at the heart of a predominantly Muslim island. The Bishop of Oxford, one Samuel Wilberforce, the son of William, whom we will encounter later, said that the Anglican presence on Zanzibar rather than the mainland was a failure. The choice of a place that had a proven record of bending to the threat of British naval power suggested there was some justice in the criticisms by the Roman Catholic Church that "The Church of England could only maintain missions . . . [where] they rest on the basis of English national power."[8] Or, put another way, however morally correct the decision to abolish slavery in Zanzibar might have been, if the Church's presence there was merely as a front for a different form of profiteering, that of British imperial and commercial interests, then it was a hollow victory indeed.

Others disagreed; to many in Britain and further afield the presence of a cathedral in place of a slave market was an undeniable good and for all the contradiction of a majority Islamic island hosting an Anglican bishop or of Christianity only being able to abolish slavery by its marriage to the geopolitical machinations of a superpower, it was still a moral good that had been done. The German philosopher Friedrich Schelling, who, along with Hegel shaped much of the thinking at the forefront of the Western elite of the nineteenth century, perhaps best summed up this mode of thinking when he wrote that "contradiction is the engine of life ... without it truly nothing would want to stir itself."[9] Construction was begun on the embodiment of that contradiction at Christmas 1873 and was completed six years later.

The building is a putting into stone of all the seemingly paradoxical truths that brought it into existence. To call it a mismatch of styles is an understatement—it is part Tyrolean tower, part Byzantine cistern, and part Moorish warehouse. Its scale cannot be denied; even today this architectural oddball rises imperiously in its orange coral stone over the little whitewashed houses that make up most of the architecture of Stone Town. Its interior, a reservoir of marble-cooled air in the midst of the heat of outside, could be that of a college chapel at Oxford, a very Church of England–style mix of whitewash and heavy wood. Today its chessboard floors and wooden columns re-echo with translations of Archbishop Cranmer's words of Common Prayer in Swahili, while hymns by stern Victorian public schoolmasters are given new leases of life and energy as they are sung with an energy rarely seen in English country churches. It sort of epitomizes some of the contrasts that are inherent both to the peculiar branch of Christianity that is Anglicanism, and to the faith more widely.

By contrast to its very English-style interior, the Moorish design of the outside was, in part, an attempt to fit into the architectural milieu of the island and to minimize further offending the Sultan who had so reluctantly acceded to British demands. The tower was built to be just a few feet shorter than the clock tower on the sultan's palace, as a show of building-based deference that belied the real relationship between local potentate and imperial hegemon. However, the tower remains taller than that of the minaret of the mosque nearby. The Moorish design was also, in its own way, a show of triumph. Here was the architecture of the slave market and of the slave marketeers, co-opted into a building antithetical both to their Islamic faith and to the practice which had made them rich. It was significant that St Monica's guesthouse was built in the same style. The guesthouse was linked to the cathedral as a place where new Christians could be housed and looked after. Its design was, if anything, even more Moorish, and in its cellars, of course, were the hellish quarters where once enslaved people had been kept. It went from being a place of horror to one where, in theory at least, its residents were treated with dignity, all inspired by the faith. The naming after St Monica was deliberate: it had been she who prayed for the conversion of her wayward son Augustine to convert from his self-centered ways. She epitomizes the belief that nobody was beyond redemption. Literally anything—and anyone—could be converted to the glory of God, was the message. Nothing was beyond the redemptive power of the cross.

Bishop Steere, under whose auspices the construction was completed, intended the cathedral to be "a monument to the triumph of faith over human suffering."[10] The site of that very same whipping post, the center of the marker where such horrors had been perpetrated, became the site on which the high altar was placed, the focal point of reconciliation. The most potent symbol of the market's inhumanity in the pursuit of profit was replaced by the most sacred location where, Christians believe, humanity is transfigured as to become partakers of the Divine. Where once physical flesh and blood had been traded for profit, now the spiritual flesh and blood of a living God who, in the words of St Paul, "took on the form of a slave," was handed out to all who came, for free.[11]

Despite its location, Christ Church, Zanzibar, is not defined exclusively by slavery. Indeed, it defies attempts to do so. Worship is at the heart of what it does—Sunday services begin at 6:30 a.m. and continue into the early afternoon. The current Bishop, Michael Hafidh, is a whirlwind of activity. A particular ministry of the cathedral is to bring together the island of Zanzibar's diverse communities to find "the common ground for peace."[12] The violence that plagues the election cycle in Tanzania, and on Zanzibar in particular, is something that the Cathedral is eager to put a stop to. Tourists—and Archbishops—might come and go to see relics of the past, but it is the building up of the future which concerns the church and its people at Christ Church today. Once again—as we saw in Canterbury, in Rome, and in Japan—there is something about the pains of the past which give a healing power to a particular place in the present.

Yet, for all the powerful symbolism of Christ Church, the story of the Church and the concept of profit is a more complicated one than its story suggests. Indeed, while its symbolic location tells a compelling story, there is perhaps more truth in its confusing architectural execution than there is in its symbolic planning. The physical structure of Christ Church speaks of tension as much as it speaks of hope. That is perhaps a good thing. Justin Welby, the Archbishop who visited it, chose to do so in the wake of the disruptions of the early 2020s, as Western institutions began to take a long and difficult look at their past engagement with various practices, slavery in particular. When asked what he had felt when entering the cellar underneath the church, the Archbishop wrote that he was "grieved." It is an interesting choice of word, speaking of sadness and regret, of a sort of emotional pain and of loss; Welby is not known for the profundity of his public statements but this was perhaps an exception, a well-chosen word. A word indicative of the complexities of the relationship between the institution of the Church and the practice of slavery.

At the time of the New Testament, slavery was a commercial and social reality. Biblical Christianity appeared to accept it as not even a moral issue but as a simple fact. In both Luke and Matthew, Jesus is approached by a Roman Centurion who asks him to heal his servant. In fact, the word used in Greek is δοῦλοσ (*doulos*), which means "the one who is bound," that is to say someone who is not free, a slave.[13] Interestingly, Matthew's telling of the same story uses a different word. The Centurion in Matthew speaks of his παίς (*pais*) being ill. While it is a word that can mean slave, it means it in a different way, as one who is dependent on or devoted to a master. It can be used for a young man or teenage child. It can also be used—reflecting the realities of homosexuality in the Greek world—to the passive partner in a male-male sexual relationship.

Regardless of the relationship, Jesus heals without judgment of it indeed seems to imply that the Centurion's relationship with this man, as well as his Gentile status and position in Rome, are irrelevant, providing he has faith. It is illustrative of just how complex Biblical morality is—and how poorly it fits into the neat battle lines of modernity, despite having been instrumental in shaping them—that the same story can be used both to suggest Jesus's support for gay couples and for the institution of slavery, all hanging on just one, possibly synonymous, word.

The Gospels are not alone in this sense of confusion. Alongside the Old Testament seeming to give clear regulatory instructions about the proper conduct of slavery in Exodus—implying that while it needs rules, it is not, according to the Bible, wrong in itself—there is a whole book of the New Testament which, while having the issue of slavery and the result of its dynamics for Christianity at its very center, manages to skirt any real moral judgment of the issue at all.[14] At some point in the middle of the first century AD, a man called Philemon's slave—whose name was Onesimus—had run away and converted to Christianity. Philemon, too, became a Christian, both men, it seems, affected by the preaching and teaching of the Apostle Paul. Paul, in light of Onesimus's skill as a minister, wrote to Philemon to ask that his former slave be forgiven his debts. But—crucially—if Philemon doesn't agree, Paul appears to be prepared to send Onesimus back to him.

It is indisputably one of the strangest books in the Bible. Paul writes in a way that is at once deeply personal and yet also oddly distant. More than that, it appears to directly contradict much of his teaching elsewhere. For instance, in 1 Corinthians 12, Paul suggests that baptism overrides the master-slave relationship, saying that "by one spirit were all baptized . . . whether bond or free."[15] Perhaps even more significantly he goes on to say that all Christians are "members of the same body" and cannot disassociate from one another: "if one member suffers, all members suffer."[16] Paul's use of fleshly metaphor throughout has led some scholars to suggest that Onesimus was in fact a younger brother of Philemon.[17] As with the Gospels, we have the same issue as we did with the Centurion's servant; those tricky words again.

While Paul appears to deliberately subvert the concept of ownership, by reminding Philemon that "thou owest unto me even thine own self besides," i.e. his new spiritual identity came about through Paul and so he owes him something, there is still an indisputable ambiguity in the text.[18] This lack of consistency seems to be, well, consistent. In the first epistle of Timothy—though his authorship of this text is disputed—Paul seems to suggest that those who had been enslaved should obey their masters. Yet this is in apparent contradiction of his line that there is no "slave or free" in his letter to the Galatians. In truth, Paul's teaching, rather like that of Christ, was never totally clear. As any good wheeler-dealer knows, where words are uncertain, then a profit can be made.

Alongside words, there has, of course, been practice. Many Christians did see the lack of absolute clarity as a chance to make a profit. Interestingly, the early history of Christian Europe, from the end of and immediately after the fall of the Roman Empire until the late Middle Ages, was "almost unique in the history of civilization" in lacking a "large scale slaving system."[19] This was due to a combination of factors. Firstly, much of Europe, where Christianity found its most considerable demographic success in this period, lacked both consistent contact with the rest of the world, as was the case in, say, Asia Minor or the African coasts of the Indian Ocean, where Christ Church, Zanzibar, now stands, and lacked the technological advances and unified military might possessed by the Islamic powers. Secondly, the dominance of Christianity, and an understanding of both Christ's command to "love thy neighbor" and Paul's instructions that the body of those of the same faith functioned as one, meant that it became impossible within the moral code of medieval Europe to enslave people who looked and, crucially, believed the same as you, and practical limitations meant it was impractical to enslave anyone else.

However, the lure of profit was great, and as the era of exploration led to European territorial expansion into America and commercial expansion into Africa, a new dynamic emerged in the slave trading done by

Christians. The Americas were a vast expanse, requiring economic development. Much of the population, already sparser than that of Europe, had died from the cruel treatment of the colonizers or from encounters with "Old World" diseases for which their immune systems were not prepared. Africa, by contrast, was a populous continent, with a very well-established Arab Muslim and pagan sub-Saharan slave trade—to which the age of Zanzibar's market bears witness. To good Christians from Europe eager to make money in the New World, the solution was simple: the "triangle trade"—which shipped enslaved labor from Africa to the Americas and then shipped the goods produced by that labor back to Europe, from whence the profits were used, in part, to buy more slaves.

Of course, aside from the obvious moral reprehensibility of this to us today and as well as its logistical issues, which led to infamous mistreatment of people on the dangerous transatlantic voyage, this "solution" presented a theological problem as well. Christianity did not, in theory, distinguish according to race and nothing in the Gospels prevented those who were enslaved from converting to the faith of those who had bought or sold them. Indeed, many of the enslaved people, when confronted with the horrors of the Caribbean plantations, like the first, freed worshippers in Christ Church, Zanzibar, found solace in a religion which ostensibly told stories of freedom from slavery: from the Israelites in Egypt to the promises of Christ that those who had little in this life would be rewarded in the next. The apparent contradiction was an obvious one: the people who whipped and mistreated them, who profited so enormously from their labor, who acted in every way as if these men and women were not men and women at all but goods and objects, claimed to believe exactly the same thing.

Justifying this required a series of contortions and theological acrobatics. Some clergy, such as the Scottish minister the Reverend John Wemyss, turned to the Bible to justify slavery. Wemyss made reference to the Book of Genesis, and the long-standing idea that Noah's three sons represented the inhabitants of the three "Old World" continents of Europe, Asia, and Africa. He wrote that the descendants of Noah's son Ham—associated with Africa—were accursed throughout all generations due to Ham's exposure of his father's naked and drunken body to public ridicule in Genesis. Noah, in his rage, had cursed Ham's children: "a servant of servants shall he be to his brethren."[20] To Wemyss, the link was obvious and immutable: "we see today that the Moors, Ham's posterity, are sold like slaves yet."[21] Often the Christianization of enslaved people was framed as a moral good: that these were new Christians who required order and control, in the way that children required it. Perhaps tellingly, similar arguments were employed to suggest the inferiority of women and the necessity of marriage: in short, God had instituted a hierarchy and slavery was a proper part of it.[22]

Many Christians, however, simply went along with it because it was a societal norm. In towns like Bristol and Liverpool, Amsterdam, and Bordeaux, where millions were made by investment in the trade, pious men who had become wealthy from it often sought to do good with their money. Churches were adorned and beautified, built and endowed with the money. It was in part in acknowledgment of this legacy that Justin Welby made his visit to that dank and grim cellar beneath Christ Church in Zanzibar. The Church, both in its buildings and its institutional wealth had—in the words of one Black British priest—"benefited in ways clearly visible today from the capture, enslavement, rape, murder, torture, sale, demoralization, and forced free labor of sacred Black bodies."[23]

It begs the question of what easy and lazy moral norms are acquiesced to by many Christians today that will be viewed with horror in the future?

Yet, as Christ Church, Zanzibar, tells us by its very bricks and mortar, the story of Christianity and slavery was and is not a simple tale of evil hypocrites, of fairy-tale goodies and baddies. While there can be no doubt that Christianity was used to justify the trade, it was also by Christianity that the greatest blows were struck against it.

In his autobiography, a crucial text in the efforts to abolish slavery that grew in vigor toward the end of the eighteenth century, the freed slave Olaudah Equiano wrote of an encounter with an elderly enslaved man on the island of Montserrat. The man, advanced in years, described how even his smallest joy, that of fishing, was robbed from him by the injustice of slavery as his master or other whites would simply take any fish he caught. Looking to people to do what was right had become an impossibility and so, he told Equiano, "I must look up to God Mighty in the top for right."[24] He was not alone in this sense that the solution to what seemed like an endless cycle of injustice lay beyond the earthly realm. The instincts of an old man on the shores of the Caribbean, tired of trying appeals to human justice, were very close to those of a very different man, who lived in the leafy suburbs of south London.

William Wilberforce was a devout man; however, he had not always been thus. His conversion to Christianity—what he called his "great change"—had occurred when he was a drinking and womanizing young Member of Parliament who was expected to go far by conforming to all of the political practices and petty corruptions of the time.[25] However, Wilberforce abandoned that life and came to believe wholeheartedly in the divinity of Christ and the truth of the Christian message. One of the most influential men he met in bringing about this change was an old and grizzled priest who served in what were then the narrow and bustling streets of the City of London. John Newton had begun his career not as a cleric but as a slave trader and—briefly—a slave himself.

Newton had been born in London in 1725 and apprenticed to his father, a merchant who had operations between London and Venice. After a period when he was forced into the service of the Royal Navy, Newton sailed several African voyages, taking advantage of the network of trade in humans which stretched from the whitewashed market of Zanzibar in the east to the coasts of Ghana in the west. However, his fiery temper, irritable nature, and obsessive energy—the combination of which had earned him several floggings in the Navy—made him a supremely annoying colleague. Finally fed up with him, the crew of the slave ship *Pegasus* left him with a slave trader in what is now Sierra Leone, and so the former slave trader became a slave himself. His father sent a ship after him and, in 1748, he was rescued and returned home in the trading ship *Greyhound*. On his way back to Britain, the ship encountered a storm; in it, Newton prayed for deliverance and felt compelled to cry the word "mercy."

It was as if he unlocked something. The cry for mercy made Newton

264 *Twelve Churches*

question where he thought mercy would come from, and whom that mercy was for. The answer he came to was God in Christ. The famous words he wrote in 1772 perhaps best described his conversion—and those of many Christians before and since:

Amazing grace! how sweet the sound,
That saved a wretch; like me!
I once was lost, but now am found,
Was blind, but now I see.

In later years, however, Newton would say that his "real" conversion didn't happen until later when he began to ask himself what the consequences of such mercy were for his own behavior. If mercy was shown to him, what did that mean for others, in particular those whom he had bought and sold? After many years of silence on the topic of his past employment, Newton turned all of his single-mindedness and, frankly, irritating obsessive tendencies to one particular purpose. In a sermon he announced that "it is no small trial for the people of God to live where wickedness prevails."[26] For Newton, righting the wrongs of the world was something that was inherent to being a Christian, to becoming, as he put it in one sermon, "one who has the Lord as his portion."[27] And for him, the greatest wrong currently evident in the world was the practice that he had once been such an enthusiastic proponent of: the buying and selling of human beings.

The old slaver-turned-priest made an impression on the young MP. From the mid-1780s Wilberforce decided that God had given him a specific purpose: to abolish the slave trade. As with so many of the changes we have seen wrought by Christianity, there wasn't a dramatic moment that triggered this, but simply a slow and growing conviction that this was the will of God. This is critical in understanding the process that led to the construction of Christ Church, Zanzibar: for Wilberforce, the abolition of slavery wasn't to do with being nice; it was nothing less than the direct divine command of Almighty God. It was a matter of insult to the Christian that men and women were enslaved when, in fact, the God that he believed in had, through the moral trajectory of the Bible, shown that the poor and dispossessed, "instead of being an inferior order in the creation, are even the preferable objects of the love of the Almighty?"[28]

As we have seen throughout, the history of Christian social engagement—from sex on Athos to faith in Japan to the cellar of Christ Church, Zanzibar—is never the story of one or two "great men." The great thing Christianity can teach history is the infinite importance of the ordinary. There were plenty of ordinary Christians who supported Newton and Wilberforce in their campaign. One such woman was Mary Prince. Mary's mother was a household slave and her father a saw operator. When her mother's owner ran into financial difficulties, she was separated from her family and sold. The descriptions of her life as slave, published in the midst of the debates of the 1820s and 1830s, proved critical in persuading people of the realities of slavery. One particular incident rightly horrified her readers.

Hetty, her sole friend in her new lodgings, was a support. One day, however, when she was heavily pregnant, Hetty tied up a cow in a way which allowed the animal to escape. Mary related what happened next. The detail is both horrific and heartbreaking:

"My master flew into a terrible passion and ordered the poor creature to be stripped quite naked, notwithstanding her pregnancy, and to be tied to a tree in the yard. He then flogged her, as hard as he could . . . till she was all over streaming with blood. He rested and then beat her again and again. Her shrieks were terrible. The consequence was that poor Hetty was delivered of a dead child . . . Ere long her body and limbs swelled to a great size; and she lay on a mat in the kitchen till the water burst out of her body and she died. All the slaves said that death was a good thing for poor Hetty."[29]

In the conclusion of her book, Mary—who had since been freed and come to Britain—pointed out the fundamental theological challenge that supporters of slavery consistently could not answer: How could those who were involved in slavery be so manifestly evil while purporting to believe in God? As Mary observed, "since I have been here, I have often wondered how English people can go out to the West Indies and act in such a beastly manner. When they go to the West Indies they forget God."[30] How could men and women who believed in a God of love, a God of the poor and dispossessed, who believed in Christ, beat a pregnant woman to death and how could that death, appalling though it was, be considered preferable by her fellow victims of enslavement to their lives. The truth was beginning to dawn on Christians in the West that the quest for profit had led to a woeful dehumanizing of people who were made in the image of God. This was a direct contravention of their faith, the means of their salvation. The stated beliefs and the commercial practices could not exist together. One—as symbolized by Christ Church, Zanzibar, itself—would have to win, and be built on the ruins of the other.

All these forces and remarkable people combined and, in 1807, slavery was abolished in Britain. More importantly, in 1833, an act was passed in the British Parliament to abolish slave trading across the British Empire. This was the very legislation which sealed the fate of the slave market in far-off Zanzibar some forty years later and spurred on abolitionist movements across the world, in particular in the United States, where it would take a war to achieve Wilberforce's aims. The bill passed in Parliament on July 22. A week later, Wilberforce, having finally achieved his aim, died, exhausted. His final affirmation was that he hoped that he had his feet set upon the rock of the Christian faith. Few now would dispute that he did.

Few places speak of the interwoven, complex human nature of that history better than Liverpool Parish Church, just around the corner from where Newton had lived. It acts as a sort of mirror on the other side of the world to Christ Church, Zanzibar. Much of its splendor was financed by slaves. It was destroyed in the Second World War, when Britain used up much of the power and treasure it had accrued over the previous century to fight the threat of Fascist Germany. One of the casualties was the Georgian parish church, its memorials to prominent slave traders mashed into dust by high tonnage explosives dropped by similarly supposedly civilized men from the air above. Today, in the area around the church, though there are a couple of headstones whose fragments make up the boundary wall, just one memorial to an individual remains in the main body of the churchyard: that of a man called Abel.[31] Abel, the first recorded Black resident of Liverpool, was a slave of Mr. Rock.

Abel was named for the wronged sibling of Cain in Genesis. When it becomes clear that Cain has killed Abel, God asks him where he is. Cain replies, "Am I my brother's keeper?"[32] It is a question that has haunted Christians ever since: How are they to treat their fellow man, their brothers and sisters made by the same God? That the same faith might both justify the appalling mistreatment of others and inspire their liberation remains one of its great paradoxes. Yet paradoxes make up Christianity. To go to the beating heart of the transatlantic slave trade and see the simple stone to Abel, one of its victims, and nobody else, is a paradox too, and yet one that is impossible without the particular power of Christianity. Abel's stone, like the cellar in Christ Church, Zanzibar, is a sermon in itself and a vindication of all those who, like the old slave in Montserrat, "look up to God Mighty in the top for right."

Of course, selling fellow human beings for money is perhaps the most extreme manifestation of prioritizing profit over the commands of God. As we have seen, plenty of other things were sold, and continue to be sold, at the market next to Christ Church, Zanzibar. If even the slave trade had its defenders from a theological perspective, it is no surprise that, throughout the history of the Church, the question of what to do with wealth, of the morality of profit full stop, has been an area of major contention. Slavery was only one part of the Church's wider struggle over what to do with human relationships which were defined not by the laws of God but by the structures of the market. Christ Church, Zanzibar, symbolizes this relationship with profit as much as it does with slavery. Today, church and market nestle in close quarters, having made an uneasy truce for the sake of that great priority of the current bishop: peace. However, Christianity's complex relationship with money goes back even further—to Christ himself.

Of the thirty-eight parables Jesus told across the four Gospels, sixteen of them involve teaching his followers about how they ought to use money. Of the social or moral issues which feature in his teaching, this is by far the largest number, considerably more than, say, sex or violence. It is perhaps because money is so obviously a worldly thing, a thing made up by humanity and therefore innately prone to misuse. Sex and violence might be seen as innate, primal stirrings from within; but money is by its very nature a placeholder for goods or services. Necessary it may well be, but it still puts it in a different, perhaps more complicated category than some of the aspects of faith and existence with which we have dealt so far. It's no surprise, then, that often Christianity has found dealing with it complicated as well.

Jesus's teaching seems to reflect a certain sense of money being the concern of other people and not really something a Christian should pay too much attention to: when challenged about the morality of paying tax, Christ famously asked to see a coin and asked whose head was on it. When receiving the coin, he famously proclaims, "Render unto Caesar the things that are Caesar's; and to God the things that are God's."[33] Indeed, this is even clearer when he commands his followers not to lay up treasure on earth, proclaiming that it is impossible to "serve both God and Mammon."[34] The question of who or what Mammon is remains fraught—the Greek used μαμωνᾶς (*mammonas*), which is thought to be a corruption of the name of a Syrian god of wealth or profit.[35] Regardless of who or what Mammon actually was in the ancient world, it has come to be a personification of profit, of a human desire for money and wealth, and, specifically, pursuit of it has come to be seen as antithetical to the Christian calling. Yet, Jesus, in perhaps his most famous saying on wealth, left what might generously be called "wiggle room": many people know the saying that "it is easier for a camel to go through the eye of a needle than a rich man to enter into the Kingdom of God." Few remember that, immediately afterwards, Jesus proclaims that "with men this is impossible, but with God, all things are possible."[36]

The earliest followers of Jesus appear to have taken his teachings literally. The very first description of the Church in the era after Jesus describes his followers as selling all their possessions and giving to each person according to their need with the goods of the community held in common.[37] Yet, as we already know, courtesy of Philemon and Onesimus, the early Church seemed to be ambivalent on the issue of buying and selling people. We also know that, while some might have lived in proto-communes, there were also plenty of polite and profitable business people in early Christian communities. One such figure was the remarkable Lydia.

Christ Church, Zanzibar, Tanzania 269

In the Book of Acts, Lydia, having been baptized along with all her household, invites Paul to make her (presumably sizeable) house in Philippi the base of his operations.[38] She had made her money selling purple fabric, the most desirable clothing for the Roman ruling classes. It was a business which would have required "a great deal of capital" due to the import costs and raw materials involved.[39] After all, purple was worn by the elite for a reason: it was eye-wateringly expensive. The presence of Lydia at the heart of the Church in Philippi is a bit like having a supplier of Gucci handbags as a lead figure in a small Christian community today. Modern analogies aside, what Lydia's presence shows is not only that women played a part in early Christian communities, but, perhaps more awkwardly, people who were filthy rich did too.

As Christianity spread to more and more people, the need to reconcile profit and faith became ever more practically important. One thinker of the early Church decided to address the matter head-on. Clement of Alexandria was a theologian of the late second century who, among titles like his "Exhortation to the Heathen," wrote a whole essay on the question of "Who is the Rich Man who may be saved?" His conclusion was, like much of Clement's other writing—in which he recommends the joys of moderate alcohol consumption and suggests men and women should be treated equally—is delightfully measured. Clement makes clear that while money can corrupt a person's soul, riches that might be used for good should not be "thrown away."[40] What goes with us, Clement says, at the end of all things, when we are made one with God, are not our riches, but love.[41] The amount of love a person displayed was, then, considerably more important than the amount of money they had. A sentiment, one suspects, Lydia, William Wilberforce, and Bishop Steere of Zanzibar would have willingly gotten behind.

Yet Clement did not have the final word and the paradoxical relationship between worldly profit and divine poverty carried on throughout Christian history. Sometimes it was embodied in one person. We first encountered St Francis of Assisi at Bethlehem, as a sheep impersonator and crib enthusiast. However, in contrast to his later simplicity, Francis began life as a very wealthy young man indeed. Yet, he found that wealth weighed heavily on his soul. Eventually he took a vow of extreme poverty. His father—who had made enormous profit as a successful merchant and so was, like many rich people, used to getting his own way—was unimpressed and sought to force young Francis back into his sybaritic existence. During a showdown in the main square of Assisi, the young man stripped off the finery his father had bought for him until he was completely naked—"not even keeping his underpants on," his admiring biographer rather breathlessly tells us.[42] Public nudity proved the final straw, and Francis went from being one of the gilded youth of medieval Italy to being, to this day, a byword for earthly poverty taken on to prove a heavenly point.

So, the tussle continued, or rather continues. If we think back to all the beauty we encountered in Renaissance Rome, such adornments were only possible by the generosity of wealthy individuals. While there were churches decorated by profit made in slavery, there were many more which were beautified by the profits of farming or wool or metalwork or any of the million other ways humans have found to make money. Wealthy Christians endowed hospitals and orphanages and housing for those who had none. They did so both because of their wealth and because of their faith. To suggest that the two are irreconcilable seems to fly in the face of reality.

Of course, even without the gifts to the poor or the beautification of churches or the funding of missions or priests, the idea that all of the ordinary Christians who turn a modest profit in a small business, or even those who are involved in making vast sums of money for themselves or others, cannot then live in a way which reflects the love of Christ is one almost all Christians would reject. As with its reconciliation to political power, it wouldn't have had a great deal of longevity as a faith if it hadn't made peace with the idea that making money wasn't an absolute moral evil.

Indeed, there are those who argue that current capitalism owes much to Christianity. From the labor-saving devices of the Cistercian monks during the agricultural expansions of the Middle Ages to Max Weber's idea of the "Protestant work ethic" creating the conditions necessary for modern capital to flourish, there are plenty of arguments which suggest that Christianity, far from being a bar to economic development, was essential to it.[43] In fact, if Christ Church, Zanzibar, shows anything, as per the fears of the Bishop of Oxford, it is that Christianity and capital did often go hand in hand, and in some cases, that replaced much wickeder systems of the past. It isn't only a question of bricks and mortar. Beyond the confines of the coral decorations of Christ Church, that clear demonstration of the complexities of this relationship, there are plenty of Christians living within the theoretical structures made by that search for profit today. I went to visit some of them.

"I've become something of a Mediterranean driver," Father Hugh Bearn said to me with a smile, as he weaved the car dangerously close to the path of a lorry filled with articulated concrete. The roads to Monte Carlo are winding ones, and the drivers are people who are used to getting their way. It might seem a very long way from the cry of the traders in the market by Christ Church, Zanzibar, but very few places are as dominated by profit as Monaco. I am there to see how profit and faith might intersect in a modern world. In Monte Carlo, money drips from every inch of the pavements, cars worth many multiples of the average suburban house sit in sun-drenched traffic jams, and then, in the harbor, super yachts float for days upon end as their billionaire owners pass the time as only the super-rich can. It is a whole sovereign state whose purpose it is to give shelter to and celebrate those who have made the acquisition of profit their primary, perhaps their sole, motivating force of their lives.

In the midst of all the glitz and the ostentation, Father Hugh and his wife and sons are a little island of normality. Welcoming, hospitable to all, and, above all else, remarkably unfazed by what is around them. When we arrive, Father Hugh is not keen to show me the Ferraris parked outside the Anglican church on the Avenue de Grande-Bretagne, but instead rushes me to see his pristine collection of first-edition Tintin comic books. In such an environment it must be hard to be a priest; to serve God in the global capital of Mammon. Yet there is much need for Father Hugh. People with what appears to be endless money are, if anything, most at risk from the dehumanizing effects of profit and from the unreal world that it creates. Or, put another way, to paraphrase both Paul McCartney and St Clement of Alexandria—"money can't buy anyone love."

I asked Father Hugh what it was like ministering in such a place, a state where Mammon seemed to have won. What were the people like? What was it he could bring to those who have everything? "People are complicated everywhere," he told me with a smile; "each one a mix of wheat and tares." I met Father Hugh's people. And they were a mix: of those who were enormously wealthy and those who were not, those who were playing at being part of the strange world of Monaco, and those who were pretending not to be part of it. Of all those whom I met, none were evil because they had, or affected to have, money. All of them wanted to be reminded of the love of that same God and, I think, to be reminded that all that was around them would one day pass away, but that that same love would remain. That, it seemed, was Father Hugh's job. And very good at it he was too.

One lady I met in the oasis-like aisles of shade in the church in Monte Carlo was particularly concerned about the issue of modern slavery. She detailed how she gave to efforts to stamp it out accordingly. She told me of its perpetuation even in places that seemed to be glittering and perfect—Monaco's fellow micro states in the Gulf, for instance. Slavery, far from being a thing of the past, was even, she told me, present in London. The place from which the visionaries went to build Christ Church, Zanzibar, was itself now a hotbed of enslavement. Father Hugh related the story he had been told by a migrant worker just a few days before of a whole group of enslaved people operating in a business near to where I lived in London. It is more common there than the advocates for that city as a beacon of tolerance would care to admit—from porters in curry houses to builders of private homes: even today, in the city of Wilberforce himself, there are people bought and sold and treated merely as things from which a profit might be made, rather than as beloved children of God.[44] It was strange to be reminded in Monte Carlo of Zanzibar. Both seem to be Neverlands—beautiful and unreal in their own ways. Both are places where money has obscured the Christian teaching of the status of each person as a child of God, equally beloved. Both ostensibly are places where those who serve Mammon seem or seemed to have won. Yet both also hide pain and a need for that most important—and unpurchasable—building block of human dignity: love.

Most importantly of all, both, in the forms of Father Hugh and in Christ Church, have reminders of that love.

Let us return to Zanzibar, and to that strange building rising out of the bustle of the market there. For all of the fact that it represents a clumsy metaphor or sometimes misplaced efforts at speaking of the love of God, Christ Church remains an important building. Indeed, as our journey throughout Christianity's tumultuous relationship with profit has shown us, it is a representation of the complexities and nuances of the strange interplay between profit and faith that has so shaped both capitalism and Christianity over the last two centuries. As we saw with sex, violence, and nationhood in earlier ages, the era when Christianity sought accommodation with the power of profit was not a simplistic morality tale, but a complex process by which our very understanding of both was changed.

Yet, for all of the clumsiness of the church in the slave market as a metaphor for that complexity, I—nor, I suspect, anyone else who has been to Christ Church—would want to say that it is not a powerful building. It is still a building that speaks. It reminds us of those who did speak out against the slave trade and it reminds us of those who still suffer under slavery today. It reminds us of the power of good which Christianity can effect in the lives of ordinary people and reminds us, too, that "good" is very rarely done without some form of moral baggage. Perhaps most importantly of all, it reminds us that there is something that affronts us when humans are treated simply as things to be bought or sold. It is a building which speaks still to the sense we get that something is wrong when, even if it is not in the form of slavery explicitly, Mammon wins out and people's worth is simply described in terms of their relation to profit.

Fundamentally, what viewing humans merely as agents of profit affronts is the idea of the soul. The sense that there is an aspect of us that is not, like the systems of profit, an earthly creation, but is of the Divine and seeking unity with the same. Whether they are millionaires in Monte Carlo or chattel slaves in Zanzibar or kitchen porters in a North London curry house, all are, according to the teaching of Christianity, beloved

274   *Twelve Churches*

children of God. All of them have a specific call of Christ that is not a denial of their humanity, but its zenith.

There was another Archbishop who went and peered into that dark cellar some years before Welby. Rowan Williams preached at Christ Church, Zanzibar, on the 200th anniversary of the abolition of the British slave trade in 2007. He asked this question: "What happens when I at last learn that I am loved?"

His answer was simple: "love makes me open my hand, the hand I tried to close on my possessions."[45] Christianity specifically tells us that God looks upon humanity in and with love, indeed, loves them to such an extent that he is, in Christ; prepared to become a slave. What believing that does is puts things into perspective: both highs and lows, feast and famine, slavery and freedom. All of them are as nothing compared to the great power of the love of God. Profit and possession are as nothing to that love. It is to this idea that Christ Church, Zanzibar—for all the failures of its aims and oddness of its structure and hypocrisies that it embodies—still stands as monument. While all earthly things, pain, profit, our very bodies themselves, shall pass away—nothing is beyond redemption. Perhaps the penultimate words ought to go to John Newton:

> Yes, when this flesh and heart shall fail,
> And mortal life shall cease;
> I shall possess, within the veil,
> A life of joy and peace.
> The earth shall soon dissolve like snow,
> The sun forbear to shine;
> But God, who call'd me here below,
> Will be forever mine.

The last words ought to go to someone else, because it is the above that perhaps best articulates a theological version of the request of Futaleh: "to be free and return home."

Chapter Eleven

16th Street Baptist Church, Birmingham, Alabama, United States of America

(Founded 1873 AD)

Much of the narrative of the West, at least as it approached the twentieth century, was one of progress. The idea that those movements—profit, secularism, science—would and could replace the ways of the past. These new movements were based in the ways of the world, not the ethereal ways of Heaven. Inevitably, Christianity became a target of such rhetoric. There no longer needed to be an elision of God and man in the person of Christ if God was, as Nietzsche claimed, dead. Those who foresaw the twentieth century as destined to be a great era of political and social progress were soon disabused by reality. It turned out that much of what had been taken for granted as part of the fabric of what that world viewed as civilization—from international law to personal morality—owed its threads to Christianity. The previous ten chapters have been about how Christianity built a world. This chapter is about how the world came to realize that only when it was threatened in new ways, and about what happened when people tried to take the things that had once been the preserve of the Church into their own hands. The question this brave new world posed Christianity was this: How can a faith which has a God of love and justice at its center remain credible in such an unjust world?

As what was "right" or good or true became a murkier, contested thing—with liberalism, fascism, communism, and almost every other political creed seeking to unpick their Christian foundations—the twentieth century, rather than being an era when humanity finally put aside the barbarism of the past, became one where untold new horrors were inflicted on the globe by angry new creeds. Justice, in particular—that concept of what was right—was suddenly "up for grabs" in a way it had not been since the days of Rome. Individuals themselves became convinced they were the arbiters of what was just. Christianity had always attracted cults and cranks, some of whom we will explore here; however, as we shall see, the seizure of truth by individuals or movements could also be a very threatening and dangerous thing indeed. Christianity was often in the forefront of the resistance to such evils, yet, as we have become familiar with, it was often complicit in their incubation and propagation as well.

Nowhere is the starkness of this truer than in the Deep American South. While the horrors of the Holocaust or the Holodomor showed the bravery of individual Christians as they sought to oppose new and wicked totalitarianisms, if we are to learn what Christian justice meant in a changing world, we perhaps have to look to somewhere with more painful nuances. As the twentieth century progressed, America had become even more resolutely Christian than Europe now was. Yet that meant vast gaps in what practice of the faith meant in a country quite so polarized. When violence or persecution broke out, as it often did in the world of Jim Crow, the question of what justice looked like inevitably followed. And that question was inevitably shaped, on every side, by the Christian faith. To see it at its most powerful—and thereby to learn something about how Christianity shaped our ideas of justice more generally—we must go to a shrapnel-marked church in the Deep South and see justice and redemption in painful practice.

16th Street North in downtown Birmingham runs from the tracks of the old Louisville and Nashville Railroad, now the means by which an occasional stop is made by the long, creeping Amtrak "Crescent" train from New York to New Orleans, up to the porches and carefully maintained lawns of the Fountain Heights suburb. About halfway between the two, on the midpoint of the street, lies a church. The building, in the style of many Baptist churches, rejects the elaborate architectural detailing that you might see as part of a Roman Catholic or Anglican church. Undoubtedly, there are Byzantine influences—the shallow domes on the two towers and the thick brick are redolent of the ruins that scatter the side streets near Hagia Sophia. However, as with those Byzantine structures, whose brick remnants could be a basilica or a bathhouse, there is little externally to differentiate it from other public buildings.

Indeed, as you approach, it isn't totally clear that it is a church at all. As you approach it from a distance, its two squat brick towers and square central glass lantern could belong to a municipal library or a high

16th Street Baptist Church, Birmingham, Alabama, United States of America 279

school or even perhaps a synagogue. As at Salem or at the Kirishitan Hokora, the absence of decoration is as much a theological statement as its presence is elsewhere. The 16th Street Church is not remarkable for this reason—indeed it is fair to say that, unlike St Peter's in Rome or the Bete Golgotha, it's not to be singled out for its architectural impressiveness. This is on purpose. Baptist churches and chapels across the world are deliberately plain, with a focus on preaching and the reading of Scripture. It might not sound like it, but they are deliberately designed this way to change lives.

The emphasis in Baptist belief is on the individual coming to salvation through belief in God. Only those who have undergone a "regeneration"— that is to say making a conscious decision to live according to Christian principles and to declare the truth of the Bible—are able to be baptized and thus become part of the community of the saved.[1] It can sound as if it is a complex, erudite faith, dependent on the whirring of the individual's brain and great long tussles to discern the truth. While there have been Baptists who fit this description, they are a minority. Very often, the Baptist faith, with its strong emphasis on equality before God, found fruitful conversions among communities which suffered from a lack of access to education or advantage.

One such community was the recently freed slaves of the American South. As our travels in Zanzibar showed us, Christianity had been crucial in inspiring the end of slavery, not only in the practical implications of the religious guilt felt by powerful white politicians but also, perhaps more importantly, by giving a coherent and indisputably theological base for the dignity of Black people as children of God. Unsurprisingly, in the aftermath of slavery's end in the United States, there was a flowering of Black churches. One such was "The First Colored Baptist Church of Birmingham," founded by two pastors—James Readon and Warner Reed—on April 20, 1873, just eight years after the end of the American Civil War.[2] Popular with the Black community from its inception, it moved to its location on 16th Street in 1880, and thence took on the name of its new geographical home.

From 16th Street the Church became involved in much more than the reading of Scripture and the business of prayer. Or rather, the reading of Scripture and the business of prayer led the church to seek justice for its community as, in the Jim Crow era, they were denied access to basic aspects of engagement in society which their white fellow believers could take for granted, such as education and legal representation. The new building, the one we can see from the corner of 16th Street North and 6th Avenue North, was built in 1909 with a network of rooms and offices underneath the main body of the church in order to provide exactly these services and so bring about small efforts to show some of the justice which the church members believed, as per the Biblical prophecy of the Hebrew prophet Amos, would "roll down like waters" from God.[3] They were determined to do their part, even if the world was proving a little slow on the uptake.

So the 16th Street Baptist Church became known for its commitment to justice. That commitment was to bring both glorification and unimaginably tragic loss.

On the morning of Sunday, September 15, 1963, Claude Wesley had dropped his fourteen-year-old daughter Cynthia off at church for the Sunday School class. After past admonitions from her mother, Cynthia had made sure to dress up especially smartly that morning, wearing one of her favorite rings on her finger. Claude took the opportunity to fill up his car at a gas station just a bit further down 16th Street. Even at 10:21 a.m., it was a hot day, and the attendant took his time over the filling hose. As he did so, suddenly a blast rang out across the calm of the Sunday morning. There had been an explosion in the basement of the church. Wesley abandoned his car and ran toward the smoke and debris that now surrounded the foundations of the building. There, in the confusion, he tried to find his daughter but in vain. Later he made his way with hundreds of others, the wounded, those seeking to help, those who were curious, and those who were angry, to the University Hospital in Birmingham. There he was led to a corpse horribly mutilated by the force of the blast. Short of other forms of recognition, Claude asked if the broken little body under the sheet in front of him was wearing a ring. "They pulled her little hand out," Claude remembered, "and the little ring was there."[4]

16th Street Baptist Church, Birmingham, Alabama, United States of America 281

The bodies of Cynthia Wesley, Carole Robertson, Carol Denise McNair, and Addie Mae Collins were propelled through the air having borne the full force of the blast from the dynamite hidden behind the steps of the 16th Street Baptist Church in Birmingham, Alabama, on that September day. Cynthia, Carole, and Addie Mae were fourteen years old. Carol Denise was just eleven. In the immediate minutes prior to the explosion the girls had been outside the bathroom adjusting one another's dresses; killed while engaged in about as innocent an activity as you might imagine.[5]

The bomb had been planted earlier that Sunday morning, and detonated just as the basement set of rooms were filling up with young attendees of the Sunday School. Those who planted it were members of the Ku Klux Klan. The 16th Street Baptist Church had been targeted because it had become known as a center for the work where the Black community sought political, legal, social, and educational justice. On April 12 that year—Good Friday—Dr. Martin Luther King Jr. and fellow clergymen Ralph Abernethy and Fred Shuttlesworth led a march to the city hall of Birmingham, which started at the 16th Street Baptist Church. They did so to protest that the treatment of Black people under the segregation laws of the American South was unjust. They had been specifically told not to do so by the city's famously brutal Commissioner for Public Safety, Bull Connor, and had been warned against it in a public letter by a number of Alabama clergy who, while sympathetic to King, felt that the march was a step too far on Good Friday.

In response, King wrote his famous "Letter from Birmingham Jail" when he sat languishing under arrest by Bull Connor's men. In it, King deliberately drew on the symbolism of Good Friday.[6] The early Church had long associated the crossing of the Israelites out of slavery in Egypt with a prefiguring, a foreshadowing of the salvation of the Cross.[7] As King had argued before in his essay "Why We Can't Wait," the Israelites' march to freedom was mirrored in Christ's march to the cross and now again mirrored, in the eternal spiral of the history of God's purposes, in the marches he was organizing from the 16th Street Baptist Church.[8] As such, King later argued, the day was not ill-timed at all but rather absolutely appropriate. In doing so he threw down the rhetorical gauntlet to those who said they supported his aims but not his methods: If these were the methods of the God of justice, then why was it wrong for the people of God to employ them? King's calling out of hand wringing was attractive to some, controversial to others. More importantly for the history of the 16th Street Baptist, it also indisputably made the starting point of the march a target for those implacably opposed to any change in circumstances at all. Six months after King assembled his supporters on its steps, the Ku Klux Klan struck the 16th Street Baptist Church with the bomb that killed Cynthia, Carole, Carol Denise, and Addie Mae.

The specific targeting of children would stir a new phase in the movement for Civil Rights in the United States of America. In many ways it achieved what King had tried to do. The horror that the targeting of children naturally elicited, the sheer injustice and evil of it all, was instrumental in converting many moderate Christian Americans to the cause of Civil Rights. In Psalms, number 82, the often primal cries for justice made to God in the heart of the Old Testament implore God to "deliver the outcast and the poor, save them from the hand of the ungodly."[9] It became clear that as much as that was a prayer of supplication to God, it was also an instruction to those who, like the majority of Americans, sought or claimed to seek to follow him.

The reaction, too, of the church community was instrumental in changing perceptions. As understandable violence threatened to break out in the bombing's immediate aftermath, the minister Pastor John Cross, himself still reeling from the blast, read out another Psalm—number 23— to calm the crowd. "The Lord is my shepherd," he intoned through a hastily found megaphone, "I shall not want."[10] Cross set the tone for the response by the church community. They would look to God. They would speak of his grace and appeal, like the Psalmist thousands of years previously, to his justice. Some 800 clergy and 3,000 mourners arrived at one of the funerals, where King himself gave the eulogy. The minister at the sermon accompanying the burial of Carole Robertson, Pastor C.E. Thomas, declared that "The greatest tribute you can pay to Carole is to be calm, be lovely, be kind, be innocent."[11]

The subject of the Sunday School lesson that fateful day was "the love that forgives."[12] As heartbreaking and difficult as it would prove to

16th Street Baptist Church, Birmingham, Alabama, United States of America 283

be, the people of the 16th Street Baptist Church were determined to put that message into practice.

However, for all of the holiness and righteousness of that sentiment, the incident and its horrors also raised questions. Not only of the movement or of moderate America or of the whole institutional basis of the southern United States, but of Christianity itself. Questions of God. If the answer to the question of where God was in all this was "working out his justice," as the 16th Street Baptist Church affirmed after the bombing, it raised the question of where that justice was. Where was this just God? Because justice in the conventional sense was not fast in coming. The FBI's internal memos of the event claimed that they had "torn Birmingham apart" trying to find admissible evidence about the four local Klansmen they suspected of the bombing, but they were met with a wall of silence among white Alabamans.[13]

In the end it would take until 1977 to indict one of the men responsible. Another two would remain free until 2000. One died thirty-one years after the bombing, having never been brought to justice. In many cases the innocence of these guilty men was maintained by people who claimed to worship the same God as the murdered little girls. When, in 1977, fourteen years after the bombs, Claude Wesley was one of those who reacted to the news that the first of the indictments was finally happening, Wesley's only response was that he hoped that "justice would be done."[14] The understandable question that followed was this: How can Christianity—a faith which has ostensibly a God of love and justice at its center—remain credible in such an unjust world? How—some would cry—could such a God, could such justice, take so long? Many echoed the words of the late Old Testament prophet, Habakkuk: "O Lord, how long shall I cry, and thou wilt not hear? Even cry out unto thee of violence, and thou wilt not save?"[15]

The fact that Habakkuk could ask such a question around 600 years before the birth of Christ suggests that the question of justice has been a major issue for any faith which maintains belief in a God who loves. There are those who feel there remains no convincing answer to such questions today. We will encounter some of the deep answers to it by some of the greatest thinkers of history presently, but first let us tarry here in Alabama, where it is not a philosophical abstract but a practical part of the Church's past and present reality.

I asked the Pastor of the 16th Street Baptist Church how the building and its members today sought to live out the answers to some of those questions. Pastor Price has a calming voice. Low, as if even its very pitch is considered carefully. He tells me, gently but firmly, that his faith in a just God is absolute: "God who is the arbitrator of justice and will distribute justice in his time, not in our time." The very building of 16th Street Baptist spoke of this. Its very continued existence speaks of "grace mercy and love," he says to me, still with that calm and steely determination of voice which shows he really means it. This depth of that faith is further shown by the constant littering of his speech with Scripture: "What some have meant for evil the Lord has turned for good, the gates of Hell shall not prevail; they'll try but they won't," he tells me, quoting the Old and New Testaments in one sentence.[16] This sense of God's purposes ultimately triumphing—but in his time, not ours, is essential to Pastor Price's understanding of both the bombing and of God.

"What the world calls justice," he says, with an implicit sense that there is a category error in thinking that God and the world operate in the same way, "didn't happen for forty years. But delay is not God's denial; in due time the Lord will repay. Justice for us is God righting a wrong in God's time, not ours."

All this leads us to a long-running theme in Christian thought: that time and justice are inherently linked together. From the earliest teaching of Jesus when he promised to "come again in his glory" to judge the world, there has been a looking ahead to a future judgment day, which will occur at the end of time as we know it. As such, Christian statements of belief invariably include an affirmation that the ultimate Divine justice can only truly be obtained when time finishes, or at least, can only be achieved outside of our own human perceptions of time, which are necessarily limited by the fact that we are, well, humans.

This is all understandable—after all, the idea that perfect justice is attainable by humans on their own doesn't really fit in with a need for a savior. However, exactly how it means that Christians should act and think in the meantime has had some very varied interpretations as we shall see. What are Christians to do? Well, for Pastor Price, the mission of the Church, not just 16th Street Baptist, but anyone seeking to live the life of following Christ, is about constantly "trying to create a space for justice." Again, he pauses and quotes Scripture to me, with deliberate weight imbued in the words of the Prophet Micah: "the role of the Christian who wants to bring about justice is this: to do justly, and to love mercy, and to walk humbly with thy God. That's it."[17] He continues, "That means not to just talk about justice, but to walk justice, as part of an active process of walking alongside God. Old folk here have a saying—the best sermon that has ever been preached is the life you live. They're right."

When it comes to the institutional life lived by a Church—both the building and the gathering of people there—Pastor Price is clear about what that looks like: "Compassion and justice are linked together." In the aftermath of that terrible injustice of 1963 and ever since, the 16th Street Baptist Church sought to create the space for God's justice by "creating a space where people could be respected. Where they were able to voice opinions and establish a common ground." These acts were the building blocks of making room for justice in our time for Pastor Price. The rest was up to God. However, there have been plenty of figures—both on the fringes of the faith and at its heart—who took a considerably more "activist" approach to bringing about Divine justice in and to an all-too-human world.

Walking back toward the railroad tracks on 16th Street North in Birmingham, Alabama, we might fairly have a question that rings around our heads: What, then, does justice mean? If it isn't that of the world, then what is it? The vision of the Old Testament is fairly clear in what justice is: "justice is what God wills because that is his nature."[18] Or put another way, whatever God does is just because he is justice itself. The Old Testament itself is perhaps one of the most difficult areas to see the logic of this. Incidents such as the massacre of the people of Ai, a Canaanite town, which Joshua executes on behalf of and apparently with the direct blessing of God, seems to be manifestly unjust.[19] There are plenty of readings of the text which explain this—either those that cast the citizens of Ai as decadent or oppressive or, more convincingly, those which place the text in the context of a succession of kings, from the Pharaoh of Egypt downwards, who seek to stand in the way of the justice of God and inevitably reap the destructive consequences.[20] Even with this in mind, the violence of it, and said violence's seeming association with justice, makes it a difficult read. Then again, as the people of 16th Street Baptist know, God's justice *is* difficult.

The destruction of Ai illustrates that, from the start of monotheistic history, there has been theological inclination to view the ways of God without any need for a reference to another moral code. What, then, exactly do believers understand the ways of God to be? If the ways of God are just *per se*, in themselves, then who gets to discern them? Surely that is a position of quite astonishing power. Much more dangerously, the extension naturally comes that if those who have discerned the ways of God have done so correctly, then they would themselves be beyond reproach or even human justice, because they too would be inherently just. The danger of such thinking is pretty clear.

Early Christians sought to avoid this by distinguishing, by types of laws, the building blocks of justice. Thomas Aquinas taught that the laws of the universe were split into three. There was human law—made by humans and knowable to them; divine law—made by God and, outside very specific areas of revelation, known only to God; and finally, natural law—the laws of the universe which draw humanity toward God's justice and so therefore made by God but, by use of our reason, knowable to humans.[21] From this Aquinas extrapolated that there was an inherent justice to the universe, which was the same for everybody and that while humans cannot be just as God was just, nor co-opt God's justice, they can use their good sense and reason to discern what the ways of that justice are. It seemed a neat solution: putting sufficient distance between fallible humans and the claim to be able to speak on behalf of God and yet also giving a pattern whereby there were still signs they could discern and follow about what God's justice might be like.[22]

However, as the fires of the Reformation burned, many of those who sought change saw Aquinas's thinking about justice and law as mere sophistry. God did have a followable law for his people: it was called the Bible. And it was up to the leaders of the Reformation to bring about justice directly. One such figure was Thomas Müntzer. He encouraged his listeners to begin the process of "striking down the godless" and to "take the enemies of God and strangle them before his eyes."[23] Müntzer believed that nothing short of a destruction of the whole worldly order could be pleasing to the Divine.

Specifically, he believed that he had a divinely ordained role to play in bringing this about. He referred to himself as "a disturber of the unfaithful."[24] One translation of Müntzer's "Prager Manifest," a letter written from his brief period in Prague in 1521, renders his epithet for the doctors of theology as "donkey-cunts."[25] Müntzer specifically thought that he needed to end earthly injustice in order to bring about the "new age" of God, rather than the other way around, and to him the world was "a battleground where God had chosen to fulfil his purposes."[26] It must have been exhausting being quite so sure of one's own reading of things to the extent that even Martin Luther thought you were a bit much. In the end, Luther wasn't alone and Müntzer—his force of peasant utopians defeated in battle—was beheaded on May 27, 1525, outside the city of Mühlhausen. His head was placed on the city walls as a reminder that trying to personally bring about God's justice might sound like a good idea, but that the world had rules too.[27]

It might all sound like good, gory Reformation story time. However, unlike other Reformers, for Müntzer, the world was not a place where disagreement was even possible: he *was* the arbiter of God's justice and that was that. Generally, while Christians are killed for their beliefs, still very rarely is it by other Christians. However, attempts by individuals who believe themselves to be specially ordained to bring about Divine justice here on earth have remained rather more regular features of the extremes of Christian—or more accurately Christian-adjacent—belief. It perhaps says something about the enduring human desire to make things about ourselves that, while we can no longer tune into heresy trials—or at least not ones centered on Christian doctrine—cult activity around apocalyptic cults promising to close that gap between justice and time remain a feature of 24/7 TV news channels.

288   *Twelve Churches*

The most famous of the last half century was the cult of the Branch Davidians, whose experiment in bringing about Divine justice ended in a maelstrom of fire, bullets, and rubble at a fortified compound at Waco, Texas, in April 1993. While, by the time of the cult's bloody end, its leader David Koresh had departed totally from any meaningful Christian belief, proclaiming that he was the Messiah, there is no doubting that Koresh's "incomparable" knowledge of Biblical texts relating to prophecy and judgment had been stepping stones to both his own descent into a controlling, apocalyptic mindset and in his ability to persuade others of his claims.[28] The Branch Davidians had already split in the mid-twentieth century from the Seventh Day Adventist Church. Out of more "mainstream" Adventism, the continued failure of various prophecies which named specific dates for the inauguration of God's reign of justice led to splits and decreasingly small churches made up of often isolated and desperate adherents. Such a context was perfect for Koresh to insert himself with his claims of a prophecy in which God's justice was in Koresh's hands. In April 1993, the FBI attempted to storm his headquarters and Koresh's attempts to bring about a new earthly reign of Divine justice ended with eighty-six people—Koresh included—dead.

The place where the final stand-off happened was called "Mount Carmel." The name came from the place where, in the Book of Micah, it was prophesied that the true remnant of Israel would "dwell solitarily" while the rest of the world and earthly justice collapsed into chaos. To there, it was prophesied, God would come and do "marvelous things."[29] A group of hermits went to live there in the era of the Crusades and, since then, it has been synonymous with places shut away from the world, for contemplation and prayer.[30] In the case of Waco, however, the name belied the real horrors of life there. Koresh had been able to take over the compound when the previous leader of the Branch Davidians, George Rosen, was committed to a mental asylum for murdering a man with an axe in a fit of religious-inspired insanity.[31]

Koresh told a negotiator from the FBI that "every single one" of the Psalms related to the apocalyptic vision of God's justice coming to earth.[32] It is testament to the astonishing breadth of Christianity that the same text, Psalm 23, could both calm the angry and upset victims of the bombing in Alabama and inspire the violence of the Waco siege. More importantly, perhaps, it shows that at the heart of the Christian faith have always been people—and people are capable of using it for good or abusing it for evil. From Müntzer to Koresh, the danger of those who believe they were specially ordained to administer the justice of God on earth is a sadly recurring aspect of Christianity. Its results, however, often seem to end up being very far from the Christian faith indeed.

Back in Birmingham, Alabama, Pastor Price reminds me that those who planted the bombs were probably churchgoers and believed they were worshipping the same God. There were those who thought that the act was justified, that they were enacting Divine justice against those who would break their previous laws. Yet there was another way. Another interpretation of human engagement with God's justice. Fourteen years after the bombing, when the first of those men were arrested, Claude Wesley was one of those who reacted to the news that indictments were finally happening. Wesley's only response—crucially in the passive rather than active voice—was that he hoped that "justice would be done."[33]

Claude Wesley's response points to a truth about the history of justice in Christianity: that not all believers have taken an extreme activist approach to bringing it about. After all, it takes quite a hefty dose of not-very-Christian ego to believe that you are God's chosen instrument for justice, especially when such "justice" involves violence or oppression. Indeed, in the Old Testament, the message is that none of the bloodshed which the people of Israel inflict on their neighbors works: they remain trapped in cycles of injustice. Indeed, God specifically sends prophets to them to say that he has "no pleasure in the death of the wicked; but that the wicked turn from his way and live."[34] For all its gore, the message of Old Testament attempts to judge by humans, even when they have interpreted such judgments as the desire of God, is that they don't work. Justice—and a justice with mercy at its heart—remains God's prerogative alone. And, for all their infamy or notoriety, men like Müntzer and Koresh stand as a minority in Christian history: the quiet hope of men

290   *Twelve Churches*

and women like Claude Wesley was undoubtedly the normative form of Christian justice.

There were those, however, who went further than just quietly hoping in the midst of an unjust world. Such is the association of the coming of God with justice that there were those who came to believe that the only way Christians could really live the ways of justice in this life was by a complete and genuine abdication from the ways of the world and a waiting for the second arrival of Christ to bring about the judgment which the world was morally incapable of leveling upon itself. Inevitably, this led to some strange practices and people.

One of the oddest of these millenarian Christian sects were the Irvingites—a group of middle-class Victorians who took the revival of High Church practice in the Church of England a little further than most. They developed a theory that the second coming of Jesus would begin when a certain number of their specially set aside priests had died.[35] Fortunately for the priests, this was to happen naturally rather than via a mass extinction campaign. The movement even prepared a special set of church vestments for Jesus to wear when he came back, as they believed his first task—before inaugurating the reign of heavenly justice—would be celebrating Holy Communion according to the rites of the Church of England at the church of Christ the King on London's Gordon Square.

The Irvingites were, however, positively mainstream compared to Joanna Southcott, a woman from Devon who left strict instructions that the twenty-four bishops of the Church of England should have a good long look at her box. The box is an actual trunk still around today. In it, Southcott claimed, are a set of prophecies given to her as she was, you guessed it, in fact the Messiah. After her death in 1814, the reading of these prophecies became the only way which the world could make itself ready to receive the coming apocalypse and judgment. Without them, humanity would face Divine justice unprepared.[36] Despite this, the bishops seemed reluctant to take Joanna and her box seriously. Others, however, did. She accrued a series of followers over the course of the nineteenth and early twentieth centuries. Perhaps the most notable of these was Mabel Barltrop, who formed "The Panacea Society" to promote Southcott's beliefs. Indeed, Barltrop went further than just promotion, adding herself to this unconventional creed as "Octavia, Daughter of God."[37] Among the beliefs she put forward were that her late husband had been Jesus and that her home, 12 Albany Road, Bedford, Bedfordshire, was in fact the real site of the Garden of Eden.

Despite Barltrop launching a letter-writing and advertising campaign, determined to try to bring about the Last Judgment, Joanna Southcott's box remained unopened. In 1927, the "psychical researcher," ghost hunter and probable conman Harry Price claimed to have X-rayed it in the presence of the distinctly uneasy Bishop of Grantham, the suffragan bishop in the Diocese of Lincoln. Price maintained that it didn't contain any prophecies at all. Instead, the items intended to help humanity in the face of Divine judgment were "a horse pistol, a dice box, purse, several books, a lottery ticket, and a night cap."[38] Today the box remains unopened, waiting in Bedfordshire for such a time when the bishops change their mind.

Tellingly, women like Barltrop and Southcott who had been denied leadership in various churches often became the messengers or prophets of these apocalyptic groups. While their beliefs were odd and always ended up straying from even the most generous descriptions of Christian orthodoxy, they often sought to bring about justice or the apocalypse by nonviolent means. Perhaps the most famous example of this was Mother Ann Lee.

Two hundred and fifty years ago, Mother Ann Lee got on a boat at Liverpool for what was not quite yet the United States of America. Lee was born in Manchester in 1736 and baptized in the Church of England. Affected by visions, she moved through the Quakers, having found them too still and silent, and founded her own religious meeting, given the gloriously Cliff Richard–like sobriquet of "the shaking Quakers" by a Mancunian journalist. The Shakers were born. Soon, the State Church made life difficult for the sect, including seeking the arrest of Mother—as the Shakers call her—for disruptive dancing. Seeking a place where her own unique vision of justice might prevail, she went across the Atlantic. Once in America, Shaker doctrine developed through "The Era of Manifestations." Ann and her immediate followers taught that a just, Heaven-like society could exist on earth, it just required a very particular way of living. Practices included celibacy, communal work, and ownership of all things, while beliefs included God as male and female, a doctrine that Mother Ann was a female Christ and a strong emphasis, again, on the coming judgment of Christ.[39] The formal name of the Shakers is, in fact, "The United Society of Believers in Christ's Second Appearing." The movement was, briefly, very popular.

However, arguably, like Koresh and Joanna Southcott, these beliefs put Mother Ann outside what we would comfortably and recognizably call Christianity, despite the obvious influences of the faith upon them. The Shakers, though, have an unlikely continued influence on Christianity today through one of their many songs. "Simple Gifts" was a popular Shaker tune that was known to millions of British schoolchildren in the mid to late twentieth century as the hymn popular in schools across the country, "Lord of the Dance."

The hymnwriter Sydney Carter had borrowed the tune from American composer Aaron Copland's ballet *Appalachian Spring*. Copland had been commissioned to evoke a very particular type of Americana and so turned to the music of the Shakers, due to their presence throughout New England and Appalachia and heyday after the Civil War. They had become known in America for their dedication to simple living, celibacy, and worship not with liturgy but through music and, historically, dance. It was this Shaker song and dance, "Simple Gifts," that inspired the composer. Copland saw the tune and the community from whence it came as emblematic of a *certaine idée* of America. However, for all their associations with that land and like so much that is emblematic of America, Shakerism didn't actually start there but with Mother Ann and her quest for justice in Georgian Manchester.

The tune might soon be the only part of the Shaker vision for the world left. At the time of writing there are only two Shakers left. I spoke to the younger one of them, who is aged a spritely sixty-seven. Brother Arnold has been a Shaker for forty-six years, having joined as a young man. I apologized to Brother Arnold of the Sabbathday Shaker Village in Connecticut for the heavy-handedness of the Established Church of which I am part. "The Congregationalists here were a hundred times worse," he reassured me. And people say you hear nothing good about the C of E these days. Despite the past and occasional present persecutions—"people throw rocks sometimes, destroy equipment. It's not nice, but it's fine." He admits Copland had a point: "Shakerism couldn't exist anywhere else but America."

He speaks in simple sentences, with a smattering of words that evoke an older English. "We let our yea be yea," he tells me, "simplicity means without folds, so truth is the only way to be." Buoyed by this, I ask directly whether he worries about the future. "I don't worry about it," he tells me. "It's in God's hands. That sounds trite but I believe it is. But we still have to be living and dying by the truth."

The truth is that Brother Arnold will, almost certainly, be the last Shaker. The sect's strict celibacy, rigorous lifestyle, and lack of proselytization led to a steady decline in numbers. Now only Brother Arnold and the elderly Sister June are left as professed members of the community. They live at Sabbathday Shaker Village and each day follows a pattern of prayers, communal breakfast, further prayers, work, more prayer, lunch, and then work again. The evenings vary. When I spoke to Brother Arnold he was about to go to song practice. "They remain where our theology is," he says of Shaker hymns. "But we don't dance anymore. As the community aged out, we stuck to sitting down."

There are 10,000 Shaker songs. Did Brother Arnold know them all? "Nay," he says, "I wish!" Instead, when asked what embodies the Shakers, what—if he is the last—they will leave behind, he picks out "Simple Gifts," the tune which became known to so many English schoolchildren as a hymn about Jesus. The original words to it are, he says, "ones to live by" and embody what it is to be a Shaker. Proclaiming that "it's a gift to be simple, it's a gift to be free," they were written by Elder Joseph Brackett, who found himself left as the sole member of a Shaker community.

"There is," Brother Arnold says, "a lot of angst in the words about his loneliness, but it's about bending to God's will until he came around." They must echo in particular to Brother Arnold, if God's will is that he is to be the last Shaker. He reminds me that vocation is about letting some things go: "sacrifice is not a big word in the twenty-first century," he says. "It's more me, me, me. Well, Shakerism abolishes pronouns: we use 'us' and 'we.'" Even when there's just one left. So it is that he will

294 *Twelve Churches*

stay looking in the very lonely vocation of seeking to bend to the ways of Divine justice via personal sacrifice, as the strain of "Simple Gifts" passes into history forever.

Most Christians, however, are not on the spectrum of either the radical action or radical submission explored above. Tellingly, be it Müntzer and Koresh or Mother Ann Lee and Joanna Southcott, the more extreme examples all involve the individuals concerned being crucial to God's plan for a more just world. By contrast, many ordinary Christians still believe, like Pastor Price, that justice is God's business. That said, for many, there *is* something they can do, which they feel brings a taste of God's justice here and now. That, in a nutshell, is by trying to live in the world shaped by love. Love and justice might seem far removed, and in the ancient world they were. However, the teaching of Christ—that the law could be summarized by love—meant that Christian concepts of Divine justice would always be complicated. In the Gospel of Matthew, Jesus is tested by a lawyer—one whose job it is to bring about justice on earth by the enforcement of God's law. He asks Jesus which of the competing and complex commandments that made up that law is the greatest. Christ's reply has come to be one of the most famous summaries of Christian ethics of them all:

"Jesus said unto him, Thou shalt love the Lord thy God with all thy heart, and with all thy soul, and with all thy mind. This is the first and great commandment. And the second is like unto it, Thou shalt love thy neighbor as thyself. On these two commandments hang all the law and the prophets."[40]

Perhaps the most significant revolution which Christianity ever affected was this: that with its spread, love became the main prism through which what was just or right was viewed in the Western world. For the ancients, justice was a matter of strength or of the capricious weight of the fates; even in Judaism it was simply the actions of God. That Christianity recast what was right as what was loving is hard to overstate as a societal change—with ramifications from Golgotha to Birmingham, Alabama, to wherever it is you are sitting and reading these words today. As the thinker Tom Holland observed, that John Lennon could say "all you need is love"—a prescription with which St Paul would not have disagreed—is testament to the triumph of Christ and the dominion of Christianity.[41]

Yet, the acceptance of love as absolute, as the ultimate justice and, as St John writes in his first epistle, as the defining characteristic of God himself, still raises questions.[42] We keep on being brought back to that street in Alabama in September 1963, to the question that doubtless came unbidden into the hearts and minds of those who were there as the dust and rubble cleared: If God is just and loving, why has this happened? Why is there a need for justice—the righting of wrongs—when surely an all-powerful and, crucially, all-loving God could simply not have created wrongs in the first place?

Two schools of thought within Christianity arose in attempts to answer this. The first came from the thought of St Irenaeus. For Irenaeus the human journey was about how we were made "gradually to partake of the divine nature."[43] It wasn't that we were made perfect by God but rather that we are being drawn toward a time when we will eventually be one with God and as we *should* be, rather than as we are in the here and now. The way we reach that is by invoking the spirit of God to choose that which is good and therefore be like Christ who "shall not consent to evil but choose the thing that it good."[44] Suffering and injustice exist as ways in which we are given opportunities to choose the good, to take the better and holier path and so be more like God to the extent that we eventually fulfill the purpose of our creation and become one with him.

St Augustine—whose *Confessions* we have already encountered—thought of things differently. For Augustine, evil was not an active substance or presence, as all things with substance were created by God and it was impossible for God not to create something good.[45] Suffering and injustice, therefore, are what happen when we fall away from what God wishes for us. Such a falling away is possible because, crucially for Augustine, humans have free will: the ability to make a meaningful choice between doing what is good and just and doing what is wrong. Our nature is fallen, however, and so, very often, we use this free will to fall away and embrace the absence of good. God can only right things by the intervention of grace. Augustine argues that this is by the Divine love shown through the death and resurrection of Jesus. Salvation—and the ultimate bringing of us to justice—is therefore accomplished not by us but by God. Our only hope of reconciliation and redemption from the fallen and unjust world we have made is to embrace that grace. For Augustine, by contrast to Irenaeus, we are incapable of making things just and good ourselves: if we want to see justice eventually, all we can do is cling to this grace.

Throughout history, Christians have reacted to injustice in ways that reflect both attitudes. Born in the years immediately following the fall of the Roman Empire, Boethius was a civil servant and politician who, though from a Roman family, rose to prominence serving the new Barbarian kings of Italy. Specifically, he became the major-domo for King Theodoric the Great. Theodoric was an Ostrogoth who had a reputation for being a little tricky to work for. Prone to violence and the brutal murder of his friends and enemies, it is said that eventually even the Devil got fed up with Theodoric's antics and sent up a demon to steer the king's horse into the crater of an active volcano.[46] Boethius, despite years of loyal service, found himself imprisoned for daring to defend a fellow senator against Theodoric's accusations of treason.

In prison, Boethius wrote *The Consolation of Philosophy*. Toward the end, Philosophy sings to Boethius and reassures him that, for all the injustice of the situation, there is one who will bring things to himself because he is justice and wisdom itself, namely God. All will come back to the good, because it is "toward the good that all things tend."[47] In the end, Boethius was tortured to death, which involved being partially hanged and then clubbed to death. Contemporaries and subsequent thinkers hailed him as a martyr, whose decision to face injustice as an opportunity to live and die well, encapsulated Irenaeus's message.

Just over 1,400 years later, another man found himself imprisoned by a tyrant with scant interest in the rule of law or the concepts of justice. Like Augustine, for Dietrich Bonhoeffer, grace was everything. Bonhoeffer was a German Lutheran pastor who stood accused of complicity in a plot to overthrow Adolf Hitler. Bonhoeffer had spent his ministry warning of the perils of cheap grace. To Bonhoeffer, grace was both "the living word" and "a sanctuary from the world"—i.e. it had to be lived by Christians in a meaningful way but, because of its strangeness and opposition to the lack of justice in the world, it necessarily involved conflict with the world in which it was lived out.[48] Such grace, for Bonhoeffer, was necessarily costly. Cheap grace would involve assenting to the idea of God as just without following through on it, not making the costly choice to accept a costly salvation: exactly what Augustine said was the only way in which true reconciliation to good and away from evil might be achieved.

Bonhoeffer practiced what he preached. His refusal to flee Nazi Germany, despite his outspoken opposition to the regime, spoke of his belief that in this fallen world the only salvation was found through grace and grace that sacrificed, like Christ, everything to the point of imprisonment and death. On April 9, 1945, he was hanged by the Nazis at the Flossenbürg concentration camp, in his death proving his utmost belief in the absolute costliness of grace in the pursuit of justice.

At the end of the Bible there is a vision. In the Book of Revelation, John describes what he sees:

"And I saw a new heaven and a new earth: for the first heaven and the first earth were passed away."[49]

It is a vision which has justice at its center. For in its middle, Jesus sits upon a throne and dispenses justice. What does that justice look like? Well, the vision continues:

"And God shall wipe away all tears from their eyes; and there shall be no more death, neither sorrow, nor crying, neither shall there be any more pain: for the former things are passed away."[50]

Whether they have an Irenaean understanding of suffering as bringing us closer to God through good choices or an Augustinian understanding of the ultimate triumph of grace, whether they think it is up to them personally to help bring it about, or whether, most likely of all, they simply hope and pray, like Claude Wesley, that justice might one day be done, the ultimate end for which Christians pray when they come to their churches is the same. That Christ will cast those former things—tears, sorrow, death, crying, and pain—away.

298   *Twelve Churches*

This vision of heavenly justice is a universal and comforting one. However, what this chapter has shown and what remains astonishing even in its final sentences is that, through history, Christians have sought so many different ways of bringing it about. Across centuries and contexts, yes, but sometimes even in the same times and places, in the same cities and churches. That points to a more difficult Christian truth. That every church is necessarily a place where past, present, and future meet. Justice, therefore, is both something that we look forward to and also work toward. A concept in which past, present, and future are in conversation or, more accurately, in communion with one another. Let us take one last walk up 16th Street North in Birmingham, Alabama, and listen to the calming voice of Pastor Price. He puts it like this, in the specific context of the 16th Street Baptist church:

"We are a mix of past, present, and future. Now some people only see us as 'that church' where a horrific and horrendous terrorist act took place, but we're also a place where people can be revived, refreshed, and renewed every week. We are called to embrace the past, to retell the stories; but we do so in light of God's justice and then reimagine how the future will be."

Pastor Price believes that the part of the building which best tells this tale is the sanctuary, where the pulpit and table for Communion are found. "It is a space designed for worship. And we do worship there, every Sunday. But under Jim Crow, folks couldn't go to a theater or speak out or seek justice in public: but there they could. So, the place where we prayed for justice, we used for others to voice their pain about the injustices and lack of equity. Worship and justice are tied together."

This is perhaps the lesson of the twentieth century and its horrors. That to separate justice from worship renders both vulnerable to incoherence and, ultimately, collapse. What enabled the people of 16th Street to pursue justice, and what enable them to tie that justice to a radical forgiveness, was their faith. As the Church weathered the storms of a century filled with ethnic, religious, and political violence, it became increasingly clear that it was at its most convincing, in a world of conflicting claims, not when it accrued power for itself in worldly terms but when it pursued a justice, often necessarily sacrificial, which was inspired by its teaching.

The pursuit of justice is therefore best understood as a prayer, but, like all Christian liturgy, a prayer that is lived and acted upon as well as spoken and hoped for. Perhaps the answer to the final question—that has dogged us throughout—of whether justice itself is possible this side of Heaven—should go to Pastor Price.

"Surely it is possible—Jesus shows it *is* possible. After all, through the power of the Holy Spirit, all things are possible. It's important to remember that we have that same power inside of us now—it's not unattainable if we yield to God's way. But the thing with that is: it's difficult."

Amen.

Chapter Twelve

Canaanland, Ota, Nigeria

(Founded 1999 AD)

What, then, of the future of Christianity? We have seen, across the world and in many churches, through the ages and in the lives of many individuals, how Christianity has shaped the world we now live in. There can be little doubting from our survey the role that Christianity has played in our understanding of all sorts of topics, from beauty to violence, to the very questions of life and death themselves. We now stand in the first decades of a new millennium, the third Christian one. The question that inevitably spurs is, how will this faith which has so formed yesterday and today shape the world of tomorrow? Linked to that is another question, deeper, more theological in nature: Does Christianity still give cause for hope?

To find out we must go to a place which is, by any measure, part of the demographic future of the world and, by extension, of the demographic future of Christianity too. We must go to Nigeria. There, in a mirror of the themes throughout this book, in order to work out what the future looks like, we must go to a church which seeks to evoke a place from before Christianity's very beginning. We must go to Canaanland.

Bound for the land of Canaan, Canaan yes I am.[1]

The above line from a hymn, dating from the heady days of American twentieth-century evangelical revival, is about the hope of glory. It has hope at its heart as the singer puts all the trials and tribulations of this life into the context of a journey to a place of "love and pure delight." That is the land of Canaan.

Canaan features prominently in the Bible. As a geographical entity it appears to be flexible—in some cases it is presented as being a generic term for the land to the west of the River Jordan.[2] In others it has tighter geographical limits, being associated with specific hills,

304 *Twelve Churches*

valleys, and settlements, such as that of Megiddo.[3] Whatever its historical extent—and borders were more likely to be porous in the age of the
Old Testament than they might be now—it became synonymous with
the idea of "the promised land," a place where the promises of God
came true. It was, in short, a place of hope. The reality of that promise,
in the Old Testament, was one of conquest: the Biblical Books of Joshua
and Chronicles tell of violence as the physical realities of taking that land
and expelling the people who lived there became clear. As ever in Scripture, it is a part of the story of the Abrahamic faiths that contains both
beauty and violence: life and death existed side by side. However, with
the teaching of Christ focused not on a geopolitical promise made to a
specific people, but a hope in changed hearts, minds, and souls, Christianity no longer used Canaan as a term for a place on a map, but as a
metaphor: Canaan became a byword for that hope. Being "bound for
the land of Canaan," as the song made clear, meant expressing a hope
that all things will be made right in the end by the purposes of God, who
will bring those who follow him to a time and a place where suffering
shall be no more.

I watched a group of elderly ladies sing the song in South Africa. It
was intensely moving. Many were of an age where they had already seen
and known enough tragedy for several lifetimes. Many lived in circumstances which might, I reflected, very well have made me give up hope
in change for the better, even perhaps in the good purposes of God.
But there they were, still hoping and repeating the chorus over and over
again:

Bound for the land of Canaan, Canaan yes I am.[4]

Christianity's transformation of global culture is such that now Canaan's
name is applied to a myriad of things: "Canaan: Official" is the world's
leading producer of Bitcoin miners, Canaan is also a thirteen-part Japanese anime cartoon series from 2009, and Canaan is a registered pet
breed with the American Kennel Club; a quick, medium-sized pasture
dog which is ranked as "less likely to drool" on the organization's special drooling scale. It is also the name of an olive oil brand, a town in

Connecticut, and of a British homelessness charity. All these names, however, draw their nomenclature from the original Canaan, that which was first "the promised land" to the ancient people of Israel and then, as Christians sought to explain the Old Testament in terms that pointed to the promises of Christ, the place synonymous with that future "promised land." A place of hope, where God's promises will come true.

For all this variety, the sense of Canaan as the "promised land"—the place and time of final fulfillment of the purposes of God in Christ—became the extended Christian metaphor for hope over the centuries. We have seen it in many guises and called it many names as we have journeyed through the world. We have seen hopes fulfilled and cruelly dashed; we have seen hopes clung to in the most trying of circumstances and hopes lost in the midst of the pains of human experience. We have seen hopes of the eternal and simpler, more day-to-day hopes. We have seen hopes written in the stone of buildings and heard of hopes that by their very nature cannot have attainment on this earth or even within the confines of human time.

Such a variety of hope, in terms of its nature and the times and places in which it was found, begs an obvious question as we reach the end of our journey around these twelve places of worship which so differently reflect the varied history of the Christian faith. Unlike many of the questions we have encountered so far, it is a question less about the past and more about the future: Where, twenty-one centuries after the babe at Bethlehem, do Christians find hope today?

One of the many industrial lots off the main highway that passes through Ota, Nigeria, might not sound like an obvious place to go to find Christian hope for the future. Ota is a town now swallowed into the continuous run of simple houses, commercial lots, and traffic that make up the wider conurbation of Lagos, the nation and continent's largest city.

While it is presently more often driven through than visited, Ota was once a focal point for the Yoruba people and specifically the Awori clan. It was at Ota from the seventeenth century onwards that people would gather to observe the Gelede ritual, where men purporting to be animate ancestral spirits, the Egungun, would perform elaborate masquerades and thus dispense blessing and curse.[5] With the arrival of British rule and the spread of Christianity, while these rituals declined, Ota remained important as the marking point of what Queen Victoria held to be "the limits of our dominions."[6]

For all this past importance Ota is now a low-rise sprawl spreading into the sunset. Lagos has long eclipsed it, rendering it part of its ever-growing borders. Despite—or more probably because of—this there are signs of development, or rather, of capitalist prosperity in Ota: it is replete with shopping malls which proudly advertise themselves as bringers of social benefits.[7] There is poverty, too, and signs of life being both cheap and difficult. The Idiroko road, which cuts through the settlement, is "notorious" for fatal car crashes.[8] Its central reservation is not a reservation at all, but a collation of rubbish, both domestic and commercial. The promise of hope for the future Kingdom of God in the Prophecy of Isaiah came to my mind as I gazed on the mound of rubbish: "Prepare ye the way of the Lord, make straight in the desert a highway for our God."[9] It is off this unlikely highway that a place named for the land of hope and promise lies. On the edge of where Ota gives way to the less densely populated wetlands of the region—Queen Victoria's "limits"—is a complex known as "Canaanland."

It is September 2024 and I am watching Bishop David O. Oyedepo preach a sermon at Canaanland's main church. The building's official name is the "Faith Tabernacle," which claims to be one of the largest churches on the face of the earth, with capacity for just over 50,000 people inside the aircraft-hangar-like proportions of the building. It is not even twenty-five years old, and yet almost every Sunday it is totally full, worshippers gathered there in their finest clothes praising the Lord alongside a football stadium's worth of fellow worshippers. Its red roof is deliberately visible on satellite images of the area. The interior is almost like that of a conference center—plain, white, cavernous. Of course, the churches we have visited so far have necessarily been varied in their style, but none of them could quite compare to the almost sterile interior of the Tabernacle. In fact, the buildings it reminded me of most were not the other churches in this book but the shopping malls on the other side of Ota. Yet, that's a message in itself: hope is adornment enough, so it seems, to glorify that same God whom the people of Israel sought to call upon all those many years ago in their tabernacles on the edge of the promised land.

Dotted around the space are screens and speakers, the odd neon sign, a twenty-four-hour clock—all things designed to further broadcast the central message. The start of the service features a choir, robed in crimson-and-gray matching outfits. There must be three or four hundred of them. They have a lead singer, backing singers, a conductor, and a band featuring several drum players, pianists, and a saxophone. It is monumental in its scale. The choir move as they sing, like a murmuration: that is to say seemingly randomly, as directed by either their emotions or the Holy Spirit, and yet in a sort of perfect harmony. The song this Sunday focuses on the power of God: "What can't you do, Jesus?" the chorus goes, repeating again and again for minutes on end. The answer, very clearly, in the minds of those gathered there is "Nothing."

There are three wings to the building, and long, wide corridors that converge on a central point where there is a stage made up of seven layers of steps leading up to a platform. After the choir have sung, it is onto this platform that Bishop David O. Oyedepo emerges to preach his sermon. He wears an all-white suit, in contrast to the darker formal attire of the congregants. His style is informal. He wanders between the aisles of those who are privileged enough to sit closest to the stage and engages them in what appears to be conversation but is really a monologue punctuated by "Amens." He talks about his own journey, the books he has written. He talks about the fact that he hasn't had to withdraw any of those books to date. He has, he claims, a "prophetic agenda." He liberally quotes scripture. Jeremiah 3:15, Ephesians 4:8, Mark 16:20 all come in quick succession. They are quoted as proofs of his message. I confess I struggle to follow what it is other than a very clear sense of the purpose of God in his own life.

Toward the end of the sermon, which, interspersed with music and other prayers, lasts for six hours, the purpose becomes clear. He is offering the people gathered there hope that their problems will be solved. Each member of the congregation is encouraged to bring their "enough is enough list." At the end, "every item on your list will return

308 *Twelve Churches*

as testimonies." This will be done, the Bishop assures his listeners, in the precious name of Jesus.

The promises come thick and fast: a new realm of wealth, a new realm of health. People rise to their feet as the promises of healing and of professional success are made, even life itself is offered; there is a particularly loud cry of affirmation when the Bishop pronounces the word "longevity." The list is so broad and varied that he even decreed an end to "the siege of procrastination," which I felt might have been personally directed at me. For all the very modern things on the lists of the people who have gathered there to hear Bishop Oyedepo, he makes clear that he is doing nothing less than continuing the story of the Bible. All of his promises are simply the fulfillment of Biblical mandate. Or, put another way: If it could happen then, why can't it happen now? To demonstrate this, he interpolates the tale of Nicodemus or of the woman with a flow of blood with tales of people being cured of bone marrow cancer, the modern language of scans and therapy alongside the stories of the Bible. One Canaan colliding with another.

The faith here is undoubtedly real, the hope tangible. The people in the aisles hold their lists tightly, they close their eyes. Some of them, I notice, are weeping. They respond with vigorous "Amens." No matter how different their requests, how varied the contents of those lists, all have hope that at Canaanland, miracles do happen.

Canaanland has something for everyone, and not just in terms of answered prayers. There is a hotel, a number of restaurants, and a microfinancing bank. The most considerable non-worship-related enterprise is the Covenant University, whose halls of residence are shaped so that they appear as either stars of David or crosses from the air and are all named after Biblical men or women. Indeed, Biblical naming is a constant theme. Even the compound's iced drink store, where freezers upon freezers' worth of ice is kept in order to keep the beverages of worshippers cool in the intense Nigerian heat, is called "Hebron Drinks" after the place at which Abraham purchased the cave of Machpelah from Ephron the Hittite, the first moment where the people of Israel laid claim to a specific part of Canaan.[10] There could be perhaps few better metaphors for the enormous reach and impact of the Christian faith than the fact that a cold drinks store in the most populous nation in sub-Saharan Africa is named after the place where an Old Testament Patriarch was purported to have conducted a property deal.

When it comes to growth, like Nigeria itself, Canaanland shows no sign of slowing down. Next door to the already monumental Tabernacle itself is an even bigger building site. Resembling a half-completed football stadium, this enormous site is "The Ark," the future home of worship at Canaanland. The aim will be to accommodate over 100,000 worshippers at any one time. Such will be its size that, if it is completed as planned, its planners claim it will break ten Guinness World Records.[11] It will cost in excess of 160 billion Nigerian Naira, roughly equivalent to a $100 million.[12] It is anticipated to be finished in November 2025—which might well be when you are reading this book. Let us see whether Bishop Oyedepo's hopes have come true.

The Ark is billed as a "legacy project," but is arguably symbolic of an aspect of twenty-first-century Christianity wider than just the ministry of Bishop Oyedepo. The movement known as the "Prosperity Gospel" developed over the last fifty years or so. It grew out of the Pentecostal movement. Pentecostalism is named after the Feast of Pentecost—the moment related in the Book of Acts when the Holy Spirit came down upon the first disciples and enabled them to do signs and wonders in Jesus's name.[13] Pentecostals necessarily emphasize the continued reality of the Holy Spirit's power in the lives of believers today. The Prosperity Gospel goes a step further and suggests that, rather than being a faith which promises future hope, Christianity is one where credit can be redeemed in the here and now. At its heart is the idea that the Christian God will "grant material prosperity to all believers who have enough faith."[14]

It has become particularly popular in West Africa. Many Nigerian pastors learned their trade in the United States, where sects had combined the American Dream's promises that anyone can become a millionaire or the President with that zeal for purity we saw at Salem. It was no longer that just *anybody* could achieve worldly success, but rather that anybody who came to the right church and gave the right amount of money could. Men like Bishop Oyedepo's mentor, Kenneth Copeland, had made a fortune in the United States selling the most valuable asset of all: hope. They brought that to Africa, where it has proved even more popular, perhaps because, as a drive down Idiroko Road shows, other forms of hope are in very short supply.

Perhaps it is my Western cynicism, perhaps a cold Colonial heart still beating within my breast, unrepentant and unreformed despite my best efforts to learn otherwise, but Canaanland to me remains the most inscrutable of the churches in this book. It all just seems very far from the specific instructions of Jesus: "whosoever shall exalt himself shall be abased; and he that shall humble himself shall be exalted."[15] Now, I and millions of the other Christians that we have encountered at every stage of our journey, in all ages and all countries, fall short of that expectation every day. But none, I think, from Bethlehem onwards, would seek to put forward a faith that seems to actively reverse it. Then there's the consistent observation that has come up from Rome to Japan to Dominica to Canterbury: that Christianity isn't about building the perfect life in the here and now but striving in hope. Fundamentally, I think it also makes Christianity theologically incoherent and unconvincing. A faith of childish wish fulfillment is what its greatest enemies paint it to be. After all, not all of those desires on the "enough is enough" lists can possibly come true.

That is not to say that criticism of the Prosperity Gospel is just an Old World vs New World, Global North vs Global South sort of a dispute. There are plenty of those in Nigeria who view what goes on at Canaanland as at odds with Christianity. It has clashed with the more established forms of the faith. One Roman Catholic priest described the Prosperity Gospel as "a satanic scam" doomed to fail because the prayers and supplications are made with the "wrong motivations."[16] It has also attracted criticism from other Pentecostals, the particular difference relating to the nature of Christian ministry. While Pentecostals view it as the calling of all Christians to discern where the Holy Spirit might move, in the Prosperity Gospel, the function of the pastor as the "man of God" who dispenses this blessing seems to cut out God and Christ altogether, establishing instead a "client relationship" more redolent of the Egungun who dominated the Ota of old.[17]

The response given to these sorts of criticisms by many who adhere to it is twofold, both parts hard to answer. Surely a God capable of rising from the dead is capable of anything and, when there are so many Christians in the West who live in what is, to many of the people I saw clutching their lists in the Faith Tabernacle, unimaginable luxury, who are they to critique their co-religionists for hoping and praying that they might share in part of that plenty as well?

The issue, as we have seen from Hagia Sophia onwards, is that, in practice, the wicked and cruel can turn the hope of the faithful into a mockery. Pastors become millionaires while the people in the pews continue to clasp their "enough is enough" lists. It is more explicitly a business than a religion. Now, of course, there have been those who have decried all religion as the meeting of "the con man and the fool."[18] Such a view is hardly a fair representation of the two millennia of history we have encountered on our journey. It doesn't accurately speak of the beauty, glory, kindness, and care committed on behalf of the hope of faith. It also assumes that what is hoped for and what is true must necessarily always be different: folly indeed.

Let us return to the question we began this chapter with: Where do Christians find hope? In reality, what the Prosperity Gospel encourages isn't really hope at all; it's expectation. At Canaanland it is the expected norm that members give at least 10% of what they have to the church. Most are expected to give more if they wish to be blessed. Bishop Oyedepo is very clear that the need for Canaanland to make money is an integral part of ministry in the same way that he preaches that gaining wealth and health are an integral part of the "deal" of being a Christian. This works both ways: in 2021 he sacked forty pastors whom he deigned had failed to bring sufficient income into the coffers of Canaanland.[19] There are few hedge funds which have quite so merciless a hire-and-fire policy. In the Christianity that we have seen, "strength is made perfect in weakness" and hope is found not in moments of success but in moments of failure.[20] Christ said "blessed are the poor," after all.[21] Let us think back to our first stop, in Bethlehem: the manger, after all, was not a sign of prosperity.

In some ways, while the hope put on offer at Canaanland might seem distant from some of the Christianities which we have encountered elsewhere on our journey—almost alien, even, to the sensibilities of much Christianity that I had encountered in particular—in fact, we might suggest that some of the promises made by Bishop Oyedepo are already coming to pass. His church is full every Sunday without fail and he clearly expects that the vast space of the Ark will be too. It is easy to see why people are willing to see the direct movement of the Christian God in a place where Christianity is so obviously growing. The hope for the future in terms of a sheer numbers game is very clear. As Africa demographically expands—the prediction is that there will be 2.5 billion Africans by 2050, representing a quarter of the global population—so too will all faith, but in particular Christianity.[22] It is thought that somewhere over 1.1 billion of that growing population will be Christian.[23] However, as we observed in the Templo de las Américas, that might well change Christianity more than we can possibly imagine.

This might not necessarily go in the way that the advocates of the Prosperity Gospel expect. There are those who are working hard within Africa itself to set out a different vision for the Christian future. Specifically, there are groups working to set out what might be done, given that Christianity's future seems set to be more African, not less, to set out a vision for it that casts off "misleading theologies in the continent."[24] There is, leaders in the African Church claim, a new hope for Christianity as it seeks to escape some of the past failings we have seen chronicled in churches across the rest of the globe. In such thinking, theologians are keen on quoting the one-time chaplain of the Unites States Senate, the Reverend Richard Halverson, who summed up the journey which we have seen played out in bricks and mortar, flesh and blood, thus:

"In the beginning the Church was a fellowship of men and women centering on the living Christ. Then the Church moved to Greece, where it became a philosophy. Then it moved to Rome, where it became an institution. Next, it moved to Europe, where it became a culture. And, finally, it moved to America, where it became an enterprise."[25]

Again, such a characterization is an oversimplification, with each of those stages having far more interrelation and continuity than we might initially think. However, there is no doubt that the question of what the

Church might become next, as it enters its most global ever manifestation, is a matter of hope.

The idea of hope for the future rooted in Christianity is not just a twenty-first-century phenomenon. Canaanland is not the first church to have existed in Ota; Bishop Oyedepo is not the first bishop to call the town home. About five miles from Canaanland, off the main road and into the maze of streets which make up the older town of Ota proper, there is a seemingly unremarkable yellow building. Two stories high, the old Vicarage of St James's Anglican cathedral was one of the first Western-style buildings in this part of Nigeria. The Anglican Church Missionary Society maintained it as a center of operations on the very limits of colonial authority in their attempts to convert the peoples they encountered in its environs. Alongside being an office and a place of worship, it was also a home to successive missionaries, who buried wives and children in its back garden.

Most of the clergy who ministered there were white; however, one freed slave who took advantage of the CMS's offer of accommodation there in the early 1860s would change Nigeria forever. Bishop Samuel Ajayi Crowther had been born into a powerful family, perhaps even royalty, in the hill country of latter-day Nigeria's Oyo state. The history of the Yoruba peoples in the early nineteenth century was one of war and counter-war, with the primary purpose being the capture of sections of opposing clans and tribes, either to then be killed as part of rituals or sold into slavery. The latter was the fate of the teenage Crowther, who—via the slave gangs who operated in the same way across West Africa as the ones we encountered at Zanzibar did for the East—found himself sold in the early 1820s and destined to cross the Atlantic. His ship, however, was intercepted by the British Royal Navy and Crowther and his fellow slaves were freed and resettled hundreds of miles away in Sierra Leone. There, Crowther converted to Christianity, a decision which would change his life.

His natural skill for languages and zeal for his new faith drew the attention of local Anglican missionaries, who were interested in the evangelization of Nigeria. Crowther, along with his fellow freed slaves Henry

Johnson, William Allen, and Daniel Olubi, joined with a white couple—the wonderfully named Anna and David Hinderer—and, after being ordained a priest by the Bishop of London on Trinity Sunday of 1843, returned to the lands of the Yoruba people to preach Christianity. He almost immediately began work in what he felt was the most important barrier to missionary efforts—the lack of a coherent codification of the Yoruba language, which made the Bible a major stumbling block for the people who spoke it. Having started with a grammar and a vocabulary, it was at the simple mission house in Ota in the 1850s that Crowther worked on his magnum opus, the translation of the scriptures into Yoruba. In 1864, at Canterbury Cathedral itself, he was consecrated Bishop of the Niger, a vast area of land, ill-defined and unchartered by Westerners.[26] There, humbly and quietly, he continued to try and bring the hope to others which had so affected him.

As the 1880s progressed, ideas among European Christians began to change. The rise of theories about race and Darwinian concepts of "superiority," which replaced the earlier wholehearted embrace of Crowther as a convert first and foremost, resulted in his being undermined and his administrative abilities questioned.[27] His health broken, he eventually died in Lagos in 1891. Undoubtedly, Crowther's life was one of "contrasts" and, even, contradictions.[28] The debate about him—was he a pioneer in and of himself or a tool of colonialism?—rages to this day. However, there can be no doubting that he was a priest who viewed faith as transformative, someone whose understanding of Christianity was one of a religion which gave people a transformative hope, both in their own lives and in the future. Indeed, it was this that inspired his transformative work in translating the Bible into Yoruba and, fundamentally, codifying the language for future use.

For Crowther, the act of giving people a way to express their faith and their hope was a life-giving act, an act, quite literally, of God. One of Crowther's earliest biographers put it like this in describing how Crowther expressed the purpose of his literary work to the clergy who assisted him:

"He assured his clergy that, apart from gifts of tongues, of healing and miracles, which God gave as credentials of their Divine mission, the

Apostles found it a great advantage that the age in which Christianity was introduced into the world was that of literature."[29]

Crowther wasn't alone in being a Christian cleric instrumental in shaping a language. We have already encountered Saints Cyril and Methodius, Thomas Cranmer, and Bishop Colenso, all of whom did the same to varying degrees and in ways that affect communication to this very day. There is so much more we can tell about the lives of the people of that part of the world—from their economic status to their customs to their very concepts of what society was like—because we know what words they used.[30] More than this, Crowther made explicit that the act of giving people a language was an inherently hopeful one. It isn't that Crowther denied the belief that God could and indeed might well act in the ways of which the preachers at Canaanland are so convinced, but that there is something subtler present too. Crowther's aim speaks of a different sort of hope present in Christianity. That it might inspire.

Our journey through these twelve churches has undoubtedly dealt more with this manner of hope than with the more mechanistic expectations of Canaanland. The churches we have encountered have been monuments to hope—whether they were hidden shrines on a Japanese mountainside, testament to the hope that, even in suffering, God would not let those who loved him down—or if they were the great architectural shrines of Christendom in Constantinople or Rome. It was belief in the fundamental hope offered by Christianity—that it might inspire an elevation of human nature—that inspired multiple works of music, art, learning, and literature in places across the world as distant in time, geography, and other types of culture as you could imagine.

Unsurprisingly, then, Crowther wasn't alone in seeing Christianity as a hope-giving faith in Nigeria. Sarah Forbes Bonetta began life similarly to Crowther: she was born named Aina, as a princess of a minor Yoruban kingdom. At some point in 1848, during one of the many internecine conflicts between those kingdoms—the first Okeadon War—she was captured by the notoriously bloodthirsty King Ghezo of the Dahomey, who had conquered her people and killed her parents. Ghezo had, like many men in the nineteenth century, a fixation with Queen

Victoria. He viewed her as the greatest European monarch and himself as the greatest African one and, therefore, believed that a relationship between the two of them was not only desirable but inevitable.

The issue with Ghezo's fixation was that Queen Victoria's representative in the Kingdom of Dahomey had been told by his superiors to give as much support as he possibly could to the faction at the Dahomey royal court (The Flies) who opposed Ghezo's own faction (The Elephants), specifically because they, unlike Ghezo, wanted to abolish slavery. Captain Frederick Forbes was a quiet, Christian man who had hoped for a simple life in the naval service rather than having to spend his time watching the "horrifying" rituals of Dahomey. Forbes spent his time being treated to elaborate displays of violence that Ghezo thought would impress him. In fact, his most regularly repeated phrase in his journals was "My God forgive them in the world to come."[31]

Mistaking Forbes's horror at the deaths of the innocent for a desire for more persuasion, Ghezo invited him to the "watering of the graves" ceremony. In this, prisoners were taken to the graves of the king's ancestors, violently beheaded, and their blood allowed to soak the soil of the previous Dahoman monarchs. One such potential victim was none other than Aina—"a girl of about six years of age." The thought of watching her beheaded was a horror too far and so Forbes quickly lied to the King and said that Queen Victoria herself would be furious were he to behead the child. Ghezo struck upon a compromise and presented the little enslaved girl as a present to the somewhat taken aback Forbes to present to Queen Victoria: she would, in his words, be a gift "from the King of the Blacks to the Queen of the Whites."[32]

Freed from this horror, Aina was given a new name—Sarah Forbes Bonetta—the surnames coming from her rescuer and the ship in which he finally made his escape from Dahomey in 1851. On arrival she was baptized as a Christian, with Queen Victoria herself becoming her godmother.[33] I wonder what King Ghezo might have made of the little child becoming closer to the most powerful woman on earth than he—the greatest king in Africa—ever could have dreamed. Sarah married a wealthy Nigerian businessman at the church of St Nicholas in Brighton, accompanied by ten carriages. She then returned to Africa where she had a child of her own, baptizing her in a church at Badagry, once a wealthy slave port for those captured in the Dahoman wars. Her name was Victoria, and the Queen agreed to become her godmother too.[34] Her faith became a central part of her life until her death in Madeira in 1880, giving her, as it undoubtedly had, hope that even the very darkest hours could be redeemed by light and life.

While Sara's story is—like all the stories we have encountered—a complex one, bound up with the realities of time and place, as much colonial political narrative as it is human fairy tale, it is easy to see why she herself saw it as a narrative of hope. To go from a cage prepared for sacrifice to the court of the most powerful woman on earth is the sort of transformation against the odds which even Bishop Oyedepo might hesitate to promise. It isn't only the materialist hope of Canaanland that might struggle with stories like Sara's and Bishop Crowther's: hope realized in the actions of others might not sit well with our modern sense of achievement—which prizes agency above all else. Yet its power is undeniable. Christian hope, as an inspiration in the manner understood by Bishop Crowther, in Sara's life as in so many lives, has not been a scam or a fairy tale but both a promise and a reality.

That idea of hope, against the odds of the world, is found in another modern Canaan, on the other side of the world from Ota. It can be tempting to see that hope as only relevant or necessary in the far-off past, in lands and times marred by horrors like human sacrifice and slavery or places where there is an existing culture of materialism or monetary need. Yet, at the heart of the world's probable next super power, one of the most popular underground publications is a collection of hymns. These songs of hope are circulated around the hidden churches in China, those which refuse to register with either of the officially tolerated (and often controlled) representations of Catholicism and Protestantism, but instead meet in houses and apartment blocks and are in constant fear of oppression.

It is hard to know precisely how many Christians exist in this way. China has almost certainly well over 100 million and growing.[35] Having suffered being tortured to death in living memory and still at

318 *Twelve Churches*

enormous risk, it is no surprise that hope has such currency in their meetings. It is no surprise that the songs they use come from a collection named after the Biblical land of hope: they are known as *The Songs of Canaan.*

Many of the hymns seem to subvert or mimic the workers' songs associated with the Cultural Revolution. The purpose of these monumental changes wrought on China in the 1960s and 1970s was to create a Communist "monoculture," with the dominant message of Communism preeminent in every area of life.[36] That Christianity can adapt to and overcome even such a totalitarian cultural vision—or, even more impressively, can redeem the cultural products of totalitarianism—is undoubtedly a source of hope for those who believe.

The tunes are easy and the lyrics simple, with titles like "Lord You Are My Best Friend" and "Follow the Holy Spirit."[37] Their composer is a woman in her fifties named Lu Xiaomin. From a family of peasant farmers and completely untaught in music or poetry, she was converted to Christianity surreptitiously when a teenager by an aunt who was an underground Christian. She then wrote both lyrics and music to the Canaan hymns in her head while working in the fields of Northern China. As such, they, like the future Christianity hoped for by those opposing the Prosperity Gospel in Africa, speak authentically of "local idiom."[38] Whether that means they will be free of the past mistakes other Christians have made, or simply destined to repeat them, is a matter, like so much, of hope. Among Chinese Christians, she is known as "God's Gift to China."[39] She is barely known in the West, but when it comes to thinking about the question "Where do Christians find hope?", to many in China the answer is through her words and music.

This hope is perhaps best demonstrated in one of Lu Xiaomin's own compositions. Drawing on the imagery of the Ark in Genesis and on the association of the Holy Spirit with the form of a dove, it expresses hope for a new era for Christianity in China.

> Night comes, the dove returns, carrying a newly
> plucked olive leaf in her mouth.
> It represents hope.[40]

At the heart of China, there are Christians who put their hope in the simple melodies that came from the work of the farm field. While agriculture is an activity many thousands of years older than Christianity itself, there are Christians elsewhere who are looking to the very newest technologies available as places where their hopes for a Christian future might be grounded.

Prakash Parthipan does not walk like the Bishop in Canaanland. He smiles as he makes the odd step across his tiny stage. All that is on it is a sideboard, a lectern, and some plastic garden furniture. Brother Prakash—for so it is that he styles himself—has Bollywood looks and a knack for technology. He is also the evangelist of the Canaan TV Network. Based in the city of Shah Alam in Malaysia, the young Christian leader streams on WhatsApp, YouTube, Facebook, Instagram, and other channels which I hadn't even heard of. His ministry is largely directed toward the Tamil minority in Malysia and is mostly in their language. His hundreds of hours of broadcasts vary from direct one-on-one videos to the revival service which I watch thousands of miles away from the comfort of my home and computer. Above his head are four words which summarize the hope of the other people watching: JESUS: HEALS, DELIVERS, SAVES.

Other parts of English, as well as Hindi and Malay phrases, break through the Tamil in the way that so often happens when polyglots speak off the cuff: "We are talking about the heavenly places," Brother Prakash tells the audience. Then a word sneaks in which has its etymology in Hebrew. Brother Prakash pronounces it softly, like it is a delicate, sacred thing. Which, in many ways it is. It is a word of comfort, of hope: "Hallelujah."

Toward the end of Brother Prakash's broadcast, his live audience stand up. I notice that they are almost all women, with a smattering of children. Many of them will live lives where they are practically invisible: Malaysia is ranked 114th out of 146 for female equality in 2024.[41] And yet here they were, with Brother Prakash, their hands in the air, their hopes not only seen but heard as well.

Televangelism has its opponents. In many cases it has been seen as a way of entering the homes of the vulnerable or lonely and milking them for cash. Ironically, one of the most recent satires of the industry—for that is what it can be—is called none other than *Canaan Land*. The land of promise can be turned into a tragic and shattered illusion for some. Organizations like the Trinity Broadcasting Network in Texas have allegations leveled against them ranging from sexual assault by pastors to massive financial corruption.[42][43] Such crimes are shocking, of course, but not unique to televangelism, to which parts of this book can testify. There is also a more existential criticism that it replaces something that is integral to Christianity. Christ specifically reshapes the concept of the Divine. This is not just a God of distant broadcasts, as if from a heavenly TV studio, but a God who allows his followers to wash his feet, who touches the bier of a dead man at Nain, who allows the nails and spear to be thrust through his flesh on the Cross. The God, to return again to our beginning, of the manger. Something is lost when that in-person, incarnate reality is replaced by a broadcast.

However, in an increasingly technologically linked world, it ought not to be surprising that Christians are present—using new technology, as they always have, be it the printing press or television, or the internet—to spread their message of hope. Brother Prakash's Canaan TV Network is not the largest nor the most famous televangelist network in the world but it illustrates the reach of a message of hope better than those that are. That places like the slums where many Malaysian Tamils, still confined by the oppressive practices of the rubber industry, have their homes, which can now be places that broadcast evangelism across the world, is astonishing.[44] Not for the first time, Christianity and technology both seem to have futures that are interwoven, extra-European, and impossible to predict.

Such is the pace of technological change that there are areas where the very assumptions of Christian concepts of the human seem to be challenged. Contact between humans of all types—financial, sexual, even religious—is increasingly happening digitally, via social media. What are the consequences of that for a religion which states that God is found in the flesh not in fiberoptic cables? Of course, there are positive aspects to this: social media has been revelatory in linking Christians to one another and in promoting the activities of various churches. While it is obvious that a phone or a computer or a television might be used to spread the message of hope that a human soul can be saved by the love of Christ, what happens when at the other end of the technology there is not a human soul at all?

The question of what Artificial Intelligence and other types of "machine learning" might mean for the future is being asked in almost every sphere of life in the early twenty-first century. In Christianity it is no different. Some Christians argue that AI will prove to be like all the other technology and is capable of being turned into a tool for the Gospel, capable of helping to spread hope. There are suggestions it could help with sermons or produce relatable content for children. Then there is the argument of provenance, or as one author has put it, "Our Father already knows more about this new technology than we ever will."[45] For many Christians, hope in a new technology and trust in the purposes of God necessarily have to go hand in hand. Elsewhere there has been a suggestion that Christianity has as much to teach AI as vice versa. The Anglican Bishop of Oxford has even produced "The 10 Commandments for Robots," a set of rules designed to try to ensure that machine learning continues in a way that remains broadly ethical. They include the instruction that the primary purpose of such technology must "be to enhance and augment, rather than replace, human labor and creativity."[46]

However, many Christians have sounded caution about new technology which seems to turn on its head the ideas which Christians have long had about the purpose of life on earth. It is all well and good for St Augustine to write that "you have made us for yourself O Lord and our hearts are restless until we find our rest in you," but what are the implications for seemingly sentient robots?[47] How can something not made by God function for worship? Where is the hope in an algorithm?

As a young researcher on the overlap between faith and science, the Reverend Dr. Andrew Davison was consulted by NASA on what the ramifications might be for faith if alien life was discovered in outer space. Now, as Regius Professor of Divinity at Oxford, he sounds a more cautious tone on the consequences of machine learning for Christianity here on earth. He quotes Thomas Aquinas, who wrote that "the tools are for the worker": that is to say that the purpose of AI, or any other technology, ought always to be a human one.[48] "Any greatness to technology is human greatness," Davison observes.[49] And any faith with the manger, cross, and tomb at its center must necessarily be a human one too.

Yet, even in a world of fast-changing—if not necessarily advancing—technology, Christian hope still offers something profound and different. We can pursue as much learning as we want, can create technology which is functionally no different from magic in terms of the astonishing things it might achieve, but still there will be a need for something more. C. S. Lewis, who was explicitly trying to present the complexities of the idea of Christian pre-existence to children and young people described it thus in his book *The Lion, the Witch and the Wardrobe*:

"the Witch knew the Deep Magic, [but] there is a magic deeper still which she did not know. Her knowledge goes back only to the dawn of time. But if she could have looked a little further back, into the stillness and the darkness before Time dawned, she would have read there a different incantation."[50]

His character Aslan goes on to describe the existence of a deeper and more powerful magic, from before the dawn of time.

If this book has demonstrated anything it is, I hope, that the power of sacred places, of churches where people have sought solace for centuries, still gives hope to Christians—and others—even in a century of technological advance where worship might now happen anywhere.

In 1948, at the start of the Cold War, a radio station in Washington, DC, contacted the ambassadors of the Great Powers resident there and asked them what they were hoping for that Christmas. The French Ambassador, echoing the message of the angels at Bethlehem, replied saying that he hoped for peace on earth and goodwill to all men, while the Soviet Ambassador, keen to stick to Communism's ideology, said he hoped for freedom for all peoples enslaved by imperialism and capitalism. The British Ambassador, Sir Oliver Franks, replied with a written note, saying simply, "That's very kind of you to ask. I'd quite like a box of crystallized fruit."[51]

The story, though sadly probably apocryphal, illustrates a truth:

there is always a slight English embarrassment about expressing hopes. That is not to say that I do not have hope—I am instructed to as a Christian. Now, of course, there is hope in the fact that Christianity is at the forefront of making the developing world a more equitable place: feeding the hungry, clothing the naked, fighting for those who are otherwise forgotten. There is hope in things I see Christianity doing every day. But I can't only hope in it as a practical faith. Instead, my hope is of an order a little different to that of Bishop Oyedepo or Lu Xiaomin or Prakash Parthipan or inhabitants of those other Canaans.

I don't hope for instant answering of my prayers, in the way that the Bishop does, I don't hope for—and I am lucky enough that I don't need to hope for—mere survival like Lu Xiaomin does. Indeed, to me, prayer is a bit more like a baring of oneself to the Divine, a making known the innermost parts of the soul, the things we would normally hide or suppress or reason ourselves out of. Rather, my hope is that God does not glorify us in our prosperity but sits alongside us in our suffering. Hope is based on what it must be: my experience of God. It was best expressed by the Anglican Divine, Jeremy Taylor. Taylor lived through persecution, exile, and tragedy during the bloody days of the English Civil War. Yet he still kept hope—though counseled that it should be of things "possible, safe, and useful." He perhaps put it best of all when he described hope as being the thing that "makes our prayers reasonable."[52]

I am sure there are those who would say that is a sign of a "lukewarm faith." The Bible ends with a book which has much to say about hope. The Revelation of Saint John the Divine talks about what will happen at the end of the world, when that hope is realized.[53] Those whose faith in the purposes of God is not strong enough—"lukewarm, neither cold nor hot"—will be "spat out."[54] I suppose the only thing that I can do is hope that, despite this, in the words of the song that started this chapter:

> Some happy day with all the ransomed I will stand
> And sing his praise 'way over in Canaan's land.

Let us return to Canaan. As with Bethlehem, its history remained a complex entanglement of life and death until even the most recent years. The

British general who defeated the Ottoman Empire in the First World War—that conflict which felt like the end of the world to so many—was honored by being made a member of the British House of Lords. Field Marshal Allenby was asked to choose a geographical location which would be linked to the title he would take in the peerage. Allenby chose two. The first was Felixstowe, an unassuming seaside town on the Eastern coast of England, favored by those with respiratory diseases as a gentle place for recuperation. The other was Megiddo in Palestine, or, to give it the name that it had been known by when part of the Biblical Canaan: Armageddon.

Allenby's choice was not accidental. It is at Armageddon that St John predicted that, God having gathered angels and men there, "thunders, lightnings, earthquakes" that indicate the end of the world would occur.[55] What is described is fearful: all moving skies and rebel angels thrown down to the earth. Death, war, famine, and pestilence are predicted to stalk the earth. It doesn't sound very cheery. Yet, the end times—whatever form they take—are not something that are necessarily scary for Christians, because they promise a conclusion of time and a return of—and to—Christ in the new promised land, the final Canaan. What is hopeful about them is that they will pass away and be replaced by something better. They promise the dawning of an age where all those hopes—for peace, justice, grace, and love—are made a reality.

In Revelation, then, as in the streets of Ota or across the internet, hope for the future and the realities of the past and present are entirely interwoven. Life and death are too. Indeed, we could say that this has been the theme which has tied together each and every building and site which we have visited across this book. Each of them tells the story of a place where humans have failed and fought, have been proud and partial, and generally exhibited all of the characteristics of an imperfect human nature and yet still have dared to hope in something beyond all that. That is what is crucial about hope in Christianity—it doesn't deny the messy parts of life but claims that even they can be redeemed. It is why—to return to its origins and to our first church on this journey—the symbols of this faith are not a crown or sword but a manger, a cross, and an empty grave.

Canaanland, Ota, Nigeria 325

• • •

I find hope, therefore, in Christianity's strangeness. In its paradox. In that it might bind together all the times and places and people mentioned here into an eventual, hopeful whole. Each week, in my little church near Oxford, I silently pray a prayer that perhaps best encapsulates that promise:

Almighty God, Father of all mercies, we your unworthy servants give you humble thanks for all your goodness and loving-kindness to us and to all whom you have made. We bless you for our creation, preservation, and all the blessings of this life; but above all for your immeasurable love in the redemption of the world by our Lord Jesus Christ; for the means of grace, and for the hope of glory. And, we pray, give us such an awareness of your mercies, that with truly thankful hearts we may show forth your praise, not only with our lips, but in our lives, by giving up ourselves to your service, and by walking before you in holiness and righteousness all our days; through Jesus Christ our Lord, to whom, with you and the Holy Spirit, be honor and glory throughout all ages. Amen.[55]

The hope of glory. If Christianity is about anything, it is that. We end, therefore, where we began, with that song of the angels and the message of the manger. With Jesus Christ. The idea that frail and flawed humanity might, by hope in that same Christ, be transformed into vessels for God's glory. Sometimes that idea has led to immense beauty and wonder, sometimes to power and corruption; it has motivated hope and faith, it has caused quests for expansion and for purity, it has affected how we think about sex, profit, violence, nationhood, and justice. It has shaped people's lives and people's deaths. It is no surprise, then, that its churches and the people who have built and prayed in them reflect that.

Epilogue:
Surprise, Service, Belonging

San Pantalon, Venice, Italy

Delhi Brotherhood, Delhi, India

St Mary's, Charlbury, and All Saints, Shorthampton,
Oxfordshire, United Kingdom

"The boiler's broken." One of my churchwardens breaks the bad news to me. We go into the toilet—a convenience carefully shaped from the ancient structure of the church—and he shows me the basin of water, which ominously fills up by means of a steady drip from the boiler. This is often the reality of a church. The prosaic run of life in the midst of the Divine.

This is my church—or rather one of my churches: I have the care of St Mary's in Charlbury and All Saints, Shorthampton, in the countryside just north of Oxford. The tower of St Mary's dominates the little town, which is fiercely proud of its charter, granted to it by King Henry III in 1256. The church, like the pubs, shops, and houses that line the gentle incline of the street which leads from it, is in Cotswolds stone and golden in the right light. It was added to by various generations: Roman remains in the graveyard, Saxon foundations, Norman pillars, medieval walls, the scars of the Reformation in the form of beheaded gargoyles, a seventeenth-century porch, eighteenth-century marble, nineteenth-century glass, and, due to an outbreak of dry rot and woodworm, a starkly functional twentieth-century interior. The church is both an astonishing survival of parts of the past and a completely ordinary example of the sort of building found in much of Europe.

I find myself back there, in Oxfordshire, listening to the bells of St Mary's while completing this book. It has been quite a journey, but, at the end of it, I am only sorry that there is not enough space for more of the stories that churches hold and of which the stones sing. What have these churches shown us? What have I learned about them, ever since that first foray into an English country church and having been to some of the most astonishing examples of them on the planet?

Firstly, I have learned that churches have the infinite capacity to surprise. Every church in this book surprised me in one way or another. Even churches that you think you know have this capacity. I think of San Pantalon, a church on an unremarkable square just where the quarter of Dorsoduro meets that of San Polo in Venice. It is made up of an ugly brick-wall facade and is walked by, unnoticed and unloved, by thousands of people every day. They are in Venice to be submerged in beauty, and San Pantalon, devoid of external decoration, jolts them out of that submersion. For this, it is punished by being ignored.

Or at least it was by me, during two decades spent visiting the city regularly. Then, one day, lost on a wander, I went in and looked up. San Pantalon has the most remarkable ceiling in Venice. John Ruskin called it "the rags and ruins of Venetian skill, honor, and worship exploded all together sky high." Not all churches have a physical interior like San Pantalon, but all, undoubtedly, have an interior life. They hold stories and secrets, highs and lows. It should not be surprising—they speak of humanity and the Divine after all—and both of those are capable of being infinitely surprising.

The other thing that has defined all these churches is service. I saw this most acutely at the Delhi Brotherhood. They are an Anglican religious order in India whose church is a squat brick building, almost with the look of a fortified bunker. It is undoubtedly not pretty, but it is serviceable. When I visited, one of the brethren was engaged in the Augean task of sweeping dust from the main steps. From the gaps between the thick stones of the exterior, trees and plants poke out. The interior is a strange mix of modern India and the building's past as a center for missionary work: the Prayer Book in Sanskrit and an Archbishop Rowan Williams commemorative plate jostle with an internet router. Money is not often spent on repairs or renovations, but rather on others. Service defines everything they do: from running helplines for women fleeing domestic violence to funding schools to simply painting the houses of those who cannot afford to paint them. The Delhi Brotherhood take to heart the radical idea that churches are buildings which explicitly do not exist for their own sake. Or even for the sake of the people immediately using them. This is true not only in the way exhibited in Delhi, but in a metaphysical sense too. They exist for those who seek shelter from the ways of the world, who need help, either physical or spiritual; they exist to serve as reminders that we are not alone.

Finally, I have found that all of these churches speak of a sense of belonging. Belonging both to a particular place, with all its history and baggage and beauty, but also to something bigger. To Christ and the faith he continues to inspire. What else can link the Vatican, Canaanland, Salem, and the hillsides above Kasuga?

My churches, St Mary's and All Saints, illustrate all of these qualities, sometimes in quite quotidian ways: the surprises are likely to be archaic coinage in the collection bowl, or bat droppings near the high altar. Its sense of service is unfussy; people come and give of time, money, and effort both to God and their fellow humans in a way that is distinctly undramatic. Even the sense of belonging is a gentle one, not tribal or sectarian, but a gentle sense that the church has been there for the community for nearly 1,500 years and so they ought to be there for it as well. One regular member of my quiet eight o'clock Communion service walks pasts the graves of his parents each Sunday morning to pray in the same place where they did. A simple act, repeated in communities all over the world, but one that inevitably ties a person to a place in ways that it is hard to map, in terms of economics or politics or even a more doggedly doctrinal faith, as measures of identity.

All this is to say that in many ways, the places to which I am called to serve are about as run-of-the-mill churches as you could find; in others, however, what goes on there is anything but ordinary. In them, astonishing things happen. I am endlessly surprised by their people and their capacity to point to a sense of Divine love using the physical space of the church. From them, the community—that is to say the ordinary people of God present here in this generation—run a foodbank for those who

330   *Twelve Churches*

struggle to feed themselves, a drop-in café for people with dementia, a care group for children, a choir for members of the wider community; they cook for monthly breakfasts and lunches and, above all else, they come to these places every day, with me, their parish priest, to worship God. In short, unlikely as it seems, these churches are where the intimate and the universal meet. I am, of course, biased, but if you were going to find a place that best expresses that strange and beautiful unity of the human and the Divine that is Christianity, then I think you could do far worse than look to this ordinary pair of churches.

St Mary's is a hive of activity, but to go back to where we began—with buildings—then All Saints, in particular, is a gem. It is a tiny chapel in the middle of a field, like something from a fairy story. People see it from across the rolling landscape and sometimes wonder if it's really there at all. Even I have wondered, as the haze of late summer shimmers over the harvest, whether it is a figment of my imagination or a visitor from another era, evidence for a slip in the fabric of time. It is reached by a warren of lanes and paths that cut through wheat and corn. It is always kept open because, as impressive as its exterior is, it is the wall paintings inside that people travel miles and miles to see.

Shorthampton's wall paintings are thought to date from between the thirteenth and fifteenth centuries. Some, like the Doom painting, are incomplete, little snippets of a medieval view of what the end of the world might have looked like preserved in the Oxfordshire countryside. Others, better preserved and fuller in scale, tell their own stories. There is an image of St Zita, an Italian servant woman of the thirteenth century whose deep faith and care for the poor earned her the role as patron saint of Lucca. What on earth had brought a devotion to her to this little part of rural England is anyone's guess. Perhaps she was commissioned by a one-time servant made good or married well, who wanted to thank a fellow serving girl for her intercession? Or perhaps she was painted by a priest, come to Oxford from Italy to study, and then exiled to the countryside for a misdemeanor, seeking a reminder of his sunnier homeland? We will never know, I suspect. But we can tell that her presence speaks of the connections Christianity has always engendered—not only across countries and oceans but across centuries as well.

Epilogue

It is, however, the roof of All Saints that is my favorite part of the church. This is because its corbels—the six supporting blocks of stone on the top of the interior walls which support the roof—are carved with faces. We suspect they were all people who had a part to play in the life of the church here during the high medieval period: the priest, the man in charge of the masonry, a woman with a rather glorious hat. The original inspirations for these carvings are long dead, but those types still come to that place and seek the solace of the Divine and the fellowship of one another. And there, above them, is a reminder of something we've seen throughout our journey: that people and place are one. At Shorthampton, this finds its expression in stone: the roof of the church is quite literally kept up by the people who worshipped here.

What are the lessons, then, of this survey, which has taken us from Japan to Dominica, the United States to Ethiopia, Tanzania to Turkey, and finally led us here, to a quiet country church? Well, that Christianity is a faith of surprises. Not a single one of these churches has told a simple story; not a single one of the themes we have dealt with has been straightforward. They have shown us, too, that Christianity has been at its most appealing when it has served. Service and a counter-cultural subversion of the powers of the world, whether in the jungles of Mesoamerica or in the courts of Europe, have been the most effective evangelistic methods for the faith which began at the manger. Finally, each of these churches is a place where people have felt a profound sense of belonging. A sense of being part of something bigger than just themselves. Of course, plenty of organizations or beliefs manage that, but Christianity, through that same manger and the incarnation found therein, suggests that frail and fallen humanity—which is on display in all its beauty and horror throughout this book—might be taken into the very heart of God. That is a promise of belonging which is, necessarily, greater than any other.

Surprise, service, and belonging. They aren't always done right and they aren't always simple. But such are the characteristics which define so many churches and the lives of the people who have loved them. And, as we have discovered, they might serve as defining characteristics for global Christianity as well.

Acknowledgments

I'd like to thank all those involved in getting this book to publication. In particular to Max Edwards for his vision and advocacy as an agent and to Jack Ramm for the same as well as taking on a project midway through. My thanks go also to Gus Brown and Checkie Hamilton at Aevitas. I'd like to thank Tom Perrin and Naomi Morris Omori in the UK and Caroline Sutton and Megan Noes in the US for their brilliance and consummate professionalism. I am also enormously grateful to Sophie Bristow Symonds and Anna Hervé for their work on copy and proof editing. My profound thanks to James Oses, Luke Adam Hawker, and Lucy Scholes for their artistic talent and vision and to Juliette Winter as well in making such a beautiful book. I'd also like to thank Mila Melia-Kapoor and Melissa Grierson for all their amazing work in getting it out there.

My thanks too to those who traveled with me to various places: to Julian, Henry, James, and the sixth form theologians and classicists, to Tom, to Ellis, to Marcus, to Simon, and Dylan. To colleagues for their tolerance as this book was prepared, in particular David. To Paul for his classical talent. Once again my deepest thanks goes to everyone named and referred to only in passing who helped me upon my way in these amazing places.

To the people of Charlbury and Shorthampton for their unceasing kindness and ordinary holiness. To the Bishop and Archdeacon of Dorchester for their support and tolerance.

To my friends, my siblings, my parents, and especially to Maddy for all their love.

Appendix: Dramatis Personae

Each chapter has at its heart the stories of the people who lived and prayed within the vicinity of the churches mentioned or whose thought or faith intersected with the places and themes discussed. This list of characters is provided as an aid to the reader, and to set the book in its proper context, which is as a story.

Chapter One

Caliph Al-Hakim (985–1021)—Sixth Caliph of the Fatimids, he ruled a large Empire across North Africa, the Middle, and Near East, putting in place punitive measures against Christians.

Gertrude Bell (1868–1926)—British author, Arabist, and adventurer. Instrumental in the creation of modern Iraq and in the protection of ancient monuments. Spent Christmas at Bethlehem at the turn of the twentieth century.

The Brawling Monks of the Nativity—monastic brothers of various denominations—Greek, Roman Catholic, and Syriac—have been fighting, sometimes physically, over access to the Church of the Nativity since the medieval period.

Bishop Brooks (1835–1893)—American clergyman and author, the Sixth Episcopal Bishop of Massachusetts, and author of "O Little Town of Bethlehem." He visited Bethlehem in 1865.

King Charles III (1948–)—Monarch of the United Kingdom, Canada, Australia, New Zealand, etc., and Supreme Governor of the Church of England, he described his visit to Bethlehem in his first Christmas speech in 2022.

Aurelius Prudentius Clemens (348–413)—Born in modern-day Spain, a Roman administrator, lawyer, and poet who wrote hymns about Bethlehem.

Gemma Collins (1981–)—A British reality television star who spoke of her emotion at visiting Bethlehem at Christmas 2022.

Saint Francis of Assisi (1181–1226)—Italian saint and mystic who gave up a life of luxury to serve Christ. Known for his visits to the Holy Land and love of animals.

The Empress Helena (c. 247–330)—the mother of the Emperor Constantine and imperial convert to Christianity. Claimed to have discovered the true sites of the manger and the cross.

Jesus Christ—believed by Christians to be God and Man, Alpha and Omega, Beginning and End.

Mrs. Favell Lee Mortimer (1802–1878)—English children's author and visitor to the

Holy Land, including Bethlehem. Her books—including *Latin without Tears* and *More about Jesus* were described as "outspokenly sadistic."

Fra Niccolò da Poggibonsi (fl. 1340s)—A Franciscan friar who went on pilgrimage to the Holy Land, in particular Bethlehem, during the period 1345–50, writing an account of his travels.

Barack Obama (1961–)—44th President of the United States of America and one of multiple recent holders of that office to visit the Church of the Nativity.

The Reverend Dr. Yazid Said (*c.* 1978–)—An Anglican priest and academic who is the Professor of Arabic at Liverpool Hope University and a native of Nazareth.

Kaiser Wilhelm II (1859–1941)—Last reigning Kaiser of the German Second Reich. He visited Bethlehem and Jerusalem in 1898 resulting in major structural work to accommodate his visit.

Chapter Two

Saint Agnes (*c.* 291–304)—Roman virgin and martyr who was brutally killed for refusing to renounce her faith. The site of her death is now a major church in Rome.

Bernini (1598–1680)—a pioneer of the Baroque and prominent architect of Rome, it was his vision which gives us much of the city as we see it today.

Bonnie Prince Charlie (1720–1788)—Jacobite Pretender to the British Throne. After the failure of his invasion of Britain in 1745, he escaped to the continent and lived in Rome.

Christina of Sweden (1626–1689)—Queen of Sweden who abdicated her throne when she converted to Roman Catholicism in 1654. She later lived in exile in Rome.

Unworthy John—the unknown patron of one of the wall paintings in the ancient basilica of San Clemente in Rome.

Pope Julius II (1443–1513)—Roman Catholic Pope, politician, general, and primary mover behind the construction of the new St Peter's.

Martin Luther (1483–1546)—German monk, author, and scatologist. Furious at the imposition of indulgences that St Peter's rebuilding required, he set in motion the start of the Protestant Reformation.

Michelangelo (1475–1564)—Florentine artist and sculptor who came to prominence during the Renaissance and was responsible for much of the ornamentation of the new St Peter's basilica.

The Emperor Nero (37–68)—Roman Emperor: the last of the Julio-Claudian dynasty who ruled from 54 until his death. A vigorous persecutor of Christianity.

Pope Nicholas V (1397–1455)—Roman Catholic Pope who first suggested the idea of rebuilding the medieval St Peter's basilica in a new style.

Saint Peter (died *c.* 65)—disciple of Christ, first Bishop of Rome, and erstwhile fishing entrepreneur. His death was thought to have occurred on the site of the current Vatican.

The weeping woman of St Peter's—a woman who stood, silently and with tears in her eyes, by the statue of the Pietà at St Peter's.

Appendix: Dramatis Personae 337

The naked bathers of the Swiss Guard—the Swiss Guard have been the personal bodyguard of the Pontiff since 1506. Recruited from Swiss men aged between nineteen and thirty and at least 5 ft 9 inches tall, they maintain the custom of swimming nude during the summer.

Johann Tetzel (1465–1519)—German friar, inquisitor, and door-to-door salesman tasked with collecting indulgences in the electorates of Brandenburg and Saxony in the early sixteenth century.

Lazslo Toth (1938–?)—Hungarian-born Australian geologist and independent thinker. Responsible for damaging the Pietà in St Peter's at Pentecost 1972.

Chapter Three

Alexios Angelos (1182–1204)—the exiled pretender to the Byzantine throne whose mismanagement of the intrigues he had started contributed to the sack of Constantinople in 1204.

Atatürk (1881–1938)—born Mustafa Kemal, he took advantage of his position as an Ottoman military commander to seize power and become the first president of a secular Turkish republic.

The tea man on the Bosphorus ferry—passenger boats have crossed the Bosphorus since ancient times. The first steam ferries made the journey in 1837; however, people have been offering refreshment on the voyage, usually in the form of hot, sweet tea, for much longer.

Constantine the Great (272–337)—Roman Emperor, Christian convert, and founder of the city of Constantinople. Crucial in the "Constantinian Shift," which saw Christianity become a political as well as religious power. Very close to his mother.

Constantine XI Palaeologus (1404–1453)—last Byzantine Emperor, who died defending the city of Constantinople from the Turks and remains the source of much myth and legend.

Enrico Dandolo (1107–1205)—the long-lived and extremely politically manipulative Doge of the Venetian Republic. Dandolo's cunning was crucial in the Latin conquest of Constantinople in 1204. He was buried at Hagia Sophia.

Diana of Ephesus—an image of the Graeco-Roman goddess of hunting, childcare, and vegetation found at the large temple at Ephesus in the ancient world.

Recep Tayyip Erdogan (1954–)—President of Turkey since 2014, in 2020 he succeeded in fulfilling his long-held political goal of returning Hagia Sophia to Muslim worship.

The caretaker of the Gül Camii—the Gül Camii or Rose Mosque was, prior to 1453, the Church of St Theodosia and one of the most important Byzantine buildings in Constantinople. It is rumored that the last Emperor was buried there. Now it is something of a backwater, cared for by a kindly old man.

Cardinal Isidore (*c.* 1390–1462)—an illegitimate member of the Byzantine Imperial family who sought preferment in the Roman Catholic Church, escaping the sack of 1453 in disguise. Not to be confused with the contemporaneous Patriarch Isidore of Kyiv who invented vodka.

338   *Appendix: Dramatis Personae*

Justinian I (482–565)—statesman, soldier, and workaholic who ruled the Byzantine Empire from 527. He wanted to be known for restoring the territories in the Western Mediterranean; his most lasting legacy is in fact Hagia Sophia itself.

Empress Maria (1145–1182)—the wife of the Emperor Manuel I Komnenos, who had been born to the French princes of Antioch in the Holy Land; she was killed during the "massacre of the Latins" by either strangulation or drowning.

Mehmet the Conqueror (1432–1481)—Sultan of the Ottoman Empire and military commander who finally conquered Constantinople.

Saint Paul (*c.* 5–65)—former persecutor of the Church turned apostle. Responsible for the authorship of many of the books of the New Testament and central to the shaping of early Christian thought.

Thomas Whittemore (1871–1950)—flamboyant American scholar and archaeologist who was instrumental in converting Hagia Sophia into a museum in 1935.

Chapter Four

Saint Alphege (953–1012)—Archbishop of Canterbury and Anglo-Saxon statesman. Taken prisoner by the Vikings at Canterbury, he was beaten to death with ox bones near the River Thames.

Thomas Becket (1119–1170)—English statesman and cleric who fell out with his onetime friend and employer and was murdered in his own cathedral as a result.

The Sisters of Boxley (fl. late 1100s)—two sickly sisters from a village near Maidstone in Kent, England. Their healing by and berating of Thomas Becket features in the stained glass of Canterbury.

Elicia Butler (died *c.* 1542)—Abbess and strict disciplinarian. From the Anglo-Irish Butler family, she was subject to a series of complaints by her own nuns due to her heavy-handedness. An effigy at St Carnice's Cathedral in Kilkenny is thought to be of her.

The Dean of Canterbury (1968–)—The Very Reverend David Monteith has been Dean of Canterbury since 2022.

Thomas Cranmer (1489–1556)—Archbishop of Canterbury in the Tudor period, a scholar and liturgist but ultimately an unsuccessful politician as he was burned at the stake under Queen Mary I.

Eilward of Westoning (fl. early 1200s)—a man accused—he maintained wrongly—of theft who was castrated as a result. He prayed to Thomas Becket at Canterbury and found his testicles miraculously healed.

Mary Sameh George (1989–2014)—a young Christian aid worker who was killed by a sectarian mob in the suburbs of Cairo for having a cross tied to the rearview mirror of her car.

King Henry VIII (1491–1547)—English monarch, Defender of the Faith, and probable syphilis sufferer. Henry's marriage problems helped to precipitate the English Reformation.

Appendix: Dramatis Personae

Pope John Paul II (1920–2005)—Roman Catholic Pope, sportsman, and widely traveled religious leader. His visit to Canterbury Cathedral in 1982 was highly symbolic.

Josce of York (died 1190)—Jewish leader and financier who died, along with his family and other members of the Jewish community, in a mass suicide at Clifford's Tower during the pogrom in the city of York.

Mad Matilda of Cologne (fl. early 1200s)—a woman from continental Europe who arrived in Canterbury to seek healing during the early days of Becket's cult.

Mileto of Sardis (c. 100–180)—Bishop of Sardis in modern-day Turkey. Mileto's writings sowed the seed for much latter Christian antisemitism.

Robert Runcie (1921–2000)—Archbishop of Canterbury in the 1980s. Instrumental in improving ecumenical relations, he had been awarded the MC for his actions as a tank commander in the Second World War.

Leonie Seliger (1965–)—a stained-glass artist and the director of stained-glass conservation at Canterbury Cathedral, who showed the author the medieval glass up close.

Chapter Five

Saint Augustine (354–430)—Bishop of Hippo in North Africa and instrumental philosopher and theologian who shaped Western and Christian concepts of self, time, and sex.

Saint John Cassian (360–435)—early monk, mystic, and writer who crossed East and West in his pursuit of asceticism. Crucial in forming monastic rules for later communities.

Brother Cassianos—an elderly, smiling monk at the Monastery of the Pantokrator.

Maryse Choisy (1903–1979)—French journalist and writer who was also, variously, a psychoanalyst, occultist, and recipient of the French Order of Merit. She disguised herself as a man and spent a month on Athos in the 1920s.

The women of the Crossbones Graveyard—the remains of those women (and their unwanted children) who worked as prostitutes in the Liberty of the Clink, a red-light district in medieval London administered on behalf of the Bishop of Winchester.

Aliki Diplarakou (1912–2002)—a Greek model, socialite, and lecturer who snuck onto Mount Athos dressed as a man in the 1930s.

Finnian (470–549)—Irish saint and father of Celtic monasticism, renowned for his learning, discipline, and organizational skills.

Saint Gregory of Nyssa (335–394)—Bishop in modern Turkey who made significant contributions to philosophy, theology, and wider thought.

Helena of Serbia (1315–1375)—Bulgarian-born wife of King and later Emperor of Serbia, Stefan Dušan, she was refused entry to the holy mountain by the monks in the 1340s.

Innocenzo Ciocchi del Monte (1532–1577)—beggar, gay sex symbol, monkey-keeper, murderer, and cardinal of the Roman Catholic Church.

340 *Appendix: Dramatis Personae*

The Blessed Virgin Mary—mother of Jesus Christ, venerated throughout the world but in particular on Mount Athos.

Michael—a fellow guest of the author's at the Pantokrator monastery on Mount Athos.

Michael the Stammerer (1020–1105)—Byzantine scholar, medic, and satirist. A tutor to the future emperor Michael VII Doukas. He was the first person to correctly identify strabismus of the eye, so wrote a 1,732-line poem about it.

Father Nikitos—the kindly guest master of the Pantokrator Monastery on Mount Athos. An enthusiast for tennis, an excellent linguist, and a clearly holy man.

Viscountess Stratford de Redclive—born Eliza Charlotte Alexander, she was the wife of the Viscount who served as British Ambassador to the Sublime Porte in Constantinople from 1842 to 1858. Her visit to Mount Athos reflected Britain's power at the time.

Chapter Six

Francisco Alvarez (1465–*c.* 1540)—Portuguese priest and explorer who visited Ethiopia for a prolonged period in the 1520s. He wrote the first European account of Lalibela's churches, for which he was worried people would accuse him of exaggerating.

Katherine Chidley (1616–*c.* 1653)—English Puritan, political radical, and all-around troublemaker, who made life difficult with her sermons, publications, and personal arguments for Church and state alike.

Gebre Mesqel Lalibela (1162–1221)—King of the Zagwe dynasty in Ethiopia, he commissioned the ornate collection of rock churches which now bear his name.

Princess Libuše—the mythical founder of the Czech nation after she fell in love with the rugged ploughman Přemysl and they spent several days having sex.

Lucy—40% of the skeleton of a female of the hominin species Australopithecus afarensis found at Hadar in Ethiopia in 1974. The remains date from roughly 3.2 million years ago.

Narendra Modi (1950–)—Prime Minister of India since 2014 and leader of the nation's Hindu nationalist party.

Patriarch Nikon (1605–1681)—Seventh Patriarch of Moscow, he was instrumental in the formation of modern Russia. Throughout his stormy career—going from the son of peasant farmer to the most powerful man in the country—he maintained a devotion to nation and Church, eventually building his own "New Jerusalem" monastery near Moscow.

Plato (*c.* 427–328 BC)—Greek philosopher instrumental in forming Western ideas about matter, reality, and the soul. An enormous influence on the growth of Christian thought.

Bishop Leonidas Polk (1806–1864)—First Episcopal Bishop of Louisiana and later notably incompetent but popular Confederate General in American Civil War, who was killed at the Battle of Pine Mountain.

Appendix: Dramatis Personae

The Queen of Sheba—a figure, also known as Makeda and Bilqis, who appears in Biblical, para-scriptural, and mythological sources and represented far-off and exotic power. Subsequent Ethiopian dynasties claimed her as an antecedent.

Saint Thomas Aquinas (1225–1274)—Italian philosopher and author of the *Summa Theologica*, he was instrumental in the development of political theology.

Margaret Thatcher (1925–2013)—Prime Minister of the United Kingdom from 1979 to 1990, the first woman to hold the role and the daughter of a Methodist local preacher.

Sir Christopher Trychay (*c.* 1490–1574)—Parish Priest of the tiny English village of Morebath in Devon, where he tried to protect his people from the rages of national politics over the turbulent years of the English Reformation.

John Winthrop (1588–1649)—English lawyer and Puritan, he was credited with first applying the term "A City on a Hill" to the nascent colonies in the Americas. He served as governor of the Massachusetts Bay Colony four times.

Andries Wouters (1542–1572)—Dutch Catholic priest, fornicator, and martyr killed during the Dutch revolt for refusing to recognize the new political entity. Despite being known as a ladies' man in his life, Wouters became an icon of Catholic obedience in death.

Chapter Seven

Fr Bartholomew de las Casas (1484–1566)—Spanish cleric, author, and politician who became the first "Protector of the Indians" when he protested against Spanish mistreatment of the indigenous populations in South America.

Catherine the Great (1729–1796)—Empress of Russia from 1762 to her death, responsible for the expansion of Russia into a global empire and—despite her often hostile attitude to the Church—Russian Orthodoxy into a cross-continental faith.

Christopher Columbus (1451–1506)—Genoese, or possibly Spanish, explorer and colonial administrator in the service of Isabela of Spain, who was the first man to establish permanent European settlement in the Americas. To say his legacy is contested would be an understatement.

Juan Diego Cuauhtlatoatzin (1474–1548)—peasant farmer from the indigenous Nahua people, he saw a vision of the Blessed Virgin Mary at the foot of Tepeyac Hill in Mexico in the year 1531.

The Prophet Ezekiel (*c.* 623–*c.*571 BC)—the purported author of the Biblical prophecy of Ezekiel, which deals with the concepts of universality and exile.

Pope Francis (1936–2025)—Pope of the Roman Catholic Church from 2013, the first South American cleric to hold the role.

Guaticabanu (died 1497)—thought to be the first indigenous person baptized in the Americas in September 1496.

Queen Isabela (1451–1504)—co-monarch of Spain with her slightly less zealous husband, Ferdinand, she oversaw both the ejection of Islam from the Iberian Peninsula and the expansion of Spanish power to America.

342
Appendix: Dramatis Personae

Matoaka (1596–1617)—Powhatan woman also known as Pocahontas, who was kidnapped by English settlers, baptized, and then married an English settler John Rolle. She went with him to England, where she died.

Fr Antonio Montesinos (1474–1540)—Spanish friar who was an early colonizer of the Americas but became a vocal advocate for indigenous rights, including preaching the sermon which changed the mind of Las Casas.

The chocolate-making nuns of Oaxaca—the nuns of the Franciscan order at Oaxaca, Mexico, who first added honey and spices to cocoa to make something approaching the drink we know today.

Rose of Lima (1586–1617)—born to a wealthy family in Colonial Spanish Peru, her intense asceticism led to her being acclaimed the first saint to be born in the Americas, heralding a new era for global Catholicism.

Grigorii Shelikhov (1747–1795)—Russian fur trader, adventurer, and expansionist who convinced the Russian state to expand eastward into Asia.

Reverend Joel Vedamrutharaj—priest in charge of the Bombay Afghan Memorial Church.

John Wesley (1702–1791)—English preacher, orator, and founder of the Methodist movement; like many Englishmen since, Wesley found his time in America deeply frustrating.

Chapter Eight

Richard Dawkins (1941–)—British evolutionary biologist who has also written amateur work on religion. Previously of the opinion that all faith was the root of all evil, he has since claimed to be a "cultural Christian."

G. K. Chesterton (1874–1936)—British critic and author of detective stories, a convert to Roman Catholicism, he wrote extensively on issues of faith and nation.

Cristovão Ferreira (1580–1650)—Portuguese Jesuit and missionary who, under torture by Japanese authorities, renounced his faith and then wrote a number of tracts attacking Christianity.

Kate Forbes (1990–)—Scottish politician who attracted publicity in the early 2020s for her strong Christian faith, leading some commentators to suggest that it was not appropriate for someone with her beliefs to lead Scotland. At the time of writing, she is the nation's Deputy First Minister.

Francisco de Olandia (fl. 1595–6)—captain of the ill-fated ship San Felipe, whose blithering and over-confidence in interviews by the Japanese authorities turned them once and for all against Christianity.

Luis Frois (1532–1597)—Portuguese Jesuit and early missionary to Japan who spent much of his ministry in Nagasaki, and author of works describing the customs, politics, and language of Japan at that time.

Jennie Geddes (1600–1660)—Scottish trader and radical Presbyterian who threw a stool at a clergyman using the new Scottish Prayer Book in Edinburgh Cathedral.

Michael Gove (1967–)—Scottish-born politician who held numerous high-ranking

Appendix: Dramatis Personae 343

cabinet jobs in successive governments between 2010 and 2024. At the time of writing, he is the editor of *The Spectator* magazine.

The villagers of Kasuga—Kasuga is a tiny village of rice terraces and single-story dwellings on the west coast of Hirado Island, about seventy miles from Nagasaki. It was Christianized very early on and remained so during the years of persecution.

John Knox (1514–1572)—Scottish Reformed minister, politician, and misogynist famed for his opposition to Mary, Queen of Scots, and determination to enforce an extreme Calvinism on Scotland.

Toyotomi Hideyoshi (豊臣 秀吉) **(1537–1598)**—Japanese samurai and eventual chancellor and de facto ruler of Japan who was instrumental in its second "unification," a key policy of which was the rejection of Christianity.

Janani Luwum (1922–1977)—Anglican Archbishop of Uganda who was killed—perhaps personally by the dictator—for opposing the rule of Idi Amin.

Magdalene of Nagasaki (長崎のマグダレナ) **(1611–1634)**—Japanese woman who was the daughter of Christians killed for their faith, she became an assistant to the clergy ministering in the midst of persecution until she too was killed.

Mashita Nagamori (増田 長盛) **(1545–1615)**—Japanese aristocrat and politician who was tasked with investigating the true nature of Jesuit presence in Japan in the light of the San Felipe incident.

Tertullian (155–240)—early Christian writer with a voluminous output. He wrote at length about the power of martyrdom alongside treatises on subjects as diverse as the composition of the Bible and whether it's possible to have sex with extraterrestrial beings.

Chapter Nine

Arius (250–336)—Presbyter from North Africa supposed to have propagated the heresy which now bears his name, which suggested that Jesus Christ was not one with the Father.

Bishop Colenso (1814–1883)—British bishop, the first of Natal in South Africa, mathematician, and Zulu linguist whose writing on the subject of scriptural inerrancy caused his deprivation from his see.

Sarah Good (1653–1692)—resident of Salem who was convicted of witchcraft during the trials at the Old Meeting House and later executed.

Bishop Gray (1809–1872)—First Bishop of Cape Town in South Africa and doughty defender of orthodoxy against what he saw as Bishop Colenso's excesses.

Little Sir Hugh of Lincoln (1246–1255)—a child from Lincoln, England, whose murder was blamed on the Jewish community of that city, resulting in persecution and the development of the blood libel.

Cotton Mather (1663–1728)—Congregationalist minister and Harvard academic who wrote an account legitimizing the Salem witch trials and encouraged the execution of the victims.

344 *Appendix: Dramatis Personae*

St Nicholas of Myra (270–343)—Bishop in modern-day Turkey, controversialist at multiple early Church councils, and the inspiration for Santa Claus.

Rebecca Nurse (1621–1692)—born in England, a homeowner and matriarch in Salem who, despite being known for her piety, was convicted of and executed for witchcraft.

Sarah Osborne (1643–1692)—resident of Salem who was accused of witchcraft during the trial but died in prison before she could be executed.

Dolly Parton (1946–)—American Country singer and philanthropist, many of whose songs have overtly Christian themes.

Sir William Phips (1651–1695)—Royal governor of the Province of Massachusetts who forced the trials at Salem to end and thus brought a close to the witch panic.

King Saul (reigned *c.* 1010–1030 BC)—Israelite monarch who initially had the favor of God but later descended into madness having lost it, during which he consulted a witch.

Socrates Scholasticus (389–440)—Greek historian of the early Church councils who provided much gory detail about what happened to supposed heretics.

Tituba (fl. 1690s)—an enslaved woman perhaps from the Caribbean or modern-day Venezuela who was owned by Samuel Parris in Salem and around whose tales many of the initial witchcraft allegations were centered.

Abigail Williams (1681–?)—a key accuser in the Salem witch trials, Williams was resident with her relative, the minister Samuel Parris, when she began making accusations about various women in the town. Her fate after the trials is unknown.

Chapter Ten

Abel (died 1717)—the first known black resident of Liverpool in England, who now is one of the few people to have a memorial to him in one of the city's parish churchyards.

Father Hugh Bearn (1962–)—British priest, currently the chaplain to St Paul's, Monte Carlo. A cleric of deep holiness, boundless hospitality, endless energy, indefatigable good humor, and increasingly continental driving habits.

Saint Clement of Alexandria (150–215)—Early Church theologian and philosopher who wrote on a number of subjects, including on the role of wealth in Christianity.

Futaleh (fl. 1847)—an enslaved woman, probably from East Africa, whose testimony was recorded by British authorities in Bombay after the slave ship in which she was being transported was intercepted.

Poor Hetty (died early 1800s)—a fellow enslaved woman with Mary Prince, whose description of her death at the violent hands of their master remains shocking to read today.

Lydia (fl. *c.* 40)—regarded as the first named and documented convert to Christianity in Europe, she was a trader in purple cloth who lived at Philippi in modern-day Greece.

Appendix: Dramatis Personae 345

Saint Monica (332–387)—mother to St Augustine, whom she nagged endlessly to become a Christian; the patron saint of pushy parents.

John Newton (1725–1807)—one-time slaver and then slave himself, Newton left seafaring and became a Church of England clergyman and committed abolitionist. He described his conversion in the words of the hymn "Amazing Grace."

Onesimus (died c. 68)—an escaped and later freed slave mentioned in the epistle to Philemon; tradition states that Onesimus later became Bishop of Byzantium.

Philemon (fl. c. 50)—the owner of Onesimus, to whom the letter in the New Testament is addressed.

Mary Prince (1788–1833)—former enslaved woman in the Caribbean who became an author who shocked Britain with the details of life for the enslaved.

Bishop Steere (1828–1882)—British bishop of Central Africa who was the driving force behind the construction of Christ Church cathedral in Zanzibar.

Archbishop Justin Welby (1956–)—105th Archbishop of Canterbury between 2013 and 2024, he visited Christ Church, Zanzibar, as part of his role as head of the Anglican Communion.

William Wilberforce (1759–1833)—British Member of Parliament and slavery abolitionist, his faith inspired him to take a lead in the campaign against the slave trade.

Reverend John Wemyss (1579–1636)—Scottish cleric and Old Testament scholar who made a Christian case for slavery based on a literal reading of the story of Noah in Genesis.

Chapter Eleven

Brother Arnold (1957–)—American Shaker, the younger of the last two surviving members of the movement, both of whom live at Sabbathday, Maine.

Mabel Barltrop (1866–1934)—British woman who believed herself to be "God the Daughter" and that the Garden of Eden had been located at 12 Albany Road, Bedford.

Boethius (480–524)—Roman senator, philosopher, and poet who wrote his greatest work, "The Consolation of Philosophy," while awaiting execution.

Dietrich Bonhoeffer (1906–1945)—German Lutheran minister and anti-Nazi dissident who wrote extensively on justice, discipleship, and grace before being executed by the Nazi regime.

Addie Mae Collins (1949–1963)—Sunday School student at the 16th Street Baptist Church, killed in the bombing of September 15.

Saint Irenaeus (130–202)—Greek Bishop and thinker who ministered in modern-day France; famed for coming up with his Irenaean explanation for human suffering in the context of a loving God.

Dr. Martin Luther King Jr. (1929–1968)—American Baptist pastor and civil rights leader who officiated at a number of the funerals of the victims of the bombing at the 16th Street Baptist Church.

346 *Appendix: Dramatis Personae*

David Koresh (1959–1993)—American cultist, murderer, and self-appointed exegetist, it was his cult of the Branch Davidians who were at the heart of the Waco massacre.

Mother Ann Lee (1736–1784)—British founder of the "Shaker" movement whose beliefs about male and female, God and man, and her own destiny as a prophet forced her out of various free-thinking groups in Britain and to the Americas.

Carol Denise McNair (1951–1963)—Sunday School student at the 16th Street Baptist Church, killed in the bombing of September 15.

Thomas Müntzer (1489–1525)—German preacher and revolutionary, whose radical interpretation of the Reformation ended with his violent death.

Pastor Price (1964–)—the present pastor of the 16th Street Baptist Church.

Carole Robertson (1949–1963)—Sunday School student at the 16th Street Baptist Church, killed in the bombing of September 15.

Joanna Southcott (1750–1814)—Devonian dairy worker, entrepreneur, self-declared Messiah, and box enthusiast, Southcott became something of a celebrity due to her claims to be able to sell people the seals of eternal life.

Cynthia Wesley (1949–1963)—Sunday School student at the 16th Street Baptist Church, killed in the bombing of September 15.

Chapter Twelve

Aina (alias Sarah Forbes Bonetta) (1843–1880)—a Yoruba woman rescued from slavery and from becoming a victim of human sacrifice, she subsequently became the ward and goddaughter of Queen Victoria.

Field Marshal Allenby (1861–1936)—British commander in the Middle East during the First World War who was later awarded a peerage and took "Armageddon" as part of his title.

Canon Professor Andrew Davison (1974–)—British priest, scientist, and academic who is currently the Regius Professor of Divinity at the University of Oxford.

Bishop Samuel Ajayi Crowther (1809–1891)—the First African Anglican bishop and Yoruba linguist, crucial in setting up the means for Christian mission in Nigeria as well as codifying the Yoruba language.

Captain Forbes (1819–1851)—Royal Navy officer, unwilling diplomat, and even more unwilling hero who rescued a girl from being sacrificed by the King of the Dahomey.

Sir Oliver Franks (1905–1992)—British ambassador to the United States of America between 1948 and 1952.

King Ghezo (1787–1858)—King of the Dahomey from 1818, his interests included the perpetuation of slavery, ritual mass murder, and trying to impress Queen Victoria.

Saint John the Divine (*c.* 8–*c.* 100)—the purported author of both the Gospel of St John and the Book of Revelation, and traditionally associated with "the Beloved Disciple," John the son of Zebedee in the synoptic Gospels.

Appendix: Dramatis Personae   347

Bishop David O. Oyedepo (1954–)—Nigerian cleric and author who is the founder of the Living Faith Church Worldwide, Presiding Bishop of the Faith Tabernacle and the Winners Church. He is very mobile during his sermons.

Prakash Parthipan—Malaysian TikToker, broadcaster, and Christian evangelist who runs the Canaan TV Network.

The Tamil women of Shah Alam—many of them textile workers, the women of Shah Alam in Malaysia are the main recipients of the Canaan TV Network's message of hope.

Jeremy Taylor (1613–1667)—Anglican author and clergyman who spent much of his career in political and religious exile.

Queen Victoria (1819–1901)—British Empress and long-standing figurehead of the nation's Empire, her interests included her husband, having things named after her, and annoying her son.

Lu Xiaomin (吕小敏) (1970–)—Chinese author of nearly 2,000 hymns and worship songs despite having no musical training and the practice of Christianity being under threat in China.

References

Chapter One

1. St John, in typical metaphysical style, takes us back to before the very **beginning** of creation in his masterful prologue, but given that this can reasonably be assumed to be talking of a time before there was a Bethlehem, we might defer discussion to later chapters.

2. A classic proposition of this thesis can be found in B.H. Streeter, *The Four Gospels: A Study of Origins Treating of the Manuscript Tradition, Sources, Authorship, & Dates* (London, 1930)

3. See Jonathan Bernier, *Rethinking the Dates of the New Testament: The Evidence for Early Composition* (Grand Rapids, 2022)

4. Luke 2:4–20

5. "according to his house and lineage of David," διὰ τὸ εἶναι αὐτὸν ἐξ οἴκου καὶ πατριᾶς Δαυίδ, Luke 2:4

6. "behold a virgin will conceive and give birth to a son," ἰδοὺ ἡ παρθένος ἐν γαστρὶ ἕξει καὶ τέξεται υἱόν, Matthew 1:23, Isaiah 7:14

7. "and they came into the house and found the child there with Mary his mother," καὶ ἐλθόντες εἰς τὴν οἰκίαν εἶδον τὸ παιδίον μετὰ Μαρίας τῆς μητρὸς αὐτοῦ, Matthew 2:11

8. Of course, it took a little while to get there, via various heresies, some of which we will deal with later—but the one most pertinent to our discussion here is Docetism, the idea that Christ only appeared to be human and first identified and condemned by Bishop Serapion of Antioch, *c.* 190 AD, as the work of Δοκηταί (illusionists). See "Letter concerning the Gospel of Peter," part of the *Fragments of Serapion of Antioch*, in Vol. IX, *Ante-Nicene Christian Library*.

9. "fecit oloronis Ledam recubare sub alis addidit, ut satyri celatus imagine pulchram Iuppiter inplerit gemino Nycteida fetu," Ovid *Metamorphoses*, Book VI, Part 103

10. See Ian Paul, "Not in That Poor Lowly Stable," *Tyndale House*, December 2021

11. Thomas Jefferson, *Letter to John Adams*, April 11, 1823

12. Numbers of Roman Catholics, see "Global Catholic Population Rising," *Vatican News*, October 22, 2023

13. John 21:25

14. See the complexity of the rules laid out in L.G.A. Cust, *The Status Quo in the Holy Places* (London, 1929)

15. J. Andrew Overman, *Church and Community in Crisis: The Gospel according to Matthew* (Valley Forge, PA, 1996)

16. Eusebius, *Vita Constantinii* [Life of Constantine], Book III, Part XLVII

17. See A.R. Birley, "St Helena: Discoverer of the True Cross," *The Breaking Ground Project, Brown*, 2004

18. διὸ δὴ βασιλὶς ἡ θεοσεβεστάτη τῆς θεοτόκου τὴν κύησιν μνήμασι θαυμαστοῖς κατεκόσμει, παντοίως τὸ τῇδε ἱερὸν ἄντρον φαιδρύνουσα in Eusebius, ibid., Part XLIII

19. Najam Haider, "On Lunatics and Loving Sons: A Textual Study of the Mamluk Treatment of Al-Hakim" in *Journal of the Royal Asiatic Society*, Third Series, Vol. 18, No. 2, April 2008

20. Raymond Cohen, "Conflict and Neglect: Between Ruin and Preservation at the Church of the Nativity," in *Toward World Heritage: International Origins of the Preservation Movement, 1870–1930*, ed. Melanie Jane Hall (London, 2011)

21. "more balantis ovis Bethleem dicens" in Thomas of Celano, *Vita Prima Franciscus de Assisi* [First Life of Francis of Assisi], Ch. XXX, 1229, edition "Dal Canonico Leopoldo Amoni," (Rome, 1880)

22. "labia sua etiam . . . quasi lanniebat lingua felici palato degustans," ibid.

23. Favell Lee Mortimer, *Far Off Asia Described* (London, 1890)

24. Gertrude Bell, Diary Entry, December 24, 1899, in The Gertrude Bell Archive, Newcastle University

25. See photograph by Giuseppe Brugo, from *L'Illustrazione Italiana* [The Italian Illustration], Year XXV, No. 47, November 20, 1898, in La Biblioteca Ambrosina

26. Matthew Fitzpatrick, *The Kaiser and the Colonies*, Ch. 3, "A Pilgrim to the Holy Land" (Oxford, 2022)

27. "Bush Visits Jesus Birthplace," *The Times of Malta*, January 10, 2008

28. "Obama visits Bethlehem's Nativity Church," Reuters, March 22, 2013

29. Text of the Speech of HM King Charles III, BBC, December 25, 2022

30. See Collins's own Instagram reel of January 2, 2023: https://www.instagram.com/gemmacollins/reel/Cm7ElOSq7lm/

31. "e grande edifizio e rilevato" in Fra Niccolò da Poggibonsi, *Libro d'Oltramare* [The Book of Outremer], (1346–50) edition published Alberto Bacchi della Lega (Bologna, 1881)

32. Raymond Cohen, "Conflict and Neglect," op. cit.

33. Ralph S. Hattox, "Mehmed the Conqueror, the Patriarch of Jerusalem, and Mamluk Authority," in *Studia Islamica*, No. 90 (2000)

34. Lucy-Anne Hunt, "Art and Colonialism: The Mosaics of the Church of the Nativity in Bethlehem (1169) and the Problem of 'Crusader' Art" in *Dumbarton Oaks Papers*, Vol. 45 (Harvard, 1991)

References 351

35. Alonzo Ketcham Parker, "Jerusalem and Thereabouts," in *The Biblical World*, Vol. 7, No. 5, May 1896

36. François-René de Chateaubriand, *Itinéraire de Paris à Jérusalem et de Jérusalem à Paris* [Journey from Paris to Jerusalem and vice versa] (Paris, 1811)

37. Micah 5:2

38. Prudentius's Latin is "sola magnarum urbium, maior Bethlehem, cui contigit, ducem salutis caelitus, incorporatum gignere."

39. "Priests brawl in Bethlehem's Church of the Nativity," BBC, December 28, 2011

40. Brison D. Gooch, "A Century of Historiography on the Origins of the Crimean War," in *The American Historical Review*, Vol. 62, No. 1, October 1956

41. Τότε Ἡρῴδης ἰδὼν ὅτι ἐνεπαίχθη ὑπὸ τῶν μάγων ἐθυμώθη λίαν, καὶ ἀποστείλας ἀνεῖλεν πάντας τοὺς παῖδας τοὺς ἐν Βηθλεὲμ καὶ ἐν πᾶσι τοῖς ὁρίοις αὐτῆς ἀπὸ διετοῦς, Matthew 2:16

42. Exodus 1:16

43. For statistics of late Medieval England, see Barabara A. Hanawalt, "Childrearing among the Lower Classes of Late Medieval England," *The Journal of Interdisciplinary History*, Vol. 8, No. 1, Summer 1977

44. "End to Bethlehem siege in sight," *Guardian*, May 6, 2002

45. "Church emerges unharmed from siege," BBC, May 11, 2002

46. Mitri Raheb, *Bethlehem Besieged: Stories of Hope in Times of Trouble* (ELCA, 2004)

Chapter Two

1. That Tiberius was a sourpuss is widely attested to in Roman literature, even in seemingly unrelated texts. The description of him as "tristissimum hominum," the most gloomy of men, comes from a scientific handbook, *Naturalis Historia* [Natural History], Book 28, Part 23, by Pliny the Elder.

2. Suentonius, *De Vita Caesarum* [The Lives of the Caesars], Book 6, Ch. 31

3. "Nero tamen, ut erat incredibilium cupitor," in Tacitus, *Annals*, Book 15, Ch. 42

4. "omni parte vitae detestabilem," in Suetonius, ibid., Ch. 5

5. "inter gratulationes amicorum negantis quicquam ex se et Agrippina nisi detestabile et malo publico nasci potuisse," ibid., Ch. 6

6. Tacitus, *Annals*, Book 15, Ch. 44

7. Cassius Dio Cocceianus, *Historiae Romanae*, Book 62, Ch. 16, Part 3

8. Tacitus, *Annals*, Book 15, Ch. 40

9. See R.F. Newbold, "Some Social and Economic Consequences of the A.D. 64 Fire at Rome," in *Latomus*, Vol. 33, Issue 4, 1974

10. "Nero subdidit reos . . . invisos vulgus Christianos appellabat, "Nero fixed the blame . . . on a group known popularly as the Christians," Tacitus, *Annals*, Book 15, Ch. 44

11. Suentonius, *De Vita Caesarum*, Book 6, Ch. 16

12. Multiple sources attest to Peter's crucifixion: in particular Eusebius, *Church History*, however the specific detail of the upside-down crucifixion comes from *The Acts of Peter (Actus Petri cum Simone)*, a text found in fragments—the earliest in the Codex Vercellensis—from an unknown source, but now in manuscripts in Latin, Coptic, and other languages. It is assumed to be from the mid to late 100s AD, perhaps a century or so after its purported events. The description of the martyrdom comes in part 37—and is the most widely attested to episode in the Acts. A translation exists in M.R. James (trans.), *The Apocryphal New Testament* (Oxford, 1924).

13. The exact numbers are unclear—the statistic of somewhere between 40,000 and 50,000 people per day is the official Vatican estimate. Eleven million people annually is one other estimate, although the sources for this are not totally reliable. This would make it the second most visited building on earth after the Forbidden City in Beijing. Fortunately, statistics for this destination are provided by the Communist Party of China, who are, of course, a byword for statistical honesty and probity.

14. Cassilly eventually put his inspiration into practice at his enormous public art installation "Cementland," a celebration of all things cement. Cassilly died tragically at Cementland in 2011 when he accidentally drove a bulldozer off a hill.

15. *The St Louis Post Dispatch*, St Louis, Missouri, Friday, August 11, 1972, p. 40

16. See a testimony by Toth's sometime roommate, "Notes and Queries," *Guardian*, June 8, 2006

17. See "Can Italy be Saved from Itself?", *Time*, June 5, 1972

18. J.J. Teunissen and Evelyn J. Hinz, "The Attack on the Pietà: An Archetypal Analysis," in *The Journal of Aesthetics and Art Criticism*, Vol. 33, No. 1, Autumn 1974

19. Lisa M. Rafinelli, *Michelangelo's Vatican Pietà and Its Afterlives* (Routledge, 2022)

20. Roger Dunsmore, *Lazslo Toth: An Improvisational Text* (Vancouver, 1977)

21. Robert S. Liebert, "Michelangelo's Mutilation of the Florence Pietà," in *The Art Bulletin*, Vol. 59, No. 1, March 1977

22. Kevin Twine, "The City in Decline: Rome in Late Antiquity," in *Middle States Geographer*, Vol. 25, 1992, pp. 134–36

23. Hilary of Poitiers, *De Trinitate*, Book 1, Part 7

24. R. McKitterick, J. Osborne, C.M. Richardson, J. Story, Introduction to *Old St Peter's, Rome*, part of the British School at Rome Studies series (Cambridge, 2013), p. 2

25. Ibid., p. 6

26. See the eyewitness account of Maffeo Veggio's *De rebus antiquis memorabilibus Basilicae sancti Petri Romae* from the late 1450s, as trans. Christine Smith and Joseph O'Connor, 2019

27. "De clericis peregrinantibus," as found in Book 2, Ch. 29 of the Liber Extra, a collection of canon law by St Raymond Penyafort

28. "submiserunt eum per quandum strictam fenestram et fugit cum uno clerico spuer decta domorum," from the testimony of Cardinal de Britannia in Stephanus Baluzius, *Vitae Paparum Avionensium*, Vol. 1, Column. 1227 (Paris, 1693)

29. Janus Pannonius, "Pjesme i epigram," in *Hrvatski latinisti*, ed. Nikola Šop, Vol. 2 (Zagreb: JAZU, 1951), p. 319, as quoted in Zoran Ladić, *Criminal Behavior by Pilgrims in the Middle Ages and Early Modern Period*, p. 64

30. See J. Allen, "Nicholas V's Tribuna for Old St. Peter's in Rome as a Model for the New Apsidal Choir at Padua Cathedral," in *Journal of the Society of Architectural Historians*, Vol. 72, No. 2, June 2013

31. In fairness to Julius, there is some dispute as to whether this was actually something said by him or by the bloodthirsty Cardinal Cisneros at the siege of Oran in 1509. If it was the latter, it perhaps says something that Julius was renowned as being a little over the top in his love for the militaristic even in a Curia populated by cardinals like Cisneros.

32. Erasmus, *Iulius exclusus e coelis* [Julius barred from Heaven] (1514)

33. For these and other insults from contemporary chroniclers, mainly French, see Robert W. Scheller, "Ung fil tres delicat: Louis XII and Italian affairs, 1510–11," in *Simiolus: Netherlands Quarterly for the History of Art*, Vol. 31, No. 1/2, 2004–2005

34. N. Machiavelli, *Il Principe*, Ch. 13, Part 2

35. See Peter Partner, "Papal Financial Policy in the Renaissance and Counter-Reformation," in *Past & Present*, No. 88, August 1980

36. A.A.M. Duncan, "Documents relating to the Priory of the Isle of May" in *Proceedings of the Scottish Society of Antiquaries*, 1956–57, p. 59

37. Robert W. Shaffern, "Indulgences and Saintly Devotionalisms in the Middle Ages," in *The Catholic Historical Review*, Vol. 84, No. 4, October 1998

38. Walter S. Gibson, "Prayers and Promises: The Interactive Indulgence Print," in *Push Me, Pull You: Imaginative, Emotional, Physical and Spatial Interaction in Late Medieval and Renaissance Art*, eds. Laura Gelfand and Sarah Blick (Brill, 2011), p. 321

39. Certainly, it was underway by 1507, as per the copy of one reading: "Universis presentes litteras inspecturis pateat. Quod propter contributionem elimosinariam factam in subsidium favrice Appostolorum Principis," in *Romana Urbe: Concessum est*, held in the Bridwell Library in Dallas, Texas.

40. Thesis 50, *Ninety-Five Theses* of Martin Luther

41. Ibid., theses 62 and 63

42. Part XX, in Luther's *Sermon On Indulgences and Grace*, from the spring of 1518

43. For more detail, see Elizabeth J. Leppmann, "Appalachian Churchscapes," in *Southeastern Geographer*, Vol. 45, No. 1, May 2005

44. For designs, see Paul A. Underwood, "Notes on Bernini's Towers for St Peter's in Rome," in *The Art Bulletin*, Vol. 21, No. 3, September 1939

45. Margaret A. Kuntz, "Questions of Identity: Alexander VII, Carlo Rainaldi, and the temporary façade at the Palazzo Farense for Queen Christina of Sweden," in *Memoirs of the American Academy in Rome*, Vol. 58, 2013, p. 143

46. When congratulated by a friend on his likely elevation to the Papacy, Alexander quoted Virgil's *Aeneid*: "Jamque dies, ni fallor, adest, quem semper acerbum, Semper honoratum (sic di voluistis) habebo."

47. Bruce P. Lenman, "Some Recent Jacobite Studies," in *The Scottish Historical Review*, Vol. 70, No. 189, April 1991

48. Percy Bysshe Shelley, *Adonais*

49. It was said the Pius had to change his white cassock three times a day because of the amount of snuff he managed to spill down it.

50. This was recounted to me directly during a visit by some members of the English College to the Anglican Center at the Palazzo Doria Pamphilj in the summer of 2016, but I cannot for the life of me recall which seminarian it was who told the story. This amnesia is, perhaps, probably for the best, or at least for the benefit of his clerical career.

Chapter Three

1. Which means "the Hagia Sophia Mosque" in Turkish, meaning that this building which was once a church and is now a mosque has a name in Turkish which is, confusingly, a transliterated Greek-Christian name for a church. So, as we will see, go the circles of power transposed onto Hagia Sophia.

2. See part 15 of Heyschius of Miletus, ΠΑΤΡΙΆΑ ΚΩΟΝΣΤΑΝ- ΤΙΝΟΥΠΟΛΈΦΣ [On the Origins of Constantinople], "Μετὰ δὲ τὴν τοῦ τείχους στεφάνην χαὶ τὰ τεμένη τῶν θεῶν ἀπειργάζετο," Greek edition of Th. Preger (1901)

3. Often given as "IN HOC SIGNO VINCES," the Latin translation. The original account is found in the work of Eusebius, Vita Constantini, Part 1, Ch. XXVIII, "ἀμφὶ μεσημβρινὰς ἡλίου ὥρας, ἤδη τῆς ἡμέρας ἀποκλινούσης, αὐτοῖς ὀφθαλμοῖς ἰδεῖν ἔφη ἐν αὐτῷ οὐρανῷ ὑπερκείμενον τοῦ ἡλίου σταυροῦ τρόπαιον ἐκ φωτὸς συνιστάμενον, γραφήν τε αὐτῷ συνῆφθαι λέγουσαν· τούτῳ νίκα."

4. 2 Corinthians 12:9

5. See St Jerome, *Chronicon*, 279th Olympiad, "Constantinus extremo vitae suae tempore ab Eusebio Nicomedensi episcopo baptizatus'

6. See Nihat Tekdemir, *Theodosius II's Church: Hagia Sophia*, History of Architecture at the Istanbul Technical University (Istanbul, 2016)

7. First referenced as "ἐνίκησά σε, Σολομών" in Διήγησις περὶ τῆς οἰκοδομῆς τοῦ ναοῦ τῆς μεγάλης τοῦ Θεοῦ ἐκκλησίας τῆς ἐπονομαζομέγης ἁγίας Σοφίας (The Narration of the Building of the Hagia Sophia), an anonymous popular text from eighth century, reproduced in *Scriptores originum Constantinopolitanarum*, ed. Preger (Leipzig 1901)

References   355

8. Geoffrey Greatrex, "The Nika Riot: A Reappraisal," in *The Journal of Hellenic Studies*, Vol. 117 (1997)

9. Donald E. Queller and Irene B. Katele, "Attitudes Toward the Venetians in the Fourth Crusade: The Western Sources," in *The International History Review*, Vol. 4, No. 1, February 1982

10. See Niketas Choniates, Annals, "μετὰ δὲ βραχείας ἡμέρας τῷ διὰ πνιγμονῆς ἐλεεινῷ μόρῳ ὑποδικάζει τὴν κακοδαίμονα, ἐπιστατησάντων τῷ ὑπουργήματι τοῦ Τριψύχου Κωνσταντίνου, ὃς τὴν τῆς ἑταιρειαρχείας ζώνην εἶχε, καὶ τοῦ ἐκτομίου Πτερυγεωνίτου," and Roger of Hovenden, Chronica [The Chronicle], *"et post longam carceris macerationem, ligatam in sacco submergi fecit in mare quod dicitur Mare Majus, ancbora alligata collo ejus"*

11. See *The Chronicle of Novgorod*, published as part of The Royal Historical Society's Camden Third Series, Vol. 25, December 1914

12. For further detail see Jonathan Phillips, *The Fourth Crusade* (London, 2005)

13. See full description in Niketas Choniates, *Annals*

14. Both Greek accounts and the Latin letter of Leonard of Chios, an eyewitness to the fall, are expertly distilled by Marios Phillippides, "The Fall of Constantinople: Bishop Leonard and the Greek Accounts," in *Greek, Roman and Byzantine Studies*, Vol. 22 (1981).

15. Much source material for the death of Constantine IX is found in the various writings of Gennadisu Scholasticus, found in *Patrologiae Cursus Completus, Series Graeca* (Paris, 1866). Credit is due to Donald M. Nicol for his distillation and cohering of them in *The Immortal Emperor* (Cambridge, 1992).

16. See Nicol, ibid.

17. Work of the Persian Poet, ﺷﯿﺮﺍﺯﯼ ﺳﻌﺪﯼ Saadi Shirazi (1210–*c.* 1291); the original seems to be lost but Mehmet's recital is widely attested to the source below.

18. *Endowment deed of Fatih Sultan Mehmed Khan*, held (and partially digitized) as the waqf deed, registered under number 2202 (formerly 666) in the Turkish and Islamic Works Museum

19. Whittemore's own rather camp description of the circumstances of 1920s archaeology in Turkey can be found in Thomas Whittemore, "Archaeology during the Republic in Turkey" in *The American Journal of Archaeology*, Vol. 47, No. 2, April–June, 1943.

20. "Erdoğan leads first prayers at Hagia Sophia," *Guardian*, July 24, 2020

21. For full technical details, see Nilay Ozlu, "Hagia Sophia and the Demise of the Sacred" in *Design Philosophy Papers*, Vol. 8, No. 1, April 2015

22. Philippians 3:21

Chapter Four

1. See S. Frere, "The Roman Theater at Canterbury," in *Britannia*, Vol. I, 1970

2. As opposed to today, where London's West End has simply elided the two concepts and it is the plays themselves that act as torture.

356   *References*

3. See J. Cox Russell, "The Clerical Population of Medieval England," in *Traditio*, Vol. 2, 1944

4. Anne Latowsky, " 'I Think This Bacon is Wearing Shoes': Comedy and Murder in the Old French Fabliaux," in *Medieval and Early Modern Murder: Legal, Literary and Historical Contexts*, ed. Larissa Tracy, 2018

5. See Dianne Hall, "Women and Violence in Late Medieval Ireland," in *Studies on Medieval and Early Modern Women: Pawns or Players?*, eds. Christine Meek and Catherine Lawless (Four Courts Press, 2003)

6. "posito pede super collum sancti sacerdotis et martyris pretiosi, (horrendum dictu), cerebrum cum sanguine per pavimentum spargens," in Part 82 of Edward Grim's *Vitae S. Thomae, c.* 1175

7. See Ch. 1 in Rachel Koopmans, *Wonderful to Relate: Miracle Stories and Miracle Collecting in High Medieval England* (University of Pennsylvania, 2011)

8. Some chroniclers record that the miraculous healing of the sisters actually occurred at Boxley itself, where there was an abbey with various attractions for the medieval pilgrim, including the immovable statue of St Rumbold. The monks at Canterbury, when it came to their meticulous recording of the healings associated with Becket, were sure to transfer the miracle to Canterbury, not only to get more credence for their own shrine, but also to get one over on the immovable St Rumbold.

9. I am immensely grateful to Leonie Seliger, director of glass at Canterbury Cathedral, who showed me these panels up close during a period of their restoration and cleaning. To see medieval craftmanship at the end of one's nose is absolutely magical.

10. 1 Corinthians 15:54

11. Mileto of Sardis, *Peri Pascha* [About Easter], Part V, *c.* 170 AD, fragments in the Roberts-Donaldson translation 1872

12. Matthew 5:39

13. Matthew 10:34

14. See R. Cox, *John Wycliff on War and Peace* (Martlesham, Boydell and Brewer, 2014)

15. As quoted in contemporary chronicler William of Newburgh's *Historia Rerum Anglicarum*, Book II, Ch. XVI

16. John Foxe, *Actes and Monuments*, Part 331 (1563)

17. See documents collated in *Archaelogia Cambrensis—The Journal of The Cambrian Archaeological Association*, 1918

18. Proclamation of Henry VIII at Westminster, November 16, 1538

19. Elkan Nathan Adler, "The Inquisition in Peru," in *Publications of the American Jewish History Society*, No. 12, 1904, p. 32

20. Crucially, the Inquisition always handed those they had condemned to the state for the actual administration of the punishment, especially in the case of the

death penalty; however, there is good evidence that inquisitors made use of torture to extract confession.

21. "famosissimus ille Joceus Annae uxori carissimae cultro praeacuto guttur incidit, et propriis quoque filiis non pepercit," in *William of Newburgh, Historia Rerum Anglicarum*, Book IV, Ch. 10

22. B. Johnson, Martyr for *Deism: Cayetano Ripoll*

23. Crispin Pailing, *God's Town: Liverpool and her Parish since 1207* (2019), p. 196

24. 1 Corinthians 1:23

25. Isaiah 19:18

26. Almost all the earliest papyri evidence of the Gospels—the earliest being the Rylands fragment of John, currently on display in Manchester, UK, thought to date from the second century—come from Egyptian sources.

27. Eyewitness to the murder of Mary Sameh George, originally appearing in Arabic on the Egyptian news program "90 دقيقة," later transcribed in *The Christian Post*, Monday, March 31, 2014

28. Most scholars accept that Isaiah is actually three different books, with the third in particular having multiple authors. The difference in dates could be as broad as three or four centuries. However, the themes, of exile, restoration, and salvation, are consistent throughout.

29. Isaiah, 50:6. This is part of the "Suffering Servant" sections of the prophecy of Isaiah, thought by many Christians to directly predict the death and suffering of Christ. They are crucial prophecies in the Bible, providing as they do a shift in the view of the Messiah from being a triumphant political and military figure to being one who suffers violence and is rejected.

30. *The Christian Post*, Monday, March 31, 2014

31. "Approval and Mood of the Country," Harvard Caps Harris Poll, October 19, 2023

32. Karl Marx, final editorial of *Neue Rheinische Zeitung*, 1849, edition transcribed by the Marx-Engels Institute

33. For more see David Little, "Some Justifications for Violence in the Puritan Revolution," in *Harvard Theological Review*, Vol. 65, Issue 4, October 1972

34. Revelation 14:14

35. See Isaiah 2:4

36. I am immensely grateful to the Reverend David Vannerly, a gentle, kind, and immensely knowledgeable priest who acted as my guide that day.

37. Seamas Heaney, *The Cure at Troy* (1990)

Chapter Five

1. Attested to in multiple places, esp. C. Maunder, *The Oxford Handbook of Mary* (OUP, 2019), p. 126, and in Kallistos Ware and Graham Speake, *Mount Athos, Microcosm of the Christian East* (Peter Lang, 2011)

2. Moses the Athonite was a monk who wandered the mountain in the late twentieth

century. Suffering from various ailments—he once said he "ate pain with a spoon"—he still traveled to the various hermitages and monasteries and compiled one of the best recent set of essays and accounts of life on Athos: *Athonite Flowers* (Holy Cross Orthodox Press, 2000).

3. Ch. 3 of No. 133 of *The Novels of Justinian*. As per the translation in S.P. Scott, *The Civil Law*, XVII (Cincinnati, 1932). Manuscripts of various ages and levels of completeness exist in France and Germany, but the oldest is thought to be in the Monastery of Monte Cassino.

4. An early copy of the *typikon* authorized by a later Patriarch of Constantinople in 1096 can be found in the Iveron Monastery on Athos (*Codex Iveron.ms*, images in D. Papachryssanthou, *Actes du Protaton* (Paris, 1975)). The Emperor himself encouraged his male courtiers and chroniclers to focus on his personal physical beauty and bodily proportions in their descriptions of him, so it is just possible there was an element of projection going on here.

5. 1 Corinthians 7:1

6. As per Chadwick's *Introduction* to C. Luibheid, *John Cassian: Conferences* (New York, 1985), p. 7, which is filled with exactly these sorts of frank asides that make the great professor's writing such a joy to read

7. St John Cassian, *Institutes*, Book II, Ch. 5

8. Ibid., Book VI, Ch. 18

9. St Clement of Alexandria, *Paedogogus*, Book III, Ch. 3

10. St John Cassian, *Institutes*, Book VI, Ch. 17

11. Ibid., Ch. 11

12. See St Augustine, *On the Good of Marriage*, Chs. 2–3

13. St Augustine, *Confessions*, Book 3, Ch. 1

14. Ibid., Book 7, Ch. 17

15. See *Chambers English Dictionary*, ed. James Donald (2023), p. 568

16. Indeed, one of the most complete sculptures we have surviving from the 79 AD eruption of Mount Vesuvius is of Pan vigorously rogering a goat. Found in the Villa of the Papyri in Herculaneum, it was exhibited in a separate room from its discovery in 1752 until 2013, such was the extreme erotic nature of the piece.

17. See Dio Chrysostom, *The Sixth Discourse: Diogenes or On Tyranny* (Loeb Classical Library, 1932)

18. Plutarch, *De Defectu Oraculorum*, translated as *Plutarch's Morals*, ed. W. Goodwin Section 17 (Cambridge, 1874), p. 23

19. Eusebius, *Church History*, Book 6, Ch. 8

20. "Greece: The Climax of Sin," *Time of Monday*, July 13, 1953 (*see Time Magazine Archive*) suggests the latter; the reporting of J. Sanidopoulous at the Mystagogy Resource Center suggests the former. Both, I suspect, are as reliable as one another.

References

21. M. Choisy, "Psychoanalysis and Catholicism," in *CrossCurrents*, Vol. 1, No. 3, Spring 1951

22. See D. Souhami, *No Modernism without Lesbians*, Head of Zeus, 2021

23. See the Mystagogy Resource Center's report as per above

24. Tom Holland, *Dominion* (2019), is superlative on this phenomenon.

25. See details in his *Auctarium Aquicinese*, further expounded on by J. Riley Smith, "The First Crusade and the Persecution of the Jews," in *Studies in Church History*, Vol. 21, 1984

26. Not to be confused with the Emperor of the 800s with the same name. See *Dramatis Personae*.

27. I am immensely indebted to the scholarly work of Tomasz Labuk in this area, in particular his doctoral work for the University of Katowice, *Gluttons, Drunkards and Lechers: The discourses of food in Twelfth Century Byzantine literature. Ancient themes and Byzantine innovation* (Katowice, 2019).

28. See the work of Johnathon Jodamus at the University of the Western Cape, whose work makes a convincing case for Paul's subversion, rather than invention of masculine norms, esp. "Redeeming Paul? Disruptive Masculinity, Sexual Autonomy, and Sexual Freedom in 1 Corinthians 7," in *The African Journal of Gender and Religion*, Vol. 26, No. 2, 2020.

29. See, inter alia, Romans 3:28, Ephesians 2:8–9, etc.

30. Galatians 3:28

31. St Gregory of Nyssa, *On the Making of Man*, Part XVI, Ch. 9

32. See *The Statistical Yearbook of the Church*, as published by the Vatican

33. Rowan Williams, *The Body's Grace*, delivered as the 10th Michael Harding Lecture, 1989

Chapter Six

1. Matthew 28:19, the Great Commission to the disciples

2. 1 John 2:2

3. As recorded in an Ethiopian manuscript translated by Rosita McGrath in "Lalibala" in *The Geographical Journal*, Vol. 66, No. 6, 1925

4. See details of the dating of Sembrouthes in Stuart C. Munro-Hay, "A Tyranny of Sources: A History of Aksum from its Coinage," in *Northeast African Studies*, Vol. 3, No. 3

5. 2 Chronicles 9

6. Tigab Bezie, "The Ethiopian religious community and its ancient monastery, Dier es Sultan in Jerusalem from Foundation to 1850s," in *Journal of Ethiopian Church Studies*, 2013

7. Yikunnoamlak Mezgebu Zerabiruk, "Lalibela and Gädlä Lalibela: The Making and Unmaking of an Ethiopian Holy Land," in *International Journal of Ethiopian Studies*, Vol. 12, No. 2

8. McGrath, in "Lalibala" in *The Geographical Journal*

9. *Gädlä Lalibela*, Perruchon edition of the Gädlä (1892), p. 59
10. Although I did notice that one reviewer on Google Maps had declared that, in fact, the tomb of Adam was "nothing special."
11. See Marco Polo, *The Travels of Marco Polo*
12. Francisco Alvarez, *Narrative of the Portuguese Embassy to Abyssinia during the years 1520–27*, Part 13, trans. Lord Stanley of Alderley (1881) for the Hakluyt Society
13. Ibid.
14. Perruchon edition and French translation of the *Gädlä Lalibela* (1892), p. 6
15. See S. Mitchell, "Pepuza and Tymion: The Discovery and Archeological Exploration of a Lost Ancient City and Imperial Estate," in *Journal of Early Christian Studies*, Vol. 17, No. 3, 2009
16. See the *Vitae Sancti Bonifatii* by the excellently named Willibald, where he refers to the sacred tree collapsing after only a tiny cut in its trunk: "sed ad modicum quidem arbore praeciso, confestim inmensa roboris moles, divino desuper flatu exagitata, palmitum confracto culmine" (Levison, 1905)
17. "conconiatur ad agrestes viros: 'O plebs miseranda nimis!" in Cosmas of Prague, *Chronica Boeorum*, p. 65 of the digitized manuscript in the Documenta Catholica Omnia
18. "Cerere et Bachho corpori reficiunt, cetera noctis spatia Veneri et Himenæo indulgent," ibid., p. 68
19. "quorum autem morum, quam honestorum vel quantæ simplicitatis," ibid., p. 6
20. "et quoniam haec antiquis referentur evenisse temporibus, utrum sint facta an ficta," ibid., p. 79
21. See W. Eugene Kleinbauer, "Charlemagne's Palace Chapel at Aachen and Its Copies," in Gesta, Vol. 4, Spring 1965
22. Voltaire, *Essai sur l'histoire générale et sur les mœurs et l'esprit des nations* [Essay on the general history and on the mores and spirit of the nations], Ch. 70
23. See C.R. Cheney, *King John and the Papal Interdict* (Manchester, 1948)
24. Peter D. Clarke, "The Interdict on San Gimignano *c.* 1289–1293: A Clerical 'Strike' and Its Consequences," in *Papers of the British School at Rome*, Vol. 67, 1999
25. Anthony Wright, "Republican Tradition and the Maintenance of 'National' Religious Traditions in Venice," in *Renaissance Studies*, Vol. 10, No. 3
26. L.A. Pavleva, "Смутное время в России," in *Страницы Истории*, Vol. 27, No. 165, 2004
27. *The Replies of the Humble Nicon, by the Mercy of God Patriarch, against the Questions of the Boyar Simeon Streshneff and the Answers of the Metropolitan of Gaza Paisius Ligarides*
28. J. Willson and A. Morse, "Transferring Jerusalem to Moscow: Maksim Grek's Letter and its Afterlife," in *The Russian Review*, Vol. 82, No. 2, 2023

References 361

29. Gary K. Waite, "Reimagining Religious Identity: The Moor in Dutch and English Pamphlets, 1550–1620," in *Renaissance Quarterly*, Vol. 66, No. 4, Winter 2013

30. See E. Duffy, *The Voices of Morebath*, 2001

31. John Klassen, "Images of Anti-Majesty in Hussite Literature," in *Bohemia Band*, No. 33, 1992

32. Manuscript edition of Vavřinec z Březové, ed. Jan Skutil, Prague

33. Katherine Gillespie, "A Hammer in Her Hand: The Separation of Church from State and the Early Feminist Writings of Katherine Chidley," in *Tulsa Studies in Women's Literature*, Vol. 17, No. 2, 1998

34. Judges 4

35. Katherine Chidley, *Good Counsell, to the Petitioners for Presbyterian Government* (London 1645)

36. See F. Quinn, "Henry Yates Satterlee, First Bishop of Washington, Builder of National Cathedral," in *Anglican and Episcopal History*, Vol. 88, No. 1, March 2019

37. Polk's Pastoral letter to his diocese, January 30, 1861

38. Initially the song was most popular with members of the Suffragist movement, who campaigned for women's votes.

39. Eliza Filby, *God and Mrs. Thatcher: The Battle for Britain's Soul* (2015)

40. Thatcher Archive: CCOPR 534/92

41. Maimire Mennasemay, "Utopia and Ethiopia: The Chronicles of Lalibela as Critical Reflection," in *Northeast African Studies*, Vol. 12, No. 2, 2012

42. John 18:36

43. Jacques Maritain, *St. Thomas Aquinas*, trans. J. Evans and P. O'Reilly (New York, 1965)

44. See *Times of India*, January 9, 2023

45. George Orwell, "England, Your England," in *The Lion and the Unicorn: Socialism and the English Genius* (1941)

Chapter Seven

1. "pues esto fue el fin y el comienzo del propósito, que fuese por acrecentamiento y gloria de la religión cristiana, ni venir a estas partes ninguno que no sea buen cristiano," November 27, 1492, in *Diario de Cristóbal Colón* [Diary of Christopher Columbus], El Prima Viaje A Las Indias, de las Casas copy

2. Ezekiel 27:35—"All the inhabitants of the isles shall be astonished at thee'

3. See Roger A. Johnson, "To Conquer and Convert: The Theological Tasks of the Voyages of Columbus," in *Soundings*, Vol. 76, No. 1, Spring 1993

4. The *Pesquisa* was, remarkably, rediscovered in the Archivo General de Simancas in 2005, having been presumed lost.

5. Matthew 2:1–12

6. Scholars increasingly think that the distinction between the peoples the Spanish

362   *References*

referred to as the Taino and Carib may not, in fact, relate to actual distinct tribes as understood in a Western anthropological sense but to the way in which different caciques—or leaders—conducted their responses to the Spanish presence on the islands, with those who resisted being identified as "Caribs" and those who acquiesced to being "Taino." In truth, reconstructing the exact social structures of pre-Columbian society is exceptionally difficult, not least as our sole written sources are those such as that of Fray Ramon Pané.

7.   Price et al., *Home is the sailor: Investigating the Origins of the Inhabitants of La Isabela, the First European Settlement in the New World* (Wisconsin, 2020)

8.   The archaeology of the site of the church at Isabela is exhaustively and incredibly skillfully detailed in Kathleen Deagan and Jose Maria Cruxent, *Archaeology at Isabela, America's First European Town* (Yale, 2002), to which I am much indebted.

9.   Sitio Arqueológico de la Villa La Isabela on the UNESCO World Heritage database

10.   Price et al., ibid.

11.   Fray Ramon Pané, *An Account of the Antiquities of the Indians*, 1498, Ch. XV, ed. J.J. Arrom, trans. Susan C. Griswold (Duke University, 1999)

12.   Ibid., Ch. XXVI

13.   "los cuales yo vide entónces en Sevilla, y posaban junto al arco que se dice de las Imágenes, á Sant Nicolás," in B. de las Casas, *Historias de las Indias* [History of the Indies], Book I, Capítulo LXXVIII (1527)

14.   See L. Hanke, "Bartolomé De Las Casas and the Spanish Empire in America: Four Centuries of Misunderstanding," in *Proceedings of the American Philosophical Society*, Vol. 97, No. 1, February 1953

15.   Timothy J. Yeager, "Encomienda or Slavery? The Spanish Crown's Choice of Labor Organization in Sixteenth-Century Spanish America," in *The Journal of Economic History*, Vol. 55, No. 4, December 1995

16.   H.E. Braun, "Genocidal Massacre in the Spanish Conquest of the Americas: Xaragua, Cholula, and Toxcatl (1503–1519)," in *The Cambridge World History of Genocide*, Vol. 1, ed. Ben Kiernan, Tracy Lemos, and Tristan Taylor (series editor: Ben Kiernan) (Cambridge: CUP, 2022)

17.   Sermon of Montesinos in *Historias de las Indias*, Book III, Capitulo VI, for translation see John-Charles Duffy, *Empire and American Religion* (2020)

18.   Matthew 22:39

19.   This was around the same time that a German monk, Martin Luther, was equally as powerfully struck by a line in the Book of Romans. A busy year for Biblical inspiration.

20.   Ecclesiasticus 34:18–22

21.   "eran y son obligados, como otro cualquier cristiano, á obedecer y cumplir los mandados apostólicos así como á los de Jesucristo," in *Historias I*, LXXIX

References   363

22. "omnes fratri sunt," in B. de las Casas, *Obras Completas*, ed. Paulino Delgado, Part IX (Madrid, 1988), p. 664

23. Diego von Vacano, "Las Casas and the Birth of Race," in *History of Political Thought*, Vol. 33, No. 3, Autumn 2012

24. "que como cristianos éramos obligados en punar contra los enemigos de nuestra fe," Hernán Cortés, Letter IV to Emperor Charles V, October 30, 1520, *Cartas y Relaciones de Hernan Cortes al Emperador Carlos V* [The Letters of Relation from Cortes to Charles V], ed. Don Pascual de Gayangos, p. 65

25. See Regina Grafe and Alejandra Irigoin, "A Stakeholder Empire: the political economy of Spanish Imperial rule in America," in *The Economic History Review*, Vol. 65, No. 2, May 2012

26. John M. Ingham, "Human Sacrifice at Tenochtitlan," in *Comparative Studies in Society and History*, Issue 26, No. 3, July 1984

27. "en los cuerpos desnudos y blancos que vieron sacrificar conocieron," Cortés, Letter VI, May 15, 1522, *Cartas y Relaciones*, p. 234

28. See Patricia Harrington, "Mother of Death, Mother of Rebirth: The Mexican Virgin of Guadalupe," in *The Journal of the American Academy of Religion*, Vol. 56, No. 1, Spring 1988

29. T. Matorina, "The Origins of the Guadalupe Tradition in Mexico," in *The Catholic Historical Review*, Vol. 100, No. 2, Spring 2014

30. Fidel de J. Chauvet, "Fray Juan de Zumárraga, Protector of the Indians," in *The Americas*, Vol. 5, No. 3, January 1949

31. "Rosa mira abstentia," "dum Rosa adhuc domi propriae suum de quo intra reclusorium inhabitabat," etc., in L. Hansen, *Vita mirabilis et mors pretiosa venerabilis sororis Rosæ de s. Maria Limensis* [The Miraculous Life and Precious Death of the Venerable Sister Rose of Lima], 1664, copy in the Bodleian, Oxford

32. For theories on this and the authorship of Rose's biographies, see Stephen M. Hart, "The Biographical Fashioning of the Americas' First Saint: Santa Rosa de Lima (1586–1617)," in *The Modern Language Review*, Vol. 114, No. 2, April 2019

33. The Dictionary of Methodism in Britain and Ireland, "Holy Club," https://dmbi.online/index.php?do=app.entry&id=1370

34. Geordan Hammond, "Versions of Primitive Christianity: John Wesley's Relations with the Moravians in Georgia," 1735–1737, in *Journal of Moravian History*, No. 6, Spring 2009

35. J. Wesley, *Journal*, Ch. 1, p. 58

36. Statistical information, The World Methodist Council, 2024

37. R.J. Kerner, "The Russian Eastward Movement: Some Observations on Its Historical Significance," in *Pacific Historical Review*, Vol. 17, No. 2, May 1948

38. John Chrysostom, *Homily on Colossians, Number 9*

39. See conclusion of Soterios A. Mousalimas, *The Transition from Shamanism to Russian Orthodoxy in Alaska* (Oxford, 1992)

364 References

40. Speech at the "Religion and Media Festival," June 2023
41. *Religion in Latin America*, Pew Research Center, 2023
42. *National Catholic Reporter*, May 20, 2016

Chapter Eight

1. As referenced in Emile Cammaerts, *Chesterton, The Laughing Prophet* (London, 1937)
2. "Blessed are ye, when men shall revile you and persecute you"—Matthew 5:11; "ye shall be beaten and brought before rulers and kings for my sake"—Mark 13:9; "some of you shall they cause to be put to death"—Luke 21:16; "if the world hate you, ye know that it hated me before it hated you"—John 15:18
3. Luke 8:5–15
4. "En las latrinas, nosotros nos sentamos, mientras que ellos se colocan en cuclillas," observation 20 in Ch. IX of L. Frois, *Tratado sobre las Contradicciones y Diferencias en las Costumbres entre los Europeos y Japoneses* [Tract on the Contradictions and Differences between the Habits of Europeans and Japanese], ed. Osami Takizawa (1585)
5. There is some debate, but it seems likely that the merchants Mota and Zeimoto were the very first in 1543.
6. See L. Frois, *Contradicciones y Diferencias*
7. Much of this was dependent on topography, geography, and political factors, but the undisputed success of the Jesuits compared to other orders was remarked upon even at the time. See Artur H.F. Barcelos, "Transformed Worlds: Missionaries and Indigenous Peoples in South America," in Revista: *Harvard Review of Latin America*, Vol. XIV, No. 3, Spring 2015.
8. The key point of the edict is the third of the five: 伴天連其智恵之法を以、心さし次第二檀那を持候と被思召候ヘバ、如右日域之佛法を相破事前事候條、伴天連儀日本之地ニハおかせられ間敷候間、今日より廿日之間二用意仕可歸國候。其中に下々伴天連儀に不謂族申懸もの在之ハ、曲事たるへき事。黒船之儀ハ商買之事候間、各別に候之條、年月を經諸事賣買いたすへき事。[Christian missionaries, by their wisdom, thought that they would leave it to the free will of the people to make them believers, but as I wrote earlier, they violated Japanese Buddhist law. It is not possible to have a Christian missionary in Japan, so get ready in 20 days from today and return to the Christian country. It would be a shame if anyone insisted that he was not a Christian missionary even when he is.] See copy of the edict in Matsuura Historical Museum in Hirado.
9. Luke O'Hara, "The Galleon, the Tyrant and the 26 Martyrs of Nagasaki," in *The National Catholic Register*, February 2023
10. "¿si quiere Dios que vayamos al Japón?", recounted in Noemí Martin Santo, "The Shipwreck of the Manila Galleon *San Felipe* in Seventeenth Century

Histories and Accounts on Japan," in *Shipwreck in the Early Modern Hispanic World*, ed. C.L. Ruiz and E. Rodríguez-Guridi (Bucknell, 2022)

11. M. Antoni J. Ucerler, *The Samurai and the Cross: The Jesuit Enterprise in Early Modern Japan*, June 2022

12. Santo, "The Shipwreck of the Manila Galleon *San Felipe*"

13. "era necesario darse verdadera informacion," in Marcelo Ribadeneira, *Historia de las islas del Archipiélago Filipino y reinos de la Gran China, Tartaria, Cochinchina, Malaca, Siam, Cambodge y Japón* [History of the Philippines and of the Kingdoms of Greater China, etc.] 1601, ed. Juan de Legísima (Madrid: La Editorial Católica, 1947)

14. For horrifically detailed engravings of these methods made by Melchoir Küssel in 1675, see C. Osswald, *On Christian Martyrdom in Japan* (University of Porto, 2021)

15. See *St Magdalene of Nagasaki*, OSA Curia of the Augustinian Order

16. Haruko Nawata Ward, "Women Martyrs in Passion and Paradise," in *Journal of World Christianity*, Col. 3, No. 1, 2010

17. Imazato Satoshi 今里悟之, "Spatial Structures of Japanese Hidden Christian Organizations on Hirado Island: A Comparative Study of Three Villages and Ikitsuki Island," in *Japanese Journal of Religious Studies*, Vol. 44, No. 2, 2017

18. Roger Vanzila Munsi, "Kakure Kirishitan Gravestones in Nagasaki Settings," in *Annual Papers of the Anthropological Institute of Nanzan University*, Vol. 12, 2021

19. Ibid.

20. Hubert Cieslik SJ, "The Case of Christovão Ferreira," in *Monumenta Nipponica*, Vol. 29, No. 1, Spring 1974

21. Text available in *Deus Destroyed: The Image of Christianity in Early Modern Japan*, ed. George Elison (Harvard, 1973)

22. Ferreira is, of course, a character in the most famous description of this period, Shusaku Endo's Silence (沈黙).

23. See *Religious Persecution and the World Watch List 2024*, report filed by "Open Doors" to the UK House of Commons subcommittee at Westminster Hall by Fiona Bruce MP, January 25, 2024

24. M. Twaddle, "The Emergence of Politico-Religious Groupings in Late Nineteenth-Century Buganda," in *The Journal of African History*, Vol. 29, No. 1, 1988

25. Letter by Janani Luwum to President Amin, 1977, as quoted in Kisekka Wilson, *A contextual interpretation of Archbishop Janani Luwum's model of non-violence resistance and church-state relations in contemporary Uganda* (Pietermaritzburg, 2008)

26. *The New York Times*, February 22, 1977, p. 3

27. As quoted in the work of a contemporary Roman Catholic priest, Fr. Emmanuel M. Katongole, *A Future for Africa: Critical Essays in Christian Social Imagination* (University of Scranton, 2005)

28. Φόβος οὐκ ἔστιν ἐν τῇ ἀγάπῃ ἀλλ' ἡ τελεία ἀγάπη ἔξω βάλλει τὸν φόβον, 1 John 4:18

29. Malachi 3:2–3

30. See the work of Professor Linda Woodhead on this in the specifically British context

31. Pew Research Survey, December 2018

32. J. Knox, "On Predestination," *Complete Works*, Vol. V

33. J. Knox, "A Vindication of the Doctrine that the Sacrifice of the Mass is Idolatry," *Selected Writings of John Knox: Public Epistles, Treatises, and Expositions to the Year 1559*

34. The posited stool—subject to some skeptical debate as to its origins—is available to view with the full story in the National Museum of Scotland.

35. Kenny Farquharson, "Whoever Leads Scotland Next: It Can't Be Kate Forbes," *The Times*, April 30, 2024. The irony of this being published on Easter weekend was not lost on many.

36. P.R.J. Duffy, Iraia Arabazaola, and Maureen Kirkpatrick, *Draft Report on the Human Remains from the Kirk of St Nicholas Uniting, Aberdeen* (Open Space Trust, 2018)

37. See J. Hebditch, "Life expectancy falls for north-east residents," *Aberdeen Live*, September 22, 2022, Report of the Integration Joint Board of Aberdeen City Council, February 6, 2024, and *Employment, unemployment and economic inactivity in Aberdeen City*, Office for National Statistics, updated May 14, 2024

38. See inter alia, *The Catholic Herald*, April 5, 2024

39. Luke 5:49 and Matthew 7:26

40. Hebrews 11:1

Chapter Nine

1. The production was *Three Sovereigns for Sarah*, part of PBS's American Playhouse series. See details provided by the Salem Witch Museum in both their published and online materials.

2. 1 Corinthians 5:13

3. 1 Corinthians 5:7

4. Matthew 11:28: the invitation of Christ for all to come to him is also a central part of the Communion liturgy of the Book of Common Prayer, a text which the Puritans such as those in Salem particularly despised and rejected.

5. The dating in this account follows that of the original documentation and primary sources (i.e. that of the Julian rather than the Gregorian calendar).

6. For an eyewitness account of one of the men who questioned them, see John Hale, *A modest enquiry into the nature of witchcraft, and how persons guilty of that crime may be convicted: and the means used for their discovery discussed, both negatively and affirmatively, according to Scripture and experience* (Boston, 1702),

in the digital collection Early English Books Online, University of Michigan Library Digital Collections.

7. Exodus 22:18

8. 1 Samuel 28

9. Galatians 5:12

10. See the engraving of Jan van de Velde, *The Witch*, 1626, Cleveland Museum of Art

11. "etliche in dem Reyhen waren so Geiss und Kuhfuss hatten," from Bernhadt's description of witches in Lorraine in 1589, as recorded in M.A. Murray, "Witches Transformation into Animals," in *Man* (1918)

12. "Panties Mystery Solved," *The Herald*, Harare, July 27, 2012

13. Geoffrey Burton Russell, *Witchcraft in the Middle Ages*, Ch. 8 (Cornell, 1974)

14. See the excellent Francis Young, *Magic as a Political Crime in Medieval and Early Modern England: A History of Sorcery and Treason* (London, 2017)

15. Paul B. Moyer, *Detestable and Wicked Arts: New England and Witchcraft in the Early Modern Atlantic World* (Cornell, 2020)

16. John Callow, *The Last Witches of England: A Tragedy of Sorcery and Superstition* (London, 2021)

17. Edward Bever, "Witchcraft Prosecutions and the Decline of Magic," in *The Journal of Interdisciplinary History*, Vol. 40, No. 2, 2009

18. In all of the direct quoting of the original texts from the court records which appear in this chapter, spelling has been modernized to aid comprehension for the general reader.

19. *Examination of Tituba*, March 1, 1692, Salem Selections, Massachusetts Box, Essex Co., Manuscripts & Archives, New York Public Library, New York, NY

20. See Elaine G. Breslaw, "Tituba's Confession: the Multicultural Dimensions of the Salem Witch-Hunt," in *Ethnohistory*, Vol. 44, no. 3, Summer 1997

21. *Jonathan Corwin's Examination of Sarah Good*, March 1, 1692, Essex County Court Archives, Salem—Witchcraft, Vol. 1, No. 14, Massachusetts Supreme Judicial Court, Judicial Archives, Massachusetts State Archive, MA

22. Deodat Lawson, *A brief and true narrative of some remarkable passages relating to sundry persons afflicted by witchcraft at Salem Village, which happened from the nineteenth of March to the fifth of April, 1692*, Boston 1692, University of Michigan

23. *Letter of Thomas Brattle, 8th October 1692*, reproduced in George Lincoln Burr, *Narratives of the Witchcraft Cases*, 1648–1706 (Virginia, 1914)

24. *Petition of John Proctor*, Essex County Court Archives

25. Warrant for the arrest of Sarah Good, February 29, 1692, Essex County Court Archives

26. Increase Mather, *Cases of conscience concerning evil spirits personating men, witchcrafts, infallible proofs of guilt in such as are accused with that crime. All considered according to the scriptures, history, experience, and the judgment of many*

368   *References*

learned men, (Boston, 1693), in the digital collection Early English Books On-line, University of Michigan Library Digital Collections

27. John Hale, *A modest enquiry,* etc.

28. *Letter of William Phips to the Privy Council, 12th October 1692,* ed. George L. Burr, Narratives of the Witchcraft Cases, pp. 198–202

29. *Petition of Elizabeth Proctor to the General Court at Boston, 27th May 1696,* Mass. Archives, Vol. 135, No. 109, Massachusetts State Archives, Boston, MA

30. Mark 12:31

31. Calvin, *Institutes,* Ch. 3

32. "The Jew's Daughter," no. 155 in *The Child Ballads* (Boston, 1860). There are several versions of the ballad collected by Francis James Child.

33. "convocarunt de unaquaque civitate aliquos Judseorum, ut in contumeliam et obprobrium esu Christi interessent sacriflcio suo Lincolnire," in Matthew Paris, *Chronica Majora* [Main Chronicle], *c.* 1255, Royal MS 14 C VII, British Library

34. Matthew 23:13

35. Matthew 9

36. "ο θεος εκαθαρισεν συ μη κοινου," Acts 10:15

37. See work of the Venetian Bishop, Petrus de Natalibus, *Catalogus sanctorum et gestorum eorum* [A Catalogue of the Saints and their Works] (Vicenza, 1493)

38. See Socrates Scholasticus, Ἐκκλησιαστική Ἱστορία [Church History], Ch. XXXVIII, in *Post Nicene Fathers,* Vol. II, ed. P. Schraff

39. "every hut, almost, would be the scene of some enforced separation, and of the hideous consequences that must follow, where so many married women, released from the law of their husbands and the strict discipline of their na-tive customs—with their best feelings outraged, and their passions inflamed, themselves and their children branded, in their people's eyes, with a name of dishonor—are turned loose upon their tribes?", in J. Colenso, *Remarks on the Proper Treatment of Cases of Polygamy As Found Already Existing In Converts From Heathenism* (Pietermaritzburg, 1855)

40. J. Colenso, *The Pentateuch and Book of Joshua Critically Examined* (London, 1865)

41. Matthew Arnold, *Preface to Essays in Criticism* (London, 1865)

42. See Hlonipha Mokoena, "Zuluness on Trial: Re-reading John W. Colenso's 1874 Langalibalele and the Amahlubi Tribe being Remarks Upon the Official Record," in *The Journal of African History,* Cambridge, Vol. 60, Issue 1, May 2019

43. Diocesan Report of the Diocese of Natal, 2004

44. Colossians 3:13

45. See Madalyn Bell, *Dolly Parton and Southern Womanhood / Race, Respectability and Sexuality in the Mid-Century South* (College of William and Mary, 2017)

46. Irish Census, 2022, as reported in *The Catholic Herald,* May 6, 2024

References 369

47. Interview with *The Hollywood Reporter*, November 2, 2023, https://www.hol lywoodreporter.com/news/general-news/dolly-parton-interview-new-album -rockstar-superbowl-halftime-show-1235634785/

Chapter Ten

1. Chhaya R. Goswami, "Professor P.S. Gupta Prize Essay: The Slave Trade at Zanzibar at the Role of the Kutchis," in Proceedings of the *Indian History Congress*, Vol. 64, 2003

2. μετὰ δύο δρόμους νυχθημέρους παρ᾽ αὐτὴν τὴν Αὐσινίτην ἠιόνα Μενουθεσιὰς, in the *Periples of the Erythean Sea*, first century AD, Greek text of Hjalmar Frisk, Part 15 (1912)

3. Μέγιστοι δὲ ἐν σώμασιν περὶ ταύτην τὴν χώραν ἄνθρωποι 6 πειραταὶ κατοικοῦσιν καὶ κατὰ τὸν τόπον ἕκαστος ὁμοίως τιθέμενοι τυράννοις, ibid., Part 16

4. See J. Alexander, "Islam, Archaeology and Slavery in Africa," in *World Archaeology*, Vol. 33, No. 1, The Archaeology of Slavery, June 2001

5. *Measures Adopted for Suppressing the Slave Trade*, Account of the India Office, December 31, 1847, [375r] (145/336), Digital Archive of the National Library of Qatar

6. See A. Bremner, "The Architecture of the Universities' Mission to Central Africa: Developing a Vernacular Tradition in the Anglican Mission Field, 1861–1909," in *Journal of the Society of Architectural Historians*, Vol. 68, No. 4, Edinburgh, 2009

7. Colossians 1:14–16

8. *Mem. of Bishop of Oxford's Address at a Conference of Members of the Committee of Central African Mission, held at 79 Pall Mall Tuesday 9th Feb 1864*, UMCA Archive, A4(I)–62, as quoted in Bremner, 2009

9. Friedrich Schelling, *Die Weltalter*, draft of 1815 as quoted in the translation of his *Philosophical Investigations into the Essence of Human Freedom*, trans. J. Love and J. Schmidt (State University of New York, 2006)

10. See The World Monuments Fund, *Zanzibar's Story: Remembering the Past, Securing the Future*

11. Philippians 2:7

12. See the Cathedral's social media presence for photos of such events: https://www.facebook.com/p/Christ-Church-Cathedral-Zanzibar-100023464585765

13. Luke 7:2, Matthew 8:6

14. Exodus 21

15. 1 Corinthians 12:13

16. 1 Corinthians 12:26

17. Allen Dwight Callaghan, "Paul's Epistle to Philemon: Toward an Alternative Argumentum," in *The Harvard Theological Review*, Vol. 86, No. 4, October 1993

18. Philemon 19

19. Jeffrey Fynn-Paul, "Empire, Monotheism and Slavery in the Greater Mediterranean Region from Antiquity to the Early Modern Era," in *Past & Present*, No. 205, November 2009

20. Genesis 9:25

21. J. Wemyss, *The Portraiture of the Image of God in Man* (London, 1632), manuscript digitized by Princeton Theological Seminary, 2012

22. Matthew Wills, *How Antebellum Christians Justified Slavery*, JSTOR, June 27, 2018

23. J. Robinson Brown, "Why should Christians care about reparations?: Black Bodies and the Justice of God," *St Mary Magdalen School of Theology*, November 2019

24. O. Equiano, *The Interesting Narrative of the Life of Olaudah Equiano*, first published London, 1789, reprinted as *Sold as a Slave* (London, 2009)

25. Anne Stott, *Wilberforce: Family and Friends*, Ch. 2 (Oxford, 2012)

26. J. Newton, *Sermon on Lamentations 3:24*, preached March 10, 1765, at Olney, Cowper & Newton Museum, Newton's Notebook, N17

27. Ibid.

28. W. Wilberforce, *An Appeal to the Religion, Justice and Humanity of the Inhabitants of the British Empire, in Behalf of the Negro Slaves in the West Indies* (London, 1823)

29. Mary Prince, *A History of Mary Prince, a West Indian Slave, related by herself* (London, 1831), p. 7

30. Ibid., p. 23

31. C. Pailing, *God's Town: Liverpool and her Parish since 1207* (Lancaster, 2019)

32. Genesis 4:9

33. Matthew 22:21

34. Matthew 6:24

35. For a sense of the mystery of the etymology of Mammon, see B.A. Mastin, "Latin Mam(m)ona and the Semitic Languages: A False Trail and a Suggestion," in *Biblia*, Vol. 65, No. 1, 1984

36. Matthew 19:24–26

37. Acts 2:44

38. Acts 16:14–15

39. Margaret Mowczko, "Wealthy Women in the First Century Roman World and in the Church," in *New Testament Women*, Volume 32, Issue 3, Summer 2018

40. Οὐκ ἄρα ἀπορριπτέον τὰ καὶ τοὺς πέλας ὠφελοῦντα χρήματα, in Part IX, "The Rich Man's Salvation," in *Works of Clement of Alexandria*, Loeb Classical series, ed. W Butterworth (Harvard, 1919)

41. ἀγάπη δέ εις πλήρωμα συνέρχεται, ibid., Part XXXVIII

42. Thomas of Celano, *First Life of St Francis*, Ch. V, Part XV

43. M. Novak, "How Christianity Created Capitalism," in *Religion and Liberty*, Vol. 10, No. 3, July 2010

References

44. See "Home Office raids restaurant over 'modern slavery' conditions," *The Kilburn Times*, June 11, 2023

45. Rowan Williams, *Sermon Preached at Zanzibar Cathedral*, Wednesday, February 7, 2007

Chapter Eleven

1. See the 1660 *Standard Baptist Confession*

2. "From Early Days, Blacks bound to the Church," *The Birmingham News*, December 19, 1971, archive of the Birmingham Public Library (Alabama)

3. Amos 5:24

4. "Inside Birmingham's Sixteenth Street Baptist Church on Sept. 15, 1963," *Birmingham Post-Herald*

5. Sarah Collins Rudolph and Tracy Snipe, *The 5th Little Girl: Soul Survivor of the 16th Street Baptist Church Bombing* (Africa World Press, 2021)

6. Edward Berry, "Doing Time: King's 'Letter from Birmingham Jail,'" in *Rhetoric and Public Affairs*, Vol. 8, No. 1, Spring 2005

7. E.g. John Chrysostom in Homily 43, *The Homilies on the Gospel of John*

8. Dr. Martin Luther King Jr., "Why We Can't Wait," (1963, reprinted New York, 2000), p. 60

9. Psalm 82:4

10. "Her Most Devastating Day," *The Alabama Baptist*, August 5, 2021

11. See https://www.al.com/news/birmingham/2016/07/family_of_16th_street_bombing.html

12. "Tragic blast ends children's Sunday lesson: The love that forgives," *Birmingham Post Herald*, September 16, 1963, archive of the Birmingham Public Library (Alabama)

13. FBI Archive, "Famous Cases—Baptist Street Church Bombing," updated October 21, 2022

14. "Indictments Recall Terror of Birmingham Sunday in 1963," *The New York Times*, October 4, 1977

15. Habakkuk 1:2

16. Genesis 50:20 and Matthew 16:18, respectively

17. Micah 6:8

18. N. Snaith, *The Distinctive Ideas of the Old Testament* (London, 1944), p. 77

19. Joshua 8

20. For details of the patterns of the Hebrew in this regard, see Lawson G. Stone, "Ethical and Apologetic Tendencies in the Redaction of the Book of Joshua," in *The Catholic Biblical Quarterly*, Vol. 53, No. 1, January 1991

21. See N.H.G. Robinson, "Natural Law, Morality and the Divine Will," in *The Philosophical Quarterly*, Vol. 3, Issue 10, January 1953

22. "Sic igitur patet quod, quantum ad communia principia rationis sive speculativae

sive practicae, est eadem veritas seu rectitudo apud omne," in *Summa Theologica*, first part of the second part, question 94, "de lege naturali'

23. T. Müntzer, *Schriften, liturgische Texte, Briefe*, edited and translated by Rudolf Bentzinger and Siegfried Hoyer (Berlin, 1990) Source of English translation: *Spiritual and Anabaptist Writers*, edited by G.H. Williams and A. M. Mergal (Philadelphia, 1957)

24. T. Müntzer, "Letter to Frederick the Wise at Allstedt, 4th October 1523," in *Revelation and Revolution: The Basic Writing of Thomas Müntzer* (Associated University Press, 1993)

25. See Michael G. Baylor's translation, *The Basic Writing of Thomas Müntzer*

26. Paul P. Kuenning, "Luther and Muntzer: Contrasting Theologies in Regard to Secular Authority within the Context of the German Peasant Revolt," in *Journal of Church and State*, Vol. 29, No. 2, Spring 1987

27. See Andrew Drummond, *The Dreadful History and Judgment of God on Thomas Müntzer: The Life and Times of an Early German Revolutionary* (London, 2024)

28. Kenneth G.C. Newport, *The Branch Davidians of Waco: The History and Beliefs of an Apocalyptic Sect* (Oxford, 2006)

29. Micah 7

30. *Carmel and Contemplation: Transforming Human Consciousness*, ed. R. Culligan and R. Jordan (Institute of Carmelite Studies, 2000)

31. List of Indictments published in *The Odessa American*, January 10, 1990

32. Tape 218 of the Waco Siege, April 13, 1993, as quoted in Eugene V. Gallagher, "David Koresh's Christian Millenarianism," in *Christian Millenarianism: From the Early Church to Waco*, ed. Stephen Hunt (London, 2001)

33. "Indictments Recall Terror of Birmingham Sunday in 1963," *The New York Times*, October 4, 1977

34. Ezekiel 33:11

35. Pierce Butler, "Irvingism as an Analogue of the Oxford Movement," in *Church History*, Vol. 6, No. 2, June 1937

36. See Peter Street, "Open the box! Take the prophecies!", *The Church Times*, December 12, 2014

37. *History of the Panacea Trust*, The Panacea Trust, Bedford 2012

38. "Whatever became of Joanna Southcott's Box?", in *Notes and Queries, Guardian*, February 10, 2011

39. R. Francis, *Ann the Word: The Story of Ann Lee, Female Messiah, Mother of the Shakers, The Woman Clothed with the Sun* (New York, 2000)

40. Matthew 22:37–40

41. See Tom Holland, *Dominion: The Making of the Western Mind*, Ch. 20 (London, 2019)

42. 1 John 4:7

43. "capere Deum," in Irenaeus, *Adversus Haereses*, Book V, Ch. 32

44. Ibid., Book III, Ch. 21

References 373

45. "malumque illud, quod quaerebam unde esset, non est substantia, quia, si substantia esset, bonum esset," in Augustine, *Confessions*, Book VII, Ch. 12

46. Dario Fo, *La Vera Storia di Ravenna* (Rome, 1999)

47. "Hic est cunctis communis amor/repetuntque boni fine teneri," Boethius, *De Consolatio Philosophiae*, Book IV, Metrum 6 (Weinberger edition, Vienna, 1935)

48. Dietrich Bonhoeffer, *The Cost of Discipleship*, published in German as *Nachfolge* (1937)

49. Revelation 21:1

50. Revelation 21:4

Chapter Twelve

1. Hymn written by Albert Brumley, copyright 1960 by The Hartford Music Co., in "Let Us Sing"

2. E.g. Numbers 33:51: "When ye are passed over Jordan into the land of Canaan"

3. Judges 1:27: "Neither did Manasseh drive out the inhabitants of Beth-shean and her towns, nor Taanach and her towns, nor the inhabitants of Dor and her towns, nor the inhabitants of Ibleam and her towns, nor the inhabitants of Megiddo and her towns: but the Canaanites would dwell in that land."

4. Hymn written by Albert Brumley, ibid.

5. John Thabiti Willis, "Bridging the Archival-Ethnographic Divide: Gender, Kinship, and Seniority in the Study of Yoruba Masquerade," in *History in Africa*, Vol. 44, 2017

6. Jesse Page, *Samuel Crowther: The Slave Boy who became Bishop of the Niger*, Ch. X (London, 1892)

7. Olawale Yinusa Olonade et al., "Megamalls and lifestyles of urban dwellers in selected cities in southwest Nigeria," in *African Journal of Reproductive Health / La Revue Africaine de la Santé Reproductive*, Vol. 25, No. 5, November 2021

8. "Many Accidents on Ogun Highways," *The Daily Trust*, August 21, 2022

9. Isaiah 40:3

10. Genesis 23

11. "THE ARK TO BREAK AT LEAST 10 GUINNESS WORLD RECORDS," *ChurchGist*, September 10, 2024, https://churchgist.org/the-ark-to-break-at-least-10-guinness-world-records/

12. "The Ark: How two church members sowed ₦1bn, $1m seeds," *PM News*, Lagos, April 19, 2021, https://pmnewsnigeria.com/2021/04/19/the-ark-how-two-church-members-sowed-n1bn-1m-seeds-oyedepo/

13. Acts 2

14. See *Spirit and Power—A 10-Country Survey of Pentecostals*, Pew Research Center, October 5, 2006

15. Matthew 23:12

16. "Why Prosperity Gospel Is Scam, Satanic—Catholic Priest," *Premium Times*, Abuja, February 18, 2024

17. Marius Nel, "Changing the Narrative Language of Prosperity in Africa: A Pentecostal Hermeneutical Challenge," in *Journal for the Study of Religion*, Vol. 34, No. 2, December 2021

18. "Mais qui fut celui qui inventa cet art? Ce fut le premier fripon qui rencontra un imbécile," Voltaire, "Des Oracles," in *Œuvres complètes*, Garnier, tome 11

19. "Why Oyedepo sacked 40 pastors," *Vanguard News*, July 19, 2021

20. 2 Corinthians 12:9

21. Luke 6:20

22. Report of the United Nations Economic Commission for Africa, July 12, 2024

23. Report on The Future of World Religions: Population Growth Projections, 2010–2050, Pew Research Center, April 1, 2015

24. Fidon R. Mwombeki, "Report of the All Africa Conference of Churches," as quoted in the foreword of *Complexities of Theologies of Wealth and Prosperity: Africa in Focus* (Oxford, 2022)

25. The quote is accredited to Halverston (1916–1995), who served as Chaplain to the US Senate between 1981 and 1995 in multiple sources. Its exact provenance, however, is unclear.

26. Owen C. Nwokolo and Victor Counted, "The First Indigenous Anglican Diocese of Western Africa: Contested Legacy of the Diocese on the Niger and CMS Mission in Igboland," in *The Journal of Anglican Studies*, Vol. 22, Issue 1, May 2024

27. "Samuel Ajayi Crowther," in *The Dictionary of African Christian Biography* (Boston, 2012)

28. Oluwatoyin Oduntan, "Samuel Ajayi Crowther, 1806–1891," in *The Oxford Research Encyclopaedia of African History* (Oxford, 2021)

29. See Page, op. cit., as quoted in Stephen Ney, "Samuel Ajayi Crowther and the Age of Literature," in *Research in African Literatures*, Vol. 46, No. 1, Spring 2015

30. See e.g. John Illife, "Poverty in Nineteenth-Century Yorubaland," *The Journal of African History*, Vol. 25, No. 1, 1984

31. Frederick E. Forbes, *Dahomey and the Dahomans: Being the Journals of Two Missions to the King of Dahomey, and Residence at His Capital, in the Years 1849 and 1850*, Vol. 2 (London, 1851)

32. Ibid.

33. See Caroline Bressey, "Of Africa's brightest ornaments: a short biography of Sarah Forbes Bonetta," in *Social & Cultural Geography*, Vol. 6, Issue 2, 2005

34. Camille Silvy, "The African Princess: Sarah Forbes Bonetta," *Black History Month Magazine*, February 2021

35. Mark Chalufour, "What's behind the Boom of Christianity in China?", in *The Brink: Pioneering Research from Boston University* (Boston, 2023)

36. See Barbara Mittler, *A Continuous Revolution: Making Sense of Cultural Revolution Culture* (Harvard, 2012)

37. Canaan Hymn #34 and #205, *The Love of the Cross* album

38. Irene Ai-Ling Sun, "Songs of Canaan: Hymnody of the House-Church Christians in China," in *Studia Liturgica*, Issue 37, March 2007

39. Xiaoli Yang, "Canaan Hymns: Songs from the fields—A grassroots missiology of the Chinese church movement," in *Missiology: An International Review*, January 2022

40. 到了晚上，鴿子飛回來，口中銜來一個新擰的橄欖葉。它代表希望，它代表和平，它代表又是一個更新的年代。我們踏著血，踏著淚走過來，大雁飛北飛南，唱不完神的愛。今日的中國，已不再荒涼，你看到處處都是蘇醒的草木。Canaan Hymn #546, "Xiao Min Introduction," China Soul for Christ Foundation [accessed May 2, 2025], https://www.chinasoul.org/en_US/xiao min-introduction

41. "Malaysia falls 12 places in Global Gender Gap Report 2024," *The Star*, Malaysia, June 21, 2024

42. "Molestation scandal is latest setback to once-mighty Trinity Broadcasting Network," *LA Times*, June 6, 2017, https://www.latimes.com/local/lanow/la-me -tcn-history-20170606-story.html

43. Peter Beaumont, "World's largest Christian TV channel 'funds owners' exorbitant lifestyle," *Guardian*, March 23, 2012, https://www.theguardian.com /world/2012/mar/23/us-christian-tv-channel-owners-lawsuit

44. Sangeetha Thanapal, "Tamil Artists resisting poverty and discrimination in Malaysia," *The Interpreter*, Malaysia, March 15, 2018

45. Simon Hope, "AI: How could Christians use it?", *The Salvationist*, November 4, 2023

46. "Bishop of Oxford's ten commandments for robots," *The Times*, March 5, 2018

47. "Quia fecisti nos ad te domine et inquietum cor nostrum donec requiescat in te," Augustine, *Confessions*, 1.1.1.

48. Thomas Aquinas, *Summa Contra Gentiles* [Summary Against the Gentiles]

49. Andrew Davison, "Tools are for the worker: Machine Learning as an Instrumental Cause," in *Philosophy, Theology and the Sciences*, Vol. 11, Autumn 2024

50. C. S. Lewis, *The Lion, the Witch and the Wardrobe* (London, 1950)

51. As quoted in *Daily Telegraph*, "Peace on earth and a box of fruit," December 23, 2007

52. Jeremy Taylor, *Holy Living*, Ch. IV, Section 2 (Dublin, 1650)

53. There are plenty of theories about who wrote Revelation, but even if it's not "The Beloved Disciple" of the Gospel of St John, a figure of "St John the Divine," who is after all self-identified in the text, seems as reasonable a placeholder name as any other.

54. Revelation 3:15

55. Revelation 16:16–18

56. The General Thanksgiving from *The Book of Common Prayer*

Index

Aachen, 156–157
Aaron (Biblical figure), 153
Abel (Biblical figure), 266–267
Abel (Liverpool resident), 266–267, 344
Aberdeen, Scotland, 218–219
Abernathy, Ralph, 281
abolitionism, 253–256, 262–267
abortion, 136–137
Abraham (Biblical figure), 308
abstinence, *see* celibacy
accidental incest, 120
Acts (Biblical book), 269, 309
Acts of Peter, The, 352n.12
Adam (Biblical figure), 121, 150, 360n.10
Adrian IV, Pope, 218
adultery, 136
Afghan Memorial Church (Mumbai, India),
 197–198
Africa
 Anglicanism in, 199
 Christian vision in, 312–313
 European expansion in, 177
 meaning of swastika in, 151
 Methodism in, 196, 199
 monasticism in sub-Saharan, 131
 nationhood in, 147
 triangle trade in, 260–261
 see also specific countries
African Church, 152, 312
"Against the Monk Jacob" (Psellus), 135
Agnes, Saint, 53–54, 336
Agrippina, 27
Ai, massacre of, 285–286
Aina (Sara Forbes Bonetta), 315–317, 346
Ain Shams neighborhood (Cairo, Egypt),
 103–106
Alaska, 196–197
Alberti, Leon Battista, 39
al Bu-Said, Sayyid Barghash bin Said, 254,
 256–257
Aleut people, 197
Alexander VI, Pope, 40
Alexander VII, Pope, 49–50, 354n.46

Alexandria, Egypt, 8
Alexios V, 68
Al-Hakim, Caliph, 9–10, 335
Allen, William, 314
Allenby, Field Marshal, 324
Allenby, Field Marshall, 346
All Saints (Shorthampton, England), 327,
 329–331
All Saints (Wittenberg, Germany), 44–45
Alphege, Saint, 90, 338
Alutiiq people, 197
Alvarez, Francisco, 152, 340
American Civil War, 166–167, 279, 292
Amin, Idi, 214–216
Amos, Prophet, 280
Amtrak, 278
anarchy, 122, 162–164
anathema, 125
ana-tsurushi, 211, 213
Anderson, John, 218
Angelos, Alexios, 68–69, 337
Anglican Church Missionary Society, 313
Anglicanism and Anglicans
 benediction of the blessed sacrament for,
 170–171
 Bonnie Prince Charlie's conversion to, 50
 debate over doctrinal purity, 243–244
 demographics of, 199
 on ethical machine learning, 321
 Matoaka's conversion to, 195
 in Ota, Nigeria, 313–314
 Ugandan persecution of, 214, 215
 visitors of Church of Nativity, 7
 see also specific churches
Anne, Queen, x
Aphrodite, 116
apocalyptic cults, 287–289
Apocrypha, 188
Appalachian Spring (ballet), 292
Aquinas, Saint Thomas, 170–172, 174, 185, 186,
 286–287, 321, 341
Aragon, kingdom of, 98, 184
Arius, 243, 343

Index

Ark, at Canaanland, 309, 312
Ark of the Covenant, 149
Armageddon, 324
Armenian Apostolic Church, 7, 14, 17
Arnold, Brother, 292–293, 345
Arnold, Matthew, 244
artificial intelligence, 321–322
asceticism, 119–120
Atatürk (Mustafa Kemal), 76–79, 84, 337
atheism, 219–220
Athena, 116
Athens, Greece, 124, 125, 127
Athos peninsula, 116–117, 124–125, 127–128
Augustine, Saint, 339
   and dignity for the individual, 136
   and *encomienda* system, 185
   St Monica and, 257
   on sex and monastic life, 121, 123, 132, 135, 140
   on suffering and injustice, 295–297
   teachings of, in future of Christianity, 321
Australia, 246
Australopithecus afarensis, 149, 340
Avignon, France, 38
Awori clan, 305
Ayasofya Camii (Istanbul, Turkey), 58
ayate, 192
Aztec Empire, 190–193

Baptist faith, 278, 279
Barltrop, Mabel, 290–291, 345
Barnabas, Saint, 200
basilica, meaning of term, 81
Basilica of San Clemente (Rome, Italy), 53–54
"Bateran Tsuiho Rei," 208
"Battle Hymn of the Republic, The" (song), 166
Bearn, Hugh, 271–273, 344
beauty, 25–54
   ban on beauty contests, 125
   of Basilica of San Clemente, 53–54
   Bernini's vision of, 47–48
   of Domus Aurea, 25–27
   for monarchs exiled in Rome, 48–51
   and Nero's persecution of Christians, 27–31
   of Old St Peter's, 37–38
   for Pope Julius II, 40–44
   for Pope Nicholas V, 38–40
   Protestant ideal of, 44–47
   redemptive power of, 51–53
   during Roman Empire's decline, 34–37
   within St Peter's, 37–44, 47–48
   Lazslo Toth's destruction of, 31–34
Becket, Thomas, 89–97, 99–100, 102, 103, 107–111, 338, 356n.8

Bell, Gertrude, 10, 335
belonging, sense of, 329, 331
benediction, of the blessed sacrament, 170–171
Benedict of Peterborough, 94
Benedict XVI, Pope, 173
Bernini, Gian Lorenzo, 47–49, 53, 336
Bete Golgotha (Lalibela, Ethiopia), 145, 149–152, 160, 163, 165, 167, 169, 279
Bete Maryam (Lalibela, Ethiopia), 151
Bete Mikael (Lalibela, Ethiopia), 151
Bethlehem, Namibia, 7
Bethlehem, Palestine, 3–5, 7–8, 12–20, 92, 193, 311
   see also Church of the Nativity (Bethlehem, Palestine)
Bethlehem, Penn., 7
Bethlehem mental hospital (London, England), 7
"Bethlehem of Noblest Cities" (Clemens), 16
Bideford, England, 231
Black community, 279–283, 298–299
Black Death, 90, 133
Black theology, 198
Blake, William, 167–169
Bobadilla, 186
bodily autonomy, 136–137
Boethius, 296, 345
Bohemia, 155–156, 162–164
Bonetta, Sara Forbes (Aina), 315–316, 346
Bonhoeffer, Dietrich, 296–297, 345
Boniface, Saint, 154
Book of Common Prayer, 366n.2
"Book of Prophecies" (Columbus), 178–179
Bosphorus Strait, 58–59, 84–85, 337
Boxley, sisters of, 94, 95, 338, 356n.8
Brackett, Joseph, 293
Bramante, Donato, 41
Branch Davidians, 288–289
Brattle, Thomas, 234
Brawling Monks of the Nativity, 335
Brazil, 182, 186
Brielle, Netherlands, 161
British Empire, 197–198, 244, 255–257, 265–266, 274, 306
   see also England
British Royal Navy, 253–255, 263, 313
Brooks, Bishop, 13, 15, 19, 335
Buddhism, 110
Buganda, 214
Buil, Bernardo, 182
Burgundy, Duchy of, 14
Burroughs, George, 234, 236
Bush, George W., 11
Butler, Elicia, 91, 338

Index

Byzantine Empire, 10, 14, 58, 61–72, 79, 120, 123, 154, 159, 278
Byzantine Institute of America, 77

Cain (Biblical figure), 97, 266–267
Caligula, 26, 30
Calvin, Jean, 46, 98
Calvin, John, 238
Calvinism, 161–162
Cambridge, England, 91
Canaan, 303–305, 323–324
Canaan, Conn., 305
Canaan anime series, 304
Canaan Dog breed, 304
Canaan Land (film), 320
Canaanland facility (Ota, Nigeria), 301, 303, 306–311, 313, 315, 317
Canaan: Official Bitcoin miners, 304
Canaan TV Network, 319, 320
Canterbury, Dean of, 93, 110–111, 338
Canterbury Cathedral (England), 87, 89–95, 97–98, 101–103, 108–111, 150, 166, 314, 356n.8
Canterbury Tales (Chaucer), 135
capitalism, 251–274
   Church's relationship with money, 251
   and construction/mission of Christ Church, 255–258
   during Crusades, 67–68
   dehumanizing effects of profit, 271–273
   economic activity by monks, 133
   encomienda system, 185–188
   European expansion and, 207, 260–262
   indulgences in Catholic Church, 41–45
   interplay of profit and faith, 273–274
   for medieval Catholic Church, 41–44
   morality of profit, 267–271
   in Ota, Nigeria, 306
   and Prosperity Gospel, 309–313
   and televangelism, 319–320
   see also slavery
Capitoline Museum (Rome, Italy), 60
Carib people, 180, 362n.6
Carnival period, 50
Carter, Sydney, 292
Cassian, Brother, 143
Cassian, Saint John, 36, 119–120, 123, 125, 127, 131, 132, 136, 139, 140, 339
Cassianos, Brother, 115–116, 119, 141, 339
Cassilly, Bob, 32, 352n.14
Castile, kingdom of, 184
catacombs, 34
Catalonia, 36
Catherine of Aragon, 98
Catherine of Siena, Saint, 193

Catherine the Great, 196, 341
Celebrity Big Brother (TV series), 12
Celestine III, Pope, 38
celibacy, 115, 118–120, 128, 138, 141, 293
cellarer, 95
"Cementland" (Cassilly), 352n.14
Central America, authority over, 191
Chadwick, Owen, 119
Chapel of the Manger, 11
charity, law of absolute, 97
Charlemagne, 156–157
Charles I, King, 217
Charles III, King, 11, 12, 18, 335
Charles V, King, 188
Charlie, Bonnie Prince, 50, 336
Chateaubriand, François-René de, 15
chattel slavery, *see* slavery
Chaucer, Geoffrey, 135
Chesterton, G. K., 205, 206, 342
Chidley, Katherine, 164–165, 167, 340
children
   as church bombing victims, 280–285
   Jews blamed for deaths of, 239–241
   Mad Matilda and, 108, 109
   priests' abuse of, 246–247
   in Salem Witch Trial, 231, 233, 235
   sexual exploitation of, 120, 121, 136
China, 6, 317–319
Choisy, Maryse, 125–126, 339
chosen people, 148, 150, 152–154, 169, 225
Christ Church (Zanzibar, Tanzania), 249, 251, 255–258, 261, 262, 266, 267, 271–274
Christian Anarchism, 162–164
Christianity and Christians (in general)
   beauty and truth in, 25–54
   capitalism and, 251–274
   as cause for hope, 303–325
   conversion of slaves to, 259, 261–264, 313, 316
   credibility of, in an unjust world, 283–285
   current violence targeting, 104–106
   decline of, in European countries, 216–220
   diversity of, 6–8
   in European expansion, 177–200
   future of, 140–141, 303, 321–322
   global expansion of, 198–200, 225, 251
   hidden communities of, 203–205, 213–214, 317–319
   influence of, xii, 226–227, 295, 308–309
   on justice, 277–299
   micro and macro levels in, 4–5
   nationhood and, 147–174
   new history of, xii–xiv
   in Nigeria, 313–317
   as official religion of Roman Empire, 59–60, 119–120

Index

Christianity and Christians (in general) (*cont.*)
  origin of, 3–22
  persecution of, 10, 27–31, 203, 205–206, 210–216
  post-Reformation fragmentation of, 225
  power in, 57–85
  purity in, 225–248
  reversal of the expected in, 31, 103
  role of, in Western society, 219–220
  sacrifice in, 203–221
  in Salem Witch Trials, 237–238
  on sex, 115–143
  stories of, in churches, ix, xi–xiv
  surprise, service, and belonging in, 327–331
  as threat to totalitarianism, 203, 214–216
  violence in, 89–111
Christian Shrine, *see* Kirishitan Hokora (Kasuga, Japan)
Christina of Sweden, 48–50, 53, 336
Christmas, 10, 11
Christ the King church (London, England), 290
Chronica Boemorum (Cosmos of Prague), 155
Chronicles (Biblical book), 304
Chrysostom, John, 197
church(es) (in general)
  as communities of believers, 25, 53
  death of, 219
  defined, ix
  global, 66
  layout of early, 81
  memories of, x
  as monuments to hope, 315
  nationalist violence against, 172–173
  orientation of, 181–182
  past, present, and future in, 298
  as places of hope, 322
  stories of Christianity in, xi–xiv
  surprise, service, and belonging in, 328–329
  wealth used for beautification of, 270
  see also specific buildings by name
Church of England, 136, 153, 164, 168, 226, 255–256, 278, 290–293
Church of Mary (Lalibela, Ethiopia), 151
Church of Scotland, 217–218
Church of St George (Gravesend, England), 195
Church of St Theodosia, 72
Church of the Holy Sepulchre (Jerusalem), 10
Church of the Holy Wisdom, *see* Hagia Sophia (Istanbul, Turkey)
Church of the Nativity (Bethlehem, Palestine), 1, 3–22
Church of the Virgin Mary and the Archangel Micheal (Cairo, Egypt), 104

Cicero, 36
Circus Maximus, 28, 36
Cisneros, Cardinal, 353n.31
Cistercian monks, 270
Civil Rights Movement, 281–282
Clamecy, France, 15
Claudius, 26
Clemens, Aurelius Prudentius, 16, 335
Clement of Alexandria, 269, 271, 344
Clement VII, Pope, 46, 99, 102
Clopin, 240
Cluny, France, abbey at, 42
Codex 234, illustration of, 135
Codex Vercellensis, 352n.12
Cold War, 322
Colenso, Bishop, 243–245, 248, 315, 343
Collins, Addie Mae, 281, 282, 345
Collins, Gemma, 11–12, 18, 335
Colosseum (Rome, Italy), 21
Columbus, Bartholomew, 184, 185
Columbus, Christopher, 100, 178–183, 185, 186, 188–190, 200, 207, 341
Communism, 6, 107, 318, 322
compassion, 285
Confessions (Augustine), 295
Connor, Bull, 281
Consolation of Philosophy, The (Boethius), 296
Constantine I (Constantine the Great), 60, 337
  church as symbol of power for, 62, 79
  churches built by, 14, 37, 43, 61
  conversion of, 35, 59 (*see also* Constantinian Shift)
  Eastern Orthodox Church under, 197, 200
  God's power revealed to, 65
  Hagia Sophia for, 84
  Empress Helena and, 9, 14
  hidden Christian worship prior to rule of, 203
  power of Christianity under, 206
  Roman authority and empire of, 154
  vision for, 59
Constantine II, 61, 62
Constantine IX Monomachos, 117, 355n.15
Constantine XI Palaeologus, 70–74, 79, 84, 337
Constantinian Shift, 58–62, 81, 154, 206
Constantinople, 35, 39, 60–61, 63–64, 66–69, 71–72, 74, 120, 315
  see also Hagia Sophia (Istanbul, Turkey); Istanbul, Turkey
Constantinople, Patriarch of, 68, 124, 125, 137, 358n.4
contraception, 139
Copeland, Kenneth, 309
Copland, Aaron, 292, 293
Coptic Orthodox Church, x, 7, 104–106
Corey, Giles, 236

Index

Corinthians, 118, 122, 127, 259–260
corruption, xi, 40, 45, 131, 139, 226, 229, 238, 247, 269, 320
Cortés, Hernán, 189, 190, 193
Corwin, Jonathan, 232
Cosmas of Prague, 155–156
Council of Jerusalem, 242
Council of Nicaea, 242–243
Covenant University, 308
Coventry, England, 18–19
Cranmer, Thomas, 98–100, 102, 160, 256, 315, 338
Crimean War, 17
Cromwell, Thomas, 99
Cross, John, 282
cross, symbol of, 70–71, 104, 111, 173
Crossbones Graveyard (London, England), 134–136, 339
Crowther, Samuel Ajayi, 313–315, 317, 346
crucifixion, 4, 26, 27, 29–30, 36, 60, 96, 105, 150, 210–211
Crusades, 10, 14, 20, 65–70, 133–134, 288
Cuauhtlatoatzin, Juan Diego, 190–192, 198, 341
Cuba, 186–188
Cultural Revolution, 318
Cyril, Saint, 154, 155, 315
Czech people, 155–156, 162–164

Dahomey people, 315–316
Dandolo, Enrico, 66–68, 70, 337
Danvers, Mass., 225–227
David, King, 4
Davison, Andrew, 321–322, 346
Dawkins, Richard, 219–221, 342
Delhi Brotherhood (India), 328–329
del Monte, Giovanni, 139
del Monte, Innocenzo Ciocchi, 139, 339
De Olandia, Francisco, 208–210
Destruction of the Indies (Las Casas), 188
Deuteronomy (Biblical book), 97
dhimmi system, 253, 254
Diana of Ephesus, 337
Diario (Columbus), 178, 189
dignity, 136, 167, 199, 279
Dio, Cassius, 28
Diplakarou, Aliki, 125, 339
"Disputation on the Power and Efficacy of Indulgences, A" (Luther), 44–45
diversity, of church leadership, 198–199
divorce, 136
Docetism, 349n.8
doctrinal purity, 242–245
Domesday Book, x
Dominican Order, 44, 170, 186–188, 193–194, 211–212

Domitius, Gnaeus, 26, 27
Domitius Ahenobarbus, Lucius, *see* Nero, Emperor
Domus Aurea (Rome, Italy), 25–27, 29, 31, 53
Doom painting, 330
Door of Humility, 12, 13
doulos, 258
Durovernum (Canterbury, England), 90

Easter, 41, 96
Eastern Orthodox Church (Church of the East), 61, 67, 68, 71, 105, 115, 196–197
see also specific jurisdictions
Ecclesiasticus (Biblical book), 188
Echo, 122
Edict of Milan, 59
Edict of the Padres, 208
Edict of Thessalonica, 119
Egungun, 305–306, 310
Egypt, 8, 103–106, 120
Egypt, Pharaoh of (Biblical figure), 18, 286
Eilward of Westoning, 94, 95, 338
Eliza, Viscountess Stratford de Redcliffe, 124
Elizabeth II, Queen, 11
encomienda system, 185–188
England
    Christmas Day speech in, 11
    Church of England's influence on, 226
    Church of the Nativity repairs funded by, 15
    Church–state relationship in, 158, 160–162, 164
    expressions of hope in, 322–323
    expulsion of Jews from, 239–241
    faith and nationality in, 173
    monastic life in, 131
    Mount Athos tour for wife of diplomat from, 124
    nationhood for, 147, 155
    papal sanctions against, 158
    Puritanism in America and, 231
    Reformation in, 98–100
    strength of Christian faith in, 217
    term "Jesuit" in, 208
    Margaret Thatcher's vision of, 167–168
    views of slavery in, 253–254
    see also British Empire; Church of England; *specific locations*
English civil law, 136
English Civil War, 164, 323
English College (Rome, Italy), 51–52, 354n.50
English Parliament, 164
Ephesians (Biblical book), 307
Ephesus, Turkey, 8
Ephron the Hittite, 308
Epiphany, 12, 179–180

382 Index

Episcopal Church, 166–167
Equestrian Order of the Holy Sepulchre, 30
Equiano, Olaudah, 262–263
"Era of Manifestations, The," 291–292
Erasmus of Rotterdam, 40
Erdoğan, Recep Tayyip, 78–79, 84–85, 337
Ethiopia and Ethiopians, 149–150, 152–154
  see also Bete Golgotha (Lalibela, Ethiopia)
Ethiopian Orthodox Church, 7, 150
Eucharist, 28, 180
Europe
  Church's control over life in, 251
  Crusaders from, 67
  cultural exchange with Japan, 206–207
  nationhood in, 147, 154–157
  role of monks in, 131–133
  triangle trade in, 260–261
  violence against Jews in, 96, 101
European expansion, 177–200
  accounts of Lalibela during, 152
  Christianity's shaping of, 177–179
  complexity resulting from, 197–198
  diversity of leadership due to, 198–199
  impact of, on Catholicism, 183–185,
    189–193
  Japanese view of, 208–210
  protecting faith during, 101
  Russian settlement in Alaska, 196–197
  and slavery, 260–262, 315–317
  Spanish settlement of Isabela, 179–183
  Templo de las Américas as symbol of,
    199–200
  theological movements due to, 198
  and trade with Japan, 207
  and translation of Scripture, 313–314
  see also New World
European Union, 168
Eusebius, 9
evangelical Protestantism, 245–246
Eve (Biblical figure), 121
"Every Sperm is Sacred" (song), 139
Exodus (Biblical book), 18, 97, 229, 259
Ezekiel (Biblical book), 179
Ezekiel, Prophet, 180, 200, 341

faith
  defining, 205, 221
  in hidden communities, 213–214
  in a just God, 284
  "keeping the," 205–206, 215–221
  and nationhood, 147, 167, 173–174
  paradox of, 238
  and power, 80, 81
  practical, 219
  and profit, 273–274

  Prosperity Gospel on, 309
  purity as parameter of, 225
Faith Tabernacle Church (Ota, Nigeria),
  305–309, 311, 312
Fascism, 107, 277
fear, 109, 233–236, 240
Federal Bureau of Investigation (FBI), 283, 288
Felipe II, King, 209–210
Felixstowe, England, 324
Ferdinand, King, 184, 188
Ferreira, Cristovão, 213, 342
Fife, Scotland, 42
Finnian, 132, 133, 339
First Colored Baptist Church of Birmingham
  (Ala.), 279
First Meeting House site (Salem, Mass.), 223,
  226–228, 232, 233, 235, 244–245, 247
First Okeadon War, 315
First World War, 76, 324
"Florentine Pietà" (Michelangelo), 33
Flores de Oliva, Isabel, 193–194
Flossenbürg concentration camp, 297
"Follow the Holy Spirit" (song), 318
Football World Cup, 173
Forbes, Frederick, 315–316, 346
Forbes, Kate, 218, 342
Forbidden City (Beijing, China), 352n.13
forgiveness, 42, 245, 248, 282–283
fornication, 118, 119, 161–162
Forum (Rome, Italy), 36
Four Seasons (Rome, Italy), 30
France, 15, 17, 38, 40, 42, 147, 155, 161, 217,
  322
Francis, Pope, 20, 173, 198, 208, 341
Franciscan missionaries, 210
Francisco de Olandia, 342
Francis of Assisi, Saint, 10, 12, 18, 269–270, 335
Franconian dialect, 109
Franks (tribe), 154
Franks, Oliver, 322–323, 346
Free Church of Scotland, 218
free will, 295–296
French Revolution, 15
Frere, Bartle, 254
Freud, Sigmund, 125
Frois, Luis, 206, 213, 342
Fulshear, Tex., 35
fumi-e, 212–213
Futaleh, 253–254, 274, 344

Gauls, 36
gay community, 140, 246, 259
Geddes, Jenny, 217, 342
Gelede ritual, 305
gender, 138–140

Index

Genesis (Biblical book), 97, 155–156, 261–262
George, Mary Sameh, 103–106, 111, 338, 357n.27
Georgia colony, John Wesley in, 195–196
Germany, 11, 44, 154, 217, 296–297
Ghezo, King, 315–316, 346
Gibbon, Edward, 195
God
 abolition of slavery as work of, 254, 264–266
 certainty about belief in, 217
 Christian allegiance to, 215
 in Christian Anarchism, 163
 church as place for being with, x, 8, 20–22
 in Church of Scotland, 217
 death and drawing closer to, 103
 empiricism as mission from, 178–179, 209
 hierarchies instituted by, 262
 hope in, 304, 325
 Jerusalem as symbolic dwelling of, 148
 Jesus and, 5, 21, 325
 as just, 282–286, 295–297
 justice as prerogative of, 289–290, 294
 Kingdom of, 97, 148, 268, 306
 legitimatizing nation with blessing of, 154–155, 157, 165
 love of, 271–274
 monastic vows as command of, 130
 participation of, in all things, 196–197
 power of and from, 65, 80, 82–84
 in Prosperity Gospel, 309–312
 purity's importance to, 245
 Reformed Church's view of, 217
 salvation through belief in, 279
 sex as distraction from, 129–130
 of the small and powerless, 16
 transcendence of gender in, 138–139
 violence in name of, 95, 107
God Delusion, The (Dawkins), 219–220
Golden Horn, of Bosphorus, 58–59, 61, 84
Golden House (Rome, Italy), 25–27, 29, 31, 53
Golgotha, 9, 111, 150, 210, 216
Good, Dorcas, 234
Good, Sarah, 232, 233, 236, 343
Good Friday, 281–282
Gordon Square (London, England), 153, 290
Gospels, 3–4
 Empress Helena's tour of sites from, 9
 papyri evidence of, 357n.26
 parables on use of money in, 267
 on persecution of Christians, 205
 on purity of outward action, 242
 on reversal of human power, 80
 rock as symbols in, 220
 on sex, 117
 on slaves and slavery, 258–261

on suffering of Jesus, 105
 see also specific Gospels by name
Goths, 154
Gove, Michael, 218–219, 342–343
grace, 44, 45, 296–297
Grand Hotel de Londres (Istanbul, Turkey), 77
Grantham, Bishop of, 291
Gravesend, England, 195
Gray, Bishop, 243–244, 343
great imperial door, Hagia Sophia, 65
Greece, 20, 161, 252–253
 see also specific cities
Greek Orthodox Church, 6, 7, 14, 17, 123, 127, 130, 197
Greenwich, England, 90
Gregory of Nyssa, Saint, 138–139, 339
Gregory the Great, Pope, 37, 43
Greyhound (trading ship), 263
Grim, Edward, 91–92
Guadalquivir River, 185
Guarionex, 184
Guaticabanu "Juan Mateo," 185, 189, 341
Gül Baba, 73–74
Gül Camii (Istanbul, Turkey), 72–74, 78, 337
Gunpowder Plot, 47

Habakkuk, Prophet, 283
Hadar, 149
Hafidh, Michael, 257–258
Hagia Eirene (Istanbul, Turkey), 60–61
Hagia Sophia (Istanbul, Turkey), xii, 55, 57–58, 61–71, 73–85, 123, 137, 197, 204–205, 311, 354n.1
Hakusan-hime shrine (Mount Yasumandake, Japan), 204
Hale, John, 236
Halverston, Richard, 312, 374n.25
Ham (Biblical figure), 261–262
Hamilton, Lady, 98
Hartford, Conn., 231
Harvard University, 107
head, as center of power, 72
healing, 93–96, 103, 108–111, 258
Heaney, Seamus, 111
Heaven, Jerusalem and, 153, 169–172
Heber (Biblical figure), 164
Hebrews (Biblical book), 221
Hebron Drinks (Ota, Nigeria), 308
Helena, Empress, 9, 124, 335
Helena of Serbia, 339
Heliopolis, 104
Henry II, King, 91, 97–98, 107
Henry III, King, 240, 327
Henry VIII, King, 98–100, 338

384   *Index*

Herman, the Wonderworker of All America, 197
Hermes, 122
Herod (Biblical figure), 5, 18–19
Hetty, Poor, 265–266, 344
Hideyoshi, Toyotomi, 208–210, 343
Hilandar, Serbia, monastery at, 124
Hilary of Poitiers, 36
Hinderer, Anna, 314
Hinderer, David, 314
Hinduism, 172–173
hippodrome, Constantinople, 63–64
History of the Indies (Las Casas), 188
Hitler, Adolf, 296
Holland, Tom, 294–295
Holocaust, 278
Holodomor, 278
Holt, John, 231
Holy Communion, 153, 160, 170, 212, 290
holy orders, 119
Holy Roman Empire, 134, 156–157
Holy Scriptures
    kissing of, 128
    Yoruba translation of, 313–314
    see also specific books
Holy See, 34
Holy Spirit, 118, 243, 299, 307, 309, 310
hope, 20–22, 303–325
    Bethlehem as symbol of, 20, 21
    breaking cycle of violence with, 109–110
    Canaan as the promised land, 303–305, 323–324
    Christianity as source of, 313–317
    churches as monuments to, 315
    discomfort expressing, 322–323
    and faith, 221
    Faith Tabernacle service on, 305–308
    in future of Christianity, 321–322
    of God's glory, 325
    in hymns of hidden churches, 317–319
    persecution to suppress, 212
    prayer and, 322–323
    in Prosperity Gospel, 309–313
    symbols of, in violent acts, 106, 111
    technology to spread, 319–321
House of the Place of the Skull, *see* Bete Golgotha (Lalibela, Ethiopia)
Hubbard, Elizabeth, 229
Huei Tlamahuiçoltica, 192
Hugh of Jervaulx, 95
Hugh of Lincoln, "Little Sir," 239–241, 248, 343
Hugh of St Cher, 42
humility, 12, 13, 65, 74, 120, 310
Hus, Jan, 163

hypocrisy
    of clergy who commit violence, 91
    of monks, 131, 133–136, 139–140
    in pursuit of purity, 242, 245–246

Iacobum Monachum (Psellus), 135
identity, 138, 161–167, 188
Idiroko road (Ota, Nigeria), 306
idolatry, 10, 118, 184, 190
Ierissos, 125
Ignatius Loyola, 207
Inca Empire, 193
incarnation, 5, 18
incest, 27, 120–122, 136
India, 172–173, 197–198, 253, 328–329
indigenous people
    conversion of, 184–185, 189–190, 195–196
    in *encomienda* system, 185–186, 188
    enslavement of, 253
    treatment of, 185–188, 191, 196, 199
indulgences, 41–45
Innocent III, Pope, 158
Innocent Metropolitan, 197
Innocent X, Pope, 48
Inquisition, 100–101, 179, 184, 356–357n.20
Institutes (Cassian), 119, 120
Ireland, 91, 131–133, 246
Irenaeus, Saint, 295–297, 345
Irving, Washington, 226
Irvingites, 153, 290
Isaac II, Emperor, 69
Isabela, Queen, 179, 341
Isabella, Queen, 184, 188
Isaiah (Biblical book), 105, 357nn.28–29
Isaiah, Prophet, 4, 104, 306
Isidore, Cardinal, 71, 337
Islam and Muslims
    in Ain Shams neighborhood, 104
    conquest of Bethlehem by, 14
    conversion of churches to mosques, 57–58, 62, 64, 66, 67, 70–71, 74–76
    future role of, in the West, 220
    Inquisition of converted, 184
    nationalist attacks on, in India, 173
    slavery for, 253, 257
    Turkish political power of, 79
Isle of May, 41–42
Israel, 3, 8, 10, 11, 14, 19–20, 147–148, 167–169
Istanbul, Turkey, 76–78, 82, 85
    see also Constantinople; Hagia Sophia (Istanbul, Turkey)
İstiklal (Istanbul, Turkey), 76–78

Jacob the Monk, 135, 136
Jael (Biblical figure), 164

Index

James, Saint, 242
Japan, 203, 206–208, 210–213, 220–221, 364n.8
  see also Kirishitan Hokora (Kasuga, Japan)
Jefferson, Thomas, 5–6
Jeremiah (Biblical book), 307
Jerome, Order of St, 184, 186
Jerusalem
  arrival of, from Heaven, 153
  call to build a new, 147–151, 153, 156–157,
    159, 163, 165–166, 193, 226
  and Ethiopians as real chosen people,
    152–154
  fall of Kingdom of, 14
  Israeli city of, 8, 10, 11, 147–148, 167–169
  as metaphor for Heaven, 169–172
  as state of mind, 167–169
  as symbol, 147–148
"Jerusalem" (Blake), 167–168
Jesuits, see Society of Jesus
Jesus Christ, 31–33, 335
  birth and birthplace of, 3–8, 121
  burial place of, 10
  call to follow good over evil from, 237
  centrality of, to Christianity, 205
  Constantine's fear of, 60, 61
  Council of Nicaea on, 243
  crucifixion of, 4, 26, 27, 30, 60, 96, 105, 150
  healing of a slave by, 258–259
  Herod's fear of, 18–19
  hidden Japanese shrines to, 213
  on humility, 310
  as incarnation of God, 5, 21
  innumerable acts of, 7
  justice dispensed by, 297–298
  on keeping the faith, 220
  on Kingdom of Heaven, 169–170
  lawyer's testing of, 294
  on loving your neighbor, 238
  on making disciples of all nations, 148
  march to salvation for, 281
  Moravians' relationship with, 195
  nuns as brides of, 127
  as Pantokrator, 62, 123, 128
  parables on money from, 267–269
  on persecution of followers, 205–206
  on power, 80–82, 85
  on price of penance, 42
  on protecting the vulnerable, 246–247
  on purity, 242
  reshaping of Divine by, 320
  resurrection of, 4
  Roman beliefs vs. teachings of, 60
  second coming of, 97, 110, 153, 179, 284,
    290–292
  on sex, 117

Shakers' views of, 292
suffering of, 108, 216
Lazslo Toth's belief that he was, 31–32
treading on images of, 212
as vessel for God's glory, 325
on violence, 96–97, 102–103
visions of, 43
Jews, see Judaism and Jews
"Jew's Daughter, The" (song), 239
John, Gospel of, 3, 7, 169–170, 357n.26
John, King, 158
John, Saint, 116, 215, 295, 297, 324, 349n.1
John, Unworthy, 54, 336
John Paul II, Pope, 102, 338–339
Johnson, Elizabeth, 237
Johnson, Henry, 313–314
John the Divine, Saint, 323, 346, 375n.53
Josce of York, 101, 339
Joseph (Biblical figure), 4, 5
Joshua (Biblical book), 304
Joshua (Biblical figure), 285–286
Jubilee, of Pope Nicholas V, 39
Judaism and Jews
  Christian violence against, 96, 100, 101,
    133–134
  conflict with Jewish authorities, 25, 242
  expulsion of Jews from England, 239–241
  in Holy Land, 8
  Inquisition of converted, 184
  Jerusalem as symbol for, 148
  members of Jewish society at the Nativity,
    4–5, 180
  persecution of, 10, 50
  power struggle between Christianity and, 57
  purity laws in, 118, 122
  view of justice in, 294
Judges (Biblical book), 373n.3
judgment day, 284, 288, 291
Julius Caesar, 40
Julius II, Pope, 40–47, 52, 336, 353n.31
Julius III, Pope, 139
June, Sister, 293
Jung, Carl, 32
justice, 277–299
  Book of Revelation on, 297–298
  credibility of Christianity in an unjust world,
    283–285
  for indigenous people, 187
  individuals as arbiters of, 277–278, 287–289
  Sts Irenaeus and Augustine on, 295–297
  in Jim Crow American South, 278–280
  meaning of, 285–286
  and quest for purity, 235, 240
  quiet methods of seeking, 289–290
  at second coming of Christ, 290–291

386 *Index*

justice (*cont.*)
for the Shakers, 291–294
for 16th Street Baptist Church, 278–285
and slavery, 263
in a world shaped by love, 294–295
and worship, 298–299
Justinian I, Emperor, 62–67, 69–71, 75, 82–84,
117, 123, 125, 338
Jüterbog, Germany, 44
Jutes, 154

kakure kirishitan, 203, 213
Karyes, Greece, 130
kasaba, 15
Kasuga, Japan, 212, 213, 343
see also Kirishitan Hokora (Kasuga, Japan)
Kemal, Mustafa (Atatürk), 76–79, 84, 337
Kilculliheen, Ireland, abbey of, 91
King, Martin Luther, Jr., 110, 281–282, 345
Kingdom of God, 97, 148, 268, 306
Kirishitan Hokora (Kasuga, Japan), 201,
204–206, 213, 217, 218, 220–221, 279
kissing, 128–129
Knox, John, 46, 98, 217–218, 343
Koresh, David, 288, 289, 292, 294, 346
Ku Klux Klan, 281–283
Küssel, Melchoir, 365n.14
Kyushu, 212

Labuk, Tomasz, 359n.27
Lagos, Nigeria, 305, 306
La Isabela, Dominican Republic, 179–183, 193,
194, 199, 200
see also Templo de las Américas (La Isabela,
Dominican Republic)
Lake Texacoco, 192
Lalibela, Ethiopia, 147, 150, 152, 153, 161, 165,
171, 173, 174
see also Bete Golgotha (Lalibela, Ethiopia)
Lalibela, Gebre Mesqel, 149–153, 156, 158, 160,
162, 168–169, 226, 340
La Navidad, Haiti, 179–181
Langton, Simon, 158
language, 156, 314–315
Las Casas, Bartholomew de, 185–191, 198, 341
Lateran Treaty, 51
Latin American, Roman Catholicism in, 183,
199
see also specific countries
Laud, William, 164
law of absolute charity, 97
laws, justice and, 286–287
Lawson, Deodat, 233–234
Lee, Mother Ann, 291–292, 294, 346
Lennon, John, 294–295

Lent, 50
Leo IV, Pope, 37
Leonard of Chios, 355n.14
Leo the Great, Pope, 37
Leo the Wise, Emperor, 65
Leo X, Pope, 43–44, 46
lesbianism, 125
"Letter from Birmingham Jail" (King), 281
Leviticus (Biblical book), 97
Lewes, England, 47
Lewis, C. S., 6, 322
lex caritatis, 97
Liberation Theology, 198
Liberty of the Clink, 134–135
Libro de las Profecías (Columbus), 178–179
Libuše, Princess, 155–156, 340
Lima, Peru, 100, 193–194
Lincoln, England, 239–241
Lion, the Witch, and the Wardrobe, The (Lewis),
322
Lipany, Czech Republic, 163
Liverpool Parish Church (England), 102, 266
Livingstone, Dr., 254
London, England, 7, 134–136, 153, 166, 272,
290, 339
"Lord of the Dance" (song), 292
"Lord You Are My Best Friend" (song), 318
Lorraine region, 230
Louisville and Nashville Railroad, 278
love, 187, 238, 271–274, 294–295
Lucy (skeleton), 149, 151, 174, 340
Luke, Gospel of, 3–5, 80, 220, 258
lust, 121
Luther, Martin, 44–46, 49, 98, 139, 287, 336,
362n.19
Lutheran faith, 7, 49
Luwum, Janani, 214–215, 343
Lu Xiaomin, 318, 323, 347
Lydia, 268–269, 344
Lyngsjö, Sweden, 92

Machiavelli, Niccolo, 41
machine learning, 321–322
Magdalene of Nagasaki, 211–212, 343
Magi (Biblical figures), 4–5, 9, 12, 18, 156, 180
Magna Carta, 158
Mahler, Gustav, 44
Major, John, 173
Malachi, Prophet, 216
Malaysia, 313, 319, 347
Mammon, serving, 268
mammonas, 268
Manila, Philippines, 209
Maria, Empress, 338
Maria of Antioch, 68

Index

Mark, Gospel of, 3, 307
Marmetine prison (Rome, Italy), 36–37
marriage, 118–119, 127, 142
martyrdom and martyrs
  St Agnes, 53–54
  for Thomas Becket, 89, 93, 94, 99
  Boethius, 296
  for Christians in Japan, 210–213, 215
  hidden worship at tombs, 34
  Jesus's predictions about, 206
  St Peter, 30, 31
  places dedicated to, 36–37
  redemption of violence in, 96
Martyrdom chapel, 102
Maruoyama hill, 212
Marx, Karl, 107
Marxism, 198
Mary (Biblical figure), 340
  and birth of Jesus, 4, 5, 9, 10
  hidden Christian shrines to, 213
  images of, in Hagia Sophia, 66
  kissing of icons of, 128
  in Michelangelo's "Pietà," 31–33
  at Mount Athos, 116, 124
  Our Lady of Guadalupe, 189–193
  statues of, at Crossbones Graveyard, 134
  sweating column of Hagia Sophia, 83
  treading on images of, 212
Mary I, Queen, 100
Mary II, Queen, 235, 237
Mary Magdalene, 211
masturbation, 122
Mather, Cotton, 236–238, 343
Mather, Increase, 235–236, 238
Matilda of Cologne, "Mad," 108–111, 339
Matisse, Henri, 77
Matoaka, 195, 342
Matthew, Gospel of, 3–5, 15, 18, 96–97, 156, 180, 187, 220, 242, 258–259, 294
Mazarin, Cardinal, 49–50
McNair, Carol Denise, 281, 282, 346
Medici family, 43, 46
mega churches, x, 306–309
Megiddo, Palestine, 304, 324
Mehmet the Conqueror, 71, 72, 74–75, 79, 84, 338
Menelik I, 149–150
Menuthias (Menuthesias), 252–253
mercy, 263–264
Messiah syndrome, 32
Methodism, 7, 46–47, 194–196, 199
Methodius, Saint, 154, 155, 315
Mexico, 186, 191
Micah (Biblical book), 288
Micah, Prophet, 4, 15, 285
Michael (monastery guest), 137–138, 340

Michael the Stammerer, 135, 340
Michael VII Doukas, 135
Michelangelo, 31–34, 41, 44, 47, 52, 336
Mileto of Sardis, 96, 101, 339
millet, 197
Milvian Bridge, Battle of, 35, 59
minbar, 73
miracles, 82–83, 93–96, 108–110, 192, 308
misanthropy, 121
missionaries, 184, 186, 200, 206–210, 213, 243, 313, 314
  see also specific orders
mistrust, 233–236, 240
Mithras, 53
Modi, Narendra, 172–173, 340
Mohammed Zahir Shah, 50
Mois Chez les Filles, Un (Choisy), 126
Mois Chez les Hommes, Un (Choisy), 126
money, 251, 267–269
Mongols, 152
Monica, Saint, 257, 345
monks
  asceticism of, 119–120
  at Canterbury Cathedral, 89, 93–94, 108–109
  daily life for, 119, 129–130
  in European society, 131–133
  hypocrisy of, 131, 133–136, 139–140
  influence of, on sexual norms, 136–137
  kissing for, 128–129
  at Mount Athos, 117
  population of, 90, 131–133
  violence involving, 17, 19, 90–91
  vow of chastity for, 115–117, 123
Monreale, Sicily, 92
Montanists, 153
Monte Carlo, Monaco, 271–272
Monte di San Giovanni Campano, 170
Monteith, David (Dean of Canterbury), 93, 110–111, 338
Montesino, Antonio, 187–188, 342
Month among the Girls, A (Choisy), 126
Month among the Men, A (Choisy), 126
Monty Python, 139
Moorish architecture, 256–257
Moravian Church, x, 195
More, Thomas, 99
More about Jesus (Mortimer), 10
Morebath, England, 162
Mortimer, Favell Lee, 10, 335–336
Moscow, Russia, 159
Moses (Biblical figure), 153, 229
Moses the Athonite, 117, 357–358n.36
Mountain Springs Church (Rome, Ga.), 46–47
Mount Athos, 113, 115–117, 123–130, 132, 133, 135, 137, 141–143

388   *Index*

Mount Carmel, 288
Mount Vesuvius, 358n.16
Mount Yasumandake, 204, 211–212
Mount Zion, 148
Muhammad, Prophet, 67, 253
mulukhiyah, 9–10
Mumbai, India, 197–198, 253
Müntzer, Thomas, 287, 289, 294, 346
Muslim Brotherhood Party, 104
Muslims, *see* Islam and Muslims
Mussolini, Benito, 46, 51

Nagamori, Mashita, 209, 343
Nagasaki, Japan, 208–210, 212
Nakaenoshima, 212
Naples, Italy, 49
Napoleon II, 50
NASA (National Aeronautics and Space
    Administration), 321
National Aeronautics and Space Administration
    (NASA), 321
nationhood, 147–174
    after fall of Roman Empire, 154–157
    Anglicanism and English, 255–257
    Bete Golgotha as symbol of, 149–151
    blessing of God to legitimize, 154–155, 157,
      165
    conflicts between Church and nations,
      157–161
    for Czech people, 162–164
    expansion by European nations (*see*
      European expansion)
    nationalist violence, 172–173
    and power of monasteries, 131
    relationship of faith and, 147, 173–174
    religion and national identity, 161–167
    for Russia, 159–160
    separation of Church and state, 164–167
    for Turkey, 76–78
    for United States, 165–167
    see also Jerusalem
Nativity scene, 10, 20, 180
Nativity story, 4–5, 180
Nazareth, Israel, 3, 8
Nelson, Admiral, 98
Nero, Emperor (Lucius Domitius
    Ahenobarbus), 26–31, 34, 37, 40, 41, 45,
    47, 53, 206, 336
Netherlands, 161–162, 229–230
New Atheists, 219–220
New Jerusalem monastery (Moscow, Russia),
    159–160
New Spain, 101
New Testament, 229, 258–259
    see also Gospels; *specific books by name*

Newton, John, 263–266, 274, 345
New World
    belief in witchcraft in, 229–231
    first native saint in, 193–194
    first vision in, 189–193
    freedom of worship in, 194–196, 227
    God's blessing for nations in, 165–166
    influence of, on Christianity, 178, 183–185
    religious violence in, 100–102
    Spanish priests in, 185–189
    triangle trade in, 260–261
    see also specific countries
Niccolò da Poggibonsi, 13, 336
Nicholas of Myra, Saint, 185, 243, 344
Nicholas V, Pope, 38–41, 46, 47, 336
Nigeria, 6, 313–317
    see also Canaanland facility (Ota, Nigeria)
Nika incident, 63–64
Nikitos, Father, 126–128, 137, 141, 142, 340
Nikon, Patriarch, 159–160, 340
Ninety-Five Theses (Luther), 44–45
Noah (Biblical figure), 155, 261–262, 318
nocturnal emission (wet dreams), 120, 136
Norman Conquest, 240
North Korea, 214
nuns, 91, 117, 127, 131, 135, 140, 159
Nurse, Rebecca, 227–228, 234, 236, 238, 344

Oaxaca, chocolate-making nuns, 191, 342
Obama, Barack, 11, 18, 336
obedience, vows of, 117, 136
O'Connor, Cormac Murphy, 51–52
oidores, 191
Old St Peter's (Rome Italy), 37–38
Old Testament
    Canaan as promised land in, 304, 305
    on justice, 282, 285, 289
    sex in, 122
    on slavery, 259
    Solomon and Queen of Sheba, 149
    violence in, 97
    witchcraft in, 229
    see also specific books by name
"O Little Town of Bethlehem" (song), 13, 15,
    22
Olubi, Daniel, 314
Onesimus, 259–260, 268, 345
On the Making of Man (Gregory of Nyssa), 138
Oran, siege of, 353n.31
Orange Order, 102
Order of St Jerome, 184, 186
Origen, 123
origin of Christianity
    in Bethlehem, 3–5
    birth of Jesus as, 5–8

in Church of the Nativity, 8–12
conflict and death in location of, 16–20
hope brought on by, 20–22
and marks of humanity on Bethlehem, 12–16
Orwell, George, 173
Osborne, Sarah, 232, 233, 236, 344
"O Sola Magnarum Urbium" (Clemens), 16
Ota, Nigeria, 305–306, 324
    see also Canaanland facility (Ota, Nigeria)
Ottoman Empire, 8, 15, 17, 39, 71–76, 79, 124, 197, 324
Ouranoupoli, Greece, 116–117, 141, 142
Our Lady of Guadalupe, 189–193
Ovando, Nicolás de, 186
Oxford, Anglican Bishop of, 321
Oxford, England, 91, 100
Oyedepo, David O., 306–309, 311–313, 317, 323, 347

pacifism, 96, 97, 102–103
paganism
    Aztec, 192
    Christianity's co-opting from, 82, 116
    in Constantinople, 57–59, 61
    in Cosmas's chronicle of the Czech people, 155–156
    death of, 122, 141, 143, 156
    Egyptian, 104
    gods in disguise in, 5
    of Indigenous Africans, 253
    sexual norms under, 118, 121–123, 137
pais, 258–259
Palazzo della Rovere (Rome, Italy), 30
Palazzo Farnese (Rome, Italy), 50
Palestine, 19–20, 119–120, 304, 324
    see also Bethlehem, Palestine
Palmerston, Lord, 124
Palodes, 122
Pan, 121–123, 141, 143, 156
Panacea Society, 290–291
Pané, Ramon, 184–185
panikos, 122
Pannonius, Janus, 39
Pantokrator Monastery (Mount Athos, Greece), 115–117, 123–130, 132, 133, 135, 137
Papacy
    economic power of, 42
    home of, 30–31, 38, 39
    Inquisition and, 101
    interventions with nations by, 157–159
    political power of, 37, 51
    sexual acts by, 139
    see also specific Popes by name
Parable of the Sower, 206
Parris, Betty, 228–229

Parris, Samuel, 228, 229, 233, 238
Parry, C. H. H., 168
Parthipan, Prakash, 319, 320, 323, 347
Parton, Dolly, 246, 248, 344
Passion Sunday, 158
Patmos, 116
Paul, Saint, 295, 338
    on death, 95, 103
    death of, 83, 206
    on faith and human suffering, 257
    on forgiveness, 245
    on grace and salvation, 44
    and Lydia, 269
    missionary work by, 200
    on Onesimus and Philemon, 259–260
    opposition to Jewish purity standards by, 242
    on power of Christ, 59
    preaching of, 37
    on purity, 228, 229, 246
    on redemption, 255
    on relationships, 115
    on rights of the individual, 136–138
    on strength and weakness, 85
    subversion of norms by, 359n.28
    teachings on Christian living by, 118, 119, 122, 123, 127, 139, 140
    on witchcraft, 229
Paul II, Pope, 139
Paul V, Pope, 47
Paul VI, Pope, 32
Paxos, 122
Pegasus (slave ship), 263
penance, 41–44, 54, 97–98, 132
penitentials, 132
Pentateuch and the Book of Joshua Critically Examined, The (Colenso), 244
Pentecost, 309
Pentecostalism, 309, 310
Pepuza, Turkey, 153
Pera Palace (Istanbul, Turkey), 77
Periplus of the Erythraean Sea, The, 252
Pesquisa de Bobadilla, 179
Peter (Biblical books), ix
Peter, Saint, 29–31, 34, 36–37, 206, 242, 336, 352n.12
Pharisees, 242
Philemon, 259–260, 268, 345
Philippines, 209
Phips, William, 237, 238, 344
Photius II, 125
"Pietà" (Michelangelo), 31–34, 40, 50, 52
Pilate, Pontius, 81, 169–170
pilgrimages, 10, 13, 38, 42, 108, 116, 127–128, 150

Pius IX, Pope, 51, 354n.49
Pius XII, Pope, 51
Pizarro, Francisco, 193
Plato, 169, 171, 340
Plaza Mayor (Lima, Peru), 100–101
Plutarch, 122
Pocahontas, 195, 342
pogroms, 101, 134, 241
polis, 57
political power, 57–85
   of Atatürk, 76–78
   Christianity's relationship with, 58–62, 80–81, 89
   of Church vs. state, 91, 97–99
   of Constantine XI Palaeologus, 70–74
   and Constantinian Shift, 58–62
   in Crusades, 65–70
   of Erdoğan, 78–79
   Hagia Sophia as symbol of, 57–58, 62–70, 75–76, 79–85
   of Justinian I, 62–65
   of Mehmet the Conqueror, 74–75
   missionaries and, 208–210
   monks who strove for, 134
   of Papacy, 37, 51
   of Rome and Constantinople, 35–36
   vulnerability and, 81–84
Polk, Leonidas, 166–167, 173, 340
Polo, Marco, 152
polygamy, 243–244
Pontypridd, Wales, 35
Porta Pia (Rome, Italy), 51
Portugal, 152, 182, 186, 206, 208–210
poverty, 117, 136, 268–270
"Prager Manifest" (Müntzer), 287
Prague, 162–164, 287
Přemsyl, 155–156
Prester John (character), 152
Price, Harry, 291
Price, Pastor (16th Street Baptist Church), 284, 285, 289, 294, 298, 299, 346
Prince, Mary, 265–266, 345
Priory of St Mary Overie (London, England), 134–135
Proctor, John, 234–236, 238
Proctor's Ledge (Salem, Mass.), 236
profit, 258, 260–262, 267–274
Prokop the Great, 163
promised land, 303–305, 323–324
Prosperity Gospel, 309–313
prostitution, 69, 134–136
Protestantism and Protestants
   Book of Ecclesiasticus for, 188
   Catholic attempts to reconvert, 194
   in Christina's Sweden, 48–49

Church–state under, 160–161
   sacking of Rome by, 45–46
   sanctioned form of, in China, 317
   view of contraception in, 139
   view of women in, 140
   violence between Catholics and, 100, 102
   witchcraft as crime for, 230
   work ethic associated with, 270
   see also Reformation; *specific denominations*
provenance, 321
Psalms (Biblical book), 282, 288, 289
Psellus, Michael, 135, 340
Puerto Rico, 136
Purgatory, 43
Puritanism, 101, 231
purity, 225–248
   adherence to social norms as, 231–233
   as basis for Salem village, 225–227
   and belief in witchcraft, 228–231
   Christian views of Jewish, 239–241
   doctrinal, 242–245
   focusing on own failings, 241, 248
   as heart of Salem Witch Trials, 228–238
   as illusion, 247–248
   Jews laws regarding, 118
   mistrust, fear, and obsession with, 233–236
   as parameter of faith, 225
   sexual abstinence and, 245–247
purity culture, 245–246
Putnam, Ann, 229

"Q," Gospel writer, 4
Quakers, 291

race, 188, 261–262, 314
rape, 5, 54, 69, 121–123, 136, 181, 253, 262
Reading, England, abbey at, 42
Readon, James, 279
reconciliation, 102–103, 167, 237
redemption, 81–84, 92, 96, 106, 111, 255, 257, 324
Reed, Warner, 279
Reem al-Bawadi (Bethlehem, Palestine), 8
Reformation, 44–47, 98–100, 139, 160–161, 225, 241, 251, 286–287, 327
Reformed Church, 217, 226, 230, 237–238
relics, of saints, 93–95, 128
Remus, 46
Revelation (Biblical book), 110, 130, 297–298, 324, 375n.53
Ribadeneira, Marcelo, 210
River Jordan, 303
Robertson, Carole, 281, 282, 346
Robin Hood, 90

Index

391

Roman Catholic Church (Church of the West) and Catholics
  attempts to reconvert Protestants, 194
  benediction of the blessed sacrament in, 170–171
  in Bethlehem, 14–15, 17
  Book of Ecclesiasticus in, 188
  on British Empire and Church of England, 255
  Maryse Choisy's conversion to, 126
  Christina of Sweden's conversion to, 49
  and Church of Scotland, 217
  conflict between nations and, 157–159
  in Crusades, 67
  death and human remains in, 34
  demographics of, 199
  economics of Early Modern, 41–44
  encomienda system and, 186
  English College for priests of, 51–52
  Hagia Sophia as symbol for, 70
  impact of European expansion on, 183–185, 189–193
  leader of, 40 (*see also* Papacy)
  Liberation Theology and, 198
  massacre of Catholics in Constantinople, 68
  monastic life in, 131, 140
  in Netherlands, 161–162
  New World's influence on, 183–185, 193–194
  number of Catholics, 6, 182–183
  and Prosperity Gospel, 310
  pursuit of purity and decline of, 246
  reunification of Church of the East and, 67, 71
  sanctioned form of, in China, 317
  split and between Eastern Orthodox and, 67, 68, 115
  Ugandan persecution of, 214
  Vatican as center of, 30–31
  view of Jesuit missionaries in, 207–208
  view on contraception in, 139
  violence between Protestants and, 100, 102
  violence of Inquisition within, 100–101
Roman Empire
  Bethlehem's church during, 14
  census in, 5
  Christianity as official religion of, 59–60, 119–120
  Church's power during decline of, 36, 147
  concern for the individual in, 21
  Domus Aurea as symbol of beauty in, 25–27
  English churches dating back to, 327
  European nations after fall of, 154–157
  fall of, 72, 121, 147, 260
  Hagia Sophia as pagan shrine in, 58
  Jesus as threat to norms of, 4

justice in, 277
  legalization of Christian worship in, 59–60
  St Paul's death under, 83
  persecution of Christians in, 27–31
  power and influence of, 81
  rules for Christian living in, 119
  shift in center of political power of, 35
  slave markets of, 255
  spread of Christianity in, xii
  violence in, 89, 90
  see also Byzantine Empire
Roman Republic, 36
Romans (Biblical book), 362n.19
Rome, Italy, 8, 15–16, 25, 28–29, 31, 35–40, 45–46, 48–54, 63, 67, 147, 315
  see also Roman Empire; St Peter's Basilica (Rome, Italy)
Romulus, 46
Rose Mosque (Istanbul, Turkey), 72–74, 78, 337
Rosen, George, 288
Rose of Lima, 193–194, 198, 342
Rumbold, Saint, statue of, 356n.8
Runcie, Robert, 102, 168, 339
Ruskin, John, 328
Russia, 17, 159–161, 196–197
Russian Orthodox Church, 196–197
Russian Revolution (1917), 160
Rylands fragment, 357n.26

Sabbathday Shaker Village, 292, 293
sacrifice, 203–221
  for building of a new Jerusalem, 167
  in countries with former Christian majority, 216–220
  by hidden communities, 203–205, 213–214
  justice and, 293–294, 297
  to "keep the faith," 205–206, 220–221
  by missionaries in Japan, 206–208
  by persecuted Christians, 27–31, 59, 96, 104–106, 210–215
  and political impact of conversion, 208–210
  and totalitarianism, 215–216
Sacristain II (folk tale), 90
Said, Yazid, 3, 8, 18, 336
Saladin, Sultan, 67, 150
Salem village (Mass.), 225–227, 234–236, 248
  see also First Meeting House site (Salem, Mass.)
Salem Witch Trials, 228–238
San Felipe (merchant ship), 208–210
San Gimignano, Italy, 158
San Nicholas de Bari (Seville, Spain), 185
San Pantalon (Venice, Italy), 328
Santa Croce (Gerusalemme, Italy), 43
Santo Domingo, Hispaniola, 185–189

Saracens, 37, 137
Satterlee, Henry Yates, 166
Saul, King, 229, 344
Saxons, 154
Schelling, Friedrich, 256
Scotland, 217–218
Scottish Civil War, 217
Scottish National Party, 218
Scottish Parliament, 218
scurvy, 180
Sea Beggars, 161
Second Intifada, 19–20
Second Vatican Council, 183, 198
Second World War, 51, 124, 126, 160, 198, 266, 296–297
Secretaire, of St Peter's, 34
secularism, 21, 251, 271
Selassie, Haile, 149
Seliger, Leonie, 339, 356n.9
Sembrouthes, King, 149
Serapion of Antioch, Bishop, 349n.8
service, 328–329, 331
Seventh Day Adventist Church, 288
Seville, Spain, cathedral at, 64
sex, 115–143
    Christian writers' views of, 117–121
    deprivation and appreciation of, 141–143
    desecration of Hagia Sophia with, 69
    as distraction, 129–130
    and future of Christianity, 140–141
    idealism and realism about, 115, 142
    Jesus's parables on, 267
    and kissing as intimate act, 128–129
    monastic hypocrisy related to, 133–135
    monks' influence on attitudes about, 136–137
    in paganism vs. Christianity, 121–123
    and purity, 243, 245–247
    relationship of Christianity and, 137–140
    and role of monks in society, 131–133
    in story of Czech people, 155
    and visitors at monasteries, 123–128
    vow of chastity for monks, 115–117
Shah Alam, Malaysia, 313, 347
Shakerism, 291–294
shamanism, 197
Sheba, Queen of, 149, 150, 158, 341
Shelikhov, Grigorii, 196, 342
Shelley, Percy Bysshe, 50
shepherds, 4, 5, 9, 124
Shintoism, 204, 210, 213
Shrewsbury, England, 164
Shuttlesworth, Fred, 281
Sierra Leone, 313
Sigebert of Gembloux, 134
Sigismund, King, 163

Simon Peter, see Peter, Saint
"Simple Gifts" (song), 292–294
Sisera (Biblical figure), 164
Sistine Chapel, 41
16th Street Baptist Church (Birmingham, Ala.), 275, 278–285, 295, 298
Sixtus IV, Pope, 40
Skellig Michael (Ireland), 132–133
slavery and slaves, 253, 315–317
    abolition of, 253–255, 262–267
    and American Civil War, 166–167
    conversion of slaves, 259, 261–264, 313, 316
    and European expansion, 186, 260–262
    freed slaves, 261, 279
    modern forms of, 271–273
    New Testament references to, 258–260
    slave trade in Zanzibar, 252–253
Slavs, 154
social media, 320–321
social norms, 136, 139, 231–233, 245–246, 262
Society of Jesus and Jesuits, 206–208, 210, 213, 364n.7
Socrates Scholasticus, 243, 344
Solomon, King, 63, 64, 81, 149–153
Songs of Canaan, The (Sun), 318
South Africa, 243–244, 304
South America
    first native saint in, 193–194
    Inquisition in, 100–101
    Las Casas on indigenous people of, 188
    Liberation Theology of, 198
    Roman Catholicism in, 183, 198
    in Spanish Empire, 182
    see also specific countries
Southcott, Joanna, 290–292, 294, 346
Southwark Cathedral, Dean of, 135
Soviet Union, 322
    see also Russia
Sower, Parable of the, 206
Spain, 6, 100–101, 147, 155, 161, 179–194, 207–210
Spanish Civil War, 6
Steere, Bishop, 257, 269, 345
Stein, Gertrude, 77
St James cathedral (Ota, Nigeria), 313–315
St John Lateran (Rome, Italy), 35
St Margaret's church (Bethersden, Kent), ix–x
St Mary's church (Charlbury, England), 327–330
St Michael's Church (Mumbai, India), 172–173
St Monica's Guest House (Zanzibar, Tanzania), 252, 254, 257
St Neots, England, 35
St Nicholas Church (Aberdeen, Scotland), 218–219

Index

St Nicholas Church (Brighton, England), 316
St Panteleimon monastery (Mount Athos, Greece), 124
St Peter's Basilica (Rome, Italy), 23, 31–34, 37–48, 50, 51, 54, 279, 336
Stratford de Redclive, Viscountess, 340
Suetonius, 26
suffering, 96, 105, 198, 215–216, 257, 295–297, 304, 315, 323
surprise, 328, 331
swastika, 151
Sweden, 48–50, 92
Swiss Guard, 51–52, 337
Switzerland, 217
Symmachus, Pope, 37
syncretism, 192–193, 204
Syria, 9, 26
Syriac Orthodox Church, 7, 17

Tabard Inn (London, England), 135
Tacitus, 26, 28
Taino people, 180, 181, 184–185, 362n.6
Taksim Square (Istanbul, Turkey), 77
Tamil ethnic group, 319, 320, 347
tapia pisada, 181
taxation, 4, 15, 17, 42, 45, 186, 197, 253, 268
Taylor, Jeremy, 323, 347
technology, 319–321
televangelism, 319–320
Temple of Diana (Ephesus, Turkey), 82
Temple of Solomon (Jerusalem), 64, 81, 150, 156
Templo de las Américas (La Isabela, Dominican Republic), 175, 177–178, 194–200, 204, 362n.8
"Ten Commandments of Robots, The" (Bishop of Oxford), 321
Tenochtitlan, 190, 191
Tertullian, 343
Tetzel, Johann, 44, 45, 337
Thamus, 122
Thatcher, Margaret, 168–169, 341
Theater of Nero (Rome, Italy), 30
Theodoric the Great, 296
Theodosius I, 119
Theodosius II, 61, 62, 64, 70
Thomas, C.E., 282
Thomas, Saint, 94
Three Sovereigns for Sarah (play), 366n.1
Tiberius, 26, 351n.1
Timothy (Biblical book), 260
Tituba, 232–233, 344
Tlacopan, 190
Tokatliyan Hotel (Istanbul, Turkey), 77
Tomb of Adam (Lalibela, Ethiopia), 151, 360n.10

Tonantzin, 191
Torquemada, Tomas de, 179, 184
Torre de Belem (Lisbon, Portugal), 7
totalitarianism, 203, 214–216, 318
Toth, Lazslo, 31–34, 52, 337
Tower of Babel, 155–156
trauma psychology, 110
Treaty of Tordesillas, 182
Trinity, 123, 139, 242–243
Trinity Broadcasting Network, 320
Trychay, Christopher, 162, 168–169, 341
typikon, 117, 358n.4

Uganda, 214–215
Umar ibn al-Khattab, 14
Uniates, 7
United Nations, 157, 158
United Society of Believers in Christ's Second Appearing, The, 291–294
United States
    adultery as crime in, 136
    belief in witchcraft in, 229–231
    Church and state in, 165–167
    justice in Jim Crow South, 278–280
    justifications for violence in, 107
    presidential visits to Bethlehem, 11
    Prosperity Gospel in, 309–310
    purity culture, 245–246
    Shakerism in, 291–293
    slavery in, 266
    see also specific locations
Universities Mission Society, 255
University of Cambridge, 133
University of Oxford, 7, 133, 195, 321–322
Urban VIII, Pope, 48

Vähä-Katava, Finland, 7
Vandals, 35, 154
Vannerly, David, 357n.36
Vatican, xiii, 30–31, 34, 38, 39, 49–51, 194, 352n.13
Vavřinec z Březnové, 163, 169
Vedamrutharaj, Joel, 197–198, 342
Venice, Republic of, 15, 66–69, 158–159, 177
Victoria, Queen, 254, 306, 315–317, 347
Vikings, 90, 132, 177
Villa of the Papyri (Herculaneum), 358n.16
violence, 89–111
    absolute condemnation of, 107, 110
    apportioning blame with, 99
    in Aztec Empire, 190
    in Bethlehem, 14, 16–20
    breaking the cycle of, 109–110
    in Church–state relationship, 161–162, 164
    clinging to power with, 74

violence (*cont.*)
  conquest of promised land through, 304
  in Constantinople, 68
  of European expansion, 180–181, 184–188, 199
  future of Christianity and, 106–108
  of God, in Church of Scotland, 217
  healing after, 93–96, 108–111, 258
  Jesus's parables on, 267
  and justice, 285–289, 296–297
  in medieval Rome, 38, 40
  monasteries as refuges from, 133–134
  monks' involvement in, 17, 19, 90–91
  murder of Thomas Becket, 89–96
  murder of Mary Sameh George, 103–106
  nationalist, against churches, 172–173
  in nation building, 157, 161–162
  in Nero's Roman Empire, 26–31
  in *Nika* incident, 63–64
  of Pope Julius II, 40, 41
  in quest for purity, 236–237, 240–241, 243
  reconciliation after, 102–103
  during Reformation, 45–46, 98–100
  religious, in New World colonies, 100–102
  16th Street Baptist Church bombing, 280–285
  of slavery, 265–266
  transformative power of Christianity over, 96–98
Visigoths, 35, 154
visions, receiving, 9, 43, 149, 153, 189–193, 242
Voltaire, 157

Washington National Cathedral (Washington, D.C.), 165–167
wealthy individuals, ministering to, 269–273
Weber, Max, 270
Welby, Justin, 199, 252, 258, 262, 274, 345
Wemyss, John, 261–262, 345
Wesley, Claude, 280, 283, 289, 290, 297
Wesley, Cynthia, 280–282, 346
Wesley, John, 195–196, 342
Westminster, Cardinal Archbishop of, *see* O'Connor, Cormac Murphy
Westminster Abbey (London, England), 166
wet dreams, 120, 136
whipping post, 253, 257
Whittemore, Thomas, 77–78, 338
"Why We Can't Wait" (King), 281
Wilberforce, Samuel, 255, 269
Wilberforce, William, 255, 263–266, 345

Wilhelm II, Kaiser, 10–11, 336
William III, King, 235, 237
Williams, Abigail, 228–229, 233–235, 238, 344
Williams, Rowan, 274, 328
William the Conqueror, x
William the Silent, 161
Wiltshire, Earl of, 99
Winchester, Bishop of, 134–135
Winthrop, John, 165, 341
Wise Men, *see* Magi (Biblical figures)
witchcraft, 192, 228–234, 236–237
women
  autonomy of, 193
  ban on, in monasteries, 116–117
  beauty ideals for, 49
  in early Christian communities, 268–269
  inferiority of, 262
  John Knox on, 98
  as prophets, 291
  role of, in Christianity, 140
  visibility of, 319, 347
  as visitors on Athos, 124–126, 142
  see also nuns
worship, 219
  at Christ Church, 257–258
  at Faith Tabernacle, 306–307
  freedom of, in New World, 194–196
  hidden, 31, 34–35, 53, 59, 81, 203–205, 213–214, 317–319
  and justice, 298–299
  at Pantokrator monastery, 129–130
  for Shakers, 292
Wouters, Andries, 161, 341
Wycliffe, John, 97, 102, 110

Xaragua Massacre, 186

yasak, 196
Yoruba people, 305–306, 313–316

Zagwe dynasty, 150
Zahir Shah, Mohammed, 50
Zanzibar, Tanzania, 252–253, 279
  see also Christ Church (Zanzibar, Tanzania)
Zeus, 5, 121
Zimbabwe, 230
Zita, Saint, 330
Zulu people, 243–244
Zumárraga, Juan de, 191–192
Zwingli, Ulrich, 46

About the Author

The Reverend Fergus Butler-Gallie is a writer and priest. He was born in Kent and educated at the Universities of Oxford and Cambridge. He is the author of the bestselling *Times* and *Mail on Sunday* Book of the Year *A Field Guide to the English Clergy* and the *Spectator* Book of the Year *Priests de la Résistance!* He speaks regularly on radio; has written numerous articles for *The Times, The Independent, The Guardian, Church Times, The Critic,* and *The Fence*; and won the 2022 P G Wodehouse Society Essay Prize. He is a member of both St John's College and Keble College, Oxford, and is also Vicar of Charlbury with Shorthampton in Oxfordshire, where he lives with his wife, Madeline.

Avid Reader Press, an imprint of Simon & Schuster, is built on the idea that the most rewarding publishing has three common denominators: great books, published with intense focus, in true partnership. Thank you to the Avid Reader Press colleagues who collaborated on *Twelve Churches*, as well as to the hundreds of professionals in the Simon & Schuster advertising, audio, communications, design, ebook, finance, human resources, legal, marketing, operations, production, sales, supply chain, subsidiary rights, and warehouse departments whose invaluable support and expertise benefit every one of our titles.

Editorial
Caroline Sutton, *VP and Editorial Director*
Megan Noes, *Editorial Assistant*

Jacket Design
Alison Forner, *Senior Art Director*
Clay Smith, *Senior Designer*
Sydney Newman, *Art Associate*

Marketing
Meredith Vilarello, *VP and Associate Publisher*
Caroline McGregor, *Senior Marketing Manager*
Kayla Dee, *Associate Marketing Manager*
Katya Wiegmann, *Marketing and Publishing Assistant*

Production
Allison Green, *Managing Editor*
Hana Handzija, *Managing Editorial Assistant*
Jessica Chin, *Senior Manager of Copyediting*
Alicia Brancato, *Production Manager*
Ruth Lee-Mui, *Interior Text Designer*
Cait Lamborne, *Ebook Developer*

Publicity
Rhina Garcia, *Publicist*
Eva Kerins, *Publicity Assistant*

Subsidiary Rights
Paul O'Halloran, *VP and Director of Subsidiary Rights*
Fiona Sharp, *Subsidiary Rights Coordinator*